GLOBAL  STUDIES

CHINA

SIXTH EDITION

STAFF

Ian A. Nielsen — Publisher
Brenda S. Filley — Production Manager
Lisa M. Clyde — Developmental Editor
Charles Vitelli — Designer
Cheryl Greenleaf — Permissions Coordinator
Lisa Holmes-Doebrick — Administrative Coordinator
Shawn Callahan — Graphics
Lara M. Johnson — Graphics
Steve Shumaker — Graphics
Laura Levine — Graphics
Libra Ann Cusack — Typesetting Supervisor
Juliana Arbo — Typesetter
Diane Barker — Proofreader

GLOBAL STUDIES

CHINA

SIXTH EDITION

Dr. Suzanne Ogden

Northeastern University

Dushkin Publishing Group/Brown & Benchmark Publishers
Sluice Dock, Guilford, Connecticut 06437

China

OTHER BOOKS IN THE GLOBAL STUDIES SERIES

- Africa
- India and South Asia
- Japan and the Pacific Rim
- Latin America
- The Middle East
- Russia, the Eurasian Republics, and Central/Eastern Europe
- Western Europe

Library of Congress Cataloging in Publication Data
Main Entry under title: Global Studies: China. 6th ed.
   1. China—History—1976–. 2. Taiwan—History—1945–. I. Title: China. II. Ogden, Suzanne, *comp*.
ISBN 1–56134–378–1   954   91–71258

Sixth Edition

Printed in the United States of America

China

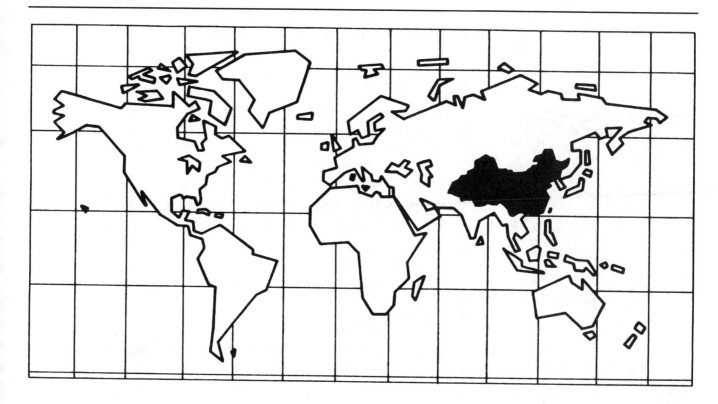

AUTHOR/EDITOR

Dr. Suzanne Ogden

Dr. Suzanne Ogden is professor and chair of the Political Science Department at Northeastern University and research associate at the Fairbank Center for East Asian Research, Harvard University. She has lived in both Taiwan and Hong Kong and has traveled frequently to the People's Republic of China. Dr. Ogden is the author of *China's Unresolved Issues: Politics, Development, and Culture* (Prentice Hall, 1989, 1992, 1995); chief editor and project director of *China's Search for Democracy: The Student and Mass Movement of 1989* (M. E. Sharpe, 1992); and the editor of *Annual Editions: World Politics* (The Dushkin Publishing Group, Inc., 1984–1991). Dr. Ogden's current research is focused on democratization in the P.R.C.

SERIES CONSULTANT

H. Thomas Collins
PROJECT LINKS
George Washington University

Contents

Global Studies: China, Sixth Edition

People's Republic of China   Page 28

Taiwan   Page 61

Hong Kong   Page 79

TAIWAN ARTICLES

HONG KONG ARTICLES

Introduction

Understanding the problems and lifestyles of other countries will help make us literate in global matters.

THE GLOBAL AGE

As we approach the end of the twentieth century, it is clear that the future we face will be considerably more international in nature than was ever believed possible in the past. Each day, print and broadcast journalists make us aware that our world is becoming increasingly smaller and substantially more interdependent.

The environmental crisis, world food shortages, nuclear weaponry, and regional conflicts that threaten to involve us all make it clear that the distinctions between domestic and foreign problems are often artificial—that many seemingly domestic problems no longer stop at national boundaries. As Rene Dubos, the 1969 Pulitzer Prize recipient, stated: "[I]t becomes obvious that each [of us] has two countries, [our] own and planet Earth." As global interdependence has become a reality, it has become vital for the citizens of this world to develop literacy in global matters.

THE GLOBAL STUDIES SERIES

It is the aim of the Global Studies series to help readers acquire a basic knowledge and understanding of the regions and countries in the world. Each volume provides a foundation of information—geographic, cultural, economic, political, historical, artistic, and religious—that will allow readers

better to understand the current and future problems within these countries and regions and to comprehend how events there might affect their own well-being. In short, these volumes attempt to provide the background information necessary to respond to the realities of our global age.

Author/Editor
Each of the volumes in the Global Studies series is crafted under the careful direction of an author/editor—an expert in the area under study. The author/editors teach and conduct research and have traveled extensively through the regions about which they are writing.

The author/editor for this volume has written the essays on each of the areas within the region being studied, has overseen the gathering of statistical information, and has been instrumental in the selection of the world press articles.

Contents and Features
The Global Studies volumes are organized to provide concise information and current world press articles on the regions and countries within those areas under study.

Country Reports
Global Studies: China, Sixth Edition, covers the People's Republic of China, Hong Kong, and Taiwan. For each of these areas, the author/editor has written a narrative essay

(Xinhua News Agency)
The global age is making all countries and all peoples more interdependent.

focusing on the geographical, cultural, sociopolitical, and economic differences and similarities of the peoples in the region. The purpose of the essays is to provide the reader with an effective sense of the diversity of the areas and an understanding of China's cultural and historical background. Each essay contains a detailed map and a summary of statistical information. In the essay on the People's Republic of China, a historical timeline provides a convenient visual survey of the key historical events that have shaped this important area of the world.

A Note on the Statistical Summaries

The statistical information provided for each country has been drawn from a wide range of sources. The most frequently referenced are listed on page 208. Every effort has been made to provide the most current and accurate information available. However, occasionally the information cited by these sources differs significantly; and, all too often, the most current information available for some countries is quite dated. Aside from these difficulties, the statistical summary for each country is generally quite complete and reasonably current. Care should be taken, however, in using these statistics (or, for that matter, any published statistics) in making hard comparisons among countries. We have also included comparable statistics on Canada and the United States, which follow on the next two pages.

World Press Articles

Within each Global Studies volume is reprinted a large number of articles carefully selected by our editorial staff and the author/editor from a broad range of international periodicals and newspapers. The articles have been chosen for currency, interest, and their differing perspectives on the region. There are 34 articles in *Global Studies: China, Sixth Edition*—24 addressing the People's Republic of China, 7 dealing with Taiwan, and 3 on Hong Kong. The articles section is preceded by an annotated table of contents and a topic guide. The annotated table of contents offers a brief summary of each article, while the topic guide indicates the main theme(s) of each article. Thus, readers desiring to focus on articles dealing with a particular theme, say, economics, may refer to the topic guide to find those articles.

Glossary, Bibliography, Index, Charts

At the back of each Global Studies volume is a glossary of terms and abbreviations, which provides a quick reference to the specialized vocabulary of the area under study and to the standard acronyms (P.R.C., R.O.C., etc.) used throughout the volume.

Following the glossary is a bibliography, which is organized into general-reference volumes, national and regional histories, and books on politics and society as well as on economic and foreign policy. There are separate bibliographic sections for the People's Republic of China, Hong Kong, and Taiwan.

The index at the end of the volume is an accurate reference to the contents of the volume. Readers seeking specific information and citations should consult this standard index.

Currency and Usefulness

This sixth edition of *Global Studies: China*, like other Global Studies volumes, is intended to provide the most current and useful information available necessary to understanding the events that are shaping China today.

We plan to issue this volume on a continuing basis. The statistics will be updated, essays rewritten, country reports revised, and articles completely replaced as new and current information becomes available. In order to accomplish this task we will turn to our author/editor, our advisory board and—hopefully—to you, the users of this volume. Your comments are more than welcome. If you have an idea that you think will make the volume more useful, an article or bit of information that will make it more current, or a general comment on its organization, content, or features that you would like to share with us, please send it in for serious consideration for the next edition.

Canada

GEOGRAPHY

Area in Square Kilometers (Miles):
9,976,140 (3,850,790) (slightly larger
than the United States)
Capital (Population): Ottawa
(920,000)
Climate: from temperate in south to
subarctic and arctic in north

PEOPLE

Population

Total: 28,114,000
Annual Growth Rate: 1.18%
Rural/Urban Population Ratio: 23/77
Major Languages: English; French
Ethnic Makeup: 40% British Isles
origin; 27% French origin; 20% other
European; 1.5% indigenous Indian
and Eskimo; 11.5% mixed

Health

Life Expectancy at Birth: 75 years
(male); 82 years (female)
Infant Mortality Rate (Ratio): 7/1,000
Average Caloric Intake: 127% of
FAO minimum
Physicians Available (Ratio): 1/449

Religions

46% Roman Catholic; 16% United
Church; 10% Anglican; 28% others

Education

Adult Literacy Rate: 97%

COMMUNICATION

Telephones: 18,000,000
Newspapers: 96 in English; 11 in
French

TRANSPORTATION

Highways—Kilometers (Miles):
884,272 (549,133)
Railroads—Kilometers (Miles):
146,444 (90,942)
Usable Airfields: 1,142

GOVERNMENT

Type: confederation with
parliamentary democracy
Independence Date: July 1, 1867
Head of State/Government: Queen
Elizabeth II; Prime Minister Jean
Chrétien
Political Parties: Progressive
Conservative Party; Liberal Party;
New Democratic Party; Reform
Party; Bloc Québécois
Suffrage: universal at 18

MILITARY

Number of Armed Forces: 88,000
*Military Expenditures (% of Central
Government Expenditures):* 8.7%
Current Hostilities: none

ECONOMY

Currency ($U.S. Equivalent): 1.39
Canadian dollars = $1
Per Capita Income/GDP:
$22,200/$617.7 billion
Inflation Rate: 1.9%
Natural Resources: petroleum; natural
gas; fish; minerals; cement; forestry
products; fur
Agriculture: grains; livestock; dairy
products; potatoes; hogs; poultry and
eggs; tobacco
Industry: oil production and refining;
natural-gas development; fish
products; wood and paper products;
chemicals; transportation equipment

FOREIGN TRADE

Exports: $134 billion
Imports: $125 billion

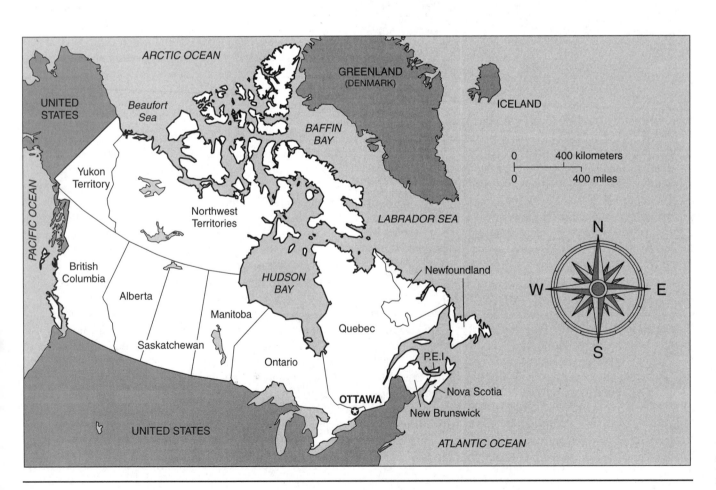

The United States

GEOGRAPHY

Area in Square Kilometers (Miles): 9,578,626 (3,618,770)
Capital (Population): Washington, D.C. (606,900)
Climate: temperate

PEOPLE

Population
Total: 260,713,600
Annual Growth Rate: .99%
Rural/Urban Population Ratio: 26/74
Major Languages: English; Spanish; others
Ethnic Makeup: 80% white; 12% black; 6% Hispanic; 2% Asian, Pacific Islander, American Indian, Eskimo, and Aleut

Health
Life Expectancy at Birth: 73 years (male); 79 years (female)
Infant Mortality Rate (Ratio): 8.3/1,000
Average Caloric Intake: 138% of FAO minimum
Physicians Available (Ratio): 1/406

Religions
55% Protestant; 36% Roman Catholic; 4% Jewish; 5% Muslim and others

Education
Adult Literacy Rate: 97.9% (official) (estimates vary widely)

COMMUNICATION

Telephones: 182,558,000
Newspapers: 1,679 dailies; approximately 63,000,000 circulation

TRANSPORTATION

Highways—Kilometers (Miles): 7,599,250 (4,719,134)
Railroads—Kilometers (Miles): 270,312 (167,974)
Usable Airfields: 12,417

GOVERNMENT

Type: federal republic
Independence Date: July 4, 1776
Head of State: President William ("Bill") Jefferson Clinton
Political Parties: Democratic Party; Republican Party; others of minor political significance
Suffrage: universal at 18

MILITARY

Number of Armed Forces: 1,807,177
Military Expenditures (% of Central Government Expenditures): 22.6%
Current Hostilities: none

ECONOMY

Per Capita Income/GDP: $24,700/$6.38 trillion
Inflation Rate: 3%
Natural Resources: metallic and nonmetallic minerals; petroleum; arable land
Agriculture: food grains; feed crops; oil-bearing crops; livestock; dairy products
Industry: diversified in both capital- and consumer-goods industries

FOREIGN TRADE

Exports: $449 billion
Imports: $582 billion

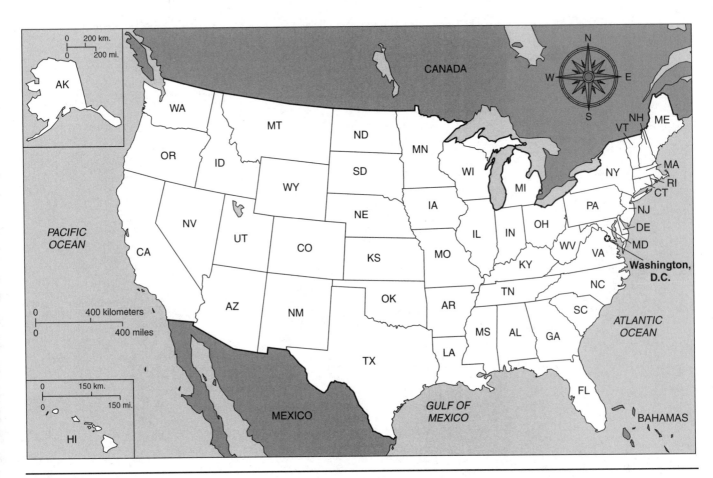

This map of the world highlights the People's Republic of China, Hong Kong, and Taiwan. The following essays are written from a perspective that will give readers a sense of what life is like in the region today. The essays are designed to present the most current and useful information available. Other books in the Global Studies series cover different global areas and examine the current state of affairs of the countries within those regions.

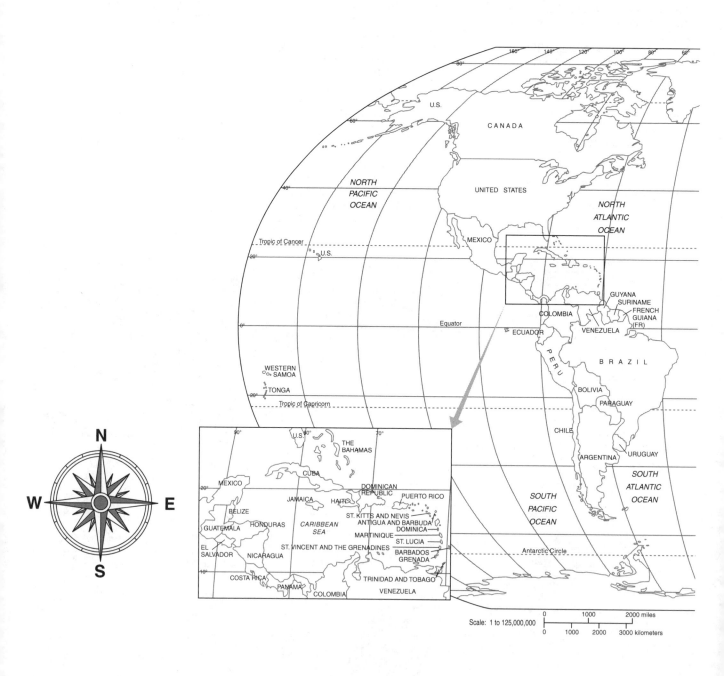

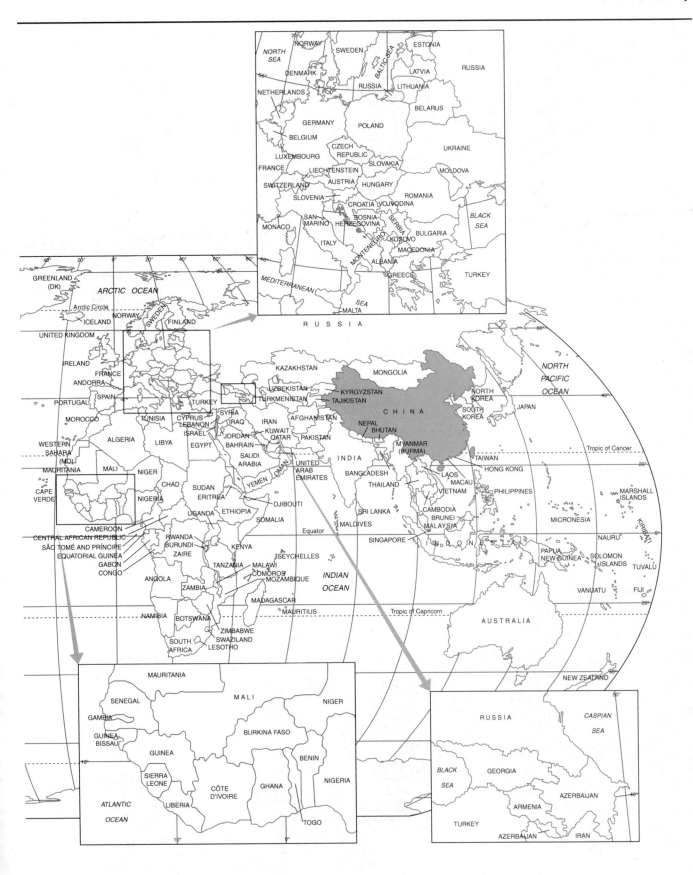

China

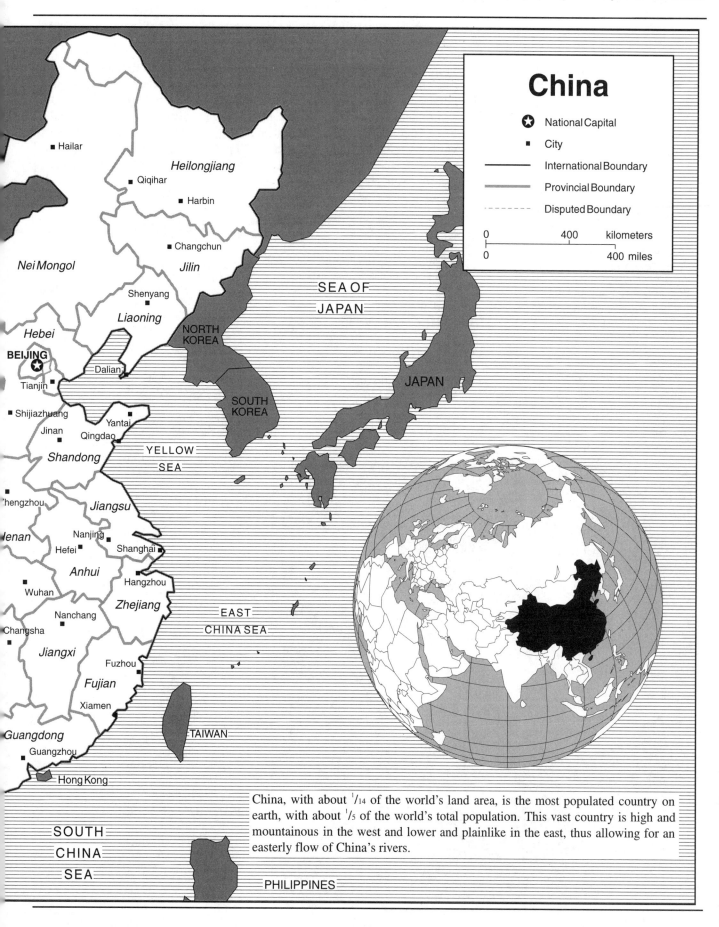

China

- ⊛ National Capital
- ■ City
- —— International Boundary
- —— Provincial Boundary
- ----- Disputed Boundary

0   400   kilometers
0   400 miles

Hailar

Heilongjiang

Qiqihar

Harbin

Changchun

Nei Mongol

Jilin

Shenyang

Liaoning

SEA OF
JAPAN

Hebei

BEIJING

Dalian

NORTH
KOREA

Tianjin

Shijiazhuang

Yantai

Jinan

Qingdao

Shandong

YELLOW

SEA

SOUTH
KOREA

JAPAN

Zhengzhou

Jiangsu

Henan

Nanjing

Hefei

Shanghai

Anhui

Wuhan

Hangzhou

Nanchang

Zhejiang

Changsha

EAST
CHINA SEA

Jiangxi

Fuzhou

Fujian

Xiamen

Guangdong

TAIWAN

Guangzhou

Hong Kong

SOUTH

CHINA

SEA

PHILIPPINES

China, with about $\frac{1}{14}$ of the world's land area, is the most populated country on earth, with about $\frac{1}{5}$ of the world's total population. This vast country is high and mountainous in the west and lower and plainlike in the east, thus allowing for an easterly flow of China's rivers.

China (People's Republic of China)

GEOGRAPHY

Area in Square Kilometers (Miles):
9,572,900 (3,696,100) (slightly larger
than the contiguous United States)
Capital (Population): Beijing (6,900,000)
Climate: extremely diverse

PEOPLE

Population
Total: 1,177,585,000
Annual Growth Rate: 1.1%
Rural/Urban Population Ratio: 73/27
Ethnic Makeup: 92% Han Chinese; 8%
minority groups (the largest being
Chuang, Hui, Uighur, Yi, and Miao)
Major Languages: Standard Chinese
(Putonghua) or Mandarin; Yue
(Cantonese); Wu (Shanghainese);
Minbei (Fuzhou); Minuan (Hokkien-
Taiwanese); Xiang; Gan; Hahka

Health
Life Expectancy at Birth: 67 years
(male); 69 years (female)
Infant Mortality Rate (Ratio): 52.1/1,000
Average Caloric Intake: 104% of FAO
minimum
Physicians Available (Ratio): 1/646

Religions
officially atheist; but Taoism,
Buddhism, Islam, Christianity, ancestor
worship, and animism do exist

Education
Adult Literacy Rate: 73%

COMMUNICATION

Telephones: 11,000,000
Newspapers: 852

THE FIRST CHINESE EMPEROR

By 221 B.C. Qin Shi Huang Di had conquered the last of the independent
states that had been fighting one another for the previous 500 years. He
thereby unified China and founded the Chinese empire. The system of
governmental institutions and social organization that he enforced
throughout the country was intended to ensure that henceforth China
would be ruled by a single emperor. All peoples, whether native Chinese
or "barbarian" foreigners, were expected to acknowledge him as the
rightful "Son of Heaven."

TRANSPORTATION

Highways—Kilometers (Miles):
1,029,000 (639,009)
Railroads—Kilometers (Miles): 64,000
(39,744)
Usable Airfields: 330

GOVERNMENT

Type: one-party Communist state
Independence Date: October 1, 1949
Head of State/Government: President
Jiang Zemin; Premier Li Peng
Political Parties: Chinese Communist
Party; several small and politically
insignificant non-Communist parties
Suffrage: universal at 18

MILITARY

Number of Armed Forces: n/a
*Military Expenditures (% of Central
Government Expenditures):* n/a
Current Hostilities: none

ECONOMY

Currency ($ U.S. Equivalent): 8.52
yuan = $1
Per Capita Income/GDP: $370/$413
billion
Inflation Rate: 20% (est.)
Natural Resources: coal; oil;
hydroelectric sites; natural gas; iron
ores; tin; tungsten
Agriculture: food grains; cotton; oil
seeds; pigs; tea
Industry: iron and steel; coal;
machinery; light industry; armaments

FOREIGN TRADE

Exports: $85.0 billion
Imports: $80.6 billion

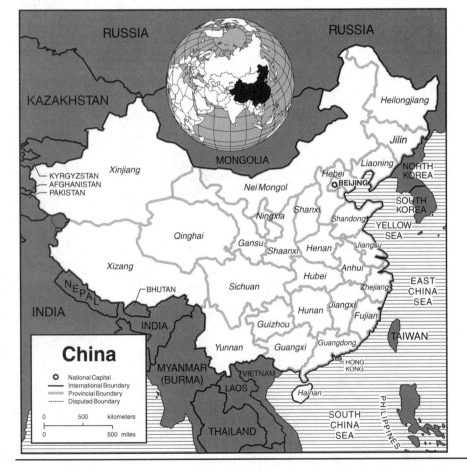

People's Republic of China

Tensions Between Modernization and Ideology

HISTORY

The history and achievements of Chinese civilization rival those of the Greek and Roman empires at their height. Chinese civilization began in the Neolithic period (beginning roughly in 5000 B.C.), but scholars know more about its exact nature during the Shang Dynasty (dating approximately from the second millennium B.C.). By this time the Chinese had developed their sophisticated ideograph system of writing—in which words are portrayed as picturelike characters, a system that continues to be used today—and they had already developed the technology and art of bronze casting to a high standard.

From the fifth to the third centuries B.C., the level of literature and the arts was comparable to that of Greece in the Classical Period, which occurred at the same time. Science flourished, and the philosopher Confucius developed a highly sophisticated system of ethics for government and moral codes for society. These were dominant until the early twentieth century, and even today they influence Chinese thought and behavior, not only in the People's Republic of China (China, or the P.R.C.), but also in Taiwan, Hong Kong, and Singapore.

THE CHINESE EMPIRE

By 221 B.C. the many feudal states ruled by independent princes had been conquered by Qin (Ch'in) Shi Huang Di, the first ruler of a unified Chinese Empire. He established a system of governmental institutions and a concept of empire that continued in China until A.D. 1911. Although China was unified from the Qin dynasty on, it was far less concrete than the term *empire* might indicate. China's borders really reached only as far as its cultural influence did. Thus China contracted and expanded according to whether other groups of people accepted the Chinese ruler and culture as their own.

Those peoples outside "China" who refused to acknowledge the Chinese ruler as the "Son of Heaven" or pay tribute to him were called "barbarians." In fact, the Great Wall, which stretches more than 2,000 miles across north China and was built in stages between the third century B.C. and the seventeenth century A.D., was constructed in order to keep marauding "barbarians" out of China. Nevertheless, they frequently invaded China and occasionally even succeeded in subduing the Chinese—as in the Yuan (Mongol) Dynasty (1279–1368) and, later, the Qing (Ch'ing, or Manchu) Dynasty (1644–1911).

However, the customs and institutions of the invaders eventually yielded to the powerful cultural influence of the Chinese. Indeed, in the case of the Manchus, who seized control of the Chinese Empire in 1644 and ruled until 1911, their success in holding onto the throne for so long may in part be due to their willingness to assimilate Chinese ways and to rule through existing Chinese institutions, such as the Confucian-ordered bureaucracy. By the time of their overthrow, the Manchu rulers were hardly distinguishable from the pure (Han) Chinese in their customs, habits, and beliefs. When considering today's policies toward the numerous minorities who inhabit such a large expanse of the People's Republic of China, it should be remembered that the central Chinese government's ability to absorb minorities was the key to its success in maintaining a unified entity called China for more than 2,000 years.

THE IMPERIAL BUREAUCRACY

A distinguishing feature of the political system of imperial China was the civil service examinations through which government officials were chosen. These examinations tested knowledge of the moral principles embodied in the classical Confucian texts. Although the exams were, in theory, open to all males in the Chinese Empire, the lengthy and rigorous preparation required meant that, in practice, the sons of the wealthy and powerful with access to a good education had an enormous advantage. Only a small percentage of those who began the process actually passed the examinations and received an appointment in the imperial bureaucracy. Those who were successful were sent as the emperor's agents to govern throughout the far-flung realm.

The Decline of the Manchus

The vitality of Chinese institutions and their ability to respond creatively to new problems came to an end during the Manchu Dynasty (1644–1911). This was due in part to internal rebellions, caused by a stagnant agriculture incapable of supporting the growing population and by increasing exploitation of the poor peasants who made up the vast majority of Chinese society. As the imperial bureaucracy and the emperor's court itself became increasingly corrupt and incompetent, they gradually lost the ability to govern the empire effectively. Further, the social class structure rewarded those who could pass the archaic, morality-based civil service examination, rather than scientists and others who could make contributions to China's material advancement.

China's decline in the nineteenth century was exacerbated by cultural "blinders" that prevented the Chinese from understanding the dynamism of the Industrial Revolution then taking place in the West. Gradually the doors erected by the Manchu rulers to prevent Western culture and technology from polluting the ancient beauty of Chinese civilization were knocked down.

The Opium War

The British began importing opium into China in the nineteenth century. Eventually they used the Chinese attack on British ships carrying opium as an excuse for declaring war on the decaying and decrepit Chinese Empire. The Opium War (1839–1842) ended with defeat for the Chinese and the forcible entry of European merchants and missionaries into China.

Other wars brought further concessions—the most important of which was the Chinese granting of "treaty ports" to Europeans. These ports inevitably led to the spread of Western values that challenged the stagnant, and by then morally impotent, Chinese Empire. As the West and Japan nibbled away at China, the Manchu rulers made a last-ditch effort at reform, so as to strengthen and enrich China. But the combination of internal decay, provincialism, revolution, and foreign imperialism finally toppled the Manchu Dynasty. Thus ended more than 2,000 years of imperial rule in China.

REPUBLICAN CHINA

The 1911 Revolution, which derived its greatest inspiration from Sun Yat-sen (even though he was on a political fund-raising trip in the United States when it happened), led to the establishment of the Republic of China—in name, if not in fact. China was briefly united under the control of the dominant warlord of the time, Yuan Shih-kai. But with his death in 1916, China was again torn apart by the resurgence of contending warlords, internal political decay, and further attempts at territorial expansion, especially by the militant Japanese, who were searching for an East Asian empire of their own. Attempts at reform failed because China was so divided and weak.

Chinese intellectuals searched for new ideas from abroad to strengthen their nation in the vibrant May Fourth period, spanning from roughly 1917 through the early 1920s. In the process, influential foreigners such as English mathematician and philosopher Bertrand Russell, American philosopher and educator John Dewey, and renowned Indian poet Rabindranath Tagore came to lecture in China. Thousands of Chinese students traveled and studied abroad. Ideas such as liberal democracy, syndicalism, guild socialism, and communism were contemplated as possible solutions to China's many problems.

(New York Public Library)

CONFUCIUS: CHINA'S FIRST "TEACHER"

Confucius (551–479 B.C.), pictured above, was the first "teacher" in China. His attempts to advise the various state governments of China were spurned, so he spent most of his life teaching his disciples. It was only 300 years later that Confucianism, as taught by descendants of Confucius's own disciples, was adopted as the official state philosophy. The basic principles of Confucianism include social harmony and hierarchy, respect for one's elders and superiors, and the responsibility of rulers to exercise their power benevolently.

The Founding of the Chinese Communist Party

In 1921 a small Marxist study group founded the Chinese Communist Party (CCP). The Moscow-based Comintern (Communist International) advised this highly intellectual but politically impotent group to link up with the more promising and militarily powerful Kuomintang (KMT, or Nationalist Party, led first by Sun Yat-sen and, after his death in 1925, by Chiang Kai-shek), in order to reunify China under one central government. Without adequate support from the Soviets or from forces within China—because there were so few capitalists in China, there was no urban proletariat, and therefore the Marxist aim of "overthrowing the capitalist class" was irrelevant—the Chinese Communists agreed to form a united front with the KMT. They hoped that once they had built up their own organization while cooperating with

OPIUM WAR: NARCOTICS SMUGGLING JUST A PRETEXT FOR WAR

Although the opium poppy is native to China, large amounts of opium were brought to China by the English-owned East India Company from the English colony of India. Eventually India exported so much opium to China that 5 to 10 percent of its revenues derived from the sale of opium.

By the late 1700s, the Chinese government had officially prohibited first the smoking and selling of opium, and later its importation or domestic production. But because the sale of opium was so profitable—and also because so many Chinese officials were addicted to it—the Chinese officials themselves illegally engaged in the opium trade. As the number of addicts grew and the Chinese government became more corrupted by its own unacknowledged participation in opium smuggling, so grew the interest of enterprising Englishmen in smuggling it into China for financial gain.

But the British government was primarily interested in establishing an equal diplomatic and trade relationship with the Chinese to supplant the existing one, in which the Chinese court demanded that the English recognize China as a superior empire. Great Britain's interest in trade, as well as its desire to secure legal jurisdiction over its nationals residing in China to protect them against Chinese practices of torture, combined to

(New York Public Library

strain relations between the two countries further.

Chinese efforts to curb the smuggling of opium and refusal to recognize the British as equals reached a climax in 1839, when the Chinese destroyed thousands of chests of opium aboard a British ship. This served as an ideal pretext for the British to attack China with their sophisticated gunboats (pictured above

destroying a junk in Canton's harbor). Ultimately their superior firepower gave victory to the British.

Thus the so-called Opium War (1839–1842) ended with defeat for the Chinese and the signing of the Treaty of Nanking, which ceded the island of Hong Kong to the British and allowed them to establish trading posts on the mainland.

---

the KMT, they could break away to establish themselves as an independent political party. Thus, it was with Communist support that Chiang Kai-shek successfully united China under his control during the Northern Expedition. Then, in 1927, he brutally quashed the Communist Party.

The Long March

The Chinese Communist Party's ranks were decimated two more times by the KMT's superior police and military forces, largely because the CCP had obeyed Moscow's advice to organize an orthodox Marxist urban-based movement in the cities. The cities, however, were completely controlled by the KMT. It is a testimony to the strength of the appeal of communist ideas at this time that the CCP managed to recover its strength each time. Indeed, the growing power of the CCP was such that Chiang considered it, even more than the

invading Japanese, the main threat to his complete control of China. Eventually the Chinese Communist leaders agreed that an urban strategy was doomed, yet they lacked adequate military power to confront the KMT head-on. They retreated in the famous Long March (1934–1935), which brought them from the southeast through the rugged interior, 6,000 miles to the windswept plains of Yanan in northern China.

It was during this retreat, in which as many as 100,000 people perished, that Mao Zedong (Mao Tse-tung) staged his contest for power within the CCP. With his victory, the Chinese Communist Party reoriented itself toward a rural strategy and attempted to capture the loyalty of the peasants, then comprising some 85 percent of China's total population. Mao saw the peasants as the major source of support for revolution. In most areas of China, the peasants were suffering from an oppressive and brutal system of

MAO ZEDONG: CHINA'S REVOLUTIONARY LEADER

(New York Public Library)

Mao Zedong (1893–1976) came from a moderately well-to-do peasant family and, as a result, received a very good education, as compared to the vast majority of the Chinese. Mao (pictured above) was one of the founders of the Chinese Communist Party in 1921, but his views on the need to switch from an orthodox Marxist strategy, which called for the party to seek roots among the urban working class, to a rural strategy centered on the exploited peasants, was spurned by the leadership of the CCP and its sponsors in Moscow.

Later it became evident that the CCP could not flourish in the Nationalist-controlled cities, as time and again the KMT quashed the idealistic but militarily weak CCP. Mao appeared to be right: "Political power grows out of the barrel of a gun."

The Communists' retreat to Yanan on the Long March was not only for the purpose of survival but also for re-grouping and forming a stronger "Red Army." There the followers of the Chinese Communist Party were taught Mao's ideas about guerrilla warfare, the importance of winning the support of the people, principles of party leadership, and socialist values. Mao consolidated his control over the leadership of the CCP during the Yanan period and led it to victory over the Nationalists in 1949.

From that time onward, Mao became a symbol of the new Chinese government, of national unity, and of the strength of China against foreign humiliation. In later years, although his real power was eclipsed, the party maintained the illusion that Mao was the undisputed leader of China.

In his declining years, Mao waged a struggle, in the form of the Cultural Revolution, against those who followed policies antagonistic to his own, a struggle that brought the country to the brink of civil war and turned the Chinese against one another. The symbol of Mao as China's "great leader" and "great teacher" was used by those who hoped to seize power after him: first the minister of defense, Lin Biao, and then the so-called Gang of Four, which included Mao's wife.

Mao's death in 1976 ended the control of policy by the Gang of Four. Within a few years, questions were being raised about the legacy that Mao had left China. By the 1980s it was broadly accepted throughout China that Mao had been responsible for a full 20 years of misguided policies. Yet since the Tiananmen protests of 1989, there has been a resurgence of nostalgia for Mao. This nostalgia is captured in such aspects of popular culture as a tape of songs about Mao entitled "The Red Sun"—an all-time best-selling tape in China, at 5 million copies—that encapsulates the Mao cult and Mao mania of the Cultural Revolution; and in a small portrait of Mao that virtually all car owners and taxi drivers hang over their rear-view mirrors for "good luck." Many Chinese long for the "good old days" of Mao's rule, when crime and corruption were at far lower levels than today and when there was a sense of collective commitment to China's future. They do not long for a return to the mass terror of the Cultural Revolution, for which Mao also bears responsibility.

landlord control; they were the discontented masses who had "nothing to lose but [their] chains." Appealing to the peasants' desire to own their own land as well as to their disillusionment with KMT rule, the CCP slowly started to gain control over the countryside.

"United" Against the Japanese

The Japanese invasion of 1937 and the subsequent occupation of the north and east coasts of China caused the CCP once again to agree to a unified front with the KMT, in order to halt Japanese aggression. Both the KMT and the CCP had ulterior motives, but according to most accounts, the Communists contributed more to the national wartime efforts. The Communists organized guerrilla efforts to peck away at the fringes of Japanese-controlled areas while Chiang Kai-shek, head of the KMT, holed up with his elite corps in the wartime capital of Chungking, taking the best of the American supplies for themselves and leaving the rank-and-file to fight bootless against the Japanese. Once the Americans and the brave, self-sacrificing Chinese masses had won the war for him,

Chiang Kai-shek believed his army would have the strength to defeat the Communists.

The Communists Oust the KMT

When World War II was over, in 1945, however, it seemed as if hard fighting had actually strengthened the Chinese Communists, while the soft life of the KMT military elite had weakened them. Moving quickly to annihilate the Communists, Chiang pursued his old strategy of taking the cities. But the Communists, who had gained control over the countryside, surrounded the cities, which, like besieged fortresses, eventually fell. By October 1949 the CCP could claim control over all of China—except for Taiwan, where the KMT's political, economic, and military elite who were loyal to Chiang had fled, with American support.

Scholars still dispute why the CCP ultimately defeated the KMT, citing as probable reasons the Communist Party's appeal to the Chinese people, its higher moral standards in comparison to those of the KMT soldiers, the Communists' more successful appeal to the Chinese sense of nationalism, and Chiang's unwillingness to undertake significant reforms. Certainly, any wartime government confronted with the demoralization within its own ranks resulting from inflation, economic destruction, and the humiliation caused by a foreign occupation would have had a difficult time maintaining the loyal support of the populace. Even the middle class eventually deserted the KMT. Those industrial and commercial "capitalists" who stayed behind in the cities hoped to join in a patriotic effort with the CCP to rebuild China.

THE PEOPLE'S REPUBLIC OF CHINA

The Chinese Communists' final victory came rapidly, far faster than anticipated. Suddenly they were in control of a nation of more than 600 million people and had to make important decisions about how to unify and rebuild the country. They were obligated, of course, to fulfill their promise to redistribute land to the poor and landless peasants. The CCP leaders, largely recruited from the peasantry, had a profound understanding of how to create revolution but little knowledge of how to govern. So, rejected by the Western democratic–capitalist countries because of their embrace of communism, they turned to the Soviet Union for support— this in spite of the Soviet leader Joseph Stalin's lackluster and fickle support for the Chinese Communists throughout the 1930s and 1940s.

The Soviet Model

Desperate for aid and advice, the CCP "leaned to one side" in the early 1950s and followed the Soviet model of development. This model favored capital-intensive industrialization and a high degree of centralized control. Such an approach to solving China's problems had some harmful long-term effects; but without Soviet support in the beginning, it is questionable whether the Chinese Communist Party would have been as successful as it was in the 1950s.

The Chinese Approach

The CCP leaders soon became exasperated with the inapplicability of the Soviet model to Chinese circumstances and with the limits of Soviet aid. Because China was unable to afford the extensive capital investments called for by the Soviet model of rapid industrialization through the development of heavy industry, Mao Zedong formulated a Chinese approach to the problem of development. He hoped to substitute China's enormous manpower for expensive capital equipment by organizing people into ever larger working units.

Ultimately, in an attempt to catch up with the industrialized states through a spurt of energy, in 1958 Mao announced a policy termed the Great Leap Forward. This bold scheme to increase production by moving peasants into still larger collective units, called *communes* (the CCP had already moved most peasants into cooperatives by 1955 and taken away almost all their land), and to accelerate industrial production in the cities and countryside was a direct rejection of the Soviet model.

Sino-Soviet Relations Sour

The Soviet leader Nikita Khrushchev denounced the Great Leap Forward as "irrational." He was also distressed at what seemed an adventurist scheme by Mao to bring the Soviets and Americans into direct conflict over the Nationalist-controlled Offshore Islands. In 1959 the Soviets picked up their bags—as well as their blueprints for unfinished factories and spare parts—and left. The Soviets' action, combined with the disastrous decline in production resulting from the policies of the Great Leap Forward and several years of bad weather, set China's development back many years. Population figures now available indicate that somewhere between 20 million and 30 million people died in the years from 1959 to 1962, mostly from starvation and diseases caused by malnutrition. Within the party, Mao's ideas were only paid lip service. Not until 1962 did the Chinese start to recover their productivity gains of the 1950s and to move forward.

The Sino–Soviet split became public in 1963, as the two Communist powers found themselves in profound disagreement over a wide range of issues: what methods Socialist countries could use to develop; policy toward the United States; and whether China or the Soviet Union followed Marxism-Leninism most faithfully and, hence, was entitled to lead the Communist world. This split was not healed until the late 1980s. By then neither country was interested in claiming communist orthodoxy.

(New York Public Library)

RED GUARDS: ROOTING OUT THOSE "ON THE CAPITALIST ROAD"

During the Cultural Revolution, Mao Zedong called upon the youth of the country to "make revolution." They were called Mao's Red Guards. Their ages varied, but for the most part they were teenagers.

Within each class and school, various youths would band together in a Red Guard group that would take on a revolutionary-sounding name and would then carry out the objective of challenging people in authority. But the people in authority, especially schoolteachers, school principals, bureaucrats, and local leaders of the Communist Party, initially ignored the demands of the Red Guards that they "reform their reactionary thoughts" or eliminate their "feudal" habits.

Since the Red Guards initially had no real weapons and could only threaten, and since they were considered just misdirected children by those under attack, their initial assaults had little effect. But soon the frustrated Red Guards took to physically beating and publicly humiliating those who stubbornly refused to obey them. Since Mao had not clearly defined precisely what should be their objectives or methods, the Red Guards were free to believe that the ends justified extreme and often violent means. Moreover, many Red Guards took the opportunity to get revenge against authorities, such as teachers who had given them bad grades. Others (like those pictured above wearing masks to guard against the influenza virus while simultaneously concealing their identities) would harangue crowds on the benefits of Maoism and the evils of foreign influence.

Mao eventually called on the army to support the Red Guards in their effort to challenge "those in authority taking the capitalist road." This created even more confusion, as many of the Red Guard groups actually supported the

people they were supposed to be attacking. But their revolutionary-sounding names and their pretenses at being "Red" (Communist) confused the army. Moreover, the army was divided within itself and did not particularly wish to overthrow the Chinese Communist Party authorities, the main supporters of the military in their respective areas of jurisdiction.

The Red Guards began to go on rampages throughout the country, breaking into people's houses and stealing or destroying their property, harassing people in their homes in the middle of the night, stopping girls with long hair and cutting it off on the spot, destroying the files of ministries and industrial enterprises, and clogging up the transportation system by their travels throughout the country to make revolution. Different Red Guard factions began to fight with one another, each claiming to be the most revolutionary.

Since the schools had been closed, the youth of China were not receiving any formal education during this period. Finally, in 1969, Mao called a halt to the excesses of the Red Guards. They were disbanded and sent home or out to the countryside to labor in the fields with the peasants. But the chaos set in motion during the Cultural Revolution did not come to a halt until the arrest of the Gang of Four, some 10 years after the Cultural Revolution had begun.

Children of school age during the "10 bad years," when schools were either closed or operating with a minimal program, received virtually no education. The Chinese frequently refer to them as "the lost generation." Many of them, because of their lack of education, have not been able to find employment; however, others have worked hard to make up for lost time and have become successful, both politically and economically, since the reforms of the late 1970s.

THE CULTURAL REVOLUTION

In 1966, whether he hoped to provoke an internal party struggle in order to regain control over policy or (as he alleged) to rid China of its repressive bureaucracy in order to restore a revolutionary spirit to the Chinese people and to prevent China from abandoning socialism, Mao launched what was termed the Great Proletarian Cultural Revolution. He called on the youth of China to "challenge authority"—particularly "those revisionists in authority who are taking the capitalist road"—and to "make revolution."

Such vague objectives invited abuse, including personal feuds and retribution for alleged past wrongs, and led to murders, suicides, ruined careers, and broken families. Determining just who was "red" (Communist) and who was "reactionary" itself became the basis for chaos, as people tried to protect themselves by attacking others, even friends and relatives. The major targets were intellectuals, experts, bureaucrats, and people with foreign connections of even the most remote sort. It is estimated that 10 percent of the population—*100 million people*—became targets of the Cultural Revolution and that tens of thousands lost their lives during the decade of political chaos.

Ultimately the Chinese Communist Party was itself the victim of the Cultural Revolution. When the smoke cleared there was little left for the people to believe in or respect. The Cultural Revolution attacked as feudal and outmoded the traditions and customs revered by the Chinese people; then the authority of the party itself was irretrievably damaged by the attacks on many of its leaders. By 1976 there was a nearly total breakdown of both traditional Chinese morality and Marxist-Leninist values. Policies had changed frequently in those "10 bad years" from 1966 to 1976, as first one faction and then another gained the upper hand.

"Pragmatic" Policies

In September 1976 the aged Mao died, and in October the so-called Gang of Four (including Mao's wife), who had been the most radical leaders of the Cultural Revolution, were arrested and removed from power. Deng Xiaoping, a veteran leader of the Chinese Communist Party who had been purged twice during the "10 bad years," was "rehabilitated" in 1977.

Once again China set off on the road of construction and put to an end the radical policies of "continuous revolution" and the idea that it was more important to be "red" than "expert." Under Deng's "pragmatic" policies, China has, in spite of readjustments and setbacks, put its major effort into modernization in four areas: science and technology, industry, agriculture, and the military.

The issue of de-Maoification has been a thorny one, as to defrock Mao would raise serious issues about the CCP's right to rule. The CCP has already admitted that after 1957 Mao made many "serious mistakes," but it insists that these errors should be seen within the context of his many accomplishments and the fact that he was a committed, if sometimes misdirected, Marxist and revolutionary.

The Challenge of Reform

The inevitable result of this endless questioning and rejection—first of traditional Chinese values, next of Marxism-Leninism and its concept of the infallibility of the party, and finally of Mao Thought (the Chinese adaptation of Marxism-Leninism to Chinese conditions)—was to leave China without any strong belief system. Such Western values as materialism, capitalism, individualism, and freedom have flowed into this vacuum to challenge both communist ideology and traditional Chinese values.

Had their ideology and values remained intact, these foreign values would appear less threatening. But as indicated by the campaign in the 1980s against "spiritual pollution" and then the crackdown on those calling for greater democracy during the spring of 1989, the "screen door" that Deng Xiaoping thought would permit Western science and technology to flow into China while keeping out the annoying insects of Western values appeared to have many large holes in it. The less "pragmatic," more ideologically oriented "conservative" or "hard-line" leadership used these problems as a rationale to challenge the economic reforms aimed at liberalization and to reverse the trend away from ideological education in the schools and propaganda in the workplace.

By 1992 policy had again shifted in favor of the more liberal reformers, with Deng Xiagoping, "retired" but still very much in control, successfully manuvering first to bypass, and then to replace, those in the central leadership resisting reform. Once again he encouraged the people to do "whatever works," regardless of ideology, to experiment until they succeeded. At the 14th Party Congress, in October 1992, the balance within the Standing Committee of the Politburo and the Politburo itself shifted in favor of those promoting reform. Although these reforms are in theory restricted to the economic realm, in practice they spill over into the political, social, and cultural realms as well.

THE PEOPLE OF CHINA

Population

By 1995 China's population was approximately 1.2 billion. In the 1950s Mao had encouraged population growth, considering its people to be China's major source of strength. No sustained attempts to limit Chinese population occurred until the mid-1970s. Even then, because there were no penalties for those Chinese who ignored them, population control programs were only marginally successful.

In 1979 the government launched a serious birth control campaign, which rewarded families having only one child with work bonuses, free health care, and priority in housing. Later the only child was to receive preferential treatment in university admissions and in job assignments. The family

(China Pictorial)

The radical leaders of China's Cultural Revolution, who came to be known as the Gang of Four, were brought to trial in late 1980. Here they are pictured (along with another radical who was not part of the Gang) in a Beijing courtroom, listening to the judge pass sentence. The Gang of Four are the first four (from right to left) standing in the prisoners' dock: Jiang Qing, Yao Wenyuan, Wang Hongwen, and Zhang Chunqiao.

THE GANG OF FOUR

The current leadership of the Chinese Communist Party regards the Cultural Revolution of 1966–1976 as having been a period of total chaos that brought the People's Republic of China to the brink of political and economic ruin. While Mao Zedong is criticized for having begun the Cultural Revolution with his mistaken ideas about the danger of China turning "capitalist," the major blame for the turmoil of those years is placed on a group of extreme radicals labeled the Gang of Four.

The Gang of Four consisted of Jiang Qing, Mao's wife, who began playing a key role in P.R.C. cultural affairs during the early 1960s; Zhang Chunqiao, a veteran party leader in Shanghai; Yao Wenyuan, a literary critic and ideologue; and Wang Hongwen, a factory worker catapulted into national prominence by his leadership of rebel workers during the Cultural Revolution. By the late 1960s, these four individuals were among the most powerful leaders in China. Drawn together by common political interests and a shared belief that the party should be relentless in ridding China of suspected "capitalist roaders," they worked together to keep the Cultural Revolution on a radical course. One of their arch enemies was Deng Xiaoping, who emerged as China's paramount leader in 1978.

Although they had close political and personal ties to Mao and derived many of their ideas from him, Mao be-came quite disenchanted with the radicals in the last few years of his life. He was particularly displeased with the unscrupulous and secretive way in which they behaved as a faction within the top levels of the party. Indeed, it was Mao who coined the phrase *Gang of Four*, as part of a written warning to the radicals to cease their conspiracies and obey established party procedures.

The Gang of Four hoped to be able to take over supreme power in China following Mao's death on September 9, 1976. However, their plans were upset less than a month later, when other party and army leaders had the Gang arrested—an event that is now said to mark the formal end of the Cultural Revolution. By removing from power the party's most influential radicals, the arrest of the Gang of Four set the stage for the dramatic reforms that have become the hallmark of the post-Mao era in China.

In November 1980 the Gang of Four were put on trial in Beijing. They were charged with having committed serious crimes against the Chinese people and accused of having had a hand in "persecuting to death" tens of thousands of officials and intellectuals whom they perceived as their political enemies. All four were convicted and sentenced to long terms in prison.

with more than two children, however, was not to receive any of these benefits and, in fact, would be penalized by a 10 percent decrease in its yearly wages.

The one-child policy in China's major cities has been rigorously enforced, to the point where it is almost impossible for a woman to get away with a second pregnancy. Who is allowed to have a child—as well as when she may give birth—is rigidly controlled by the woman's work unit. Women are required to stand in front of X-ray machines to make sure that their IUDs are still in place. Abortions can and

The Chinese government has made great efforts to curb the country's population growth by promoting the merits of the one-child family. Today China has an average annual growth rate of 1.1 percent.

will be performed throughout the period of a woman's unsanctioned pregnancy. As Christianity is not a religion embraced by many Chinese, the moral issues that surround abortions in the West concerning the rights of the unborn fetus are not issues for the Chinese.

The effectiveness of China's birth control policy in the cities is not merely attributable to the surveillance by work units, neighborhood committees, and "granny police" who watch over the families in their locales. Changed social attitudes also play a critical role, for urban Chinese now accept the importance of population control. They are all too aware of how overcrowded their cities are and of China's limited ability to provide adequately for a still-expanding population.

The one-child policy ultimately may pose another ideological issue for the Chinese: If the only children of conscientious parents are given preferential opportunities in education and in job assignments, the Chinese will be creating another elite, based not on achievement or even revolutionary credentials but on birth rights. Furthermore, the demographic issues created by the one-child policy, such as too few young people to support the elderly in future years, have since the early 1990s led to modification in the strictness of its enforcement.

The success of the one-child policy in the cities has led to another social issue: spoiled children. Known as "little emperors," the only children are the center of attention of six anxious adults (two sets of grandparents and the parents), who carefully scrutinize their every movement. It has led to the overuse of medical services by these parents and grandparents, who rush their only child/grandchild to the doctor at the first signs of a sniffle or sore throat. It has also led to children who are overfed and grow fat. Because of China's history, being overweight was considered a hedge against bad times, and the Chinese were initially pleased that their children were becoming fat. A common greeting showing admiration has been "You have become fat!" As the urban Chinese adopt many of the values associated with becoming wealthier in the developed world, however, they have started to value remaining thin. So far salad bars do not loom on the horizon, and exercise remains valued for the purpose of keeping China a strong nation, not for looking attractive.

Female Infanticide

In the vast rural areas of China, where more than 80 percent of the population still live, efforts to enforce the one-child policy have met with less success than in the cities, because the benefits and punishments are not as relevant for peasants. Under the "contract responsibility system" initiated in the 1980s, communes were disbanded and families given their

(United Nations photo/John Isaac)

The Chinese central government has pursued policies designed to get the many minorities to identify with the Han Chinese majority.

own land to till. As a result, the more family members to help with farming, the better. This is hardly conducive to family planning.

Although China's peasants have always preferred having sons because of their strength in doing farmwork, it is ironically the sons who are being rewarded with the relatively easy factory jobs now available in rural towns, thereby leaving the daughters to work in the fields. Nevertheless, males are still more valued in Chinese culture. This is because only sons are able to carry on traditional Chinese family rituals and ancestor worship. The result is that in spite of governmental efforts to stop female infanticide, it still continues in rural areas under the less rigidly enforced one-child per family policy. So does the kidnapping of young women and the practice of selling girls as brides in rural marketplaces. Again, this reflects cultural values that denigrate females; it also reflects a demand for brides in remote villages where there are not enough women to go around.

Finally, in the countryside, it is estimated that hundreds of thousands of peasants have taken steps to ensure that their

female offspring are not counted toward their one-child (and now, in many places, two-child) limit: A pregnant woman simply moves to another village to have her child. Since the local village leaders are not responsible for women's reproduction when they are not their own villagers, women are not harassed into getting an abortion in other villages. If the child is a boy, she can simply return to her native village and register him; if a girl, she can return and not register her. Thus, a whole generation of young girls are growing up in the countryside without ever having been registered. Since, except for schooling, peasants have few claims to state-supplied benefits anyway, they may consider this official nonexistence of their daughters a small price to pay for having as many children as necessary until giving birth to a boy.

China's strict population control policies have been effective: Since 1977, the population has grown at an average annual rate of 1.1 percent, one of the lowest growth rates in the developing world. Unfortunately, even this low rate has worked out to an average annual increase of China's population of more than 12 million people. This poses a challenge, and perhaps a threat, to future economic development and, therefore, to political stability.

National Minorities

Ninety-four percent of the population are Han Chinese. Although only 6 percent are "national minorities," they occupy more than 60 percent of China's geographical expanse. These minorities inhabit almost the entire border area, including Tibet, Inner Mongolia, and Xinjiang, the security of which is important for China's defense. Furthermore, China's borders with the many countries on its national borders are poorly defined, and members of the same minority usually live on both sides of the borders.

To address this issue, China's central government pursued policies designed to get the minorities on the Chinese side of the border to identify with the Han Chinese majority. Rather than admitting to this objective of undermining distinctive national identities, the CCP leaders phrased the policies in terms of getting rid of the minorities' "feudal" customs, such as religious practices, which are contrary to the "scientific" values of socialism. At times these policies have been brutal and have caused extreme bitterness among the minorities, particularly Tibetans and the large number of minority peoples who practice Islam.

In the 1980s the Deng Xiaoping leadership conceded that Beijing's harsh assimilation policies had been ill-conceived, and it tried to gain the loyalty of the national minorities through more sensitive policies. By the late 1980s, however, the loosening of controls had led to further challenges to Beijing's control. For example, the central government reimposed martial law in Tibet to quell protests and riots against Beijing's discriminatory policies toward Tibetans. Martial law was lifted in 1990, but security has remained tight in Lhasa, the capital of Tibet.

In the far northwest, the predominantly Muslim population of Xinjiang Province continues to challenge the authority of China's central leadership. The loosening of policies aimed at assimilating the minority populations into the Han (Chinese) culture has given a rebirth to Islamic culture and practices, including prayer five times a day, architecture in the Islamic style, traditional Islamic medicine, and teaching Islam in the schools.

With the dissolution of the USSR into 15 independent states, the ties between the Islamic states on China's borders (the former Soviet republics of Kazakhstan, Kyrgyzstan, and Tajikistan, as well as Afghanistan and Pakistan) are accelerating rapidly. Beijing is certainly concerned that China's Islamic minorities may find that they have more in common with these neighboring Islamic nations than with the Chinese Han majority and may attempt to secede from China. Their concern was heightened when Turkey held a summit conference in late 1992 at which it announced that the next century would be the century of Islam. Subsequent signs of a growing worldwide Islamic movement have heightened Beijing's anxieties about controlling their Islamic minority.

Events in Outer Mongolia have also led China's central leadership to keep a watchful eye on Inner Mongolia, an autonomous region under Beijing's control. In 1989 Mongolia's government, theoretically independent but in fact under Moscow's tutelage, decided to permit multiparty rule at the expense of the Communist Party's complete control. Beijing has grown increasingly concerned that these democratic inklings might spread to their neighboring cousins in Inner Mongolia, with a subsequent challenge to one-party CCP rule. As with the Islamic minorities, China's leadership is concerned that the Mongols in Inner Mongolia may try to secede from China and join with the independent state of Mongolia because of a shared culture.

Religion

Confucianism is the "religion" most closely associated with China. It is not, however, a religion in Western terms, as there is no place for gods, the afterlife, or most other beliefs associated with formal religions. But, like most religions, it does have a system of ethics for governing human relationships; and it adds to this what most religions do not have, namely, ethics and principles for good governance. The Chinese Communists rejected Confucianism until the 1980s, but not because it was an "opiate of the masses." (This was Karl Marx's view of religion, which he saw as a way of trapping people in a web of superstitions and causing them to endure their miserable lives passively.) Instead, they denounced Confucianism for providing the ethical rationale for a system of patriarchy, which allowed officials to insist on obedience from subordinates. During the years in which "leftists" set the agenda, moreover, the CCP rejected Confucianism for its emphasis on education in order to become part of the ruling elite, in favor of ideological commitment as the primary criterion for ruling. The series of reforms that began in 1979, however, have generally supported an emphasis on an educated elite, and some Confucian values are now referred to in support of the CCP's reform policies.

Buddhism and Islam have remained important among some of the largest of the national minorities, notably the Tibetans (for Buddhism) and the Uygars and Mongols (for Islam). The CCP's efforts to eradicate these religious influences have been interpreted by the minorities as national oppression by the Han Chinese. As a result, the revival of Islam and Buddhism in the 1980s was associated with efforts by the national minorities to assert their national identities and to gain greater autonomy in formulating their own policies.

For most Chinese, however, folk religions are far more important than any organized religion.[1] The CCP's best efforts to eradicate folk religions and to impart in their place an educated "scientific" viewpoint have failed.

Animism, the belief that nonliving things have spirits that should be respected through worship, continues to be practiced by China's vast peasantry. *Ancestor worship,* the belief that the living can communicate with the dead and that the dead spirits to whom sacrifices are ritually made have the ability to bring a better (or worse) life to the living, absorbs much of the excess income of China's peasants. The costs of burning paper money, of offerings, and of using shamans and priests to perform rituals that will heal the sick, appease the ancestors, and exorcise ghosts (who are often those poorly treated ancestors returned to haunt their descendants) at times of birth, marriage, and death, can be burdensome. But peasants are once again spending money on traditional religious folk practices, thereby contributing to the reconstruction of practices prohibited in earlier decades of Communist rule.

Taoism, which requires its disciples to renounce the secular world, has had few adherents in China since the early twentieth century. But during the repression that followed the crackdown on Tiananmen Square's prodemocracy movement in 1989, many Chinese who were unable to speak freely turned to mysticism and Taoism. *Qigong,* the ancient Taoist art of deep breathing, had by 1990 become a national pastime. Some 30 Taoist priests in China took on the role of national soothsayers, portending the future of everything from the weather to China's political leadership. What these priests said—or were believed to have said—quickly spread through a vast rumor network in the cities. Meanwhile, on Chinese Communist Party–controlled television, *qigong* experts swallow needles and thread, only to have the needles subsequently come out of their noses perfectly threaded. It is widely believed that with a sufficient concentration of *qi* (vital energy or breath), a practitioner may literally knock a person to the ground.[2]

The revival of Taoist mysticism and meditation, folk religion, and formal religions suggests a need to find meaning from religion to fill the moral and ideological vacuum created by the near-collapse of Communist values.

In the 1980s, under the influence of the more moderate policies of the Deng Xiaoping reformist leadership, the CCP reconsidered its efforts to eliminate religion. The 1982 State Constitution permits religious freedom; previously, only atheism was allowed. The state has actually encouraged the restoration of Buddhist temples and Islamic mosques, in part because of Beijing's awareness of the continuing tensions caused by its efforts to deny minorities their respective religious practices—and in part because of a desire to attract both tourists and money to the minority areas.

Christianity, which was introduced in the nineteenth and early twentieth century by European missionaries, has several million known adherents, and its churches, which were often used as warehouses or public offices after the Communist victory in 1949, have also been reopened for religious practice. A steady stream of Christian proselytizers flow to China in search of new converts. Today's churches are attended as much by the curious as by the devout. As with eating Western food in places such as McDonald's and Kentucky Fried Chicken, attending Christian churches is a way some Chinese feel that they can participate in Western culture.

Many of those who maintained their religious beliefs after 1949 have been targets for "thought reform" during mass campaigns. Even today anyone who openly embraces a formal religion finds it difficult to become a member of the CCP.

Marxism-Leninism-Mao Zedong Thought
Unlike religions, which the CCP leadership believes hinder the development of "rational" behavior and values that are so important to modernization, Marxism-Leninism-Mao Zedong Thought has been considered an integrated, rational thought system. Nevertheless, this core of China's communist political ideology has had many of the trappings of religions. These include scriptures (the works of Marx, Lenin, and Mao, as well as the party doctrines themselves); a spiritual head (Mao); and ritual observances (particularly during the Cultural Revolution, when Chinese were forced to participate in the political equivalent of Bible study each day). In the 1980s, as the pragmatic leadership encouraged the people to "seek truth from facts" rather than from Marxism-Leninism-Mao Zedong Thought, the role of this political ideology/religion declined, although more conservative elements in the political leadership have attempted to keep it strong. They were successful in returning the country to ideological study and control in both the schools and the workplace in the immediate aftermath of the Tiananmen Square protests of 1989; but by 1992 the "pragmatic" group within the leadership had reasserted dominance and once again directed the people's attention away from ideology. The required Friday afternoon "political study" sessions in all urban work units abandoned any pretense of interest in politics. Instead, they focused on such issues as "how to do our work better" that were in line with the more pragmatic approach to the workplace.

This is not to suggest that ideology has been entirely abandoned. In the context of modernizing the economy and raising the standard of living, the current leadership is still committed to building "socialism with Chinese characteristics." Marxist-Leninist ideology is once again being reformulated in China; but it is increasingly evident that there are few true believers in communism left.

Language
The Chinese had a written language by the time of the Shang Dynasty, in the second millennium B.C. It has evolved through 4,000 years into its present-day form, which is still ideographic. Each Chinese character, or *ideograph,* originally represented both a picture and/or a sound of a word. Before the May Fourth Movement of the 1920s, only a tiny elite of highly educated men could read these ideographs in

DENG XIAOPING = TENG HSIAO-P'ING: WHAT IS PINYIN?

Chinese is the oldest of the world's active languages and is now spoken and written by more people than any other modern language. Chinese is written in the form of characters, which have evolved over several thousand years from picture symbols (like ancient Egyptian hieroglyphics) to the more abstract forms now in use. Although spoken Chinese varies greatly from dialect to dialect (e.g., Mandarin, Cantonese, Shanghai-ese), the characters used to represent the language remain the same throughout China: dialects are really just different ways of pronouncing the same characters.

There are more than 50,000 different Chinese characters. A well-educated person may be able to recognize as many as 25,000 characters, but basic literacy today requires familiarity with only a few thousand.

Since Chinese is written in the form of characters rather than by a phonetic alphabet, Chinese words must be transliterated so that foreigners can pronounce them. This means that the sound of the character must be put into an alphabetic approximation: since English uses the Roman alphabet, Chinese characters are Romanized. (We do the same thing with other languages that are based on non-Roman alphabets, such as Russian, Greek, Hebrew, and Arabic.)

Over the years a number of methods have been developed to Romanize the Chinese language. Each method presents what the linguists who developed it believe to be the best way of approximating the sound of Chinese characters. *Pinyin* (literally, "spell sounds"), the system developed in the People's Republic of China, has gradually become the most commonly accepted system of Romanizing Chinese.

Chinese characters are the symbols used to write Chinese. Modern Chinese characters fall into two categories: one with a phonetic component, the other without it. Most of those without a phonetic component developed from pictographs. From ancient writing on archaeological relics we can see their evolution, as in the examples shown (from left to right) above.

However, other systems are still used outside China, such as in Taiwan. This can cause some confusion, since the differences between Romanization systems can be quite significant. For example, in pinyin, the name of China's dominant leader is spelled *Deng Xiaoping*. But the Wade-Giles system, which until recently was the Romanization method most widely used by Westerners, transliterates his name as *Teng Hsiao-p'ing*. Same person, same characters, but a difference in how to spell his name in Roman letters.

their classical written form, which in no way reflected the spoken language. However, this was changed in the 1920s, and the written language became almost identical in its structure to the spoken language.

Increasing Literacy

When the Chinese Communists came to power in 1949, they decided to facilitate the process of becoming literate by allowing only a few thousand of the more than 50,000 Chinese characters in existence to be used in printing newspapers, official documents, and educational materials. However, since a word is usually comprised of a combination of two characters, these few thousand characters form the basis of a very rich vocabulary: any single character may be used in numerous combinations in order to form words. The Chinese Communists have also attempted to make literacy easier by simplifying thousands of characters, often reducing a character from more than 20 strokes to 10 or even fewer.

In 1979 China adopted a new system, *pinyin,* for spelling Chinese words and names. This system, which uses the Latin alphabet of 26 letters, is still largely for foreign consumption and is not commonly used within China. The fact that so many characters have the same Romanization (and pronun-

ciation), plus cultural resistance, have thus far resulted in ideographs remaining the basis for Chinese writing. There are, as an example, at least 70 different Chinese ideographs that are pronounced *zhu,* but each of which means something different.

Spoken Chinese

Finally, the Chinese Communists decreed that all Chinese would speak the same dialect. Although the Chinese have shared the same written language for the last 2,000 years, regardless of which dialect of Chinese they spoke (the same written characters were simply pronounced in different ways, depending on the dialect), it was extremely difficult to achieve a high level of national unity when people needed interpreters to speak with someone even a few miles away. After the Communist victory in 1949, a majority of the delegates to the National People's Congress voted to adopt the northern dialect, Mandarin, as the national language, and they required all schools to teach in Mandarin (standard Chinese).

But the reality was that in the countryside, it was difficult to find teachers capable of speaking Mandarin; and at home, whether in the countryside or the cities, the people continued to speak their local dialects. The liberalization policies of the 1980s and 1990s have seemingly had as their by-product a discernible trend back to speaking local dialects, even in the workplace and on the streets. Whereas 10 years ago a foreigner could count on the Chinese speaking Mandarin in its major cities, this is no longer the case. As a unified language is an important factor in supporting national cohesion, the reemergence of local dialects at the expense of standard Chinese threatens China's fragile unity.

One force that is slowing this disintegration is television, for it is broadcast almost entirely in standard Chinese. As there is now a wide variety of interesting programming available on Chinese television, it may be that most Chinese will make an effort to acquire at least the ability to understand, if not speak, standard Chinese.

Education

Educating the Chinese people has been one of the great achievements of the P.R.C. Before 1949 less than 20 percent of the population could read and write. Today, although it is impossible even to agree on what literacy means, it is widely believed that almost all school-age children in the cities attend the 5-year program at the primary level and that 90 percent of those children living in the rural areas do. At the higher educational levels, however, few rural children attend school. Not only are they needed to help in the fields, but also, even the very low school tuition is too expensive for a poor peasant family. Rural education also suffers from a lack of qualified teachers, as any person educated enough to teach can probably get a better-paying job in the industrial or commercial sector. In the cities, those children who continue on to secondary schools go either to a vocational middle school or to what is basically a college-preparatory school.

Overeducated Students

As in the United States, there is now concern in China that too many students are preparing to go on to a university—but the reason for the concern is different. In the United States, *college graduates* who lack vocational training often find themselves poorly prepared to get a good job. In China, only about 5 percent of the senior middle-school graduates (less than 1 percent of all college-age people in China) will pass the university entrance examinations and be admitted, but far more people than this pursue a college-oriented curriculum. Thus, in China it is *high school graduates* who find themselves inappropriately educated for the workplace. The government is consequently attempting to augment vocational training at the high school level as well as to increase the number of slots available in colleges and universities. Some private high schools and colleges are also being established to address these needs.

In the context of the freewheeling small enterprise capitalist economy that has thrived since the early 1980s, many Chinese have grown cynical about the value of education.

Those making the most money have not, after all, been those with a college education but, rather, those successful at entrepreneurship. A college graduate, who is usually assigned to the low-paying state sector, still makes a mere $60 to $200 per month. An uneducated individual selling noodle soup out of his back door can often make at least that much in just a week. And workers in the state industrial sector have always earned far more money than have China's "intellectuals." At a time when moonlighting is permitted, ordinary workers often move on to a second job at the end of the day; but there are few such opportunities available to those with a liberal arts college education.

Political Education

Until the reforms that began in 1979, the content of Chinese education was suffused with political values and objectives. A considerable amount of school time—as much as 100 percent during political campaigns—was devoted to political education. Often this amounted to nothing more than learning by rote the favorite axioms and policies of the leading faction in power. When that faction lost power, the students' political thought had to be reoriented in the direction of the new policies and values. History, philosophy, literature, and even foreign language and science were laced with a political vocabulary.

The prevailing political line has affected the balance in the curriculum between political study and the learning of skills and scientific knowledge. Beginning in the 1960s, the political content of education increased dramatically until, during the Cultural Revolution, schools were shut down. When they reopened in the early 1970s, politics dominated the curriculum. When Deng and the "modernizers" consolidated their power in the late 1970s, this tendency was reversed. During the 1980s, in fact, schools jettisoned the study of political theory: Both administrators and teachers wanted their students to do well on college-entrance examinations, which by then focused on academic subjects. As a result, students refused to clog their schedules with the study of political theory and the CCP's history. Although the study of Marxism and party history was revived in the wake of the events of Tiananmen Square in 1989, with the entering classes for many universities required to spend the first year in political study and indoctrination (sometimes under military supervision), this practice was abandoned after 2 years. Today political study has again been confined to a narrow part of the curriculum in the interest of education that will help advance China's modernization.

Study Abroad

Since 1979, when China began to promote an "open door" policy, more than 80,000 P.R.C. students have been sent for a university education to the United States, and tens of thousands more have gone to Europe and Japan; for although China does have universities, they have space for only a small

DENG XIAOPING: TAKING A "PRACTICAL" APPROACH TO CHINA'S PROBLEMS

Deng Xiaoping, a controversial figure throughout his political career, was twice purged from power. Deng, pictured here, became the dominant figure in Chinese politics soon after the Gang of Four was removed from power in October 1976.

Under Deng's leadership, China implemented policies of economic liberalization (that is, the use of capitalist methods of production and free markets), many of which are in conflict with China's socialist economic system. Deng's statement, "I don't care whether the cat is black or white as long as it catches mice," illustrates his practical, nonideological approach to modernizing China. In other words, Deng would resort to capitalist methods if they would help modernize China faster than socialist methods.

Deng's methods caused considerable controversy within the Chinese Communist Party. To remain in control, Deng often had to retreat from his efforts to reform the economic and political system and to satisfy his enemies' demands for a stricter adherence to communist doctrine and Communist Party control.

In March 1990 Deng resigned from his only remaining official post, chairman of the State Military Commission. Nevertheless, he still retained considerable power within the central leadership. In Chinese politics, it is only with the death of such extraordinarily powerful leaders as Deng and Mao that their influence ends.

(Hsin-Hua News Agency)

percentage of all high school graduates. Furthermore, until the late 1980s, Chinese universities were unable to offer graduate training. Those trained abroad were expected to return to China to establish graduate education in Chinese universities.

The fate of P.R.C. students educated abroad who return to China has not always been a happy one. The elite educated in Western universities who were in China in 1949, or who returned to China thereafter, were not permitted to hold leadership positions within their fields. Ultimately they were the targets of class-struggle campaigns and purges in the 1950s, 1960s, and 1970s, precisely because of their Western education. For the most part, those students who returned to China in the 1980s after studying abroad were given the same positions that they occupied before they received advanced education abroad. This was in part because their less-well-educated seniors who had not been able to study abroad held a jealous regard for their own positions. These individuals still have the power to make arbitrary decisions about their subordinates, and they ignore the mandate from the central authorities to promote the returned students to appropriate positions. In those places where the seniority system is still the basis for promotion, therefore, it may be difficult for a returned student to get a satisfactory job in China.

Moreover, while studying abroad, Chinese students and older "visiting scholars" learn much about liberal democratic societies. When they return to China—and to date, only a small percentage of students have—they bring with them the theories, values, and concepts at the heart of liberal democratic societies. The central CCP leadership saw the danger signs of this in 1986, when student demonstrations erupted, and later, in 1989, when the student-led prodemocracy movement took on massive proportions in demonstrations in Beijing and other cities. The conservative members of the leadership placed the blame for these efforts to push for democratic political reform in China squarely on the liberalization policies that permitted an opening to the West, including the education of Chinese students abroad.

Nevertheless, much has changed since 1992, when Deng Xiaoping announced a major shift in government policy to support just about anything that would help China develop and become strong. The impact of this on students who have studied abroad is that the government is now offering them significant incentives to come back, including excellent jobs, good salaries, and even the chance to start up new companies. Chinese students who have graduated from foreign universities are also recruited for both their expertise and their understanding of the outside world by the rapidly multiplying number of joint ventures in China.

The flow of Chinese students to study in foreign countries continues unabated, even though further hurdles must now be

(Chinese News Service photo)

Although the Chinese Communist Party (shown here at its 11th National Congress) has hand-picked one candidate for each public office in the past, it is now allowing more than one person to run for the same post.

negotiated before any university student can leave China. Students who have received a university education in China must work for 5 years after college before going abroad for graduate study; otherwise, they must repay the state government for the university education that they received at state expense before they leave China. Yet this requirement has seemingly done little to stem the outward flow of China's college students, as the rapid accumulation of wealth by many Chinese in recent years has made it possible to repay what used to be considered extraordinary debts.

THE ECONOMIC SYSTEM

A Command Economy
Until 1979 the Chinese had what is known as a *centrally controlled command economy*. That is, the central leadership determined the economic policies to be followed and allocated all of the country's resources—labor, capital, and raw materials. Once the Communist Party leadership determined the country's political goals and the correct ideology to follow, the State Planning Commission and the State Economic Commission then decided how to implement these objectives through specific policies for agriculture and industry and the

allocation of resources. This is in striking contrast to a capitalist laissez-faire economy, in which there is a minimum of government control; market forces of supply and demand are the primary determinants of what is produced.

The CCP leadership adopted the model of a centralized economy from the Soviet Union. Such a system was not only in accord with the Leninist model of centralized state governance but also made sense for a government desperate to unify China after more than 100 years of internal division, instability, and economic collapse. Historically, China suffered from large regions evading the grasp of central control over such matters as currency and the payment of taxes. The inability of the Kuomintang government to gain control over the country's economy in the 1930s and early 1940s undercut its power and contributed to its failure to win control over China. Thus, the Chinese Communist Party's decision to centralize economic decision making after 1949 contributed to the state functioning as an integrated whole.

Over time, however, China's highly centralized economy became inefficient and inadequately flexible to address the complexity of the country's needs. Although China possesses a large and diverse economy, with a broad range of resources, topography, and climate, the P.R.C.'s economic planners made policy as if China were a uniform, homogeneous whole. Merely increasing production was itself considered a contribution to development, regardless of whether or not there was a market for the products manufactured.

The state planning agencies, without the benefit of market research, determined whether or not a product should be manufactured and in what quantity. For example, the central government might set a goal for a factory to manufacture 5 million springs per year—without knowing whether there was even a market for them. The factory management did not care, as the state was responsible for marketing the products and paid the factory's bills. If the state had no buyer for the springs, they would pile up in warehouses; but rarely would production be cut back, much less a factory be closed, because this would create a problem for employing the workers cut from the payroll. Economic inefficiencies of this sort were often justified because socialist political objectives were being met. Thus, even today the state worries about shutting down an inefficient factory because it would create unemployment.

Quality control has also largely been ignored by state-run industries, as the state itself allocates the finished products to other industries that need them. If a state-controlled factory makes defective parts, the industry using them has no recourse against the supplier, because each factory has a contract with the state, not with each other.

As a result, China's economic development under the centralized political leadership of the CCP occurred by fits and starts. Much waste resulted from planning that did not take into account market factors of supply and demand. Centrally set production quotas took the place of profit-and-loss issues in the allocation of resources. Although China's command economy was able to meet the country's most important industrial needs, problems like these took their toll over time. Enterprises had little incentive to raise productivity, quality, or efficiency when doing so did not affect their budgets, wages, or funds for expansion.

Unrealistic Agricultural Programs

The agricultural sector suffered most from centralized planning. Regardless of geography or climate, China's economic planners repeatedly ordered peasants to restructure their economic production units according to one centralized plan. China's peasants, who had supported the CCP in its rise to power before 1949 in order to acquire their own land, had enthusiastically embraced the CCP's fulfillment of its pledge of "land to the tillers" after the Communists took over in 1949. But in 1953 the leadership, motivated by a belief that small-scale agricultural production could not meet the production goals of socialist development, ordered all but 15 percent of the arable land to be pooled into "lower-level agricultural producer cooperatives" of between 300 and 700 workers. The remaining 15 percent of land was to be kept as private plots for the peasants, and they could market the produce from these plots in private markets throughout the countryside. Then, in 1956, the peasants throughout the country were ordered into "higher-level agricultural producer cooperatives" of 10 times that size, and the size of the private plots allotted to them was reduced to 5 percent of the cooperatives' total land.

Many peasants felt cheated by these wholesale collectivization policies. When in 1958 the central leadership ordered them to move into communes 10 times larger still than the cooperatives they had just joined, they were incensed. Mao Zedong's *Great Leap Forward* policy of 1958 forced all peasants in China to become members of large communes: economic and administrative units consisting of between 30,000 and 70,000 peasants. With communization, all the peasants' private plots and private utensils, as well as their household chickens, pigs, and ducks, were to be turned over to the commune. Resisting this mandate, many peasants killed and ate their livestock. Since private enterprise was no longer permitted, home handicraft industries ground to a halt.

CCP Chairman Mao Zedong's vision for catching up with the West was to industrialize the vast countryside. Peasants were therefore ordered to build "backyard furnaces" to smelt steel. Lacking iron ore, much less any knowledge of how to make steel, and under the guidance of party cadres who themselves were ignorant of steel making, the peasants tore out metal radiators and pipes, metal fences, pots and pans. Almost none of the final smelted product was usable. Finally, the central economic leadership ordered all peasants to eat in large, communal mess halls. This was reportedly the last straw for a people who valued family above all else. Being deprived of time alone with their families for meals, the peasants refused to cooperate further in agricultural collectivization.

When the catastrophic results of the Great Leap Forward policy poured in, the CCP retreated, but it was too late. Three subsequent years of bad weather, combined with the devastation wreaked by these policies and the Soviet withdrawal of all assistance, brought economic catastrophe. Demographic data indicate that in the "3 bad years" from 1959 to 1962, some 20 million to 30 million Chinese died from starvation and malnutrition-related diseases.

By 1962 central planners had condoned peasants returning to production and accounting units the size of the higher- and lower-level cooperatives. Further, peasants were again allowed to farm a small percentage of the total land as private plots, to raise domestic animals for their own use, and to engage in household handicrafts. Free markets, at which the peasantry could trade goods from private production, were reopened. The commune structure was retained throughout the countryside, however, and until the CCP leadership introduced the contract responsibility system in 1979, it provided the infrastructure of rural secondary school education, hospitals, and agricultural research.

(United Nations photo/A. Holcombe)

With the highly centralized or command economy in place until the 1980s, China's manufacturing energy was focused on production, with little regard to need or markets. These women in Shanghai were producing mechanical toys for no defined market.

Other centrally determined policies, seemingly oblivious to reality, have compounded the P.R.C.'s difficulties in agriculture. These include attempts to plant three crops per year in areas that for climatic reasons can only support two (as the Chinese put it, "Three times three is not as good as two times five"); and to plant twice as much grain as was normal in a field, with the result that all of it grew to less than full size or simply wilted for lack of adequate sunshine and nutrients.

A final example of centrally determined agricultural policy bringing catastrophe was the decision in the early 1970s by the Gang of Four radicals that "the whole country should grow grain." The purpose was to establish China's self-sufficiency in grain. Naturally, considering China's immense size and diverse climates, soil types, and topography, a policy ordering everyone to grow the same thing was doomed to fail. Peasants plowed under fields of cotton and cut down rubber plantations and fruit orchards, planting grain in their place.

China's planners, who at this point were largely CCP cadres, not economic experts, ignored overwhelming evidence that grain would not grow well in all areas and that, as a result, China would have to import everything that it had replaced with grain at far greater costs than it would have paid for importing grain. Peasant protests were futile in the face of local-level Communist Party leaders who hoped to advance their careers by implementing central policy. After the arrest of the Gang of Four in 1976, the self-sufficiency in grain

policy was reversed, and each region was told to specialize in growing what it grew best.

Economic Reforms: Decentralization and Liberalization

In an effort to increase productivity and speed up modernization, the Deng Xiaoping government began in 1979 to implement a program of economic reform and liberalization. In brief, although the program tried to maintain overall state control of the direction of policy and the distribution and pricing of strategic and energy resources, it introduced decentralized decision making down to the level of local enterprises. The purpose of decentralization was to facilitate more rational decision making, based on local conditions, needs, and efficiency criteria—about the best policy for any particular enterprise or part of the country. While retaining the right to set overall economic priorities, the national government allowed a greater number of goods to be produced and allocated according to local market forces of supply and demand instead of centrally determined quotas and pricing. It also encouraged enterprises to contract with each other instead of with the state, thereby limiting the role of the government as the go-between in commercial transactions.

Today most collective and individual enterprises, instead of fulfilling centrally determined production quotas, meet contractual obligations that they themselves set under the contract responsibility system. After they have fulfilled their

(United Nations photo)

The success of communes is still under debate. With the abandonment of communes in the early 1980s, a few leaders held out and refused to break up their communes. Some of these holdouts have experienced tremendous success.

contractual obligations and paid their taxes, profitable enterprises are permitted to use the remaining profits to expand production facilities, improve equipment, and award bonuses. The so-called collective enterprises (set up by individuals or small groups), which compete with state-run enterprises to supply goods and services, may become rich or go bankrupt.

This is not the case for state-run enterprises. Although they have been threatened with bankruptcy and being shut down if they operate with losses or produce goods that no one wants, fear of the political instability that might result from a high level of unemployment has left the government in an unfortunate position: It must continue to subsidize the heavy losses in the state-controlled sector. This, in turn, consumes a significant portion of the state's budget and contributes to China's growing inflation.

In agriculture, the collectivized economy has been almost completely replaced by the *contract responsibility system.* Under this system, individuals or individual households, to whom the formerly collective lands and production tools have been distributed, are responsible for planning and carrying out production on their own land. The "10,000 yuan" (about $2,000) household, a measure of extraordinary wealth in China, has now become a realizeable goal for many peasants. After fulfilling their contractual responsibilities to the state, they are free to sell remaining produce in free markets, where price is determined by the forces of supply and demand, not by a centralized state bureaucracy.

Although theoretically the collectives still own the land that they have "leased" to the peasants, in practice the land is treated as if it is owned by the peasants. Those who choose to work in the towns contract out their own land to others, so some peasants have amassed large amounts of land appropriate for large-scale farm machinery. To encourage development of the land, the government has permitted land to be leased for as long as 30 years and for leased rights to be inherited. Furthermore, peasants have built houses on what they consider their own land.

Efforts now and again since the early 1980s to revert to collectivized agriculture have repeatedly come up against a stone wall of resistance from the overwhelming number of peasants who have benefited from the reforms. Today wealthy rural towns are springing up throughout the agriculturally rich and densely populated east coast as well as along China's major transportation lines.

With the growth of free enterprise in the rural towns since 1979, some 60 million to 100 million peasants have left the land to work for far better pay in small-scale rural industry or to search for jobs in China's large cities. Many roam the country searching for work. For some, especially those able to find employment in the construction industry, which is booming in many of China's cities, this new system has meant vast personal enrichment. However, tens of millions of unemployed peasants clog city streets, parks, and railroad stations. They have contributed to a significant increase in crime and a sense of social instability.

Problems Created by Economic Reforms

Withholding of Profits and Materials

Inevitably, problems arose from the reformers' new economic policies. For example, decentralization prompted profitable industrial enterprises to refuse to hand over a fair percentage of their profits to the state. Thus, although the value of industrial output increased dramatically beginning in the 1980s, the profits turned over to the state have actually declined. Moreover, some localities and enterprises withhold materials normally allocated by the state, such as rolled steel, glass, cement, and timber, either to hoard them as a safeguard against future shortages or to resell them at unauthorized higher prices. Not only do these enterprises make illegal profits for themselves, but they also deprive the state of

(United Nations photo)

COMMUNES: PEASANTS WORK OVERTIME DURING THE GREAT LEAP FORWARD

In the socialist scheme of things, communes are considered ideal forms of organization for agriculture. They are supposed to increase productivity and equality, reduce inefficiencies of small-scale individual farming, and bring modern benefits to the countryside more rapidly through rural industrialization.

These objectives are attained largely through the economies of scale of communes; that is, it is presumed that when things are done on a large scale, they are more efficient and cost-effective than when done on a small scale. Thus, tractors, harvesters, trucks, and other agricultural machinery make sense when large tracts of land can be planted with the same crops and plowed at one time. Similarly, small-scale industries may be based on the communal unit of 30,000 to 70,000 people, since, in such a large work unit, some people can take care of agricultural needs for the entire commune, leaving others to work in commune-based industries.

Because of its size, a commune may also support other types of organizations that smaller work units would find impossible to support, financially and otherwise. A commune, for example, can support a hospital, a high school, an agricultural-research organization, and, if the commune is wealthy enough, even a "sports palace" and a cultural center for movies and entertainment.

During the Great Leap Forward, launched in 1958, peasants were—much against their will—forced into these larger agricultural and administrative units. They were particularly distressed that their remaining private plots were taken away from them. Communal kitchens, run by women, were to prepare food for everyone while workers went about their other productive work. Peasants were told that they had to eat in the communal mess halls rather than in the privacy of their own homes.

When the combination of bad policies and bad weather led to a severe famine, widespread peasant resistance forced the government to retreat from the Great Leap Forward and abandon the communes. But a modified commune system remained intact in much of China until the late 1970s, when the government ordered communes to be dissolved. A commune's collective property was then distributed to the peasants belonging to it, and a system of contract responsibility was launched. Today, with the exception of a few communes that refused to be dissolved, agricultural production is no longer collectivized. Individual households are again, as before 1953, engaged in small-scale agricultural production on private plots of land.

CHINA'S SPECIAL ECONOMIC ZONES

In 1979 China opened four Special Economic Zones (SEZs) within the territory of the People's Republic of China as part of its program of far-reaching reform of the socialist economy. The SEZs were allowed a great deal of leeway in experimenting with new economic policies. For example, Western management methods, including the right to fire unsatisfactory workers (something unknown under the Soviet-style centrally planned economy), were introduced into SEZ factories. Laws and regulations on foreign investment were greatly eased in the SEZs in order to attract capital from abroad, and export-oriented industries were established, with the goal of earning large amounts of foreign exchange in order to help China pay for the imported technology needed to hasten modernization. To many people, the SEZs looked like pockets of capitalism inside the socialist economy of the P.R.C.; indeed, they are often referred to as "mini-Hong Kongs."

The largest of the Special Economic Zones is Shenzhen, which is located just across the border from the Hong Kong New Territories. The transformation of Shenzhen over the last few years from a sleepy little rural town to a large, modern urban center and one of China's major industrial cities has been phenomenal. The city now boasts broad avenues and China's tallest skyscrapers, and the standard of living is the highest in the country.

But with growth and prosperity have come numerous problems. The pace of construction has gotten out of hand, outstripping the ability of the city to provide adequate services to the growing population. Speculation and corruption have been rampant, and crime is a more serious problem in Shenzhen than it is elsewhere in China. Strict controls on immigration have been implemented to stem

Shenzhen is the largest of China's Special Economic Zones and is located close to the Hong Kong New Territories.

the flood of people who were attracted to Shenzhen in the hopes of making their fortune. Furthermore, conservatives in the leadership of the CCP have been critical of Shenzhen as a source of decadent ideas from the West.

Steps have been taken to clean up Shenzhen, and the pragmatic leadership faction has repeated its support for the idea of the SEZs. Nevertheless, the SEZs remain a source of conflict within the central leadership.

access to building materials for its key construction projects. This reflects the problem of a mixed economy: With the state controlling the pricing and allocation of some resources and the free market determining the rest, there are many opportunities for corruption and abuse of the system.

Furthermore, the needs of the centralized state economy remain in conflict with the interests of provinces, counties, towns, and individuals, most of which now operate under the dual rules of a part-market, part-command economy. Thus, even as enterprises are determining whether they will expand production facilities based on the demands of a market economy, the state continues to centrally allocate resources based on a national plan. A clothing factory that expands its production, for instance, requires more energy (coal, oil, water) and more cotton. The state, already faced with inadequate energy resources to keep most industries operating at more than 70 percent capacity, continues to allocate the same amount to the now-expanded factory. Profitable enterprises want a greater share of centrally allocated scarce resources, but they find they cannot, without the help of middlemen and a significant

amount of under-the-table dealing, acquire them. Corruption has, therefore, become rampant at the nexus where the capitalist and socialist economies meet.

Unequal Benefits

Not all Chinese have benefited equally from the contract responsibility system. Peasants living far from cities or transportation lines or tilling less arable land have reaped few benefits from the economic reforms of the Deng period. Worse still, the commune as the basis of education and medical care in the countryside has disappeared. The peasantry in many areas suffer from even less access to education and medical care than before, whereas wealthy peasants can send their children into the larger towns and cities for schooling, and their family members can travel to the more comprehensive health clinics and hospitals farther away. In some areas, however, those peasants who have become wealthy have invested in private hospitals and schools in their areas.

In the cities, employees of state-run enterprises, who are on fixed salaries, have suffered from the double-digit inflation

Overall, however, China's economy is booming. Because of Deng's support of continued economic liberalization, it has commonly been said in China that the people would give $1 million a day to keep Deng alive.

Mortgaging the Future

Perhaps one of the most damaging aspects of the capitalist "get-rich" atmosphere prevailing in China is the willingness to sacrifice the future for profits today. The environment is literally being destroyed by uncontrolled pollution; the rampant growth of new towns, cities, and highways; the building of houses on arable land; and the destruction of forests. Some state institutions such as middle schools have turned their basketball courts into parking lots in China's crowded cities, which are unable to provide parking facilities for the huge number of newly owned private cars. And they have used state funds allocated to the schools for education to build shops all along the outside walls of the schools. Teachers and administrators deal themselves the profits, but in the meantime, classroom materials and facilities are deteriorating.

Economic Crime

Widespread corruption in the economic sector has led the Chinese government to wage a series of campaigns against economic crimes. Until energy and transportation bottlenecks and the scarcity of key resources are dealt with, however, it will be extremely difficult to halt the bribery, smuggling, stealing, and extortion now pervasive in the P.R.C. The relaxation of strong state central controls, the mandate for the Chinese people to "get rich," and a mixed economy have exacerbated what was already a problem under the socialist system. In a system suffering from serious scarcities but controlled by bureaucrats, political power, not the market, determines who gets what—not only goods, but also opportunities, licenses, permits, and approvals. In today's mixed economy, although the Chinese may now purchase in the market many essential products previously distributed only through bureaucratically controlled channels, there are still many goods that they can only acquire through the "back door"—that is, through people whom they know and for whom they have done favors. Scarcity, combined with bureaucratic control, has led to "collective corruption": Individuals engage in corrupt practices, even cheat the state, in order to benefit the enterprise for which they work. Since today's non-state-owned "collectives" survive or perish on the basis of profits and losses, the motivation for corrupt activities is stronger than under the previous system.

Liberalization of the economy is, then, providing a massive number and variety of goods for the marketplace. The Chinese people may buy almost any basic consumer goods in stores or the open markets. But corruption is continuing, and getting worse, especially where state controls over energy,

(Xinhua News Agency)
Under the economic liberalization program, shops such as this one in Sichuan were allowed to prosper.

that resulted from the state's decontrolling of prices in the agricultural sector in the 1980s. Urban dwellers, long accustomed to being the primary beneficiaries of growth, were enraged that the living standards of the peasantry should be rising faster than their own. Some of China's more conservative leaders concluded that soaring inflation, rampant corruption, and the development of a distinctly wealthy class were too high a price to pay for modernization. In the late 1980s, they were temporarily able to halt reforms in their tracks. This, however, did not resolve China's economic problems, and by the early 1990s, the leadership was moving forward with economic reforms. By the mid-1990s the standard of living in the cities was surging ahead, while, by contrast, the benefits of reform in the countryside had slowed considerably. As a result, China faces serious revolts among the peasantry, who are angered by the government's inability to pay them for their grain and to address the needs of China's massive rural population.

transportation, and limited key resources continue. In short, the nexus between continued state control and the free economy still fuels a rampant corruption that may ultimately undercut the strength of China's economy.

SOCIALIST LEGALITY

Law, Order, and Legal Rights

China's legal system must be viewed within the particular Chinese cultural context for law, and the goals of law in the context of a socialist system. If Western standards of law and justice are used to evaluate the Chinese system, it must be with the understanding that these standards have never had a foundation in China.

The Confucian system provided the basis for the traditional social and political order: Confucianism posited that ethics were based on maintaining correct personal relationships among people, not on laws. A legal system did exist; but in civil cases, the Chinese resorted to it only in desperation, for the inability to resolve one's problems oneself, or through a mediator, usually resulted in considerable loss of face. (In criminal cases, the state normally became involved in determining guilt and punishment.)

Thus, until recently most Chinese have preferred to call in CCP officials, local neighborhood or factory mediation committees, family members, and friends—not lawyers or judicial personnel—to settle disputes. Only when mediation failed did the Chinese resort to the courts. By contrast, the West lacks both this strong support for the institution of mediation and the concept of "face," or dignity and pride. So Westerners have had difficulty understanding why China has never had many lawyers, and why the Chinese lack faith in the law.

With the economic and legal reforms since 1979, however, the Chinese have undergone a rapid transformation of attitudes toward the law. This is particularly true in the area of law that relates to the economy, including contract, investment, property, and commercial laws. The Chinese have discovered that the legal system has developed into a strong protector of their rights in economic transactions. In civil law (when it relates to disputes with neighbors and family conflicts), however, the Chinese are still more likely to rely on mediation to settle their disputes.

Law as a Tool

Like Confucianism, Marxism-Leninism is an ideology that embodies a set of ethical standards for behavior. After 1949 it easily built on this cultural predisposition toward ruling by ethics instead of law. Although Marxism-Leninism did not completely replace the Confucian ethical system, it did establish new standards of behavior based on socialist morality. These ethical standards emerge in the works of Marx and Lenin, in the writings of Mao Zedong, and in the CCP's policies. State organs write up and even revise "laws" *after* the CCP has made a policy, in order to justify the state's decisions. The Chinese leadership readily acknowledges that law is a mere tool of the state, to be used for the state's own purposes. Unlike Western liberal democracies, laws do not set standards to which state policies have to conform.

Law and Politics

From 1949 until the reforms of the early 1980s, Chinese universities trained very few lawyers. Legal training consisted of learning law and politics as an integrated whole, for according to Marxism, law is meant to reflect the values of the "ruling class" and to serve as an instrument of "class struggle." The Chinese Communist regime has viewed law as a branch of the social sciences, not a professional field of study. For this reason, China's citizens have viewed law as a mere propaganda tool, not a means for protecting their rights. They have never really experienced a law-based society.

Not only are the laws and legal education highly politicized; the CCP and politics also infiltrate the judicial system. With few lawyers available, few legally trained judges in the courts, and even fewer laws to refer to for standards of behavior, China's legal system has inevitably been subject to abuse. China has been ruled by people, not by law; by politics, not by legal standards; and by party policy, not by a constitution.

After the Deng Xiaoping leadership gained ascendancy in late 1978, the government moved rapidly to write new laws. Fewer than 300 lawyers, most of them trained before 1949 in Western legal institutions, undertook the immense task of writing a civil code, a criminal code, contract law, economic law, law governing foreign investment in the P.R.C., tax law, and environmental and forestry laws. One strong motivation for the Chinese Communist leadership to formalize the legal system was its growing realization, after years of a disappointingly low level of foreign investment, that the international business community was reluctant to invest further in the P.R.C. without substantial legal guarantees.

In fact, even China's own potential entrepreneurs wanted legal protection against the *state's* interests before they would assume the risks of developing new businesses. If, for example, the state should fail to fulfill its part of a contract to supply resources to an enterprise for production, the individuals running that enterprise want a legal guarantee that the state can be sued for losses to the enterprise issuing from their nonfulfillment of contractual obligations. Since the whole purpose of economic reform was to encourage individual and collective investment in order to make more and better goods and services available, the leadership has necessarily had to supplement economic reforms with legal reforms.

These efforts to formalize the legal system have fostered a stronger legal basis for modernization. They have, moreover, helped to limit the CCP's and the state's abuse of the people's rights. Nevertheless, the CCP still continues to interfere in the legal process at will, especially when a party official or the state's interests are involved.

(UN photo by John Isaac)

Settling civil disputes in China today still usually involves neighborhood mediation committees, family members, and friends.

Presumption of Guilt

Procedures followed in Chinese courts differ significantly from those in the United States. For example, in China's socialist judicial system, it is presumed that people brought to trial in criminal cases are "guilty," for a branch of the judiciary called the *procuracy,* the investigative branch, has already spent considerable time and effort finding out the facts and establishing whether suspects are indeed guilty *before* they are brought to trial. This is important to understand when assessing the fact that 99 percent of all the accused who are brought to trial in China are judged guilty. Had the facts not substantiated their guilt, the procuracy would have dismissed their cases before going to court. For this reason, court appearances of the guilty function mainly to remind the public that criminals are punished—a morality play of sorts. Furthermore, the trial process emphasizes the importance of confessing one's crimes, for those who confess and appear repentant in court will usually be dealt more lenient sentences.

From the Western perspective, the real problem with this system is that once the procuracy establishes "the facts," they are not open to question by the lawyer or other representative of the accused. (In China, a person may be represented by a family member, friend, or colleague, largely because there are simply not enough lawyers to fulfill the guarantee of a person's "right to a defense.") A lawyer is not allowed to introduce new evidence, make arguments to dismiss the case based on technicalities or improper procedures (such as wire tapping), or make insanity pleas for the client. Instead, the lawyer's role in a criminal case is simply to represent the person in court and to bargain with the court for a reduced sentence for the repentant client.

According to China's 1982 Criminal Code, although the accused has the right to a defense, it is presumed that a lawyer will not defend someone who is guilty. The lawyer is, in fact, an employee of the state and is paid by the state. As such, a lawyer's obligation is first and foremost to protect the interests of the state, not to protect the individual's interests at the expense of the state. When lawyers have done otherwise, they have risked being condemned as "counterrevolutionaries" or treasonous. Small wonder that after 1949, the study of law did not attract China's most talented students.

In the area of civil and commercial law, however, the role of the lawyer has become increasingly important since the opening of China's closed door to the outside world. Now that the leadership views trade with other countries and foreign investment as crucial to China's development, its goal is to train at least one lawyer for every state, collective, or private organization and enterprise. Increasingly, the Chinese recognize that upholding the law is not merely a question of correctly understanding the "party line" and then following it in legal disputes but, rather, of interpreting the meaning of law according to the concrete circumstances of a case. Yet even in economic disputes in the 1980s and 1990s, lawyers who have vigorously defended their clients' interests have occasionally been condemned for being "anti-socialist."

Since China has had so little experience in dealing with civil conflicts and economic disputes in the courts, and since Western investors insist that Chinese courts be prepared to address such issues, the leadership is forced to train lawyers in Western law and to draft literally thousands of new laws. To protect itself against what is difficult to understand in the abstract, however, the Chinese often refuse to publish their newly written laws. Claiming a shortage of paper or the need to protect "state secrets," they have withheld publication of many laws until their actual impact on China's state interests can be determined. The leadership realizes that once the laws are actually published, it will be much harder to retract them for rewriting. This practice has frustrated potential investors, who dare not risk capital investment in China until they know exactly what the relevant laws are.

THE POLITICAL SYSTEM

The Party and the State

The Chinese Communist Party is the fountainhead of power and policy. But not all Chinese people are CCP members. Although the CCP has some 50 million members, this represents less than 5 percent of the population. Joining the CCP is a selective, rigorous process. Some have wanted to join out of a commitment to communist ideals, others in hopes of climbing the ladder of opportunity, still others to gain access to limited goods and opportunities. By the late 1980s, however, so many students and educated individuals had grown cynical about the CCP that they simply refused to join. Still, those who travel to China today are likely to find that many of the most talented people they meet happen to be members of the CCP.

The CCP is the ultimate institutional authority and determines the "general line." All state policies must conform to it. Theoretically, the state is distinct from the party. In practice, the two have overlapped almost completely since the late 1950s. The state apparatus consists of a State Council, headed by the premier. Under the State Council are the ministries and agencies and "People's Congresses" responsible for the formulation of policy. The CCP, however, exercises firm control over these state bodies through interlocking organizations. For example, CCP branches exist within all government organizations, and all key state personnel are also party members. Efforts to separate the CCP from the government have been under way since Deng gained power in 1978; but it is still difficult to uproot party leaders.

China's socialist system is subject to enormous abuses of power. The lines of authority within both the CCP and the state system are poorly defined, as are the rules for succession to the top leadership positions. This has allowed individuals like Mao Zedong and the Gang of Four to usurp power and rule arbitrarily.

There have been repeated efforts to reform the political system. The Chinese have tried to separate the party from the functions of the state bureaucracy and economic enterprises. For some leadership positions, there are now limits on tenure in office. There are also strict prohibitions on a leader developing a personality cult, such as that which reached fanatical proportions around Party Chairman Mao Zedong during the Cultural Revolution. Reforms have also encouraged, if not demanded, that the Chinese state bureaucracy reward merit more than mere seniority, and expertise more than political activism.

Stringent efforts have been made to control official corruption. But even now officials continue to use their power to achieve personal gain, trading official favors for other's services (such as better housing, assignment of children to good urban jobs, admission to the best schools, and access to goods in short supply). Getting things done still depends heavily upon a complex set of personal connections and relationships, all reinforced through under-the-table gift giving. This is partly because of the still heavily centralized aspect of Chinese governance and partly because China's bureaucracy remains overstaffed and plagued by red tape. Countless offices must sign off on requests for anything from buying a typewriter to getting a passport. This gives individual officials who are willing to take charge of processing an individual's or work unit's request for something, such as a license, enormous power. In today's more market-oriented China, for example, anyone with adequate funds may buy an air conditioner. Then, however, they must pay off an official to allow the electrical service to their living unit to be upgraded so that they can actually use the air conditioner.

By the late 1980s, China's bureaucracy appeared to have become more corrupt than at any time since 1949. Anger at the massive scale of official corruption was, in fact, the major factor unifying ordinary citizens and workers with students during the antigovernment protests in the spring of 1989. Campaigns to control official corruption continue. Individuals are free to suggest in the country's daily newspapers how corruption might be ferreted out. On occasion specific cases are investigated by journalists, thereby focusing public attention on official abuse.

One middle-aged, well-educated Chinese put it this way: All countries face corruption; but the Chinese will *never* be able to control corruption in China because it is a "tradition." It is simply the CCP's turn to be corrupt!

An example of the difficulty in controlling corruption is this: To cut down on the abuse of official privilege, the government issued a new regulation stipulating that governmental officials doing business could only order four dishes and one soup. But as most Chinese like to eat well, especially at the government's expense, the restaurants accommodated them by simply giving them much larger plates on which they put many different foods, and wrote it up as one dish. Another example concerns middlemen who are paid for arranging business transactions. They used to be considered corrupt. Now a government regulation says that it is all right for a middleman to keep 5 percent of the total value of the transaction as a "fee," and it is no longer called corruption. The Chinese have also adopted the custom in other countries of permitting tour guides who take tourists to a shop to receive a percentage of the total sales, behavior earlier considered corrupt by the government.

THE ENVIRONMENT FOR DEMOCRACY

When assessing the Chinese political system's level of freedom, democracy, and individual rights, it is important to remember that the Chinese do not share the values and traditions of the West's Greco–Roman political heritage. Chinese thought has run along different lines, with far less emphasis on such ideals as individual rights, privacy, and limits on state power. The Chinese political tradition is one of authoritarianism and moral indoctrination. For more than 2,000 years, China's rulers have shown greater concern for establishing their authority and maintaining unity over the vast territory and population that they controlled than in Western concepts of democratic liberalism. Apart from China's intellectuals in the twentieth century, the vast majority of the Chinese people have appeared to be more afraid of chaos than rule by an authoritarian despot.

China's limited experience with democracy in the twentieth century has been bitter. Virtually the entire period from the fall of China's imperial monarchy in 1911 to the Communist victory in 1949 (the period of the "Republic of China" on the mainland) was marred by warlordism, chaos, war, and a government masking brutality, greed, and incompetence under the label of "democracy." Although it is hardly fair to blame this period of societal collapse and externally imposed war on China's efforts to practice "democracy" under the "tutelage of the Kuomintang," the Chinese people's experience of democracy was nevertheless negative.

China's experience of democracy after 1911 as well as China's political culture help explain the people's reluctance to pursue democracy aggressively. During this period the existence of both democratic political institutions and a complete legal system (on paper) proved inadequate to guarantee the protection of individual rights. Under Communist rule after 1949, the period described as "democratic mass rule" (the "10 bad years" or "Cultural Revolution" from 1966 to 1976) was in fact a period of mass tyranny. For the Chinese, the relinquishing of power to "the masses" turned into the most horrific period of unleashed terrorism and cruelty that they had experienced since the Communist takeover.[3]

When the CCP came to power in 1949, it inherited a country torn by civil war, internal rebellion, and foreign invasions for more than 100 years. The population was overwhelmingly illiterate and desperately poor, the economy in shambles. The most urgent need was for order. Despite some serious setbacks and mistakes, Mao Zedong and his colleagues made great strides in securing China's borders, establishing the institutions of government, and enhancing the material well-being of the Chinese people. But they also severely limited the development of "democracy" as the liberal democratic West would understand it, in the name of order and stability.

Cultural Predisposition Toward Authoritarianism
The heavy weight of more than 2,000 years of Chinese history helped shape the development of today's political system. The Chinese inherited a patriarchal culture, in which the hierarchical values of superior-inferior and subordination, loyalty, and obedience prevailed over those of equality; a historical predisposition toward official secrecy; a fear of officials and official power; a traditional repugnance for courts, lawyers, and formal laws that resulted in a legal system inadequately developed to defend democratic rights; and a historical legacy of authoritarianism. These cultural factors provided the context for the introduction of Western democratic values and institutions into China from the nineteenth century onward. As a result, the Chinese people have not embraced democratic values with fervor.

The Chinese people are accustomed to "eating bitterness," not to standing up to authority. The traditional Confucian emphases on the group rather than the individual and respect for authority continue to this day in the guise of the CCP's "democratic dictatorship." The government decides which rights individuals will receive—and when to withdraw them. But at this point in history, this behavior has less to do with habits ingrained by several thousand years of Confucian culture than with state policies of punishment of those who do not obey—through threat or actual loss of jobs, ostracism, jail, labor camps, and worse.

Today, although an atmosphere of greater freedom is pervasive in China, all will admit that a gnawing fear continues of what *could* happen. As one faculty member in a university remarked, although he does not think that the atrocities of the Cultural Revolution could happen again, he still writes his diary in code. As he put it, when you feel that you have been watched every day of your life for more than 40 years, it is difficult to rid yourself of deeply ingrained fears when no one any longer is watching. Furthermore, many would admit that although those scholars and students studying abroad who protested the Chinese government's brutal suppression of the

CENTRAL GOVERNMENT ORGANIZATION OF THE PEOPLE'S REPUBLIC OF CHINA

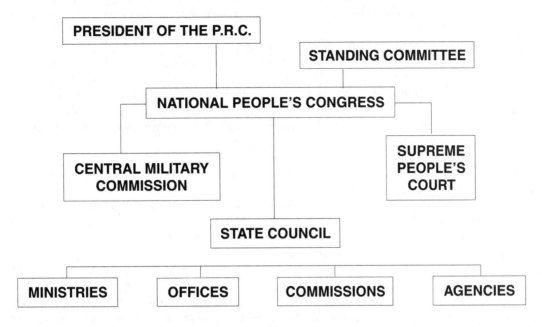

This central government organization chart represents the structure of the government of the People's Republic of China as it appears on paper. However, since all of the actions and overall doctrine of the central government must be reviewed and approved by the Chinese Communist Party, political power ultimately lies with the party. To ensure this control, virtually all top state positions are held by party members.

THE CHINESE COMMUNIST PARTY (CCP)

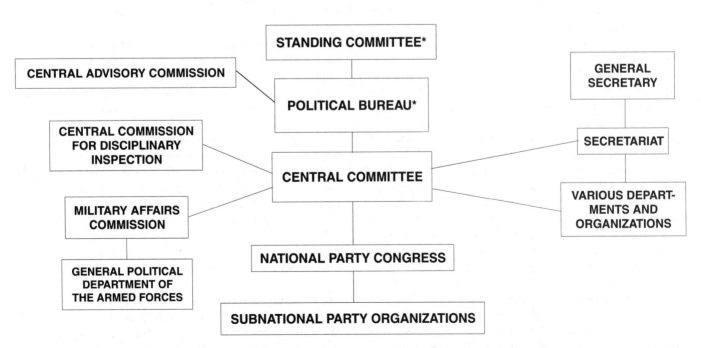

*This Political Bureau and its Standing Committee are the most powerful organizations within the Chinese Communist Party and are therefore the real centers of power in the P.R.C.

1989 Tiananmen demonstrations need not fear being jailed or persecuted if they return to China (unless, of course, like Shen Tong, an actual leader of those demonstrations, they are brazen enough to publicly advocate democratization on their return), they might well be punished in other ways, such as the state offering them jobs inappropriate for the level of education that they received abroad.

The conditions for sowing the seeds of "democracy" in China have been less than fertile in other ways. First, China has suffered as much as Western democracies from "the 'lukewarm middle' of apathetic citizens." In China in the late 1970s, those who participated only enough "to fend off charges of inadequate . . . political participation" accounted for some 80 to 90 percent of the entire population.[4] As China's creative energies were channeled away from political activism and into economic development in the 1980s and 1990s, the percentage may have grown even higher. At this point in history, the Chinese are, quite simply, more interested in improving the quality of their daily lives than in getting involved in political issues.

Second, the Chinese lack of interest in political participation is even greater than in the West, because their participation appears ineffective in getting what they want for themselves. For that purpose, they have found that under-the-table gift giving to and entertainment of local officials, together with developing a "web of connections," are far more effective. Chinese peasants and workers seem inclined to believe that policies change only when high-level officials mandate it, not in response to popular pressure.[5]

This helps explain the pervasive gift giving and outright bribery. As the impersonal market forces of supply and demand undercut the power of officials to control the distribution of resources and opportunities in the society, these patterns may change. Thus, although participation in the political process at the local level may reap perceivable results, above that level, many Chinese see their participation as meaningless or even dangerous. Memories of forced participation in the many campaigns and movements in China since 1949 "continue to give political participation a negative connotation. The result is that an active political participant is often regarded with deep suspicion."[6]

So far China has experienced only limited popular demand for democracy. When the student-led demonstrations began in April 1989, the demands for democratic reforms were confined largely to the small realm of the elite—that is, students and well-educated individuals as well as some members of the political and economic ruling elite. The workers and farmers of China were still more concerned about bread-and-butter issues: inflation, economic growth, and their own personal enrichment, not democratic ideals.

To the extent that the unwillingness of Chinese to challenge the political institutions and rulers of the CCP regime may be labeled as passive or submissive behavior, not to mention "collusion" with their oppressors, is it in any sense unique to

China? One could argue that Central/Eastern Europeans also participated in their own political oppression simply by complying with the demands of the system. Czechoslovakia's former president Vaclav Havel has stated, "All of us have become accustomed to the totalitarian system, accepted it as an unalterable fact and therefore kept it running. . . . None of us is merely a victim of it, because all of us helped to create it together."[7]

Can we say that the Chinese, any more than the Czechs, passively *accepted* totalitarianism if they did not go into exile outside of their country or did not refuse to work? Is anyone who does not actively revolt against an oppressive system necessarily in collusion with it? As one person wrote in China in 1989:

> The danger of losing jobs and the threats to survival make many people fearful. Fear also comes from the policy of implication, the personal dossiers. . . . The people, therefore, can only try to cope with the situation by burying anger deep in their hearts.[8]

Thus, to the degree that the CCP steps back from its state policies of punishment for political crimes, there is nothing in an abstract Chinese culture that will necessarily cause Chinese to remain submissive to an authoritarian regime. Rather, it is the political system that has reinforced the authoritarian qualities of Chinese culture. Nor should a lack of rules and institutions be considered an insurmountable object, as "democratic" behavioral skills can be acquired through practice.[9] In short, as the political system becomes more liberal, the political culture is likely to evolve—indeed, it *is* evolving—in a more liberal direction.

Limited Popular Demands for Greater Democracy

Minimally, the student-led demonstrations of 1989, which projected democratic slogans onto a national canvas, have made many more millions of ordinary Chinese citizens aware that the authoritarian rule of a corrupt and incompetent leadership has been responsible for the problems in the economy. Many more Chinese now realize that economic issues are at heart profoundly political. Thus, they have become open to the possibility that a more pluralistic and democratic system, one that would force the leadership to be less secretive, less able to conceal their weaknesses, and more accountable to the public, would be valuable to both the economic and the political systems.

Lack of an Evident Leadership for an Alternative Political System

One of the critical problems for democratization in China has been the people's inability to envision an alternative to CCP rule: It has been *unthinkable*. What form would it take? How would it get organized? Wouldn't the organizers be jailed? And if the CCP were overthrown, who would lead a new system? These questions are still far from being answered even today. But one thing seems clear: Those dissidents who have left China and remain abroad have lost their political influence with the Chinese people. Apart from everything else, dissidents abroad still have no way to make themselves heard in China, where their articles cannot be published.

For the 40 years of Chinese Communist rule from 1949 to 1989, no dissident leadership capable of offering an alternative to CCP leadership and laying claim to popular support had formed. The result was that in China, the students' and workers' actions of 1989 were in no sense a "rebellion" under a recognized leader. China's intellectuals were not prepared to offer any sort of comprehensive alternative policies to the CCP's; and in any event, they soon found themselves in exile abroad.

Furthermore, the democracy movement was led by neither a worker nor a peasant, nor by an intellectual with whom the common people could identify:

[C]ompared with the intellectuals of Poland and Czechoslovakia, for example, Chinese intellectuals have little contact with workers and peasants and are not sensitive to their country's worsening social crisis; they were caught unawares by the democratic upsurge of 1989, and proved unable to provide the people with either the theoretical or practical guidance they needed.[10]

In fact, during the Tiananmen protests in 1989, it was evident that the students were actually *annoyed* with the workers' participation in the demonstrations. They wanted to press their own political demands, not the workers' more concrete, work-related issues. Not a few Chinese have commented that the students' real interest in demanding respect for their own goals from China's leadership was because they wanted to enhance their own power vis-à-vis the regime: The students' major demands were for a "dialogue" with the government as "equals" and for free speech, issues of primary interest to them but of secondary interest to the workers of China.

Many Chinese believe that the leaders of the 1989 demonstrations would have differed little from the CCP elite had they suddenly been catapulted to power. The student movement itself admitted to being authoritarian, of kowtowing to its own leaders, and of expecting others to obey rather than to discuss decisions. As one Beijing University student wrote during the 1989 Tiananmen Square protests:

The autonomous student unions have gradually cut themselves off from many students and become a machine kept constantly on the run in issuing orders. No set of organizational rules widely accepted by the students has emerged, and the democratic mechanism is even more vague.[11]

Apart from students and intellectuals, the major proponents of democratic reform today hail from China's newly emerg-

ing business circles; but these two groups have not united to achieve reform, as they neither like nor trust each other. Intellectuals view venture capitalists "as uncultured, and business people as driven only by crass material interests." They in turn regard intellectuals and students as "well-meaning but out of touch with reality and always all too willing and eager to serve the state" when it suits their needs.[12]

The Impact of Global Interdependency on Democratization

There have been some positive developments in the cultural context for democracy in China that have, since the late 1970s, grown steadily stronger with each passing year. First, an increasing awareness of global interdependency, with the expansion of the global capitalist economy to include China, brought with it a social and economic transformation of China. The result is, for the first time in Chinese history, a significant challenge to the "we–they" dichotomy, of China on the one hand, against the rest of the world on the other.

Similarly, for the first time, many Chinese question the heretofore assumed superiority of Chinese civilization to all other civilizations. Such an idea does not come easily for a people long accustomed to believing in their own superiority. Hence the fuss caused by *River Elegy,* a television series first shown on Chinese national television in the summer of 1988. In this series the film producers argued that the Chinese people must embrace the idea of global interdependency—technological, economic, and cultural. To insist at this time in history on the superiority of Chinese civilization, with the isolation of China from the world of ideas that this implied, would only contribute to China's continued stagnation. The film suggested that Chinese people must see themselves as equal, not superior to, others; and as interdependent with, not as victims of, others. Such concepts of equality and of opening up China to ideas from outside China implicitly challenge the CCP's authoritarian rule and are still resisted by the more conservative reformers remaining in China's top leadership today.

The Press and Mass Media

At the time that the student-led demonstrations for democracy began in the spring of 1989, China's press had witnessed remarkable growth in its diversity and liberalization of its content. With some 1,500 newspapers, 5,000 magazines, and 500 publishing houses, the Chinese were able to express a wider variety of viewpoints and ideas than at any time since the CCP came to power in 1949. The importation and domestic production of millions of television sets, radios, short-wave radios, cassette recorders, and VCRs also facilitated the growth of the mass media in China. They have been accompanied by a wide array of "un-Chinese" and "uncommunist" audio and video materials. The programs of the British Broadcasting System and the Voice of America, the diversification of domestic television and radio programs (a choice made by the Chinese government and facilitated by international satellite communication), and the importation and translation of foreign books and magazines—all contributed to a more pluralistic press in China. In fact, the stream of publications by the end of the 1980s so overwhelmed the CCP Propaganda Department that it was simply no longer able to monitor their content.

During the demonstrations in Tiananmen Square in the spring of 1989, the Chinese press, under pressure from both students and the international press in Beijing, which freely filmed and filed reports on the demonstrations, took a leap into complete press freedom. With cameramen and microphones in hand, reporters covered in its entirety the student hunger strike that began on May 13; but with the imposition of martial law in Beijing on May 20, press freedom came to a crashing halt.

After the crackdown on Tiananmen Square in June 1989, the CCP imposed a ban on a variety of books, journals, and magazines. Vice Premier Wang Zhen ordered the "cleansing" of media organizations, with bad elements removed and not permitted to leave Beijing for reporting. All press and magazine articles written during the prodemocracy movement in the press, all television and radio programs shown during this period, were analyzed to see if they conformed to the party line. All individuals responsible for editing during this period were dismissed. And, as in the past, all press and magazine articles had to be on topics specified by the editors, who are under the control of the CCP. In short, press freedom in China suffered a significant setback because of the prodemocracy demonstrations.

In the new climate of experimentation launched by Deng Xiaoping in 1992, however, the diversity of television and radio programs has soared. China's major cities now have multiple television and radio channels carrying a broad range of programs from Hong Kong, Taiwan, Japan, and the West. These programs, whether soap operas about daily life for Chinese people living in Hong Kong and Taiwan or art programs exposing the Chinese to the world of Western religious art through a visual art history tour of the Vatican, or in news about protests and problems faced by other nations in the world, are both subtly and blatantly exposing the Chinese to values, ideas, and standards of living previously unknown to them. Round-the-clock, all-news radio stations have now been established; and radio talk shows take phone calls from anonymous viewers about everything from sex to political corruption. So far no one seems to be challenging the broadcasting of these eye-opening programs.

Even the printed press has regained substantial freedom. "Weekend editions" print just about any story that will sell, and often these are about the seamier side of Chinese life. All are undercutting the puritanical aspect of CCP rule, not to mention expanding the range of topics available for discussion in the public domain. Even China's official papers are now required to make money instead of being subsidized completely by the state. As a result, they now accept adver-

tisements and print stories that cater to public interests. So many publishing houses have sprung up that the CCP no longer has the resources to monitor the content of their publications. And even China's movies, plays, and fine arts have been able to provide commentary on heretofore prohibited topics.

International Pressures to Democratize

For more than a decade, China's government has attempted to accelerate economic development by decentralizing the economy, moving out of its isolationist position by trading in the world economy, and bringing foreign investment funds into China. Furthermore, pressures from the West and Japan of a *quid pro quo* sort (greater trade, investment, and more access to technology in exchange for greater liberalization of the economic and political system) have forced the CCP leadership to take certain steps along the road of reform, most notably in the economic and legal systems. For example, to maintain most-favored-nation (MFN) trading status with the United States, the Chinese government has capitulated to demands to stop using prisoners to make goods for export and to respect intellectual copyright laws.

Finally, Asia's four little dragons (Taiwan, Hong Kong, Singapore, and South Korea) have offered to the Chinese leadership an alternative model to the West for economic development. All four of these systems have maintained a system of tight centralized political control while decentralizing control over the economy. Obviously the CCP leadership prefers the idea of remaining in power while adopting an economic system that provides astounding economic success. With tourists and businesspeople from the four little dragons traveling and doing business in China, the Chinese people's understanding of the successes of other Asian societies has increased—as has their desire to emulate them. "Taiwan fever" on the mainland is fed by the Chinese people's access to Taiwan's music, fashions, books, and films. Taiwan is now envied in the P.R.C. for both its economic development and the diversity and richness of its culture. Perhaps most important for the enormous appeal of the Taiwan model is that it has been successful within the context of a Chinese culture. Thus, the CCP cannot dismiss the Taiwan model as easily as it does successful models of reform and development within non-Chinese cultures.

The Student and Mass Movement of 1989

Symbolism is very important in Chinese culture; and the death of a key leader is a particularly significant moment. In the case of the former head of the CCP, Hu Yaobang, his death in April 1989 became symbolic of the death of liberalizing forces in China. The students used Hu's death as an excuse to place his values and policies in juxtaposition with those of the then–increasingly conservative leadership. The suddenly deceased leader's career and its meaning were touted as symbols of liberalization, even though his life was hardly a

STOCK MARKETS, GAMBLING, AND LOTTERIES

China's first two stock markets opened just before the Tiananmen Square demonstrations of 1989. One is in the Special Economic Zone of Shenzhen; the other is in Shanghai. With only seven industries originally registered on them, strict rules about how much daily profit or loss (1.2 percent for the Shanghai exchange until July 1992) a stock could undergo, and deep public suspicion that these original issues of stocks were worthless, these markets got off to a slow start. But when these same stocks were worth 5 times their original value just 1 year later, the public took notice. Rumors—as important in China as actual news—took over and exaggerated the likelihood of success in picking a winning stock. The idea of investors actually losing money, much less a stock market crash, did not seem to be an idea whose time had come.

Soon there were so many Chinese dollars chasing so few stocks that the government began a lottery system: Anyone who wanted to buy a stock had first to buy a coupon, which was then put into a national lottery. The supply/demand ratio for stocks was so out of proportion that an individual had only a 1 in 100 chance of having a coupon chosen from the lottery. The coupon would, in turn, enable its bearer to buy a mere 5 shares of a stock that might or might not make a profit. Today, thanks to the rapid increase in stocks registered on the stock exchanges, there is now a 70 in 100 chance of getting the right to buy a stock.

When a set of new issues was scheduled to appear in 1992, literally thousands of people waited in line for as many as 5 nights until the lottery coupons went on sale in Shenzhen and Shanghai. The estimated 100,000 people in this line—a queue so tight that people in it were pressing up against those in front of them so that no one could break into it—carefully calculated their places in line as good enough to ensure their right to purchase lottery coupons for a shot at the stock market. The crowd became an angry mob when, within a short time after opening the lottery, the authorities announced that no more coupons were available for purchase. The crowd's frustration and anger combined with suspicion about official corruption, for how else could most of the shares have been sold so quickly? Violence broke out, and seven people were shot by the police or trampled to death in the resulting melee.

What had happened? Those people whom the Chinese call "the Mafia" went down the long line and offered 200 yuan in exchange for their official identification cards, cards that were required in order to buy the lottery coupons. In other words, without incurring the risk of buying a stock that might not increase in value, individuals could receive what was, for many of them, the equivalent of a month's pay. Working with corrupt officials, "the Mafia" then were allowed to purchase most of the available coupons before the vast majority of those standing in line who kept their identity cards.

As communications remain poor in China, and as it is still largely a cash economy, making a stock market transaction does not resemble what happens in a Western country. Instead of simply telephoning a broker and giving an order, with a simple bank transfer or check to follow shortly, most Chinese must still appear in person, stand in line, and pay cash on the spot. Taiwan has added its own angle to China's stock mania by selling to the Mainlanders small radios that are tuned into only one frequency—stock market news.

Issuing, buying, and selling stocks have become national obsessions. Not only do ordinary companies selling commercial goods, such as computers and clothing, issue stocks; so do cab companies and even universities. Thus far, few such stocks are actually listed on the two national stock exchanges, but employees of these work units are eager to purchase these stocks. In most cases, the original issues are sold at far higher prices than their face value, as employees (and even nonemployees) eagerly buy up fellow employees' rights to purchase stocks at grossly inflated prices. Presumably the right of employees to own stock in their own work unit will make them eager to have it do well and thus increase efficiency and profits.

Learning from Western practices and catering to a penchant for gambling, which is illegal, the Chinese have also begun a number of lotteries. Most of these have thus far been for the purpose of raising money for specific charities or causes. In addition, following Western marketing practices, companies put Chinese characters on the inside of packages or bottle caps to indicate whether the purchaser has won a prize. With a little Chinese ingenuity, the world could witness never-before-imagined realms of betting and competitive business practices that appeal to people's desire to get something for nothing.

---

monument to liberal thought. More conservative leaders in the CCP had chosen to remove him from his position as the CCP's general secretary in part because he had offended their sensibilities. Apart from everything else, these leaders clung to traditional Chinese culture. Thus, Hu's suggestions that the Chinese turn in their chopsticks for knives and forks and not eat food out of a common dish because it spread disease were culturally offensive.

The students' reassessment of Hu Yaobang's career in a way that rejected the party's evaluation of it was in itself a challenge to the authority of the CCP's right to rule China.

The students' hunger strike during the visit of then–Soviet president Mikhail Gorbachev to China was, even in the eyes of ordinary Chinese people, a humiliation to the Chinese leadership. Many Chinese later acknowledged their belief that the students went too far, as their demonstrations, by humiliating the leadership, humiliated *all* Chinese.

The students' demands changed over time. At first they merely wanted a reassessment of Hu Yaobang's career. But quickly the students added new demands: An end to official corruption, exposure of the financial and business dealings of the central leadership, a free press, dialogue between the government and the students (with the students to be treated as equals with top CCP leaders), retraction of an offensive *People's Daily* editorial, the removal of the top CCP leadership, and still other actions that challenged continued CCP rule.

The students' hunger strike, which lasted for 1 week in May, was the final straw that brought down the wrath of the central leadership. Martial law was imposed in Beijing; and when the citizens of Beijing resisted its enforcement and blocked the army's efforts to reach Tiananmen Square to clear out the hunger-strikers, both students and CCP leaders dug in; but both were deeply divided bodies. Indeed, divisions within the student-led movement caused it to lose its direction; and divisions within the central CCP leadership incapacitated it. For 2 weeks the central leadership wrangled over who was right and what to do. On June 4 the "hardliners" won out, and they chose to use military power over a negotiated solution with the students.

Did the students make significant or well-thought-out statements about "democracy" or realistic demands on China's leaders? The short and preliminary answer is no; but then, is this really the appropriate question to be asking in the first place? One could argue that what the students *said* was less important than what they *did*: They mobilized the population of China's capital and other major cities to support a profound challenge to the legitimacy of the CCP's leadership. Even if workers believed that "You can't eat democracy," and even if they participated in the demonstrations for their own reasons (such as gripes about inflation and corruption), they supported the students' demand that the CCP carry out further political reforms. This was because the students successfully promoted the idea that if China had had a different sort of system, a democratic system rather than authoritarian rule, the workers' bread-and-butter issues and corruption would have been addressed more seriously.

Repression Within China Following the Crackdown

By August 1989 the party leadership had established quotas of "bad elements" for work units and identified 20 categories of people to be targeted for punishment. But people were more reluctant to follow orders to expose their friends, colleagues, and family members than in the past, not only because such verdicts had often been reversed at a later time but also because few believed the CCP's version of what had happened in Beijing on June 4. Although many people worried about informers,[13] there seemed to be complicity from top to bottom, whether inside or outside the ranks of the CCP, in refusing to go along with efforts to ferret out demonstrators and sympathizers with the prodemocracy, antiparty movement. Party leaders below the central level appeared to believe that the central government leadership was doomed and, for this reason, they dared not carry out its orders. There would inevitably be a reversal of verdicts, and they did not want to be caught in that reversal.

As party leaders in work units droned on in mandatory political study sessions about Deng Xiaoping's important writings, workers wondered how long it would be before the June 4 military crackdown was condemned as a "counter-revolutionary crime against the people." Individuals in work units had to fill out lengthy questionnaires. A standard one had 24 questions aimed at "identifying the enemy." Among them were such questions as, "What did you think when Hu Yaobang died?" "When Zhao Ziyang went to Tiananmen Square, what did you think? Where were you?" At one university, each questionnaire had to be verified by two people (other than one's own family) or the individual involved would not be allowed to teach.[14]

In July 1989 new regulations prohibited all criticism of the Communist Party and the government; and Li Peng submitted a new law to the National People's Congress Standing Committee curtailing the right to demonstrate:

> Demonstrations can be authorised only after the names and details of every one of the organisers have been submitted to the state security apparatus. In addition, the organisers must provide in advance the planned number of demonstrators and the text of all their placards.

Also:

> Neither soldiers, nor police, nor public servants may demonstrate. If a factory or work unit manages to obtain a permit to voice their demands, no other factory or work unit may join their rally. People from outside the city are excluded, and foreigners may join a demonstration only with a special permit from the state security organs.[15]

Of course, with all names of leaders registered, the government could exert far greater control.

As part of the repression that followed the military crackdown in June 1989, the government carried out announced and unannounced arrests of hundreds of "liberal" intellectuals, students, workers, and others supporting the prodemocracy movement. Some were summarily executed, although available information indicates that most of those executed were workers, not students or intellectuals. During the world's absorption with the war with Iraq in 1991, the Chinese government suddenly announced the trials and verdicts on some of China's most famous dissident leaders during the 1989 demonstrations. Few dissidents remained in jail by 1993, although the government has occasionally arrested dissidents since that time.

The central leadership, which viewed university students as the source of the challenge to CCP rule, cut the size of the freshman university class in September 1989 and in subsequent years nearly in half. Moreover, the number of students under government sponsorship permitted to go abroad for university study dropped. This has, however, been counter-

(Photo by Liu Li)

Students from the University of Law and Politics staging a sit-in during the Tiananmen Square demonstrations in 1989.

balanced by those who now pay their own way (supported largely by relatives who have already gone abroad). Officially, only those with impeccable political credentials (as evaluated by their superiors) are eligible for government support for study abroad. Unofficially, those students with the best connections are the ones who have been, and continue to be, supported.

As for academics in the Chinese Academy of Social Sciences, who do state-sponsored research on history, economics, society, anthropology, politics, and international relations, after the 1989 crackdown, the government announced only 190 subjects on which its researchers could publish. Most of these social science researchers did not want to publish on these limited government-approved topics; and so they remained silent. Because of crowded working conditions, they were not required to appear at their offices anyway, so they were free to do whatever they chose, including nothing.

As with the mass media, many, if not all, of such repressive controls have slowly disappeared. The increasing involvement of Chinese intellectuals in international conferences, the result of China's desire to become a more respected partici-

pant in the international community of science, commerce, and economics, has led to far more innovation in scholarship than was formerly tolerated.

INTERNATIONAL RELATIONS

The historical context of China's foreign policy is fundamental to understanding its evolution. From the 1840s onward, foreign imperialists nibbled away at China, subjecting it to one national humiliation after another. As early as the 1920s, both the KMT and the CCP were committed to unifying and strengthening China in order to rid it of foreigners and resist further foreign incursions. When the Communists achieved victory over the KMT in 1949, they vowed that foreigners would never again be permitted to tell China what to do.

From Isolation to Openness

By the early 1950s, the Communists had forced all but a handful of foreigners to leave China. China charted an independent, and eventually an isolationist, foreign policy. After the end of the Cultural Revolution in 1976 and the return to power of more pragmatic "reformers" in 1978, China re-opened its door to the outside world. By the 1980s it was hosting several million tourists annually, inviting foreign investors and foreign experts to help with China's modern-ization, and allowing Chinese to study and travel abroad. Nevertheless, inside the P.R.C. contacts between Chinese and foreigners are still affected by the suspicion on the part of ordinary Chinese that ideological and cultural contamination comes from abroad and that association with foreigners may bring trouble.

Chinese sensitivity to any suggestion of foreign control and their strong xenophobia (dislike and fear of foreigners) mean that the Chinese are likely to rail at any effort by other countries to tell them what to do. Even after 1978, when China pursued an "open door" policy toward the outside world, the Chinese continued to exhibit this sensitivity on a wide variety of issues: on labeling drugs sent from China to the United States; on meeting standards set by other countries if China wishes to export those products to them; on intellec-tual property rights; on the use of prisoners for manufacturing goods for export; and especially on human rights.

China's xenophobia continues to show up in its efforts to keep foreigners isolated in certain living compounds and hotels reserved for foreigners; to limit social contacts be-tween foreigners and Chinese; to control the importation of foreign literature, films, and periodicals; and to keep foreign ideas, and diseases, out of China. The pride of the Chinese in their culture and country has been enhanced in recent years by their economic success, and by such things as their suc-cesses in the Olympic and Asian Games, music competitions, and film festivals.

By any measure, China in the 1980s and 1990s has been a much more open country than at any time since 1949. This is in spite of the concern of the more conservative wing of the CCP about the impact of China's "open door" policy on the political system (the influx of ideas about democracy and individual rights); on economic develop-ment (a market economy, corruption, foreign control and ownership, and the export of hard currency); and on Chi-nese culture ("pollution" from pornography to ideas about individualism and materialism). Although the more con-servative wing of the CCP leadership was responsible for crushing the student-led protests in June 1989, China's door remained open to foreign investment. But in the wake of the military's intervention in 1989, the domestic envi-ronment was so inhospitable to business that a large num-ber of foreign businesspeople left.

They were soon back. By 1992 foreign investment had skyrocketed to more than $12 billion. The new investment climate created by Deng's 1992 "experiment" speech accel-erated the return of foreign capital. Since then China has seemed less worried about the invasion of foreign values than it is anxious to attract foreign investments.

The Sino–Soviet Relationship

In the 1950s, while forcing most other foreigners to leave China, the Chinese Communist regime invited Soviet experts to China to give much-needed advice, technical assistance, and aid. This convinced the United States (already certain that Moscow controlled communism wherever it appeared) that the Chinese were Soviet puppets. Indeed, for most of the 1950s, the Chinese Communist regime had to accept Soviet tenets of domestic and foreign policy along with Soviet aid. But China's leaders soon grew concerned about the limits of Soviet aid and the relevance of Soviet policies to China's conditions—especially the costly industrialization favored by the Soviet Union. Ultimately, the Chinese questioned their Soviet "big brother" and turned, in the form of the Great Leap Forward policy, to a Chinese model of development.

The Chinese were also distressed about the de-Stalinization program of the general secretary of the Soviet Union's Com-munist Party at the time, Nikita Khrushchev. The Chinese feared that criticism of Stalin might have a politically desta-bilizing effect on their own heavily Stalinist-influenced sys-tem. For his part, Khrushchev warned the Chinese of the dangers to China's economy in undertaking the Great Leap Forward. Mao Zedong saw this as evidence that the Soviets had become "revisionists" and were on the road to restoring capitalism.

The Soviets' refusal to use their military power in support of China's foreign policy objectives further strained the Sino–Soviet relationship. First in the case of China's confrontation with the United States and the forces of the "Republic of China" over the Offshore Islands in the Taiwan Strait in 1958, and then in the Sino–Indian border war of 1962, the Soviet Union backed down from its promise to support China. Had the Soviets given China this support, it could have led to a direct Soviet–American military confrontation.

The final blow to the fragile relationship came with the Soviet Union's signing of the 1963 Nuclear Test Ban Treaty. The Chinese denounced this as a Soviet plot to exclude them from the "nuclear club" of the United Kingdom, France, the United States, and the Soviet Union. Subsequently, Beijing publicly broke Communist Party relations with Moscow.

The Sino–Soviet relationship, already in shambles, took on an added dimension of fear during the Vietnam War, when the Chinese grew concerned that the Soviets (and Americans) might use the war as an excuse to attack China. China's distrust of Soviet intentions were heightened when, in 1968, the Soviets invaded Czechoslovakia in the name of the "greater interests of the socialist community," which, they contended, "override the interests of any single country within that community."

Soviet skirmishes with Chinese soldiers on China's north-ern borders soon followed. Ultimately, it was the Chinese leadership's concern about the Soviet threat to China's na-tional security that, in 1971, caused it to reassess its relation-ship with the United States. The Sino–American ties that ensued made the Soviets anxious about their own security. The alleged threat of "Soviet hegemony" (dominance) to world peace became the main theme of almost every public Chinese foreign policy statement. An estimated 1 million Soviet troops on China's northern borders, the Soviet occupation of Afghanistan on China's western flank, and Soviet support for a territorially aggressive Vietnam on China's southern borders gave the Chinese reason to be concerned about Soviet intentions.

Limited Reconciliation

Beginning in 1987 the Soviets made some peaceful overtures: the reduction of its troops on China's borders and the withdrawal of support for Vietnam's puppet government in neighboring Cambodia. Moscow's decision to withdraw from Vietnam gave Beijing further evidence of a desire on Moscow's part for reconciliation. Beijing initially responded positively to the "glasnost" (open door) policy of the Soviet Communist Party's general secretary, Mikhail Gorbachev. Furthermore, ideological conflict between the two Communist giants abated, for with the Chinese themselves abandoning much of Marxist dogma in their economic policies, they no longer found it fruitful to denounce the Soviet Union's "revisionist" policies and to make self-righteous claims to ideological orthodoxy.

Thus, both the Soviet Union and China abandoned their earlier focus on laying claim to the leadership of the Communist camp, and they shifted their focus from security issues to economic issues. The more conservative wing of the CCP leadership was, however, concerned about the appeal of Gorbachev's glasnost policies, because it was not prepared to implement them in China. Gorbachev's visit to Beijing in the midst of the 1989 student-led protests, therefore, proved an embarrassment. The students viewed Gorbachev as the kind of reformer they wanted in their own government and chose to use the occasion of his summit meeting with China's leaders to hold large demonstrations to press for some of Gorbachev's kind of reforms.

The End of the Cold War

With the collapse of Communist party rule, first in Central/Eastern Europe in 1989 and subsequently in the Soviet Union, the dynamics of China's foreign policy changed dramatically. Apart from fear that their own reforms might lead to the collapse of CCP rule in China, the disintegration of the Soviet Union into 15 independent states removed China's ability to play off the 2 superpowers against each other: The formidable Soviet Union simply no longer existed. Yet its fragmented remains had to be treated seriously, for the state of Russia still shares a common border of several thousand miles with China, and Kazakhstan shares a common border of nearly 1,000 miles.

Moreover, instead of just one country on its borders having a nuclear first-strike capability against it (that is, an ability to

destroy China's retaliatory nuclear abilities if it strikes first), today China faces two countries with that ability—until such time as Kazakhstan relinquishes all its nuclear weapons under agreements signed with the United States. Russia continues to maintain at least half a million troops along its border with China and a large nuclear arsenal.

Because of the costliness of establishing a stronger defense and the sacrifices in economic development it would require, military modernization remains on the back burner. Indeed, in the face of an inadequate allocation of resources to China's military for modernization since 1979, the People's Liberation Army has struck out along the capitalist road to raise money. It has purchased considerable property in the Special Economic Zones (SEZs) near Hong Kong and has taken over ownership of major tourist hotels and industrial enterprises as a means for funding military modernization. China's military has already purchased significant military weaponry and technology from Russia as it scales back its own military in what sometimes resembles a going-out-of-business sale.

The end of the cold war has also led to a shift in focus, away from security concerns to economic issues. With China's primary interest now in becoming an integral part of the international economic, commercial, and monetary systems, it moved quickly to increase trade with its Russian and Kazakhstani neighbors. These rapidly increasing commercial links, due in large part to the paucity of consumer goods on the Russian and Kazakhstani side and the abundance thereof in China, have helped enrich China's border provinces, especially Xinjiang (bordering on Kazakhstan) in the far northwest. This area is rich in natural resources but was until recently unable to capitalize on its wealth because of its distance from the east's coastal export zone.

The Sino–American Relationship

China's relationship with the United States has historically been an emotionally turbulent one. It has never been characterized by indifference. During World War II, the United States gave significant help to the Chinese. At that time the Chinese Communists were fighting together with the Nationalists, under the leadership of the Nationalist Party (KMT) head, General Chiang Kai-shek, in a "united front" against the Japanese. Therefore, American aid was not seen as directed against communism.

After the defeat of Japan at the end of World War II, the Japanese military, which had occupied much of the north and east of China, was demobilized and returned to Japan. Subsequently, civil war broke out between the Communists and Nationalists. The United States attempted to reconcile the two sides, but to no avail. As the Communists moved toward victory in 1949, the KMT leadership fled to Taiwan. Thereafter, the two rival governments each claimed to be the true rulers of China. Since the United States was already in the throes of the "cold war" because of the "iron curtain" falling over Central/Eastern Europe, Washington pointedly decided to oppose communism throughout the world. As a result, the United States decided to support the KMT, which by then had lost control of the mainland, as the legitimate government of all of China.

The Korean War

The outbreak of the Korean War in 1950 made the United States' decision to support the Nationalists easier. The war began when the Communists in northern Korea attacked the non-Communist south. When United Nations (UN) troops (mostly Americans), led by American General Douglas Mac-Arthur, successfully pushed Communist troops back to the Chinese border and showed no signs of stopping their advance, the Chinese—who had been sending the Americans anxious messages about their concern for China's own security—entered the war. The United States labeled the Chinese Communists as aggressors, unfit for membership in the United Nations. They became a major target of America's cold war isolation and containment policies.

With the People's Republic of China condemned as an international aggressor for its action in Korea, the United States felt free to recognize the government established by force in Taiwan as the legitimate government of all of China. The United States supported the Nationalists' claim that the 600 million people then on the Chinese mainland actually wanted the KMT to return to the mainland and defeat the Chinese Communists. As the years passed, however, it became clear that the Chinese Communists controlled the mainland and that the Chinese people were not about to rebel against Communist rule.

Sino–American relations steadily worsened as the United States continued to build up a formidable anti-Communist military bastion under KMT control in the tiny Offshore Islands, just off China's coast. The hostility grew even more intense as the U.S. military involvement in Vietnam steadily escalated in the 1960s and early 1970s. China, certain that the United States was really using the war in Vietnam as the first step toward attacking China, concentrated on civil defense measures: Chinese citizens used spoons and shovels to dig air-raid shelters in Beijing and tunnels that connected central Beijing with the suburbs. Similar efforts were carried out in Shanghai. Some industrial enterprises were moved out of China's major cities in order to make them less vulnerable in the event of a massive attack on concentrated urban areas. The Chinese received a steady barrage of what we would call "propaganda" about the United States as its number-one enemy; but it is important to realize that the Chinese leadership actually *believed* what it told the people. Otherwise, it is

unlikely that they would have made such an immense expenditure of manpower and resources on civil defense measures.

Diplomatic Relations

By the late 1960s, China was completely isolated from the world community, including the Communist bloc. In the throes of the Cultural Revolution, it had withdrawn its diplomatic staff from all but one of its embassies. It saw itself as surrounded on all sides by enemies—the Soviets to the North and West, the United States to the South and in South Korea and Japan, and the Nationalists to the East in Taiwan. Internally, China was in turmoil from the Cultural Revolution. The country appeared to be on the verge of complete collapse.

In this context, then, it was the Soviet invasion of Czechoslovakia in 1968 and Soviet military incursions on China's northern borders, combined perhaps with an assessment of which country could offer China the most profitable economic relationship, that led China in 1971 to consider the United States the lesser of two evil giants and to respond positively to American overtures. With President Nixon's 1972 visit to China, the first public official American contact with China since breaking diplomatic relations in 1950, the initial steps in reversing more than 2 decades of hostile relations were taken.

A new era of Sino–American friendship was consummated in the Shanghai Communique, but full diplomatic relations were not established until January 1, 1979. This long delay in bringing the two states into full diplomatic relations reflected not only each country's domestic political problems but also mutual disillusionment with the nature of the relationship. The Americans had assumed that the 1972 opening of partial diplomatic relations would lead to a huge new economic market for American products; the Chinese assumed that the new ties would quickly bring the United States to end its diplomatic relations with Taiwan. Both were disappointed. Eventually, however, pressures from both sides brought full diplomatic relations between the United States and the People's Republic of China.

The Taiwan Issue

With both the People's Republic of China and the Republic of China claiming to be the only legitimate government of the Chinese people, the establishment of diplomatic relations with the former necessarily entailed breaking them with the latter. Nevertheless, the United States continued to maintain extensive informal ties with Taiwan, including military sales. Although the military sales are still a serious issue, American ties with Taiwan have become much less important to China,

| The Chinese Communist Party (CCP) is established **1921** | Japanese occupation of Manchuria (the Northeast Province of China) **1931** | The Long March **1934–1935** | The Japanese invasion and occupation of much of China **1937–1945** | The Japanese occupation of Hong Kong **1942–1945** | **1949** | The United States recognizes the Nationalist government in Taiwan as the legitimate government of all China **1950** | The Great Leap Forward; the Taiwan Strait crisis (Offshore Islands) **1958** |

Civil war between the KMT and CCP   The KMT establishes the Nationalist government on Taiwan   The People's Republic of China is established

as its own ties with Taiwan have grown steadily closer since 1988. Taiwan's entrepreneurs (by way of Hong Kong front companies, as certain laws still prohibit their direct investment in China) have become one of the largest group of investors in China's economy. Although Taiwan used to have one of the cheapest labor forces in the world, its workers now demand wages too high to remain competitive in international trade. Thus, Taiwan's entrepreneurs have dismantled many of its older industries and reassembled them on the mainland. With China's cheap labor, these same industries are now profitable, and both China and Taiwan's entrepreneurs are the beneficiaries.

Ties between Taiwan and the mainland have also been enhanced by the millions of tourists, most of them with relatives in China, who have traveled to the mainland since the late 1980s. They bring with them both presents and goodwill. Families that have not seen each other for 40 years have reestablished contact, and "the enemy" now seems less threatening. Furthermore, as China continues to liberalize its economic system and to raise the standard of living, the Chinese leadership hopes reunification will become more attractive to Taiwan. In this very positive context, disturbed only briefly by the military crackdown on the demonstrators in Tiananmen Square in 1989, neither side wants to do anything to disrupt a peaceful and profitable relationship in which Taiwan continues to act as an independent state, without actually declaring independence.

In short, without firing a single shot, Taipei and Beijing are coming closer together. This does not mean that the two, both claiming that there is only one China and that Taiwan is part of China, will soon be fully reunified in law; but it matters far less as their two economies continue to benefit mutually from their economic and commercial ties.

Nevertheless, there remains the black cloud of Beijing possibly using military force against Taiwan, especially if it ever appears that Taiwan would actually declare itself an independent state. Beijing refuses to make any pledge that it will never use military force to reunify Taiwan with the mainland, on the grounds that Taiwan is an "internal" affair. Hence, no other country has a right to tell China what to do about Taiwan.

(UPI/Bettmann Newsphotos)

In 1971 U.S. secretary of state Henry Kissinger made the first overtures toward reversing the hostile Sino–American relationship. In 1972 President Richard Nixon visited China, and a new era of cooperation began. Nixon is pictured above with Vice Premier Li Xiannian on the Great Wall of China during this historic visit.

Soviet withdrawal of aid to the P.R.C. 1959	The public Sino–Soviet split 1963	The Great Proletarian Cultural Revolution 1966–1976	The United Nations votes to seat the P.R.C. in place of the R.O.C. 1971	U.S. president Richard Nixon's visit to the P.R.C.; the Shanghai Communique 1972	Mao Zedong dies; removal of the Gang of Four 1976	Deng Xiaoping is restored to power 1977	The Democracy Wall movement 1978–1979	The United States recognizes the P.R.C. and withdraws recognition of the R.O.C.; the Sino–Vietnamese War 1979

Human Rights

The election of Bill Clinton as president of the United States caused considerable consternation, both to China's leadership and its people. The Chinese people were confused and distraught at the prospect of punitive economic measures that the new Clinton administration threatened to take in response to China's human rights abuses.[16] They saw their government as having taken economic measures to bring in foreign investment, integrate China into the international economy, and enhance development. China's phenomenal growth in the 1980s and early 1990s had improved the daily lives of hundreds of millions of ordinary Chinese people. They were far more interested in the prospect of an improved standard of living than in the rights of jailed dissidents.

Even China's intellectuals no longer seemed interested in politics. They did not "love the party," but they accepted the status quo. They just wanted a promotion and to make money. As one university professor put it, it is easy to be idealistic in one's heart; but to be idealistic in action is a sign of a true idealist, and there haven't been many of those in China since 1989.

The Chinese perspective is this: They only know what their government tells them; they assume it lies to them, but they nevertheless know no more than what they are told. Why should they risk their careers to fight for the rights of jailed dissidents when they really know very little about what the dissidents have done? They then argue that the American government has also brutalized its population, pointing to such matters as the Kent State killings during the Vietnam War and the brutality of the Los Angeles police against Rodney King. They have heard about the abominable behavior of several student leaders of the Tiananmen Square demonstrations in 1989, both during the movement and after, from some who escaped to the West. They wonder aloud if, upon examination, any of them were more virtuous than their own corrupt and brutal government leaders.

In defense of their own government, some Chinese intellectuals argue that the recent difficulties in the United States and in other Western democracies indicate that their respective citizens keep electing the wrong leaders, leaders who make bad policies. This, they argue, indicates that democracy does not work. And many support the view that the Chinese people are not "ready" for democracy because of inadequate education.

In any event, they do not see any point in punishing hundreds of millions of Chinese people for crimes committed by their leadership, not by themselves. Indeed, not infrequently it is the Chinese people themselves who demand ever harsher penalties for common criminals, if not political dissidents.

And many ordinary people now seem to believe the government's overall assessment of the events of the spring of 1989, which is that they posed a threat to the stability and order of China. To the Chinese people, no less than to their government, stability and order are critical to continued economic development.

In the end, of course, President Clinton decided to break the linkage between most-favored-nation trade status for China and an improvement in its human rights record. This was due to his apparent conviction—a conviction that President George Bush had had before him—that the United States dare not risk jeopardizing its relations with an increasingly powerful state containing one quarter of the world's population through measures that would probably have simply given Japan and other countries a better trading position while destroying the opportunity for Americans to do business with China.

THE FUTURE

China's agenda is daunting: It must avoid war, maintain internal political stability in the context of international pressures to democratize, continue to carry out major reforms without endangering CCP control, sustain economic growth, and limit population growth. Since 1980 China's Communist Party leadership has succeeded in all these efforts. China's name may soon be added to the list of Asia's dragons—only it will not be one of the "four little dragons," but a very large one.

The Chinese people are anxious that Deng Xiaoping's death may precipitate a major power struggle within the CCP leadership. The 14th National Party Congress, held in October 1992, witnessed a major reshuffling of leaders, with the more liberal reformers and a younger generation of leaders promoted to key positions, and older and more conservative leaders retired or demoted. These changes may more firmly anchor a leadership favorable to the continuation of Deng's reforms in positions of power, thereby diminishing the possibility of a leadership struggle that could lead to a military coup, a civil war, or both.

If China's record of economic success continues, the CCP may become more secure and allow still further political liberalization. Although "liberalization" must not be confused with "democratization," it would certainly allow China to continue in the direction of greater pluralization and freedom for its people. In fact, greater political pluralization is an almost inevitable offshoot of economic liberalization. As privatization continues, more and more groups form to com-

1980s–1990s							
Resumption of arms sales to Taiwan	Beijing announces its intention to restore Chinese sovereignty over Hong Kong	A short-lived campaign against "spiritual pollution" from the West and capitalism	Sino–Soviet relations begin to thaw	The Special Party Conference removes many aged and infirm leaders; conservative opposition to Deng's reforms grows	Student demonstrations for democracy are widespread in China's cities; political liberalization is condemned	China sells Silkworm missiles to Iran and Saudi Arabia	Student demonstrations in Tiananmen Square; military crackdown; political repression follows
The Shanghai Communique II: the United States agrees to phase out arms sales to Taiwan	The P.R.C. and United States reach agreement on textile quotas and the selling of technology	China and Great Britain sign an agreement on Hong Kong's future		Deng is named *Time* magazine's "Man of the Year"	CCP General Secretary Hu Yaobang is removed; ties with Taiwan expand rapidly	Premier Li Peng reasserts centralized economic control	Deng encourages "experimentation" and the economy booms

pete with one another economically and to pressure the government for measures to protect and enhance their economic position. The number of pressure groups and interest groups are bound to grow, resulting in a pluralization of political forces.

Finally, as the Chinese economy has become more integrated into the international economy, China's leaders have become more enmeshed in the international political system and at least slightly more sensitive to pressures from it. But it is still likely that they will insist on moving at their own pace, and in a way that takes into account China's culture, history, and institutions. In the meantime, like so many other developing countries, it must worry about the increasing polarization of the population into the rich and the poor, high levels of inflation and unemployment, uncontrolled economic growth, environmental degradation, corruption that threatens the very foundation of CCP rule, and the strident resistance by whole regions within China to following economic and monetary policies formulated at the center. These would be formidable tasks for any country; how much more so for a leadership responsible for feeding, educating, and controlling a population of 1.2 billion.

NOTES

1. For excellent detail on Chinese religion practices, see Robert Weller, *Taiping Rebels,* 1994; and Alan Hunter and Chan, *Protestantism,* 1993. The latter notes that Chinese judge gods "on performance rather than theological criteria" (p. 144). That is, if the contributors to the temple in which certain gods were honored were doing well financially and their families were healthy, then those gods were judged well. Furthermore, Chinese pray as individuals rather than as congregations. Thus, before the Chinese government closed most temples, they were full of individuals praying randomly, children playing inside, and general noise and confusion. Western missionaries have found this style too casual for their own more structured religions (p. 145).

2. Professor Rudolf Wagner of Heidelberg University. Information based on his stay in China in 1990.

3. Of course, the masses were really manipulated by power-hungry members of China's elite, an ever-shifting nouveau elite, who were in a desperate competition with other pretenders to power.

4. Victor C. Falkenheim, "Political Participation in China," *Problems of Communism* (May–June 1978), No. 27, p. 21, as referenced in Suzanne Ogden, *China's Unresolved Issues: Politics, Culture, and Development,* 2d ed. (Englewood Cliffs, NJ: Prentice Hall, 1992), p. 135.

5. Ogden, *China's Unresolved Issues,* p. 136.

6. *Ibid.*

7. Vaclav Havel, as quoted by Timothy Garton Ash, "Eastern Europe: The Year of Truth," *New York Review of Books* (February 15, 1990), referenced in Giuseppe De Palma, "After Leninism: Why Democracy Can Work in Eastern Europe," *Journal of Democracy,* Vol. 2, No. 1 (Winter 1991), p. 25, note 3.

8. Anonymous, "Letter to Friends From a County-Level Party Official" (June 4, 1992), Document 200, in Suzanne Ogden, Kathleen Hartford, Lawrence R. Sullivan, and David Zweig, eds., *China's Search for Democracy: The Student and Mass Movement of 1989* (Armonk, NY: M. E. Sharpe, 1992), p. 439.

9. De Palma, "After Leninism," p. 26.

10. Liu Binyan, "China and the Lessons of Eastern Europe," *Journal of Democracy,* Vol. 2, No. 2 (Spring 1991), p. 8.

11. Beijing University student, "My Innermost Thoughts—To the Students of Beijing Universities," May 1989, Document 68, in Ogden *et al.,* eds., *China's Search for Democracy,* pp. 172–173.

12. Vivienne Shue, in a speech to a USIA conference of diplomats and scholars, as quoted and summarized in "Democracy Rating Low in Mainland," *The Free China Journal* (January 24, 1992), p. 7.

13. "Campaign to Crush Dissent Intensifies," *South China Morning Post* (July 8, 1989).

14. Chinese student (anonymous) in the United States, conversation, summer 1990.

15. "Clampdown Sparks Rush to Beat Censors," *South China Morning Post* (July 8, 1989).

16. Based on Suzanne Ogden's observations during her lecture tour in China in the fall of 1992.

Taiwan

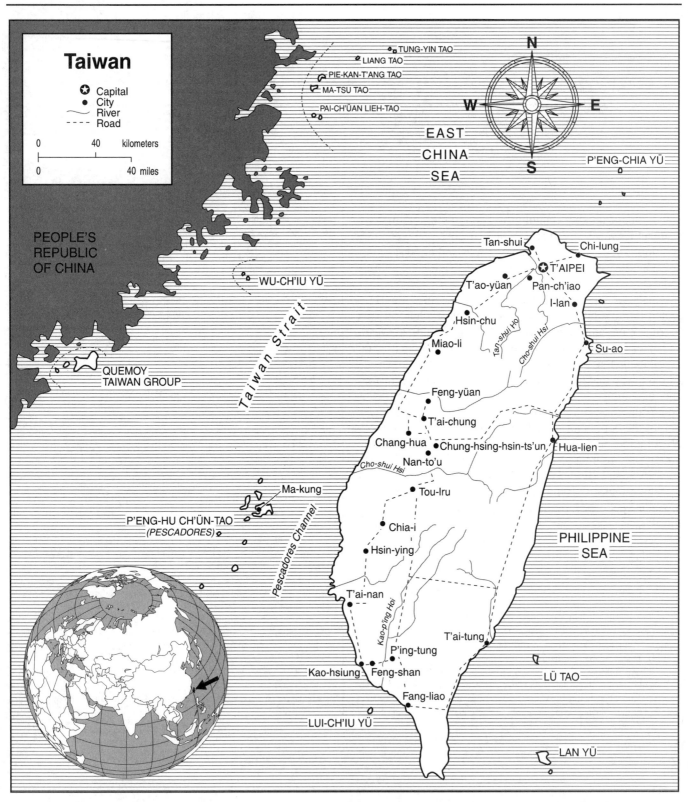

Since 1949 Taiwan has been considered the center of the government of the Republic of China (Nationalist China). The Nationalist government on Taiwan has claimed jurisdiction over all the Chinese mainland, while the People's Republic of China has claimed jurisdiction over Taiwan. Both governments agree that Taiwan is part of China. The province of Taiwan consists of the main island, 15 islands in the Taiwan group, and 64 islands in the Pescadores Archipelago. While the Pescadores are close to the main island, the islands in the Taiwan group are only a few miles off the cost of mainland China.

Taiwan (Republic of China)

GEOGRAPHY

Area in Square Kilometers (Miles):
36,002 (22,320) (about the size of West Virginia)
Capital (Population): Taipei (2,720,000)
Climate: subtropical

PEOPLE

Population
Total: 21,092,000
Annual Growth Rate: 1%
Rural/Urban Population Ratio: 25/75
Ethnic Makeup: 84% Taiwanese; 14% Mainlander Chinese; 2% aborigine
Major Languages: Mandarin Chinese; Taiwanese and Hakka dialects

Health
Life Expectancy at Birth: 72 years (male); 78 years (female)
Infant Mortality Rate (Ratio): 5.7/1,000
Average Caloric Intake: n/a
Physicians Available (Ratio): 1/910

Religions
93% mixture of Buddhism, Taoism, and folk religions; 4.5% Christian; 2.5% others

---

TAIWAN: "NONEXISTENT" BUT PROFITABLE

In 1979 the United States recognized the People's Republic of China as the sole legal government of China. Since for diplomatic purposes there could only be one China, recognition of the Nationalist government of the Republic of China on Taiwan was dropped. Officially, this made Taiwan cease to exist as a separate state in the view of the U.S. government. American business interests, however, continue to thrive in Taiwan. U.S. investment in Taiwan is now about $1 billion, and American banks have made billions of dollars in loans to Taiwan. Thus, even in the absence of formal diplomatic relations, the economic links between the United States and Taiwan remain extensive.

Education
Adult Literacy Rate: 92%

COMMUNICATION

Telephones: 7,800,000
Newspapers: 139

TRANSPORTATION

Highways—Kilometers (Miles): 20,041 (12,425)
Railroads—Kilometers (Miles): 4,600 (2,852)
Usable Airfields: 38

GOVERNMENT

Type: multiparty democratic regime
Head of State/Government: President Lee Teng-hui; Premier Lien Chan
Political Parties: Nationalist Party (Kuomintang); Democratic Progressive Party; China Social Democratic Party; Labour Party
Suffrage: universal over 20

MILITARY

Number of Armed Forces: 400,000
Military Expenditures (% of Central Government Expenditures): 5.4%
Current Hostilities: officially (but not actually) in a state of war with the People's Republic of China

ECONOMY

Currency ($ U.S. Equivalent): 26.23 New Taiwan dollars = $1
Per Capita Income/GDP: $10,566/$209 billion
Inflation Rate: 4.4%
Natural Resources: coal; gold; copper; sulphur; oil; natural gas
Agriculture: rice; tea; bananas; pineapples; sugarcane; sweet potatoes; wheat; soybeans; peanuts
Industry: steel; pig iron; aluminum; shipbuilding; cement; fertilizer; paper; cotton; fabrics

FOREIGN TRADE

Exports: $82.4 billion
Imports: $72.1 billion

Taiwan

A Dynamo in East Asia

HISTORY AND PEOPLE

Taiwan,* a powerful economic center in Asia, was once an unknown island off the coast of China, just 90 miles away. It was originally inhabited by aborigines from Southeast Asia. By the seventh century A.D., Chinese settlers had begun to arrive. The island was subsequently discovered by the Portuguese, in 1590, and Dutch as well as Spanish settlers followed. The aborigines' descendants, who have been pushed into the remote mountain areas by the Chinese settlers, number fewer than 400,000 today, a small fraction of the 21 million people now living in Taiwan. Furthermore, most of the current population are descended from those Chinese who emigrated from the Chinese mainland's southern provinces before 1885, when Taiwan officially became a province of China. Although these people originally came from China, they are known as *Taiwanese,* as distinct from the Chinese who came from the China mainland from 1947 to 1949. The latter are called *Mainlanders* and represent less than 20 percent of the island's population. After 1949 the Mainlanders dominated Taiwan's political elite; but the "Taiwanization" of the political realm that began after Chiang Kai-shek's death in 1975, and the political liberalization of the late 1980s and early 1990s, have allowed the native Taiwanese to take up their rightful place within the elite.

The Manchus, "barbarians" who came from the north, overthrew the Chinese rulers on the mainland in 1644. In 1683 they conquered Taiwan; but because Taiwan was an island 90 miles distant from the mainland, the Manchus paid less attention to it and exercised minimal sovereignty over the Taiwanese people. With their defeat in the Sino–Japanese War (1894–1895), the Manchus were forced to cede Taiwan to the Japanese. The Taiwanese people refused to accept Japanese rule, however, and proclaimed Taiwan a republic. As a result, the Japanese had to use military force to gain actual control over Taiwan.

For the next 50 years, Taiwan remained under Japan's colonial administration. Taiwan's economy flourished under Japanese rule. Japan also helped to develop Taiwan's agricultural sector, a modern transportation network, and an economic structure favorable to later industrial development. Further, by creating an advanced educational system, the Japanese developed an educated workforce, which proved critical to Taiwan's economic growth.

With Japan's defeat at the end of World War II (1945), Taiwan reverted to China's sovereignty. By this point the Chinese had overthrown the Manchu Dynasty (1911) and established a republican form of government. Beginning in 1912 China was known as the Republic of China (R.O.C.).

*Taiwan has also been known as Formosa, Free China, the Republic of China, and Nationalist China. Today the government in Taiwan calls the island "Taiwan" and the government the "Republic of China government."

Thus it was Chiang Kai-shek who, as head of the R.O.C. government, accepted the return of the island province of Taiwan to R.O.C. rule in 1945. Relations between Taiwanese and Mainlanders were, however, full of tension: The rag-tag, undisciplined KMT (Nationalist Party, or Kuomintang) military forces who arrived in Taiwan were met with hatred and contempt by the local people, who had grown accustomed to the orderliness and professionalism of the Japanese occupation forces. Angered by the incompetence and corruption of KMT officials, demonstrations against rule by Mainlanders occurred in February 1947. Relations were badly scarred when Chiang Kai-shek's troops brutally killed thousands of Taiwanese opposed to mainland rule. Among those killed were many members of the island's political elite.

Meanwhile, the KMT government of the R.O.C. had to focus its attention on the mainland, where, following a fragile peace during World War II, the civil war between the Chinese Communists under Mao Zedong and the Chinese Nationalists under Chiang Kai-shek broke out once again. Civil war, which raged from 1945 to 1949, diverted the KMT's attention away from Taiwan, which, as it had under Manchu rule, functioned fairly independently of Beijing. In 1949, when it became clear that the Chinese Communists would defeat the Nationalists, Chiang and 2 million members of his loyal military, political, and commercial elite fled to Taiwan to establish what they claimed to be the true government (in exile) of the Republic of China. This declaration was based on Chiang's determination to regain control over the mainland, and on his insistence that the more than 600 million people left on the mainland wanted the KMT to overthrow the Communists and reassert control.

Chiang was supported by the United States in the 1950s, during the McCarthy period of the "Red scare" (a period during which individuals believed to be Communists or Communist sympathizers were persecuted by the government). In response to the Chinese Communists' alleged aggression in Korea in 1950, the United States projected to Asia its cold war isolation and containment policies in order to surround the Chinese Communists with strongholds of "democracy," "capitalism," and "freedom." It was within this context that the United States committed itself to the military defense of Taiwan and the Offshore Islands in the Taiwan Strait, both by ordering the U.S. Seventh Fleet to the Taiwan Strait (in 1950) and by giving large amounts of military and economic aid to Taiwan. Chiang Kai-shek continued to lead the Republic of China government on Taiwan until his death in 1975, at which time his son, Chiang Ching-kuo, succeeded him.

Two Governments, One China

What each side believes about the relationship between Taiwan and the mainland of China is essential to understanding the issue of Taiwan's future. In 1949, when the R.O.C. government fled to Taiwan, the Chinese Communists established the People's Republic of China and claimed that the R.O.C. government was illegitimate. (Mao Zedong, the P.R.C.'s pre-eminent leader until his death in 1976, was later to say that adopting the new name of the People's Republic of China instead of keeping the old name of the Republic of China was the biggest mistake he ever made.) They claimed that the P.R.C. government governed all of China, including Taiwan. Beijing's attempt to regain control over Taiwan was, however, interrupted by the outbreak of the Korean War and later by the presence of the U.S. Seventh Fleet in the Taiwan Strait. This thwarted the Chinese Communists' final objective in their civil war against the Nationalists. For this reason, Beijing still insists that Taiwan is an "internal" Chinese affair, that international law is therefore irrelevant, and that other countries have no right to interfere. For its part, although the R.O.C. government until the 1980s had claimed that *it* should be the true government of all of China, this is no longer a pillar of its policy.

Even though the Chinese Communists' control over the mainland was long evident to the world, the United States managed to keep the Republic of China in the United Nations' China seat by insisting that the issue of China's representation in the United Nations was an important question requiring a two-thirds vote of the General Assembly, rather than a simple majority. Because of support from its allies, the United States was able to block a two-thirds vote from occurring until 1971. At this critical moment, when the R.O.C.'s right to represent "China" in the United Nations was questioned, the R.O.C. could easily have put forward the claim that Taiwan had the right to be recognized as an independent state. Instead, it steadfastly maintained that there was but one China and that Taiwan was merely a province of China. Both governments (but not the majority of Taiwanese people) still officially contend that Taiwan is a province of China.

International Acceptance of the People's Republic of China

Since the P.R.C.'s entry into the United Nations in 1971, the R.O.C.'s position in international affairs (except for the international economy) has been severely eroded as, one by one, the People's Republic of China has taken over the China seat in international organizations and agencies. The Beijing government has in most cases successfully protested against Taiwan's representation in international organizations to which it belongs. Not wanting to anger China, which has a huge and growing economy and the world's largest population, international organizations have given in to Beijing's unrelenting pressure. Similarly, Beijing insists that in bilateral state-to-state relations, any state establishing diplomatic relations with it must accept China's "principled stands." These include an acknowledgment that Taiwan is a province of China, that there is only one China (not "two Chinas," or

New York Public Library

McCARTHYISM: ISOLATING AND CONTAINING COMMUNISM

The McCarthy period in the United States was an era of rabid anticommunism. McCarthyism was based in part on the belief that the United States was responsible for losing China to the Communists in 1949 and that the reason for this loss was the infiltration of the U.S. government by Communists. As a result, Senator Joseph McCarthy (pictured above) spearheaded a "witch-hunt" to ferret out those who allegedly were selling out American interests to the Communists. McCarthyism took advantage of the national mood in the cold war era that had begun in 1947, in which the world was seen as being divided into two opposing camps: Communists and capitalists.

The major strategy of the cold war, as outlined by President Harry Truman in 1947, was the "isolation and containment" of communism. This strategy was based on the belief that if the United States attempted—as it had done with Adolf Hitler's aggression against Czechoslovakia (the first step toward World War II)—to appease communism, it would spread beyond its borders and threaten other free countries.

The purpose of the cold war strategy, then, was to contain the Communists within their national boundaries and to isolate them by hindering their participation in the international economic system and in international organizations. Hence, in the case of China, there was an American-led boycott against all Chinese goods, and the United States refused to recognize the People's Republic of China as the legitimate representative of the Chinese people within international organizations.

CHIANG KAI-SHEK: DETERMINED TO RETAKE THE MAINLAND

Until his dying day, Chiang Kai-shek (1887–1975), pictured here with his wife, maintained that the military, led by the KMT (Kuomintang, or Nationalist Party), would one day invade the mainland and, with the support of the Chinese people living there, defeat the Communist government. During the years of Chiang's presidency, banner headlines daily proclaimed that the Communist "bandits" would soon be turned out by internal rebellion and that the KMT would return to control on the mainland.

In the last years of Chiang Kai-shek's life, when he was generally confined to his residence and incapable of directing the government, his son, Chiang Ching-kuo, always had two copies of the newspaper made that proclaimed such unlikely feats, so that his father would continue to believe these were the primary goals of the KMT government in Taiwan. In fact, a realistic appraisal of the situation had been made long before Chiang's death, and most of the members of the KMT only pretended to believe that an invasion of the mainland was imminent.

Chiang Ching-kuo, although continuing to strengthen Taiwan's defenses, turned his efforts to building Taiwan into an economic showcase in Asia. Taiwan's remarkable growth and a certain degree of political liberalization were the hallmarks of Chiang Ching-kuo's leadership in Taiwan. A man of the people, he shunned many of the elitist practices of his father and the KMT ruling elite and helped to bring about the Taiwanization of both the KMT party and the government. The "Chiang dynasty" in Taiwan came to an end with his death in 1988. It was, in fact, Chiang Ching-kuo who made certain of this, by barring his own sons from succeeding him and by grooming his own successor, a native Taiwanese.

"one China, one Taiwan"), and that the People's Republic of China is the sole representative of the Chinese people.

Those who thought that commercial ventures and foreign investment in Taiwan would dry up as a result of ending diplomatic relations with Taipei have been proven wrong. Taipei responded to the change of status with a diplomatic sleight of hand: After closing one embassy after another, it opened offices that actually function as embassies of Taiwan even though they are unofficial. Their purpose is to handle all commercial, cultural, and official business (including the issuance of visas to those traveling to Taiwan).

As the KMT began to face reality in the 1990s, it adopted a new approach. Entitled "flexible diplomacy," it essentially allows Taiwan to rationalize its own decision to join international organizations to which China already belongs by calling itself "China Taipei." Beijing has, with only a few exceptions, been adamant about not letting this happen. Thus, the unresolved issue surrounding "two Chinas" still plagues Taiwan on various matters.

THE OFFSHORE ISLANDS

Since crises of serious dimensions erupted between China and the United States in 1954–1955, 1958, 1960, and 1962 over the blockading of supplies to the Taiwan-controlled Offshore Islands in the Taiwan Strait, the importance of these tiny islands grew out of all proportion to their intrinsic worth. The two major island groups, Quemoy (about 2 miles from the Chinese mainland) and Matsu (about 8 miles from the mainland) are located almost 90 miles from Taiwan. Thus, Taiwan's control of them has made them strategically valuable for pursuing the government's professed goal of retaking the mainland and for psychologically linking Taiwan to the mainland.

The civilian population is about 50,000 (mostly farmers) in Quemoy and about 6,000 (mostly fishermen) in Matsu. The lack of industry and manufacturing on the islands has led to a steady emigration of their natives to Southeast Asia for better jobs. The small civilian population in Quemoy is significantly augmented, however, by an estimated 10,000 to 100,000 soldiers. The heavily fortified islands appear to be somewhat deserted, though, since the soldiers live mostly underground: hospitals, kitchens, sleeping quarters—everything is located underground. Tunnels blasted out of granite accommodate two-lane highways in a honeycomb pattern under the surface of Quemoy. Heavily camouflaged anti-artillery aircraft dot the landscape, and all roads are reinforced to carry tanks.

In the first years after their victory on the mainland, the Chinese Communists maintained a fairly steady barrage of shelling of the islands to remind the Nationalists that the civil war was not over and that there was only one China. When there was not a crisis, their shells were filled with pro-Communist propaganda materials, which littered the islands. When the Chinese Communists wanted to test the U.S. commitment to the Nationalists in Taiwan and the Soviet commitment to its own objectives, they shelled the islands heavily and intercepted supplies to the islands. In the end, China always backed down; but in 1958 and 1962, it did so only after going to the brink of war with the United States. After 1979 and Deng Xiaoping's "peace initiatives" toward Taiwan, the contest for control over the Offshore Islands was at the level of an exchange of gifts by balloons and packages floated across the channel:

> The Nationalists load their balloons and seaborne packages with underwear, children's shoes, soap, toys, blankets, transistor radios and tape recorders, as well as cookies emblazoned with Chiang Ching-kuo's picture and audio tapes of Taiwan's top popular singer, Theresa Teng, a mainland favorite.
>
> The Communists send back beef jerky, tea, herbal medicines, mao-tai and cigarettes, as well as their own varieties of soap and toys.
>
> [There is] confirmation from the mainland of the balloons' reaching as far as Tibet. . . . Unpredictable winds make the job harder for the Communists, but enough of the packages reach Quemoy and Taiwan for the authorities to have passed a law requiring people to hand over all pamphlets and gifts.[1]

Although the brutal suppression of the Tiananmen Square demonstrators in Beijing in the spring of 1989 temporarily led to increased tensions in the Taiwan Strait and a military emergency alert, by 1992 the political situation in China had stabilized enough to make an attack unlikely. A sign of the diminished sense of threat came in November 1992, when Taiwan's military administration of Quemoy and Matsu ended. By the mid-1990s, however, a furious debate had broken out over the future of these Offshore Islands. The opposition Democratic Progressive Party (DPP) argues that given today's military technology, these islands just off the China coast could easily be taken as "hostages" by the Chinese Communists. The DPP is therefore proposing that the Quemoy and Matsu island groups be made into an international monetary zone. As such, they would attract foreign investment while simultaneously making it less likely that China would invade. As an international monetary zone, they could also compete with Hong Kong's role as the financial center in Asia. The ruling KMT considers this proposal treasonous and argues that the islands are still vital to the defense of Taiwan.[2]

CULTURE AND SOCIETY

Although the Taiwanese people were originally immigrants from the Chinese mainland, their culture, which has developed in isolation from the mainland's culture, is not the same as the "Chinese" culture of the "Mainlanders" who arrived from 1947 to 1949. Since the Taiwanese continue to speak their own dialect of Chinese, distinct from the standard Chinese spoken by the Mainlanders, and since almost all engage in Taiwanese folk-religion practices, the distinctions institutionalized in a political system that discriminated against the Taiwanese have been culturally reinforced.

The Taiwanese have in recent years grown increasingly resistant to efforts by the KMT Mainlanders to "Sinify" them—to have them speak standard Chinese and adopt the values of the dominant Chinese Mainlander elite. State-controlled television now offers programs in the Taiwanese dialect, and many more radio programs are in Taiwanese. Nevertheless, the commonalities between Taiwanese and Mainland Chinese culture are many. Generally speaking, they need not be viewed as two cultures in conflict. As Taiwanese

(Photo credit Dean Collinwood)
As Taiwan enjoys an economic boom, residents suffer the complications of having more than they know what to do with. Individuals now have easy access to owning cars, but the sheer number of private automobiles overwhelms the infrastructure's capacity.

individuals move into leadership positions in what used to be exclusively Mainlander institutions and intermarriage between the two groups grows more common, an amalgamation of Taiwanese and traditional Chinese practices is becoming evident throughout the society. As is discussed later in this essay, the real source of conflict is the desire of the Taiwanese not to be controlled by *any* Chinese from the mainland of China, whether they be KMT Nationalists or Communists.

Taiwanese culture is, however, gradually being eroded by mass education and the media, both of which emphasize Chinese cultural values. In turn, rampant materialism as well as the importation of foreign ideas and values are eroding both Taiwanese *and* Chinese values. Although the KMT government has engaged in a massive campaign to reassert Chinese values, the message seems lost in its larger message, which asks all to contribute to making Taiwan the showplace of the developing world. The government's emphasis on hard work and economic prosperity has seemingly undercut its focus on traditional Chinese values of politeness, the sanctity of the family, and the teaching of culturally based ethics (such as filial piety) throughout the school system. Materialism and an individualism that focuses on personal needs and pleasure seeking are slowly undermining collectively oriented values.[3] The "I can do whatever I want" attitude is, in the view of many, leading to a breakdown in social order.[4]

While playing a part in Taiwan's economic boom of the past decade, the emphasis on materialism has contributed to a variety of problems, not the least of which are the alienation of youth, juvenile crime, the loosening of family ties, and a general decline of community values. The pervasive spread of illicit sexual activities through such phony fronts as dance halls, bars, saunas, "barber shops," movies-on-video, and music-video establishments, as well as at hotels and brothels, grew so scandalous and detrimental to social morals and social order that the government suggested cutting off their electricity.[5]

As is noted later, in the section on Taiwan's economy, the pursuit of individual material benefit without a concomitant concern for the public good has led to uncontrolled growth and a rapid deterioration in the quality of life even as the people have become richer. Although recycling and efforts to prevent environmental degradation throughout Taiwan have begun, individuals continue to do such things as dump and burn refuse in public places. Taiwanese continue to purchase cars at the rate of 300,000 per year, even though the expansion of the island's roads has not kept pace and even though most cars can only be parked illegally, either by double parking, which further clogs traffic, or parking on sidewalks meant for pedestrians; build illegal structures that similarly obstruct sidewalks; and spit bright red betle-nut juice on the pavement.

As Taiwan struggles to catch up with its own success, the infrastructure has faltered. During the hot, humid summers in Taipei, both electricity and water are frequently shut off;

roads are clogged from 7:00 A.M. until 10:00 P.M.; and the city's air is so dense with pollution that eyes water, hair falls out, and many people suffer from respiratory illness. Inadequate recreational facilities leave urban residents with few options but to join the long parade of cars out of the city on weekends. Taiwan's citizens have begun forming public-interest groups to address such problems, and public protests about the government's neglect of quality-of-life issues have grown increasingly frequent in the 1990s. Environmental groups, addressing such issues as building more nuclear plants in Taiwan, wildlife conservation, industrial pollution, and waste disposal, have burgeoned. However, environmental campaigns and legislation have hardly kept pace with the rapid growth of Taiwan's material culture.

RELIGION

A remarkable mixture of religions thrives in Taiwan. The people feel comfortable with placing Buddhist, Taoist, and local deities—and even occasionally a Christian saint—in their family altars and local temples. Restaurants, motorcycle repair shops, businesses small and large—all maintain altars. The major concern in prayers is for the good health and fortune of the family in this world. People pray for prosperity, for luck on the stockmarket, and even more specifically for the winning lottery number. If the major deity in one temple fails to answer prayers, people will seek out another temple where other deities have brought better luck. Alternatively, they will demote the head deity of a temple and promote others to his or her place. The gods are thought about and organized much in the same way as the Chinese bureaucracy is; in fact, they are often given official clerical titles to indicate their rank within the deified bureaucracy.

Offerings of food and money are important in making sure that the gods answer one's prayers; but it is equally important to appease one's deceased relatives, for if they are neglected or offered inadequate amounts of food, money, and respect, they will cause endless problems for their living descendants by coming back to haunt them as ghosts. Thus, those having trouble getting their computer programs to work or those with car trouble will take time to go to the temple to pray to the gods and ancestors. The Chinese designate the seventh month of the lunar calendar as "Ghost Month." For the entire month, most Chinese do whatever is necessary "to live in harmony with the omnipotent spirits that emerge to roam the world of the living." This includes

> preparing doorway altars full of meat, rice, fruit, flowers and beverages as offerings to placate the anxious visitors. Temples [hang] out red lanterns to guide the way for the roving spirits. . . . ghost money and miniature luxury items made of paper are burned ritualistically for ghosts to utilize along their desperate journey. . . . The influence of Ghost Month is widespread in society, with Chinese heeding a long list of taboos that have a

(United Nations photo)

This masonry course at Taiwan University is part of a vocational arts program designed to train prospective teachers in the industrial arts.

strong impact on business activity during this cautious time.

The real estate industry feels the negative forces more so than any other business sector. Buying or moving into new houses is the last thing citizens would dare do, fearing that homeless ghosts might become permanent guests. . . . [M]any customers do not want their new cars delivered until after Ghost Month.

Traditionally, the number of newlyweds drops drastically. According to folk belief, a man who marries during the period could discover before long that his bride is actually a ghost. . . . Some pregnant women, after realizing they will most likely undergo childbirth during Ghost Month, [ask] that Caesarean sections be performed prior to the beginning of the month.

Busy lawyers on the island know they can take a breather in Ghost Month. Legal suits traditionally decrease due to the common belief that ghosts do not appreciate those who sue.[6]

Finally, there continues to be a preference for seeking medical cures from local temple priests over either traditional Chinese or modern Western medicine. The concern of local religion is, then, a concern with this life, not with salvation in the afterlife.

What is unusual in the case of Taiwanese religious practices is that as the island has become increasingly "modern" and wealthy, it has not become less religious. Technological modernization has seemingly not brought secularization with it. In fact, aspiring capitalists often build temples in hopes of getting rich: People bring offerings of food; burn incense and bundles of paper money to honor the temple gods; and burn expensive paper reproductions of houses, cars, and whatever other material possessions they think their ancestors might like to have in their ethereal state. They also pay real money to the owner of their preferred temple to make sure the gods are well taken care of. Since money goes directly to the temple owner, not to a religious organization, the owner of a temple whose constituents prosper will become wealthy. Given the rapid growth in per capita income in Taiwan over

(Photo credit Dean Collinwood)

Taiwan is almost self-sufficient in agriculture, but the amount of natural resources is quite limited and must be carefully utilized.

the last 20 years, then, temples to local deities have proliferated, as a builder of a temple was almost guaranteed to get rich if his or her constituents' wealth grew steadily.

Although the vast majority of Taiwan's citizens follow folk religions, Christianity is not left out of the melange of religions. About 4 percent of the population are Christian. Christianity does not escape local adaptations, however, such as setting off firecrackers inside a church during a wedding ceremony to ward off ghosts or putting flashing neon lights around representations of the Virgin Mary. The Presbyterian Church, established in 1865 in Taiwan by missionaries, has frequently been harassed by the KMT because of its activist stance on social and human rights issues.[7]

As for Confucianism, it is really more a philosophy than a religion. Confucianism is about self-cultivation, proper relationships among people, ritual, and proper governance. Although Confucianism accepts ancestor worship as legitimate, it has never been concerned directly with gods, ghosts, or the afterlife. In imperial China, if drought brought famine, or if a woman was thought to have given birth to a cow, the problem was ascribed to be the lack of

morality on the part of the emperor, not the lack of prayer, and required revolt.

In the KMT's efforts to restore Chinese traditional values, they have tried to reinstitute the formal study of Confucianism within the schools. Students are apathetic, however, and will usually only borrow Confucian texts long enough to study for their examinations for college entrance: Unlike the system of getting ahead in imperial China through knowledge of the Confucian classics, in Taiwan students need to excel in science and math. Yet even though the government's plea for the formal study of Confucianism has fallen on deaf ears in Taiwan, Confucian values suffuse the culture. Streets, restaurants, corporations, and stores are named after major Confucian virtues; advertisements appeal to Confucian values of loyalty, friendship, and family to sell everything from toothpaste to computers; children's stories focus on Confucian sages in history; and the vocabulary that the KMT government and party officials use to conceptualize issues is the vocabulary of Confucianism: moral government, proper relationships between officials and the people, loyalty, harmony, obedience.

EDUCATION

The Japanese are credited with establishing a modern school system in Taiwan in the early twentieth century. Under KMT rule since 1949, the system has grown steadily, to the point where today Taiwan offers 9 years of free, compulsory education. Almost all school-age children are enrolled in elementary schools, and most go on to junior high schools. More than 70 percent continue on to senior high school. Illiteracy has been reduced to about 8 percent and is still declining. In areas where night schools catering to those students anxious to test successfully and make the cut for the best senior high schools and colleges are being dismissed, traffic clogs the road at 10:00 P.M. The willingness of students to make such extra efforts attests to the great desire of the Taiwanese to get ahead through education. Taiwan has one of the best-educated populations in the world, a major factor in its dramatic economic development. Yet its educational system is coming under growing criticism by those who argue that the insistence on uniformity through a unified national curriculum, a lecture format that does not allow for participation of students, the high school and university examinations, tracking, rote memorization, heavy homework assignments, and humiliating punishments inhibit creativity. In 1994 these concerns led to a major national demonstration at which demands for reform were presented.[8]

The island has more than 100 colleges and universities, but the demand for higher education still outstrips the ability of the system to provide spaces for all qualified students. As a result, many students go abroad for study—and many never return. From 1950 to 1978, only 12 percent of the some 50,000 students who studied abroad returned, a reflection of both the lack of opportunity in Taiwan and the oppressive nature of government in that period. This outward flood of human talent, or brain drain, was stemmed in the 1980s and 1990s as Taiwan grew more prosperous and the political system more open.

WOMEN

The subordination of women in Taiwan reflects an important cultural ingredient of Confucianism. "Women in classical Chinese society were expected to obey their fathers before marriage, their husbands after, and their sons when widowed. Furthermore, women were expected to cultivate the 'Four Virtues': morality, skills in handicrafts, feminine appearance, and appropriate language."[9] In Taiwan, as elsewhere throughout the world, women have received lower wages than men and have rarely made it into the top ranks of business or government. Moreover, women are treated differently in the workplace from men. "For example, all female civil servants, regardless of rank, are expected to spend half a day each month making pants for soldiers, or to pay a substitute to do this."[10]

Today there are countervailing values and new trends toward greater opportunities and respect for women. The fact that women may now receive an education the equal of a man's has helped promote their social and economic mobility, as has the advocacy by Taiwan's feminists of equal rights for women. It has also made the typical marriage pattern, in which a man is expected to marry a woman with an education inferior to his own, far more difficult.

THE ECONOMY

As one of the newly industrialized countries, Taiwan has shed its Third World, underdeveloped image. With a gross domestic product per capita income that has risen to more than $10,500 in recent years and its highly developed industrial infrastructure and service industry, Taiwan has entered the ranks of some of the most developed economies in the world. As with the leading industrial nations, the increasing costs of manufacturing in Taiwan's economy, where labor demands ever-higher wages, have meant that the percentage of the economy in the industrial sector is steadily declining and that manufacturing jobs are being exported to other countries with cheaper wages and raw materials.

Taiwan's economic growth rate over the last 3 decades has been phenomenal, averaging more than 8 percent per year. If Taiwan's GDP per capita income continues to grow at the rate of 6 to 8 percent annually as it has for more than 20 years, it will soon find itself with one of the world's highest per capita incomes. Yet, as with Japan, this will not necessarily mean a commensurate improvement in lifestyle: The cities are crowded; housing is too expensive for most urbanites to afford more than a small apartment; and the overall infrastructure is inadequate to handle traffic, parking, sewage, electricity, and the other needs of a more advanced society.

The economy and foreign trade have grown so rapidly, in fact, that Taiwan now finds itself in the position of being the world's largest holder of hard currency reserves. Most of the critical reforms that helped Taiwan's economy grow were initiated by the KMT government elite's state-regulating policies. These have included land redistribution, currency controls, central banking, and government corporations.[11] Taiwan's success may also be attributed, however, to a largely free enterprise economy in which businesspeople have developed international markets for their products and promoted an export-led economy, and whose labor force has contributed through its high productivity. A stable political environment has facilitated Taiwan's rapid growth as well. But the growth is also in part attributable to a protected market, which has brought cries of unfair trade policies from those suffering from an imbalance in their trade with Taiwan.

The government's efforts since 1988 to remedy its trade imbalance with the United States, Taiwan's major trading partner, by permitting more agricultural imports has brought protests from farmers (most notably in a 1988 antigovernment protest). They remain angry that the remedy for a trade imbalance that was caused by the industrial sector is being sought at the expense of farmers. But the government has had to go far beyond permitting greater agricultural imports: It has begun investing heavily abroad and has even launched a "buy American" campaign. It has also established nonprofit foundations in the United States and helped fund U.S. university research centers that study Taiwan. All these efforts have helped to shrink the trade imbalance, but Taiwan still holds billions of U.S. dollars in its central reserve bank.

Agriculture and Natural Resources

After arriving in Taiwan, the KMT government carried out a sweeping land reform program: The government bought out the landlords and sold the land to their tenant farmers. The result was equalization of land distribution, an important step in promoting income equalization among the farmers of Taiwan. The land reform program was premised upon one of Sun Yat-sen's famous Three Principles, the "people's livelihood." One of the corollaries of this principle was that any profits from the increase in land value attributable to factors not related to the real value of farm land, such as urbanization, which makes nearby agricultural land more valuable, would, when the land was sold, be turned over to the government. Thus today, although the price of land has skyrocketed around Taiwan's major cities, and although many farmers feel that they are being squeezed by low prices for their produce, the farmers would get almost nothing for their land if they sold it to developers. As a result, many farmers have felt trapped in agriculture. (This was another factor behind the farmers' antigovernment protest in 1988.)

A high level of agricultural productivity has made Taiwan almost self-sufficient in agriculture. This is an impressive performance, as only 25 percent of the land is arable. Furthermore, natural resources are quite limited in Taiwan. Taiwan's rapid industrialization and urbanization have put a strain on what few resources do exist. The result is that the government has had to invest in the building of a number of nuclear power plants to compensate for the lack of other sources of energy. Popular protest against further nuclear power plants, however, has brought an energy crisis in the 1990s. Investment in developing China's vast natural resources is one way in which Taiwan is postponing its energy and resource crisis.

Taiwan as a Model of Economic Development

Taiwan is often cited as a potential model for other developing countries seeking to lift themselves out of poverty. They could learn some useful lessons from certain aspects of Taiwan's experience, such as the encouragement of private investment and labor productivity, an emphasis on basic health care and welfare needs, and policies to limit the gross extremes of inequality. But Taiwan's special advantages during its development have made it hard to emulate: its small size, the benefits of improvements to the island's economic infra-

structure and educational system made under the Japanese occupation, massive American financial and technical assistance, and a highly favorable international economic environment during Taiwan's early stages of growth.

What has made Taiwan extraordinary among the rapidly developing economies of the world is the ability—and the commitment—of the government to achieve and maintain income equality. Taiwan has been able to develop without relying on the exploitation of one economic class to support the growth of others. Admittedly, this has been achieved at the expense of a truly free economy, but the results are nevertheless admirable. Although there are surely beggars in Taiwan today, it is difficult to find them. Government programs to help the disabled and a thriving economy that offers employment to almost everyone certainly help, as does a tight-knit family system that supports family members facing difficult times. The KMT's commitment to Sun Yat-sen's principle of the "people's livelihood" deserves much of the credit.

Today the only truly major economic division within Taiwan is between farmers and urban workers, although in the last few years, the growth of Taiwan's stockmarket—a market built on the thin air of gossip and rumor—has created (and destroyed) substantial wealth almost overnight. Yet Taiwan's economic wealth is still fairly evenly distributed, contributing to a strongly cohesive social system and political stability.

Taiwan's economy, however, is not without growing pains. The government has so far seemingly been unable to address many of the problems arising from its breathtakingly fast modernization: massive pollution; an inadequate urban infrastructure for housing, transportation, electricity, and water; as well as rampant corruption as everyone tries to get ahead in a now relatively open economy. The rapid acquisition of air conditioners and automobiles has made the environment unbearable and transportation a nightmare. In spite of, and in some cases because of, Taiwan's astounding growth, the quality of life has deteriorated greatly. Complaints of oily rain, ignitable tap water, stunted crops due to polluted air and land, and increased cancer rates abound. "Garbage wars" over the "not-in-my-back-yard" issue of sanitary landfill placement have led to huge quantities of uncollected garbage.[12] Numerous public-interest groups have emerged to pressure the government to take action. In 1994 antinuclear activists even tried to use the recall vote to remove seven legislators who favored building Taiwan's fourth nuclear power plant.[13]

Inflation, although still under 5 percent per annum, has been fueled by labor's demand for higher wages. Higher wages have, in turn, priced Taiwan's labor-intensive products out of the international market. This has caused foreign investors to look elsewhere as Taiwan loses its competitive advantage. Even Taiwan's own entrepreneurs have set up shop outside of Taiwan, notably in Thailand, the Philippines, and China, where labor is far cheaper. To encourage Taiwan's manufacturers to keep their plants in Taiwan instead of movment on Tariffs and Trade in 1994; participation in GATT is a critical step for moving toward full participation in the international economy. In the meantime, by positioning itself as a major investor and financier in the international economy, Taiwan has continued to run a trade and international-currency surplus. Internationalization is also Taiwan's way of fighting China's efforts to cut off Taiwan's relationships with the rest of the world: With Taiwan an increasingly important actor in the international economy, it is virtually impossible for its trade, commercial, and financial partners to ignore. And this, in turn, saves Taiwan from the international diplomatic isolation that it might otherwise face in light of its present nonstate status.

THE POLITICAL SYSTEM

The unusual nature of Taiwan's political system is predicated on two extraordinary assumptions. First, the structure and workings of Taiwan's political system were justified for 40 years by the KMT's stance that the government of the Republic of China, under KMT leadership and merely "in exile" on China's island province of Taiwan, was the legitimate government not just of Taiwan but also of the hundreds of millions of people living on the Chinese mainland. Furthermore, the KMT believed, the people living under the control of the Communist "bandits" on the mainland would support the KMT if it invaded the mainland to overthrow the Chinese Communist Party regime.

The Constitution

In 1946, while the KMT still was the ruling party on the mainland, it promulgated a Constitution for the Republic of China. This Constitution adopted as its premises the same political philosophy as the newly founded R.O.C. adopted in 1911: Sun Yat-sen's "Three People's Principles" (nationalism, democracy, and the people's livelihood). Democracy was, however, only to be instituted after an initial period of "party tutelage." During this period the KMT would exercise virtually dictatorial control while preparing China's population for political participation.

The Constitution provided for the election of a National Assembly, with the responsibility of electing a president and vice president; a Legislative Yuan (branch) to pass new laws, decide on budgetary matters, declare war, and conclude treaties; an Executive Yuan to interpret the Constitution and all other laws and to settle lawsuits; a Control Yuan, the highest supervisory organ, to supervise officials through its powers of censure, impeachment, and auditing; and an Examination Yuan (a sort of personnel office) to conduct civil service examinations. The Examination Yuan and Control Yuan were holdovers from Chinese imperial traditions dating back thousands of years.

As this Constitution went into effect in 1947, while the KMT still held governmental power in the mainland, it was

(Photo credit Dean Collinwood)
The considerable economic wealth of Taiwan has been distributed in a judicious fashion. This street is illustrative of Taiwan's consumer economy. The result of this widespread prosperity has been a stable middle class.

ing overseas for cheaper labor, the government since 1988 has allowed businesses to import an increasing number of laborers from Southeast Asia to do work at wages too low, hours too long, and conditions too dangerous for Taiwan's own citizens. Numbering 143,000 by the mid-1990s, these workers introduce their own invisible "costs" to Taiwan; for being lonely and isolated within a society where they are considered socially inferior and where they rarely speak the language, they tend to engage in heavy drinking, gambling, and other socially dysfunctional behaviors.[14]

Taiwan is capable of addressing its problems as long as it continues to internationalize its economy. Through such actions as dropping tariff barriers on agricultural products, it has made itself eligible for membership in the General Agree-

meant to be applicable to all of China, including Taiwan. The KMT government called nationwide elections to select delegates for the National Assembly and then, in 1948, held elections for representatives to the Legislative Yuan and indirect elections for members of the Control Yuan. Later in 1948, as the civil war between the Communists and the Nationalists on the mainland continued, the KMT government amended the Constitution to allow for the declaration of martial law and a suspension of regular elections. They did this because by this time, the Communists were taking control of vast geographical areas of China. Soon afterward the Nationalist government, under Chiang Kai-shek, fled to Taiwan. With emergency powers in hand, it was able to suspend elections—and all other democratic rights afforded by the Constitution.

By October 1949 the Communists controlled the entire Chinese mainland. As a result, the KMT, living in what it thought was only a temporary exile in Taiwan, could not again hold truly "national" elections for the National Assembly or for the Legislative and Control Yuans, as mandated by the 1946 Constitution. But to foster its claim to be the legitimate government of all of China, the KMT retained the 1946 Constitution and governmental structure, as if the KMT alone could indeed represent all of China. With "national" elections suspended, those individuals elected in 1947 from all of China's mainland provinces (534 out of a total 760 elected had fled with General Chiang to Taiwan) continued to hold their seats in the National Assembly, the Legislative Yuan, and the Control Yuan—usually until death—without standing for reelection. Thus began some 40 years of a charade in which the "National" Assembly and Legislative Yuan in Taiwan pretended to represent all of China. In turn, the government of the island of Taiwan functioned as a mere provincial government under the "national" government run by the KMT.

Although the commitment to retaking the China mainland was quietly abandoned by the KMT government even before President Chiang Kai-shek's death in 1975, the 1946 Constitution and governmental structure remained in force. Over these years, of course, many members of the three elected bodies died, and special elections were held just to fill their vacant seats. But the continuation of this atavistic system raised serious questions about the legitimacy of the no-longer-elected government. The Taiwanese, who comprised more than 80 percent of the population, accused the Mainlanders of keeping a stranglehold on the political system and pressured the KMT for greater representation. Because the holdovers from the pre-1949 period were of advanced age and often too feeble to attend meetings of the Legislative Yuan (and some of them no longer even lived in Taiwan), it was virtually impossible to muster a quorum. Thus, in 1982 the KMT was forced to "reinterpret" parliamentary rules to allow the Legislative Yuan to get on with its work.

By the time a Taiwanese, Lee Teng-hui, succeeded President Chiang Ching-kuo upon his death in January 1988 as the new KMT party leader and president of the "Republic of China," 70 percent of the KMT were Taiwanese. Pressures therefore built for party and governmental reforms that would undercut the power of the old KMT Mainlanders. In July 1988, behind the scenes at the 13th KMT Party Congress, the leadership requested the "voluntary" resignation of the remaining pre-1949 holdovers: Allegedly as much as $1 million was offered for some of them to resign, but few accepted. Finally, the Council of Grand Justices forced all those Chinese mainland legislators who had gained their seats in the 1946 elections to resign by the end of 1991.

Under the Constitution, the Legislative, Judicial, Control, and Examination Yuans hold certain specific powers. Theoretically, this should result in a separation of powers, preventing any one person or institution from abusing power arbitrarily. In fact, until after the first completely democratic legislative elections of December 1992, none of these branches of government exercised much, if any, power independent of the president (himself chosen by the KMT), the premier (appointed by the president), or the KMT. The members of both the Control Yuan and Judicial Yuan continue to be appointed by the president,[15] and they are expected to reflect the KMT's philosophies.

The Provincial Government of Taiwan

Even at the height of its power, the KMT did not exercise as much control in Taiwan as the Chinese Communist Party did in China. Taiwanese, through a separate provincial government system, have always had considerable say in the nonpolitical affairs of Taiwan province. Furthermore, although top KMT leaders play a central role in all important policy decisions, the provincial-level KMT is mass-based rather than elitist. That is, membership is basically open to anyone over age 20 who accepts KMT principles. About 20 percent of this eligible age group belong to the KMT, in contrast to the 5 percent of adults who are carefully selected to join the CCP on the mainland.

MARTIAL LAW

The imposition of martial law over Taiwan from 1949 to 1987 is critical in the dynamics of Taiwan's politics. Concerned with the security of Taiwan against an invasion by the Chinese Communists, the KMT declared a state of martial law on Taiwan in 1949. Martial law allowed the government to suspend civil liberties and to limit political activity. It was also a convenient weapon against potential Taiwanese resistance to control by the KMT Mainlanders, who were by then occupying the seat of power of Taipei. In particular, the KMT felt it necessary to quash any efforts to organize a "Taiwan independence" movement. Police powers were widely abused and press freedoms sharply restricted. Dissidents were jailed. As a result, the Taiwan Independence Movement was forced to organize abroad, mostly in Japan and the

United States. Taiwan was run as a one-party dictatorship supported by the secret police. Non-KMT candidates were, however, eventually permitted to run for office under the informal banner of *tangwai* (literally, "outside the party").

The combination of international pressures for democratization, the growing confidence of the KMT, a more stable situation on the China mainland and diminished threats from Beijing led the KMT to lift martial law in July 1987. Thus ended the state of "Emergency" under which almost any governmental use of coercion against Taiwan's citizens was justified.

The Mass Media

With the official removal of martial law in July 1987, the police powers of the state were radically curtailed. The media abandoned former taboos and grew more willing to address social and political problems openly, including the "abuse of authority and unwarranted special privilege."[16] A free press, strongly critical of the government and KMT, now flourishes. Taiwan, a small island with a population of 21 million, boasts close to 4,000 magazines, about 100 newspapers with a total daily circulation of 5 million, 150 news agencies, 3 domestic television channels, and more than 30 radio stations, which now include foreign broadcasts such as CNN, NHK, and the BBC. Thus, although television and radio are still controlled by the government, they have become far more independent since 1988; and 1.2 million households receive 20 to 30 channels through satellite dishes.[17] Television stations show programs from all over the world, exposing people to alternative ideas, values, and lifestyles, and contributing to social pluralism.[18]

Nevertheless, the Central Election Commission reviews all ads to see if any violate the law or are inappropriate. In the 1992 elections, for example, it referred to the Broadcasting and Television Law, which prohibits ads that disseminate rumors or are "hate-mongering," as grounds for prohibiting the transmission of one DPP ad that ridiculed the premier and another that allegedly used " 'unsubstantiated' statistics to portray many aborigines as having sold their daughters into prostitution." In addition, the television stations muted out all references in DPP ads to "Taiwan Independence" and "the Republic of Taiwan,"[19] even while it permitted DPP ads that advocated "One China, One Taiwan." According to the leading government spokesperson, however, now, "A candidate may openly proclaim his or her support for Taiwan independence provided that he or she does not support the organized activity of armed bands using physical force to overthrow the government."[20]

Civil Rights

Until the late 1980s, the rights of citizens in Taiwan did not receive much more protection than they did on the Mainland. The R.O.C. Constitution has a "bill of rights," but as with those rights listed in China's several constitutions, most of these civil rights never really existed until recently, except to the degree that they were in accord with KMT needs and policies. Civil rights have been suspended when their invocation by the citizenry has challenged KMT power or policies. Until 1987, because the "Emergency" regulations provided the rationale for the restriction of civil liberties, the KMT used military courts (which do not use normal judicial procedure) to try what were actually civil cases,[21] arrested political dissidents, and used police repression, such as in the brutal suppression of the Kaohsiung Incident[22] (the result of *dangwai*-fomented protests). As late as May 1988, police and government intimidation were used to halt farmers' street protests against imports of American agricultural products, lack of insurance, and other concerns. And there were strict limits on what the opposition parties could say. Even today individuals may be imprisoned for political crimes, but it is far less likely than before.

Political Reform

The gradual introduction of democratic processes since 1987 has eroded much of the KMT's former authoritarian style of rule. The KMT's introduction of liberal democratic values into a heretofore authoritarian system has created tensions, but they have not been destabilizing. At first the KMT tried to control these tensions through a combination of coercion and material rewards. But by the early 1990s, the KMT discovered that it was able to ride out repeated demonstrations against government policies, and that it could still win elections even if it did not suppress the opposition.

Taiwan's economic growth and rapidly rising standard of living over several decades had lent the KMT regime the legitimacy it needed even though it did not permit democratic participation. Because the government successfully addressed economic issues, these did not provide fuel for political grievances. This, in turn, encouraged the KMT to liberalize the political realm further.

Taiwan possesses a condition important for political liberalization: a large middle class with increasingly diverse and complex social and economic interests of its own that arise from ownership of and concern for private property.[23] Moreover, because there is a remarkably egalitarian distribution of economic wealth and no large underclass, economic discontent is low. Thus, the KMT regime has grown increasingly willing and able to modify its authoritarian rule by responding to demands from an ever more politically aware and active citizenry.

One way in which the KMT has maintained dominance as it reforms is by opening itself up to a broader segment of the population. Social diversity and political pluralism may now be expressed within the KMT. The "Taiwanization" of both the KMT and governmental institutions after Chiang Kai-shek's death actually permitted the KMT not to respond to the demands of the Taiwanese until the mid-1980s, for Taiwanization allowed the KMT to undermine efforts by Taiwanese

(Photo credit Fred J. Maroon)

The signing of the Shanghai Joint Communique during President Richard Nixon's visit to China was the first of several steps by which the United States diplomatically deserted its long-time ally, Taiwan. The power of the economic relationship between the United States and Taiwan, however, eventually overcame the lack of diplomatic recognition, and Taiwan continued to do business with the West.

to establish an independent and powerful opposition. By Taiwanization and, subsequently, by *co-opting* the most appealing platforms of the Democratic Progressive Party (DPP),[24] Taiwan's political system has been able to institutionalize channels for conflict within a party–government system still under the KMT's control. In short, as Taiwan has become more socially and politically diverse, the KMT has been willing to move away from authoritarian instruments to persuasion and conciliation in order to maintain control.[25]

External pressures have played a significant role in the democratization of Taiwan's institutions. Substantial U.S. aid was accompanied by considerable American pressure for liberalizing Taiwan's economy and political institutions. Taiwan's dependence on foreign trade has made it anxious to become accepted into membership in the General Agreement on Tariffs and Trade, even though this will hurt its agricultural sector as well as other industries, such as car manufacturing. To gain acceptance, Taiwan must open up its domestic market to foreign imports, through such measures as cutting tariffs, lifting trade barriers, and the reduction of government subsidies on agricultural products.[26] Taiwanese businesspeople have added their own pressures to these, as has international

tourism, which exposed Taiwan's residents to the values and achievements of other countries.

The willingness of the KMT government to position Taiwan within the international economy has allowed Taiwan to reap the benefits of internationalization. Furthermore, the KMT has since 1987 responded positively to demands for greater contacts with China and for reform of the party and government. As a result, the KMT can continue to claim responsibility for Taiwan's prosperity and political liberalization.

With the KMT moving quickly to assume key elements of most opposition-party policies, the opposition has had to struggle to lay claim to providing an alternative to the KMT. In the December 1992 elections, the Democratic Progressive Party did so. Without making a point of pushing Taiwan's independence, an issue that could inflame Beijing's aggressive sentiments as much as those of the KMT elite (and an issue that alienated the public in the 1991 elections), the DPP took on the KMT, demanding more rapid political reforms and criticizing corrupt practices of the KMT. During these elections, moreover, the DPP was permitted to campaign against the KMT's claims to be the legitimate government of mainland China.

In the December 1994 elections, the DPP had a major victory: The DPP candidate for mayor of Taipei won over the KMT and other parties. The KMT succeeded, however, in winning massive victories for the provincial governorship of Taiwan and for the mayor's seat in Taiwan's second-largest city, Kaohsiung. The vote suggests that the KMT is still the party of choice but that people voted for the DPP because the KMT fielded a poor candidate for mayor of Taipei and because the KMT's administration of Taipei had been marked by incompetence and corruption. In short, candidates and local issues, not the broader concern for Taiwan's future relationship with the mainland of China, affected the vote in the city of Taipei.

Outside of Taipei, however, the DPP's stance on Taiwan independence has continued to alienate many potential supporters. In the wake of losing the December 1994 elections for the governorship of Taiwan, the DPP is considering revision to its 1991 Party Charter, one clause of which advocates the establishment of a "Republic of Taiwan" through a plebiscite in Taiwan.

Elections in Taiwan are by most standards successful. Voting participation in 1994 was over 70 percent, and the number of accusations of voter fraud were substantially lower than in previous elections. Still, the tradition of vote buying favored the much wealthier KMT. A vote could cost between $20 and $100. Candidates could give gifts or cash and receive no promise of a vote in exchange; but in rural areas, "the voter must swear over the image of a folk god that he will vote for the candidate whose money he takes."[27] As vote buying resonates with traditional culture and even continues in Asia's most advanced democracy, Japan, it is unlikely that this practice will disappear easily in Taiwan.

Political Parties

In late 1986, aware that continued restriction of democratic rights was creating greater resistance to KMT rule, and in the favorable environment created by widespread prosperity and economic growth, the government permitted the formation of new political parties independent of the KMT. The Democratic Progressive Party, a largely Taiwanese-based opposition party, was established and immediately captured 22 percent of the vote. It was not officially recognized, however, until 1989, when the KMT passed new laws legalizing opposition parties. Yet the KMT continued to regulate political parties strictly, rationalizing its gradualist approach by maintaining that the institutionalization of truly competitive politics could not be allowed to jeopardize political and social stability.[28]

The first real elections, for 101 of the total seats in the Legislative Yuan (Parliament), occurred in December 1989. Vote buying and general dishonesty were serious issues during this first competitive election, but the results indicated the DPP's appeal as an opposition party. However, in both these and the 1991 elections, internal differences marred the ability

THE U.S. SEVENTH FLEET HALTS INVASION

In 1950, in response to China's involvement in the Korean War, the United States sent its Seventh Fleet to the Taiwan Strait to protect Taiwan and the Offshore Islands, which were under the Republic of China's control, from an invasion by the People's Republic of China. Because of improved U.S.–P.R.C. relations in the 1970s, the improved Chinese Nationalist defense capabilities for the area, and the problems in the Middle East, the Seventh Fleet was eventually moved out of the area. The aircraft carrier *Enterprise*, a part of the Seventh Fleet, is shown above.

of the DPP to project a unified electoral strategy. Since then DPP leaders have proven more willing to compromise with one another in order to present a united front against the KMT. Yet whether out of general frustration as the minority party or a lack of socialization into democratic parliamentary procedures, DPP representatives continue to engage in physical brawls on the floor of the Legislature, ripping out microphones and throwing furniture.

For its part, the KMT has grown increasingly factionalized between progressive reformers and those reluctant to move ahead with further liberalization of the economic and political systems. It is, therefore, less able to discipline its own members to conform to party policies. One wing of the KMT, angry that the KMT was not moving more actively to bring

SUN YAT-SEN: THE FATHER OF THE
CHINESE REVOLUTION

New York Public Library

Sun Yat-sen (1866–1925) was a charismatic Chinese nationalist who, in the declining years of the foreign-ruled Manchu Dynasty, played upon Chinese-nationalist hostility to both foreign colonial powers and to the Manchu rulers themselves.

Sun (pictured at the left) drew his inspiration from a variety of sources, usually Western, and combined them to provide an appealing program for the Chinese. This program was called the Three People's Principles, which translates the American tenet "of the people, by the people, and for the people" into "nationalism," "democracy," and "the people's livelihood."

This last principle, the people's livelihood, is the source of dispute between the Chinese Communists and the Chinese Nationalists, both of whom claim Sun Yat-sen as their own. The Chinese Communists believe the term means socialism, while the Nationalists in Taiwan prefer to interpret the term to mean the people's welfare in a broader sense.

Sun Yat-sen is, in any event, considered by all Chinese to be the father of the Chinese Revolution of 1911, which overthrew the feeble Manchus. He thereupon declared China to be a republic and named himself president. However, he had to relinquish control immediately to the warlord Yuan Shih-K'ai, who was the only person in China powerful enough to maintain control over all other contending military warlords in China.

When Sun died, in 1925, Chiang Kai-shek assumed the mantle of leadership of the Kuomintang, the Chinese Nationalist Party. After the defeat of the KMT in 1949, Sun's widow chose to remain in the People's Republic of China and held high honorary positions until her death in 1982.

about reunification with the mainland of China, and in general holding more conservative views than the liberalizing KMT, broke off to form the New Party (NP). The NP took 7 percent of the vote in the 1994 elections, making it an up-and-coming third party.

The DPP and the KMT actually agree on the fundamentals. Both are committed to democracy, both vehemently oppose communism and advocate capitalism, both believe that it is important to maintain good relations with the PRC, and both support an equitable distribution of wealth, even though this requires governmental intervention. Unlike most developing countries, therefore, in Taiwan there is not a deep ideological rift between the dominant party (KMT) and the opposition (DPP).[29] As a result, the growing power of opposition parties does not significantly threaten policies that the KMT so carefully laid out during its many decades in power.

Interest Groups

As Taiwan has become more socially, economically, and politically complex, alternative sources of power have developed that are independent of the KMT. These are predominantly economic-interest groups comprised largely of Taiwanese. Their power lies in private property and wealth; but there are also public-interest groups concerned with po-

litical issues that challenge the KMT's policies in areas such as civil rights, the environment, women's rights, consumer rights, and nuclear power.

Inescapably, growing numbers of individuals and groups are coming into conflict, especially when different values and economic interests are concerned. For example, the growing tensions between farmers and urban dwellers are fueled in part by the island's more liberal import policies which can make local products less competitive in terms of quality and price.[30]

By the mid-1990s every adult in Taiwan belonged on average to one interest group, of which there are literally thousands. Themselves the result of political liberalization and economic growth, these groups have in turn added to the social pluralism in Taiwan and increased the pressures for a still greater institutionalization of democratic procedures. Two think tanks—the Parliament Monitor Foundation and the Taipei Society—monitor and publish reports concerning the performance of those in the National Assembly, the Legislative Yuan, and the Control Yuan.[31] Still, the KMT strictly regulates the personnel, budgets, and representation of interest groups in the Legislature; and if the KMT believes that any interest group is voicing support for interests inimicable

(United Nations photo/Chen)

The Chinese Communists have said that Taiwan may maintain its free market economy after reunification with the mainland, but many Taiwanese fear that the island's textile and other industries would falter under Communist control.

to its own, or that opposition forces might coalesce around them, it does not hesitate to restrict or eliminate them.[32]

With so many interest groups in existence, however, and with new ones forming every day, the KMT government finds it increasingly difficult to control all of them. Those without substantial resources and a large mass base are likely to escape close scrutiny and gain limited autonomy. The results are not always beneficial in the short run, however. For example, the impact of the success of labor unions (even though unions are heavily regulated by the government) in increasing their members' wages is that Taiwan's entrepreneurs have increasingly established their factories in other developing countries (and especially on the mainland of China) where wages remain low and the workers are less well organized. On the other hand, although this has meant the export of factory jobs, it has also led to an expansion of the service sector of the economy, where better-paying jobs are available. Given the highly educated workforce, these jobs are more appropriate.

The Future of Political Reform in Taiwan

The KMT has, then, been able to harness popular pressure, in part by allowing dissent to have an outlet through interest groups as well as opposition parties. At this point, should the KMT feel its power threatened, it could do little to remove the many democratic rights that it has bestowed on the Taiwanese people in the last decade. Undoing them would be easier, of course, if Taiwan's security were threatened—either because of internal political turmoil (resulting, say, from an economic downturn), or external political threat from Beijing. Were internal pressures to threaten KMT control, it might try to revert to authoritarian measures—and it is even plausible that the majority of the population would accept this as necessary. Since the late 1980s, however, the KMT has felt that it has *needed* and even benefited from the legitimation of its right to rule by the gradual introduction of a more democratic system.

Finally, the ability of the KMT to keep the lid on the expression of political discontent is aided by the grip of a strongly conservative ideology. Although, as compared with 1985, fewer people in a 1990 survey agreed with the statement that "Too many different thoughts result in social chaos," 63 percent still agree! In short, the majority of people in Taiwan still are politically conservative and fear the consequences for stability of too many different ideas. Similarly, a majority (58 percent) in this survey worried that "an increased number of social groups might hurt social stability." As a result, the government is not as challenged by the people to allow greater freedom as it might be in a less conservative political culture.[33]

THE TAIWAN-PRC-US TRIANGLE

Under the KMT government of the Republic of China from 1949 until the 1960s, Taiwan received significant economic, political, and military support from the United States. Even after it became abundantly clear that the Communists effectively controlled the China mainland and had the support of the people, the United States never wavered in its support of President Chiang Kai-shek's position that the R.O.C. was the legitimate government of *all* of China. Then, in 1971, U.S. Secretary of State Henry Kissinger's secret trip to China, followed by President Richard M. Nixon's historic visit in 1972, led to the gradual erosion of the R.O.C.'s diplomatic status.

Allies of the United States, most of whom had loyally supported its diplomatic stance on China, soon severed diplomatic ties with Taipei, a necessary step before they could in turn establish diplomatic relations with Beijing. Only one government could claim to represent the Chinese people; and since the KMT was in complete agreement with the Chinese Communist regime that there was no such thing as "two Chinas" or "one Taiwan and one China," the diplomatic community had to make a choice between the two contending governments. Given the reality of the Chinese Communist Party's control over 1 billion Chinese people and the vast continent of China, and, more cynically, given the desire of the business community throughout the world to do business in China, Taipei found itself increasingly isolated diplomatically.

The United States found it painful to desert its long-time Asian ally. The R.O.C. had, after all, always been a loyal ally in Asia and a bastion against Communism, if not a democratic oasis. The United States had, moreover, heavily invested in Taiwan's economy. At last, on January 1, 1979, President Jimmy Carter announced the severing of diplomatic relations with Taipei and the establishment of full diplomatic relations with Beijing. Although the disappointment and anger of the

KMT government at the time cannot be overstated, the relationship flourished between the United States and what was known as simply the "Taiwan government." American interests in Taiwan are overseen by a huge, quasi-official "American Institute in Taiwan," while Taiwan is represented in the United States by multiple branches of the "Taipei Economic and Cultural Office." In fact, the personnel in these offices continue to be treated in most respects as if they are diplomatic personnel.

Furthermore, having agreed to the Chinese Communists' "principled stand" that Taiwan was a province of China and that the People's Republic of China was the sole legal government of all of China, the United States could hardly continue to maintain a military alliance with one of China's provinces. Recognition of Beijing, therefore, required the United States to give the mandated 1-year termination notice to its mutual-defense treaty with the R.O.C. In the Taiwan Relations Act of 1979, however, the United States stated its concern for the island's future security, its hope for a peaceful resolution of the conflict between the KMT government and Beijing, and its decision to put a moratorium on the sale of new weapons to Taiwan.

Renewal of Arms Sales

By 1981 the newly ensconced Reagan administration had announced its intention to resume arms sales to Taiwan. It argued that Taiwan needed its weapons upgraded in order to defend itself. Irate, Beijing demanded that, in accordance with American agreements and implicit promises to China, the United States phase out the sale of military arms over a specified period. The issue of U.S. arms sales to Taiwan has plagued relations with Taiwan and the P.R.C. ever since. Agreements were concluded in 1992 to deliver 150 F-16 fighters to Taiwan in 1996. In the meantime Taiwan developed its own defense industry; by late 1994 it had produced its own squadron of 20 jet fighters, armed with Taiwan-made air-to-air missiles.[34]

One of the critical stumbling blocks is the insistence by the United States that Beijing agree to the "peaceful resolution of the Taiwan issue." But, "on principle," China refuses to make any such commitment, insisting that Taiwan is an "internal" affair, not an international matter over which other states might have some authority. From China's perspective, then, it has the right as a sovereign state to choose to use force to settle the Taiwan issue.

China's conflicts with the United States over its own sales of military equipment, such as medium-range missiles to the Saudi Arabians, Silkworm missiles to the Iranians—used against American ships, nuclear technology to Pakistan, and massive sales of semiautomatic assault weapons to the United States (one of which was used to attack the White House in 1994) have put it in a weak position for protesting American military sales to Taiwan. In the end Beijing seemed to put a good trade relationship with the United States ahead of its insistence that the United States cancel the sale of fighter jets, and its protests faded into mutterings.[35]

CHINA'S "PEACE OFFENSIVE"

Since the early 1980s, the People's Republic of China has pursued a "peace offensive" in an effort to get the KMT leaders to negotiate a future reunification of Taiwan with the mainland. Beijing has invited the people of Taiwan to visit their friends and relatives on the mainland and to witness the progress made under Communist rule. In the first year (1987–1988) since 1949 that Taiwan's government agreed to allow visits to the mainland, more than 170,000 people seized the opportunity. Since then many hundreds of thousands more have done so. In turn, only a few thousand individuals from China manage to receive permission from the KMT government to visit Taiwan each year. The KMT government has, however, arranged for mainland Chinese students studying abroad to go to Taiwan for "study tours." They have treated these students as if they were visiting dignitaries, and the students have usually returned to their universities full of praise for Taiwan.

Part of China's peace offensive was a 9-point proposal made in 1981. Its major points included Beijing's willingness to negotiate a mutually agreeable reintegration of Taiwan under the mainland's government; encouragement of trade, cultural exchanges, travel, and communications between Taiwan and the mainland; the offer to give Taiwan "a high degree of autonomy as a special administrative region" of China after reunification (the same status that it has offered to Hong Kong when it comes under Beijing's rule in 1997); and promises that Taiwan could keep its own armed forces, continue its socioeconomic systems, and maintain political control over local affairs—far more, incidentally than China has offered to Hong Kong. Beijing also offered to allow Taiwan's leaders to participate in the national leadership of a unified China.

Until 1988 the KMT's official response to Beijing's peace offensive was negative. The KMT's bitter history of war with the Chinese Communists, and what the KMT sees as a pattern of Communist duplicity—making and breaking promises—explain much of the government's hesitation. Since late 1992, however, Taiwan has been engaged in "unofficial" discussions (in which important "former" officials acting on behalf of their respective governments are the key participants) on topics of mutual interest. These include such issues as the protection of Taiwan's investments in the mainland, tourism, cross–Taiwan Strait communication and transportation links, and the dumping of Taiwan's nuclear waste on the mainland. Taipei remains sensitive, however, to the Taiwanese people's concern about the unification of Taiwan with the mainland implicit in Beijing's peace offensive. The Taiwanese insist that they will never accede to rule by yet another mainland Chinese government, especially a Communist one. And they insist that no deals be struck between the KMT Mainlander leadership and the Chinese Communist regime. Their concern is that until the Taiwanese people are participants in a fully democratic system, the KMT Mainlander elite could join in an agreement with the Beijing leadership, at the expense of the Taiwanese.

Any serious negotiations between the KMT Mainlanders and the Chinese Communists for reunification could, therefore, strengthen the hand of the Taiwan Independence Movement in its objective of declaring Taiwan an independent state. Those supporting Taiwan's independence realize the risks involved in doing so: Beijing has threatened the use of military force should any declaration of Taiwan's independence occur. This has muted the cries for Taiwan independence in recent years and has caused many members of the DPP to step in line with mainstream KMT policies on the issue of Taiwan's relationship with China.

As links between Taiwan and the mainland continue to grow from the "unofficial" talks, "indirect" trade between China and Taiwan by way of Hong Kong continues to soar. It had already surpassed $10 billion by 1994, making China Taiwan's third-largest trading partner, after the United States and Japan. Meanwhile, "illegal" trade between mainland fishermen and Taiwanese continues at a steady pace (as much as an estimated $2 billion a year by the mid-1990s), with fishermen trading much-coveted traditional Chinese medicines for made-in-Taiwan VCRs, televisions, and videotapes. The KMT has permitted all these aspects of its relationship with China to develop, in part, to let some of the steam out of the Taiwan Independence Movement and, in part, to counter the DPP's arguments that under KMT policies, Taiwan has essentially been removed (at least at the official level) from international diplomatic circles. With only a handful of countries recognizing it instead of the P.R.C., and with Beijing blocking its membership in most international organizations, the KMT has to be able to show some positive results in its evolving relationship with Beijing.

To keep up at least the pretense of moving toward unification with the mainland, Taiwan's government-controlled television presents travelogues about China as if it were just another place that any ordinary citizen in Taiwan could visit (no longer a land occupied by Communist "bandits"). News about China, including weather forecasts, is included under the topic of "national news" on Taiwan's radio and television programs (symbolizing the fact that Taiwan is indeed a part of China). Since 1988 individuals from China who have ailing relatives on Taiwan, or whose funerals they wish to attend, could for the first time go to Taiwan and stay for up to 3 months. By 1992 the government had formulated policies to treat more humanely those individuals who had since 1988 married citizens of Taiwan but were themselves citizens of the People's Republic of China. Several hundred each year are now being permitted to come to reside with their respective spouses in Taiwan. The government's fear that the mainland spouses would be spies is declining, but not entirely eliminated.

Meanwhile China continues to deepen and widen harbors to receive ships from Taiwan; wines and dines influential individuals from Taiwan; gives preferential treatment to Taiwan's entrepreneurs in trade and investment on the mainland; rebuilds some of the most important temples to local deities in Fujian Province, favorite places for Taiwanese to visit; establishes special tourist organizations to care solely for people from Taiwan; and refurbishes the birthplace of Chiang Kai-shek, the greatest enemy of the Chinese Communists in their history. It has even become possible to dial Taipei direct from many mainland cities and to check in luggage at Taipei's airport direct to Beijing.

Various segments of the Taiwan population view the relationship differently. Businesspeople and scholars want direct trade and personal contacts. They feel that there is little to fear and that political concerns should be separated from economic interests and international scientific exchanges. Those in the economic sector are particularly worried that unless they are allowed to penetrate the China market, others will establish control over it, at their expense. They have insisted that trade will remain limited and that the government need not fear Taiwan becoming dependent on trade with China.

For those faced with ever higher labor costs in Taiwan that price them out of the international market, and with the need for cheap raw materials unavailable in Taiwan, investing in China offers definite advantages: They can move Taiwan's now outdated labor-intensive factories and machinery to the mainland. There, significantly cheaper labor allows these same factories still to make a profit. Since the factories are not profitable if left in Taiwan, not much can be lost by moving them to the mainland.

Many are concerned, however, that Taiwan, which already has put 15 percent of its total foreign investment in the mainland, could become "hostage" to Beijing. That is, if China were to refuse to release Taiwan's assets or repay investors for their assets on the mainland in case of a political conflict between Taipei and Beijing, Taiwan's enterprises would form a pressure point that would give the advantage to Beijing. Furthermore, without diplomatic recognition in China, Taiwan's businesses on the mainland are at risk in case of a conflict with local businesses or the government. Yet so far affairs have turned out quite the opposite: China has actually *favored* Taiwan's businesses over all others. As with the issue of how Hong Kong is treated after 1997, it is unlikely that China would want to do anything to cause jitters in Taiwan over its future relationship with a mainland government.

PROSPECTS FOR REUNIFICATION

As ties with the P.R.C. blossomed, reform-minded individuals in the KMT insisted that it abandon its head-in-the-sand behavior and actively structure how that relationship evolves. In the fall of 1990, the KMT set up a "National Unification Council for the purpose of accelerating the process of "unifi-cation of all China as a free, democratic nation."[36] Taiwan's former premier proposed a "one country, two regions" model "as a means for handling legal and other disputes arising from unofficial contact."[37] This model would not necessarily be used, however, if reunification were to occur.

Resulting changes in policy have been critical to improving cross–Taiwan Strait ties. For example, the KMT ended its 40-year-old policy of stamping "communist bandit" on all printed materials from China and prohibiting ordinary people from reading them; Taiwan's government officials and others formerly prohibited from visiting relatives in China are now also permitted to go; scholars may now attend some international conferences there; and KMT retired veterans, who fought against the Communists and retreated to Taiwan in 1949, are actually encouraged to return to the mainland to live out their lives, because their limited KMT government pensions would buy them a better life there! Certainly, some members of Taiwan's upper class are acting as if the relationship will eventually be a harmonious one when they purchase large mansions in the former international sector of Shanghai.

Nevertheless, such signs of growing ties between Taiwan and the mainland as these, as well as rapidly growing economic ties, do not add up to a desire for reunification. And, with an ever smaller number of first-generation Mainlanders in top positions in the KMT and Taiwan's government, few are keen to push for reunification. Indeed, the majority of people in Taiwan still oppose reunification under current conditions. They are particularly concerned about the gap in living standards, and are fully aware of the high price that West Germany has paid to reunify with East Germany. Obviously, the price tag to close the gap with mammoth China would be prohibitive for tiny Taiwan.

Still, many of those opposed to reunification would agree that the KMT government's policy toward China should be more progressive, assertive, and forward-looking. They would also agree that lacking a long-term plan and simply reacting to Beijing's initiatives put the real power to determine the future relationship in the Chinese Communist Party's hands. Nevertheless, the KMT is caught in a dilemma, for its efforts to move more quickly toward reunification were not fast enough to avoid alienating both the military and the conservatives within the KMT, who in 1993 broke off to form the New Party, but were too fast to avoid giving the DPP more appeal in its platform encouraging greater independence for Taiwan. Over the years many have pushed the KMT to propose an alternative to a "two-Chinas" model. The fact that a divided Germany has been unified and that the divided Korea Peninsula may now also move toward reunification increases the pressure to examine the future relationship between Taiwan and the mainland.

Other forces encourage Taiwan to expand its ties, if not yet reunify with the mainland. First, both Taiwan and China would prefer the establishment of a Chinese trading zone to a Japan-dominated East Asian trading zone. A "Chinese common market" would incorporate China, Taiwan, Hong Kong, Macao, and perhaps other places with large ethnic-Chinese communities such as Singapore. Economically integrating these Chinese areas would strengthen them against the Japanese powerhouse, particularly against a Japan community that incorporates Taiwan, Hong Kong, and South Korea. Adopting common policies on taxes, trade, and currencies would be an important step toward eventual reunification of Taiwan with the mainland.[38]

Greater contacts and exchanges between the two sides may in themselves help lay the basis for mutual trust and understanding, although this is not necessarily the case. So far greater contacts have led to a greater appreciation on the mainland of an alternative to communism in a Chinese society. The Chinese Communist regime has been closely watching to see if political and economic liberalization in Taiwan will lead to the sort of chaos that followed political and economic liberalization in Central/Eastern Europe and the former Soviet Union since 1989. If Taiwan continues to maintain stability in the face of both the growing economic polarization of society into rich and poor and the increasing number of protests and demonstrations that challenge government policies, the Chinese Communist regime might consider it a possible model for reform.

At many levels, then, ties between the mainland and Taiwan are developing. China's government has displayed remarkable stability; and the likelihood of Beijing using military force against Taiwan seems less and less likely as it continues to benefit from Taiwan's trade and investment as well as remittances from Taiwan and Taiwanese visits to the mainland (more than 5 million since 1988). Yet Taiwan cannot discount the possibility that Beijing might use military force, or at least impose a naval blockade around Taiwan, if the government were to advocate independence. Thus, given Taiwan's heavy dependence on trade, Taiwan must at least "talk about unification while pursuing a policy which, if effective would create the basis for both *de facto* and *de jure* independence." It is, in short, a strategy aimed at using "the unification *process* to set up conditions advantageous for the emergence of some form of *de jure* independent Taiwan with no commitment to unification with China."[39]

No guarantee exists that reunification will ever take place. China's low level of economic development and lack of a pluralistic culture are unacceptable even to Taiwan's Mainlanders. Furthermore, the KMT would never be interested in reunification unless it would be in control of the mainland government. A situation of "coalition government," especially one in which it would be a minority voice, would at this point be unacceptable to the KMT. Since people in China would not welcome the return to power of the KMT government—a government unable to address China's problems successfully before 1949—this will be an intractable issue for reunification for the foreseeable future.

Taiwan is genuinely concerned about developments within China. Whether Mainlander or Taiwanese, KMT or DPP, the Chinese Communist Party's crackdown on Tiananmen Square demonstrators in June 1989, the subsequent repression throughout society, and the reversal of economic reforms (even though temporary) severely dampened enthusiasm for formal reunification. Beijing's threats to rip up the Sino–British Declaration on Hong Kong, which together with the Basic Law guaranteed Hong Kong certain freedoms and a continuation of Hong Kong's economic and political system for 50 years after 1997, also conjure up ghosts of duplicity.

Thus, it seems to be in Taiwan's best interests for the relationship with China to develop in a careful and controlled manner. The people in Taiwan are wise to avoid the issue of reunification—and of an independent Taiwan. In particular, with 1997 approaching, it is in Taiwan's interest to wait and see how China integrates Hong Kong under its formula of "one country, two systems." Finally, with Taiwan's high wages for labor and lack of natural resources, and with China's abundance of both natural resources and cheap labor, closer ties with China offer Taiwan a chance to continue its rapid growth into the twenty-first century.

It seems unlikely that China's leadership would be willing to risk the international repercussions of using military force to regain Taiwan. China's leadership, committed to rapid economic development, would also have to consider the risks involved in draining its limited resources into a war that it might lose. Were Beijing to attack Taiwan, however, we cannot know in advance whether the United States would intervene on behalf of Taiwan; but Beijing might well worry that the United States would intervene.

It seems unlikely that Taiwan will change its international stance, which has thus far proved so successful: acting as an independent state, while insisting it is not, and conducting business and diplomacy with other states as usual. As its relationship with China deepens and broadens, it is possible that more arrangements could be made for the representation of both Taiwan and China in international organizations without Beijing putting up countless roadblocks. But the integration of the province of Taiwan into a China under Beijing's leadership, even if Taiwan's leadership were to be offered representation in that leadership, is an eventuality that the vast majority of Taiwanese people are not likely to accept. In the meantime Beijing is not likely to threaten Taiwan militarily. Apart from concerns for its own economic development and international standing, China's hands are already full with the reversion of Hong Kong (1997) and Macao (1999) to its sovereignty.

NOTES

1. John F. Burns, "Quemoy (Remember?) Bristles with Readiness," *New York Times* (April 5, 1986), p. 2.

2. Susan Yu, "Lien Vows Defense Outposts to Stay," *Free China Journal* (November 4, 1994), p. 1.

3. Thomas A. Shaw, "Are the Taiwanese Becoming More Individualistic as They Become More Modern?" Taiwan Studies Workshop, *Fairbank Center Working Papers*, Harvard University, No. 7 (August 1994), pp. 1–25.

4. David Chen, "From Presidential Hopeful, Frank Words on Democracy," *Free China Journal* (September 9, 1994), p. 6.

5. "Premier Hau Bristling About Crime In Taiwan," *Free China Journal* (September 13, 1990), p. 1.

6. Lee Fan-fang, "Ghosts' Arrival Bad for Business," *Free China Journal* (August 7, 1992), p. 4.

7. Marc J. Cohen, *Taiwan at the Crossroads* (Washington, D.C.: Asian Resource Center, 1988), pp. 186–190. For further detail, see his chapter on "Religion and Religious Freedom," pp. 185–215.

8. See *Free China Review*, Vol. 44, No. 9 (September 1994), which has a series of articles on educational reform, pp. 1–37.

9. Cohen, p. 107.

10. *Ibid*, p. 108. For more information on women, see Cohen's chapter on "Women and Indigenous People," pp. 106–126.

11. James A. Robinson, "The Value of Taiwan's Experience," *Free China Journal*, November 6, 1992, p. 7.

12. Robert P. Weller, "Environmental Protest in Taiwan: A Preliminary Sketch," Taiwan Studies Workshop, *Fairbank Center Working Papers*, No. 2 (October 1993), pp. 1, 4.

13. Susan Yu, "Legislature Acts to Protect Lawmakers from Recall Movements," *Free China Journal* (October 14, 1994), p. 2.

14. Dianna Lin, "Alien Workers Face Problems in New Life," *Free China Journal* (September 9, 1994), pp. 7–8.

15. According to the 1992 amended constitution, the Control Yuan members are nominated by the president but the National Assembly must approve of the nominees.

16. Lee Chang-kuei, "High-Speed Social Dynamics," *Free China Review* (Taipei), Vol. 39, No. 10 (October 1989), p. 6.

17. Yu-ming Shaw, "Problems and Prospects of the Democratization of the Republic of China on Taiwan," Taiwan Studies Workshop, *Fairbank Center Working Papers*, Harvard University, No. 2 (October 1993), pp. 1–2.

18. For more detail on television programming, see Minh-ha Nguyen, "Telecommunications: Business Is Beaming," *Free China Review* (September 1994), pp. 54–59.

19. Susan Yu, "DPP Lodges Strong Protest Over Cuts to Campaign Ads," *Free China Journal* (December 11, 1992), p. 2.

20. Yu-ming Shaw, p. 3.

21. From 1950 to 1986, military courts tried more than 10,000 cases involving civilians. These were in violation of the constitution's provision (Article 9) that prohibited civilians from being tried in a military court. Hung-mao Tien, *The Great Transition: Political and Social Change in the Republic of China* (Stanford: Hoover Institution, Stanford University, 1989), p. 111.

22. The Kaohsiung rally in 1980, which was followed by street confrontations between the demonstrators and police, is an instance of KMT repression of *dangwai* activities, activities that were seen as a challenge to the KMT's absolute power. The KMT interpreted the Kaohsiung Incident "as an illegal challenge to public security." For this reason, those arrested were given only semi-open hearings in a military, not civil, tribunal; and torture may have been used to extract confessions from the defendants. See Tien, p. 97.

23. In recent years, however, Taiwan has had to cope with the effect of a growing disparity in income distribution. By 1994 the wealthiest 20 percent of the population possessed 54 percent of the total wealth of Taiwan. See Philip Liu, "Discontent with a Growing Wealth Gap," *Free China Review* (June 1994), pp. 36–41.

24. *E.g.*, DPP's demand for more flexible treatment of relations with the P.R.C.; ecology and environmental issues; including the DPP in discussions; and permitting greater freedom of the press.

25. Hung-mao Tien, p. 72.

26. Philip Liu, "Revving Up for the GATT Shock," *Free China Review* (September 1994), pp. 47–53.

27. Nicholas Kristof, "Taiwan's Parties Test Limits of New Freedom," *New York Times* (December 17, 1992), p. A19.

28. "Jiang Ping-lun, "Competition Mixed With Consensus," *Free China Review* (October 1989), p. 36.

29. *Ibid*, pp. 37–38.

30. Lee Chang-kuei, "High-Speed Social Dynamics," *Free China Review* (October 1989), p. 4.

31. Editor, "Kudos for Parliament Monitor," *Free China Journal*, December 11, 1992, p. 6.

32. Tien, pp. 43, 45ff.

33. Hei-yuan Chiu, "Reconciling Confucianism and Pluralism During the Transition of Taiwan's Society," Philip Lin, Zhiling, and Thomas W. Robinson, eds., *The Chinese and their Future: Beijing, Taipei, and Hong Kong* (Washington, D.C.: AEI Press, 1994), p. 266.

34. Peter Chen, "Taiwan-made Fighters Go into Active Service," *Free China Journal* (December 30, 1994), pp. 1–2.

35. Perhaps Beijing was wise not to clamor too much; for just before the end of his term in office, President Bush authorized the first shipments of military equipment to China since the 1989 Tiananmen military crackdown on the dissidents. This equipment, including radars, torpedos, and aviation electronics, had been kept in storage for 3 and 1/2 years after it was sold to China. The release of it at the end of 1992 was justified on the grounds that it had become outdated and of limited use to China."Arms Shipments to China Cleared," *The Boston Globe* (December 23, 1992), p. 7.

36. "NUC's Charter Approval May Hasten Unification," *Free China Journal* (September 17, 1990), p. 1.

37. "One China, Two Regions," *Free China Journal* (September 6, 1990), p. 1.

38. Willy Wo-lap Lam, "Beijing 'Reconsidering' 'Chinese Common Market,' " *Foreign Broadcasts Information Service* (FBIS-China-89-043), (March 7, 1989), pp. 58-59.

39. Alastair I. Johnston, "Independence through Unification: On the Correct Handling of Contradictions Across the Taiwan Straits," *Contemporary Issues*, No. 2, Fairbank Center for East Asian Research, Harvard University (September 1993), pp. 5-6.

Hong Kong

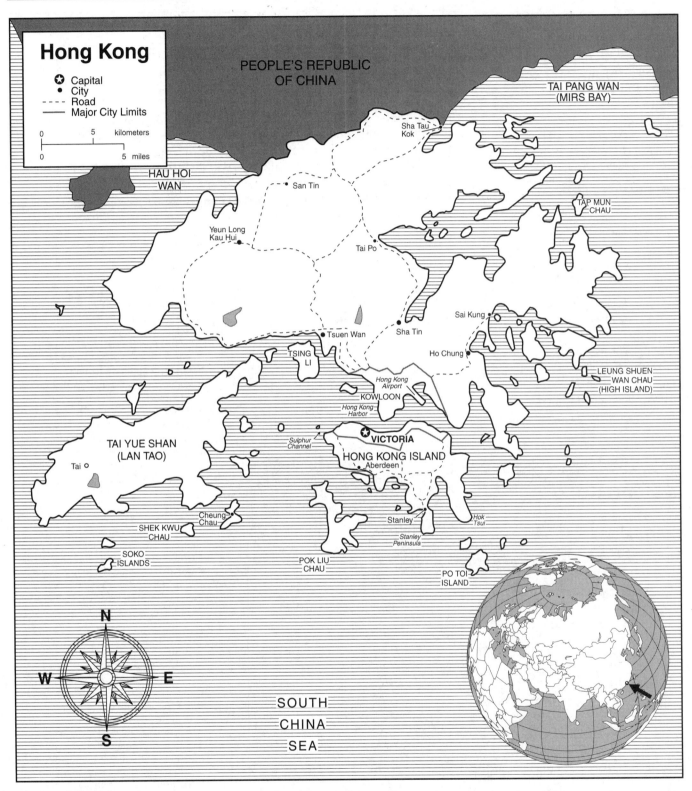

Hong Kong consists of the island of Hong Kong, adjacent islets, the Kowloon Peninsula, and the New Territories (these last two are on the mainland of China). More than 230 islands make up Hong Kong. Since land is constantly being reclaimed from the sea, the total land area of Hong Kong is continually increasing by small amounts.

Hong Kong

GEOGRAPHY

Area in Square Kilometers (Miles):
1,062 (658) (about twice the size of
New York City)
Capital: Victoria
Climate: subtropical

PEOPLE

Population

Total: 5,553,000
Annual Growth Rate: 0.06%
Rural/Urban Population Ratio: 9/91
Ethnic Makeup: 98% Chinese (mostly
Cantonese); 2% European and
Vietnamese
Major Languages: Cantonese; other
Chinese dialects; English

Health

Life Expectancy at Birth: 77 years
(male); 84 years (female)
Infant Mortality Rate (Ratio): 5.9/1,000
Average Caloric Intake: n/a
Physicians Available (Ratio): 1/1,000

Religions

90% a combination of Buddhism and
Taoism; 10% Christian

Education

Adult Literacy Rate: 77%

HONG KONG'S UNCERTAIN FATE

As 1997, the date when the United Kingdom must relinquish its colony of
Hong Kong to the People's Republic of China, nears, there are vastly
differing opinions as to what will happen. While the Chinese and the British
have signed an agreement stating that Hong Kong's way of life will remain
basically unchanged after the reestablishment of Chinese sovereignty,
some people doubt whether an enclave of capitalism can continue to thrive
under the control of the People's Republic of China.

Others feel, however, that China will do little to threaten the stability
and prosperity that have marked Hong Kong under British rule, since
the P.R.C. has so much to gain, both politically and economically, from
a smooth transfer of power. Whatever the outcome, Hong Kong is
clearly in the midst of a major period of transition.

COMMUNICATION

Telephones: 3,000,000
Newspapers: 69

TRANSPORTATION

Highways—Kilometers (Miles): 1,100
(683)
Railroads—Kilometers (Miles): 35 (22)
Usable Airfields: 2

GOVERNMENT

Type: colonial (British Crown colony)
Independence Date: Chinese
sovereignty to be reestablished on July
1, 1997
Head of State/Government: Queen
Elizabeth II; Governor Christopher
Patten (appointed by Britain)
Political Parties: United Democrats of
Hong Kong; Liberal Democratic
Federation; Hong Kong Democratic
Federation; Association for Democracy
and People's Livelihood; Progressive
Hong Kong Society
Suffrage: residents over age 21 who
have lived in Hong Kong for at least 7
years

MILITARY

Number of Armed Forces: foreign
relations and defense the responsibility
of British Armed Forces, 12,000 of
whom are stationed in Hong Kong
*Military Expenditures (% of Central
Government Expenditures):* 0.5%
Current Hostilities: none

ECONOMY

Currency ($ U.S. Equivalent): 7.72
Hong Kong dollars = $1
Per Capita Income/GDP: $14,600/$86
billion
Inflation Rate: 9.4%
Natural Resources: none
Agriculture: vegetables; livestock
(cattle, pigs, poultry); fish
Industry: light—textiles and clothing;
electronics; clocks and watches; toys;
plastic products; metalware; footwear;
heavy—shipbuilding and ship
repairing; aircraft engineering

FOREIGN TRADE

Exports: $118 billion
Imports: $120 billion

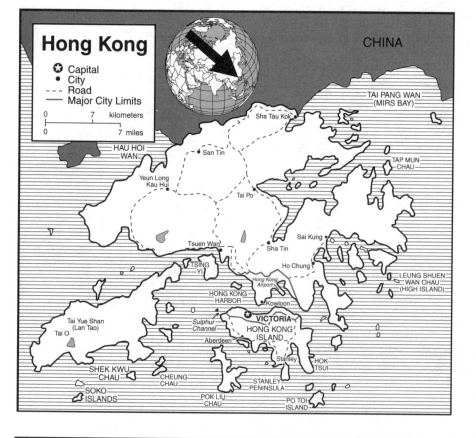

Hong Kong

From British Colony to China's Special Administrative Region

Hong Kong, the "fragrant harbor" situated on the southeastern edge of China, has been characterized as a "capitalist paradise," a "borrowed place living on borrowed time," and a "den of iniquity" as well as other epithets of dubious honor. Under a British colonial administration committed to a laissez faire economy, but in the context of a highly structured and tightly controlled political system, Hong Kong's dynamic and vibrant people have shaped the colony into one of the world's great success stories. The history of Hong Kong's formation and development, its achievements, and the complex problems that it must address today as it makes the transition to becoming integrated under the government of the People's Republic of China in 1997 affect how Beijing, London, and the Hong Kong people themselves view the

colony's future. Hong Kong's "borrowed time" is coming to an end.

HISTORY

In the 1830s the British sale of opium to China was creating a nation of drug addicts. Alarmed by this development, the Chinese imperial government banned opium; but private British "country traders," sailing armed clipper ships, continued to sell opium to the Chinese by smuggling it (with the help of Chinese pirates) up the coast and rivers. In an effort to enforce the ban, the Chinese imperial commissioner, Lin Zexu, detained the British in their warehouses in Canton and forced them to surrender their opium. Eventually Imperial

**THE SECOND ANGLO/CHINESE CONVENTION:
THE KOWLOON PENINSULA IS CEDED TO THE BRITISH**

The second Anglo/Chinese Convention, signed in 1860, was the result of a string of incidents and hostilities among the Chinese, the British, and the French. Although the French were involved in the outbreak of war, they were not included in the treaty that resulted from conflict.

The catalyst for the war was that, during a truce, the Chinese seized the chief British negotiator and executed 20 of his men. In reprisal, the English destroyed nearly 200 buildings of the emperor's summer palace and forced the new treaty on the Chinese. This called for increased payments ("indemnities") by the Chinese to the English for war-inflicted damages, as well as the cession of Kowloon Peninsula to the British.

New York Public Library

Commissioner Lin took the more than 21,000 chests of opium that he had seized and destroyed them in public.[1]

The British, desperate to establish outposts for trade with an unwilling China, used this siege of British warehouses as an excuse to declare war on the Chinese. Later called the Opium War (1839–1842), the conflict ended with China's defeat and the Treaty of Nanking.

Although many would argue that it was disgraceful for Great Britain to wage a war in order to sell a drug banned by the Chinese government, an addictive and debilitating drug that destroyed people's lives, the British saw it otherwise. Opium was available for self-medication in Britain, "was even administered by working mothers as a tranquilliser for their infants," and was not considered toxic by the British medical community at that time. As a result, the public did not generally understand that the Chinese might have a problem with addiction and thus largely ignored moral considerations.[2]

Great Britain's true reason for going to war with the Chinese was to gain free trade with a government that restricted foreign trade to one port, Canton, and to assert Britain's diplomatic and judicial equality with a country that considered itself the "Central Kingdom," superior to all other countries. At the political level, the Chinese imperial government's demand that all "barbarians," including the British, kowtow to the Chinese emperor incensed the British and gave them further cause to find an opportunity to set the record straight.

More pragmatically, the British treasury was being drained of its gold and silver species; for the British purchased large quantities of Chinese porcelain, silk, tea, and spices, while the Chinese, smug in their belief that their cultural and moral superiority was sufficient to withstand any military challenge from a "barbarian" country, refused to purchase goods being manufactured during the industrial revolution going on in Great Britain. An amusing example of the thought process involved in "Sinocentrism" (the Chinese belief that China was the center of the world, hence superior to all other countries) was Imperial Commissioner Lin's letter to Queen Victoria. Here he noted "Britain's dependence on Chinese rhubarb, without which the English would die of constipation."[3]

China's Sinocentric world view blinded its government to the growing power of the West and resulted in China's losing the opportunity to benefit from the industrial revolution at an early stage. The Opium War turned out to be only the first step in a century of humiliation for China, the step that led to a British foothold on the edge of China.

In the Treaty of Nanking, the British gained the right to trade with the Chinese from five Chinese ports; and Hong Kong, a tiny island off the southern coast of China, was ceded to them "in perpetuity." The island's total population of Chinese villagers and people living on boats numbered fewer than 6,000. From that point onward, Hong Kong became the primary magnet for Chinese immigrants fleeing the chaotic conditions of the mainland in favor of the relatively peaceful environment of Hong Kong under British rule.

In 1860, again as a result of a British victory in battle, the Chinese ceded "in perpetuity" to the British a small (3½ square miles) but significant piece of land facing the island of Hong Kong: Kowloon Peninsula. Just a few minutes by ferry (and, since the 1970s, by tunnel) from Hong Kong Island, it became an important part of the residential, commercial, and business sector of Hong Kong. The New Territories, the third and largest part (89 percent of the total area) of what is now known as Hong Kong, were not granted "in perpetuity" but were merely leased to the British for 99 years, under the second Anglo–Chinese Convention of Peking in 1898. The New Territories, which are an extension of the Chinese mainland, comprise the major agricultural area supporting Hong Kong.

This distinction between those areas that became a British colony (Hong Kong Island and Kowloon) and the area merely leased for 99 years (the New Territories) is crucial to understanding why by the 1980s the British had to negotiate with the Chinese about the future of "Hong Kong"; for although colonies are theoretically colonies in perpetuity, the New Territories were merely leased and would automatically revert to Chinese sovereignty in 1997. Without this large agricultural area, the rest of Hong Kong could not survive. The leased territories have, moreover, been tightly integrated into the life and business of Hong Kong Island and Kowloon. With the exception of the Japanese occupation (1942–1945) during World War II, Hong Kong has, then, been administered as a British Crown colony since the nineteenth century.

After coming to power on the mainland in 1949, the Chinese Communist Party held that Hong Kong was a part of China, stolen by British imperialists. The People's Republic of China has insisted that Hong Kong *not* be treated like other colonies, for the process of decolonization has in practice meant sovereignty and freedom for a former colony's people.[4]

And China was not about to allow Hong Kong to become independent. After the P.R.C. gained the China seat in the United Nations in 1971, it discovered that the UN General Assembly's Special Committee on Colonialism listed Hong Kong and Macao (a Portuguese colony) as colonies. In a letter protesting the inclusion of Hong Kong and Macao on the list, Beijing insisted that they were merely

part of Chinese territory occupied by the British and Portuguese authorities. The settlement of the questions of Hong Kong and Macao is entirely within China's sovereign right and does not at all fall under the ordinary category of colonial territories. Consequently they should not be included in the list of colonial territories covered by the declaration on the granting of independence to colonial countries and peoples. . . . The United Nations has no right to discuss these questions.[5]

(United Nations photo)

Hong Kong's economy is supported by a hard-working and dynamic population. The people in this outdoor market typify the intense entrepreneurial tendency of Hong Kong's citizens.

The Chinese Communists found it ideologically uncomfortable to proclaim China's nationalist rights and spout Communist principles while at the same time tolerating the continued existence of a capitalist and British-controlled Hong Kong on its very borders. China could have acquired control within 24 hours simply by shutting off Hong Kong's water supply from the mainland. But China profited from the British presence there and, except for occasional flareups, did little to challenge it.

As for Hong Kong's colonial subjects, declaring independence was not the option that it was for other colonies, for overthrowing British colonial rule would have led directly to the reimposition of China's control of Hong Kong. And, although there is for the Hong Kong Chinese a certain amount of nationalist sentiment as Chinese, after 1949 few wanted to fall under the rule of China's Communist Party government. Furthermore, Beijing and London as a rule did not interfere in Hong Kong's affairs, leaving these in the capable hands of the colonial government. In 1958, in fact, London ceded financial authority in Hong Kong to its colonial government. On the other hand, the colonial government did not in turn cede any significant political power to its colonial subjects.[6]

In 1982, however, the British took the initiative in responding to concerns expressed by the Hong Kong and foreign business communities over the expiration of the lease on the New Territories in 1997. They began to press China for an agreement on the future status of the colony and the rights of its people. Everyone recognized the inability of Hong Kong Island and Kowloon to survive on their own because of their dependence upon the leased New Territories for food. Everyone also knew that Hong Kong was militarily indefensible by the British. Therefore, a series of formal Sino–British negotiations over the future of Hong Kong began in mid-1983, and in September 1984, the two sides reached an agreement to restore all three parts of Hong Kong to China on July 1, 1997.

THE SOCIETY AND ITS PEOPLE

Immigrant Population
In 1842 Hong Kong had a mere 6,000 inhabitants. Today it has reached about 5.6 million people. What makes this population distinctive is its predominantly immigrant composition. Waves of immigrants have flooded Hong Kong since 1842. Even today barely half of Hong Kong's population was actually born in Hong Kong. This has been a critical factor in the political development of this colony, for instead of a foreign government imposing its rule on submissive natives, the situation has been just the reverse. Chinese people have voluntarily emigrated to Hong Kong, even risking their lives to do so, to subject themselves to alien British colonial rule.

In recent history the largest influxes of immigrants came as a result of the civil war in China (1945–1949), when 750,000 fled to Hong Kong; as a result of the "3 bad years" (1959–1962) following the economic disaster of China's Great Leap Forward policy; and from 1966 to 1976, when more than 500,000 came to escape the societal turmoil generated by the Great Proletarian Cultural Revolution. After the Vietnam War ended in 1975, Hong Kong also received thousands of refugees from Vietnam as that country undertook a policy of expelling many of its ethnic-Chinese citizens. Many Chinese from Vietnam have risked their lives on small boats at sea to attain refugee status in Hong Kong. China's improving economic and political conditions beginning in the 1980s have greatly stemmed the flow of immigrants from the mainland. Nevertheless, the absorption of refugees into Hong Kong's economy and society remains one of the colony's biggest problems, in spite of the British tightening of both legal and illegal immigration. The injection of another distinct group (the ethnic Chinese from Vietnam) has also generated tension and conflict among the Hong Kong population.

Because of a severe housing shortage and strains on the provision of social services, the British colonial government first announced that it would confine all new refugees in camps and prohibit them from outside employment. It then adopted a policy of sending back almost all refugees caught before they reached Hong Kong Island and unable to prove that they had relatives in Hong Kong to care for them. By 1988 the British had reached an agreement with Vietnam's government to return some of those Chinese immigrants from Vietnam who were believed to be economic rather than political refugees. The first few attempts at this reportedly "voluntary" repatriation raised such an international furor that the British were unable to systematize a policy meant to discourage further illegal immigration. By the mid-1990s, however, the improvement of economic and political conditions in Vietnam made it easier for the British colonial government once again to repatriate Vietnamese refugees. In the meantime the economy of southern China was expanding so rapidly that the pressure of immigrants from China dropped to a trickle.

Language
Ninety-eight percent of Hong Kong's people are Chinese, with the bulk of the other 2 percent being European and Vietnamese. Although there is a profusion of Chinese dialects spoken, the two official languages, English and the Cantonese dialect of Chinese, still are dominant. Since the Chinese written language is in ideographs and is written fairly much the same regardless of how it is pronounced in a dialect, all literate Hong Kong Chinese are able to read newspapers and other publications.

Living Conditions
Hong Kong has a large and growing middle class, but its people suffer from extremes of wealth and poverty. The contrast in housing that dots the landscape of the colony dramatically illustrates its great inequalities of wealth. The rich live in luxurious air-conditioned apartments and houses on some of the world's most expensive real estate. They are taken care of by cooks, maids, gardeners, and chauffeurs. They enjoy a social life that mixes such Chinese pleasures as mahjong, banqueting, and participation in traditional Chinese and religious rituals and festivals with British practices of cricket, horseracing, rugby, social clubs, and athletic clubs for swimming and croquet. By contrast, the vast majority of Hong Kong's people live in crowded high-rise apartment buildings, with several poor families sometimes occupying one apartment consisting of a few small rooms and inadequate sanitation facilities. Since the mid-1950s the government has built extensive low-rent public housing, which accommodates about half of the population.[7]

These government-subsidized housing projects easily become run-down and are often plagued by crime. But without them, a not-insignificant percentage of the new immigrant population would continue to live in squalor in squatter villages, with no running water, sanitation, or electricity. Shantytowns and refugee camps continue to accommodate the very poor.

The tensions that might be expected to result from the enormous gap between rich and poor have been significantly diminished by the government's commitment to social welfare programs, including public housing, social services, and education. Hong Kong's rapid post–World War II economic growth, which has improved the lives of almost all Hong Kong residents, as well as the resulting opportunities for economic and social mobility have also allayed tensions.

A poor, unskilled peasant who fled across China's border to Hong Kong, to an urban life of grinding poverty—but opportunity—would usually be rewarded before he died by a government-subsidized apartment, and his grandchildren would likely graduate from high school and move on to white-collar jobs. Why most Hong Kong Chinese wanted to maintain the status quo as a British Crown colony was the same as why refugees sought to go to Hong Kong in the first place: freedom of choice, the chance to live better, freedom of speech, and freedom to make money.[8]

But many of these opportunities are now being threatened by an uncertain political future and a change from an economy of hundreds of thousands of entrepreneurs to one dominated by large corporations in a number of sectors. Furthermore, a class of "the super rich addicted to conspicuous consumption and crass materialism" has led to a growing class consciousness.[9]

Chinese cultural values of diligence, willingness to sacrifice for the future, commitment to family, and respect for education contribute to the success of Hong Kong's inhabitants. What is more, the colonial government provides 9 years of compulsory and free education for children through age 15, helping to reinforce these cultural values. Hong Kong's people continue to view education as the key to material success. But their children are educated in schools modeled on a now

> out-of-date British grammar school, complete with uniforms, lists of rules, and a packed academic timetable. Many of the most prestigious schools are Christian foundations; their medium of instruction is English and the pupils are still given English Christian names by their teachers. . . .[10]

Since access to higher levels of education are strictly limited, students work hard to gain access to an upper middle school, and then to the even fewer places available in Hong Kong's universities. An alternative that many of Hong Kong's brightest students take is to go abroad for college education. Universities in the West have benefited from the presence of these highly motivated and achievement-oriented students in their classrooms.

Until recent years, then, the allure of Hong Kong was its combination of economic success with enlightened social welfare policies. These were possible not just because of the British colonial government's commitment to them but also because the flourishing Hong Kong economy provided the resources for them. Hong Kong has had a larger percentage of the gross domestic product available for social welfare than most places, for two reasons. First, it has a low defense budget to support its approximately 12,000 British troops

(including some of the famous Gurkha Rifles) stationed in the colony for external defense (only 0.4 percent of the GDP, or 4.2 percent of the total budget available). Second, the government was also able to take in substantial revenues (18.3 percent of GDP) through the sale of land leases.[11] With China's takeover of Hong Kong just around the corner, however, the sale of land leases that extend beyond 1997 is far more problematical.

Hong Kong does suffer from significant problems, including serious environmental pollution, ignored in the pursuit of profits, and an appallingly high crime rate. Violent crime continues to rise, as does white-collar crime, which is spreading into the highest levels of government. For more than a decade, ordinary criminality has been steadily augmented by crime under the control of competing Chinese criminal societies known as *triads*. Organized crime has moved beyond extortion from massage parlors, bars, restaurants, and clubs, illegal gambling, smuggling, the sale of handguns, prostitution, and drugs, to take advantage of a plummeting real estate market. Opium, largely controlled by the triads, continues to be used widely by the Chinese. As a commentator once put it,

> Opium trails still lead to Hong Kong . . . and all our narcotic squads and all the Queen's men only serve to make the drug more costly and the profits more worthwhile. It comes in aeroplanes and fishing junks, in hollow pipes and bamboo poles and false decks and refrigerators and pickle jars and tooth paste tubes, in shoes and ships and sealing wax. And even cabbages.[12]

Fear is growing that as 1997 approaches, triad influence and ordinary criminality will expand even further. In fact, once the British governor Christopher Patten, who took up his position in July 1992, upset Beijing with his proposals for further democratization of Hong Kong before 1997, the Chinese Communist regime (by way of its estimated 60,000 supporters working in Hong Kong) recruited triad members to begin harassing those within the Hong Kong government who were supporting Patten's proposals. (And, when Patten's dog disappeared one day in November 1992 during the crisis stage of Sino–British relations, one rumor had it that the Chinese Communists had kidnapped the dog and were going to ransom it in exchange for halting political reform in Hong Kong; the other rumor was that Patten's pet had been flown into China to be served up for breakfast to Deng Xiaoping.)

THE ECONOMY

From the beginning the British designated Hong Kong as a free port. This has meant that Hong Kong never applied tariffs or other major trade restrictions on imports. Such appealing trade conditions, combined with Hong Kong's free market economy, deep-water harbor, and location at the hub of all commercial activities in Asia, have made it an attractive place for doing business. Indeed, from the 1840s until the crippling Japanese occupation during World War II, Hong Kong served as a major center of China's trade with both Asia and the Western world.

The outbreak of the Korean War in 1950 and the subsequent United Nations embargo on exports of strategic goods to China, as well as a U.S.-led general embargo on the import of Chinese goods, forced Hong Kong to reorient its economy. To combat its diminished role as the middleman in trade with the mainland of China, Hong Kong turned to manufacturing. At first it manufactured mainly textiles. Later it diversified into other areas of light consumer products and developed into a financial and tourist center. Today it continues to serve as a critical trade center, with thousands of companies located in Hong Kong for the purpose of doing business with the P.R.C.

Hong Kong's many assets, including its hard-working, dynamic people, have made it into the world's second-largest container port, the third-largest gold-dealing center, and the third-largest banking and financial center. Yet because of Hong Kong's lack of natural resources, it has remained vulnerable to international political and economic currents, such as trade restrictions and international monetary fluctuations. For example, in the early 1980s, Hong Kong's economy, which relies heavily on exporting, suffered considerably from the protectionist measures taken by its major trading partners, including the United States. Similarly, the repeatedly threatened withdrawal of most-favored-nation (MFN) status for China put Hong Kong in as much of a state of panic as Beijing, for, as the largest single investor in China's export sector, Hong Kong would have been badly hurt by the elimination of MFN treatment for China. The favorable resolution of these negotiations brought a collective sigh of relief from Hong Kong.

Since 1979, when China initiated major internal economic reforms that opened it up to foreign investment, Hong Kong's economy has become deeply integrated with China's contiguous province of Guangdong. Hong Kong entrepreneurs have taken advantage of China's cheap labor (Hong Kong industries operating on Chinese soil employ some 3 million Chinese workers) and turned Guangdong into "a huge processing zone for Hong Kong based manufacturers."[13] Hong Kong's investment accounts for 66 percent of China's total foreign investment, and a full 80 percent of Guangdong's total. Hong Kong owns 16,000 factories in Guangdong, factories that export goods worth some $11 billion annually.[14]

More than 35 percent of China's trade is through Hong Kong. As part of its economic reform program and "open door" policy, China has created Special Economic Zones (SEZs) in areas bordering or close to Hong Kong, in order to attract foreign investment. These SEZs, under far more liberal regulations than the rest of China, have blossomed in the last decade. Various parts of China's government have themselves invested heavily in the SEZs in hopes of making a profit. Even China's military has developed an industrial area

(United Nations photo/A. Jongen)
Chinese cultural values are still very strong in modern-day Hong Kong. Here, women in traditional Chinese dress take a work break.

catering to foreign investors and joint ventures in Shenzhen, an SEZ, as part of its effort to compensate for insufficient funding for the military since 1981. It calls its policy "one army, two systems"—that is, an army involved with both military and economic development.[15] Brushing aside its earlier concern for a puritanical society, China's military is as likely to invest in nightclubs, Western-style hotels, brothels, and health spas as it is in industry.

The bulk of foreign investment in the SEZs and in the rest of China actually comes, however, from Hong Kong Chinese, either with their own money or acting as middlemen for investors from Taiwan, South Korea, the United States, and other countries. Two thirds of direct foreign investment in China, in fact, comes *through* Hong Kong. Thus, this integrated area, encompassing Hong Kong, the SEZs, and Guangdong Province, has the potential to become a powerful new regional economy on a par with other newly industrialized countries (NICs). Indeed, it is increasingly evident that before China takes over Hong Kong in 1997, Guangdong will already have become part of Hong Kong's empire.

Hong Kong's growth has been challenged by the rapidly expanding economies of the other "little dragons" of East Asia: Singapore, Taiwan, and South Korea. These robust economies compete with Hong Kong in the manufacture and export of light industrial and consumer goods. South Korea, which previously had had to use Hong Kong as an entrepôt for trade and business with China, established full diplomatic relations with China in 1992, thereby allowing it to deal directly with China. Still, Taiwan's indirect trade through

Hong Kong in 1992 was estimated at $7 billion,[16] and China remains Hong Kong's largest trading partner.

Sensitivity of Economy to External Political Events

Hong Kong's economic strength rests on the population's belief in Hong Kong's future. Its people's willingness to work hard and invest in Hong Kong, however, fluctuates with its vacillating confidence in the future. Concern over Great Britain's unwillingness to negotiate more democratic rights for Hong Kong before 1997, as well as uncertainty about the outcome of Sino–British negotiations, have periodically threatened Hong Kong's economic stability, diminished confidence, and generated an outward flow of professionals from Hong Kong.

The furor caused by Governor Patten's 1992 democratization proposals for Hong Kong resulted in Beijing threatening to retaliate and cause chaos in Hong Kong. Jitters in the Hong Kong community surged. The irony in this situation is that earlier, the people of Hong Kong were afraid that Britain would trade Hong Kong's democratic future for good relations with China. Now they are afraid that Patten's efforts to inject Hong Kong with a heavy dose of democratization before 1997 could result in China using retaliatory measures that would hurt Hong Kong's economy before 1997 and restrict its political freedom after 1997. Indeed, by 1994 China's leaders were saying that they would simply *revoke* all political liberalization measures taken since 1992.

Similarly, the student-led protest movement in China in 1989, which eventuated in a military crackdown on demonstrators on June 4, as well as China's economic retrenchment policies and partial closing of the "open door" to international trade and investment, temporarily halted Hong Kong's growth and destabilized its economy. The stockmarket collapsed, and real estate prices plummeted. Both people and capital fled Hong Kong. This volatility demonstrated once again just how vulnerable Hong Kong is to Beijing's policies and actions. China is well aware of this and is deeply concerned that Hong Kong not be destabilized either by China's own policies or by potentially destabilizing changes in Hong Kong, such as those changes that they fear greater democratization in Hong Kong might bring.

Although Hong Kong's economy has recovered since then, the resulting labor and capital shortage has fueled inflation in the 1990s. The uncertainty of economic conditions after 1997 has made it more difficult to attract the capital investment necessary for continued strong growth. Indeed, although much of the potential imbalance is redressed by international capital flowing in, capital continues to flow out of Hong Kong.[17]

Much of this investment abroad is, however, in China. Since the value of these investments depends on a stable political and economic environment in China, Hong Kong's wealthy entrepreneurs are far less interested in supporting a quest for democratic rights in China if these would come at the expense of political stability.

Emigration from Hong Kong (at the rate of about 60,000 per year since 1990) largely comes from among its better-educated, wealthier class.[18] Thus, both talent and investment dollars leave. Once emigrants gain a second passport (a guarantee of residency abroad in case conditions warrant flight), however, they often return to Hong Kong, where there is still money to be made and opportunities available for professional success (e.g., for architects, engineers, dentists, doctors, and businesspeople). Furthermore, this outflow of talent is largely counterbalanced by an inflow of immigrants as well as by the education of new professionals in Hong Kong's excellent schools.[19]

POLITICS AND POLITICAL STRUCTURE

From a developmental perspective, Hong Kong's record of combining economic growth with political stability has been remarkable. This has not been due to any effort on the part of the British to transplant a form of Western-style democracy to Hong Kong. Instead, the colonial Hong Kong government "deliberately created hundreds of consultative committees at various levels of the bureaucracy, through which the views and feelings [of the population] fed back into the administrative decision-making processes." Similarly, the Legislative and Executive Councils function to get Hong Kong's socioeconomic elites to participate in the administration. The administration has also absorbed more than 300 advisory groups and numerous partly elected bodies, such as the Urban Council (for Hong Kong Island and Kowloon), the Rural Committees (for the New Territories), and district boards, all of which have considerable say in managing the affairs under their jurisdiction. By institutionalizing consultation among Chinese administrators and the colonial government, Hong Kong "developed a unique brand of political system which can be characterized as one variant of elitist politics." Political dissent outside the government was, therefore, almost unnecessary.[20]

Hong Kong is different from other ethnic-Chinese societies: In most other Chinese societies, personalities, personal rule, factional politics, and personified political arrangements loom large, and the crucial problem in political development is the establishment of viable political institutions. In Hong Kong political institutions have thrived at the expense of political personalities as well as of "politics" in the commonly understood sense of the term.[21]

The problem remains, however, one of finding competent leaders trusted by the people of Hong Kong to take charge as the colonial government closes down. In a 1988 survey, 69.9 percent of those queried replied that there were no trustworthy political leaders among the Hong Kong Chinese. Among those who did believe that Hong Kong could produce acceptable leaders, the largest number named David Wilson, at that time *the British governor* of Hong Kong, as the single most trustworthy leader! Similarly, the

(United Nations photo)

The refugees who came to Hong Kong and settled in squatter communities such as the one shown above voluntarily subjected themselves to foreign (British) rule.

Hong Kong Chinese place extraordinary trust in their British-controlled political institutions: 75 percent endorsed the statement that Hong Kong's political system, while not perfect, was "already the best under existing circumstances."[22] Nevertheless, since the mid-1980s they have become increasingly concerned about the commitment to Hong Kong's welfare on the part of those who hold foreign passports or rights of residence abroad as well as about the competency of the colonial government.[23]

Hong Kong's government has remained stable, then, in large part because it has functioned well and has been perceived to be trustworthy and capable of addressing the needs of its people. A solid majority of Hong Kong's citizens believe, in fact, that a strong political authority is indispensable to prosperity and stability; and that the formation of multiple political parties could disrupt that strong authority. Thus, what in the West is seen as a critical aspect of democracy is viewed by the people in Hong Kong as suspect: "Political parties conjure up pictures of conflict, sectional interests, political repression and corrupt government."[24] This is, inci-dentally, a view they share in common with their neighbors in China.

Hong Kong's government is well-institutionalized. The British monarch, acting on the advice of the prime minister, appoints a governor, who presides over the Hong Kong government's colonial administration. Colonial rule in Hong Kong may be characterized as benevolent, consultative, and paternalistic, but it is nonetheless still colonial. Although local people are heavily involved in running the colony and the colonial government interferes very little in the business activities and daily lives of Hong Kong Chinese, the British still control the major levers of power and fill the top ranks in the government. As has been common to British colonial administration elsewhere, the lower levels of government are filled by local people.

The concern of many Hong Kong Chinese that democratic political reforms be institutionalized before the Chinese Communists take over in 1997 has led since the late 1980s to greater political demands. In turn, the ability of the departing colonial government to deal with these increased pressures has declined because it is viewed as a "lame duck" government. Moreover, the people of Hong Kong have awakened to the fact that their interests and those of the colonial government, which has since the signing of the Joint Declaration in 1982 become a mere appendage of British policy toward China, are no longer compatible.[25] Indeed, the Joint Declaration and the 1990 Basic Law have "basically frozen the status quo and hence [have] circumscribed the policy-making sphere of the government."[26]

Thus, although the people of Hong Kong have since 1982 steadily increased pressure on the colonial government to address their own interests, rather than Great Britain's, they have done so largely by trying to get the support of the two governments that are really in charge—Beijing and London—for the Hong Kong colonial government is now perceived to have lost its independence to these more powerful governments.[27]

Executive and Legislative Councils

The Constitution of Hong Kong provides for a separation of powers among the executive, legislative, and judicial branches of government as a check on the arbitrary use of power by any single individual or institution of the government. The separation of powers in Hong Kong's government does not, however, exist within the framework of a representative democracy. Hong Kong's people still do not elect their most important leaders.

A number of "policy secretaries" assist the governor in administration of the colony. An Executive Council, composed of several top civil servants and "unofficial" (that is, non-civil servant) members appointed by the governor, functions as a cabinet of sorts, although sole decision-making authority is vested in the governor.

A 60-member Legislative Council advises the governor on laws and exercises considerable control over the colony's finances. Until recently all Legislative Council members were appointed by the governor, who is also a member. Under the 1990 Basic Law, Hong Kong's future constitution, 40 of these slots were to be filled through a process of indirect elections, with only 20 being directly elected. The right of the Hong Kong people to elect their own representatives directly, however, hardly reflects a democratic process: Of those eligible to vote (all residents over age 21 who have lived in Hong Kong for at least 7 years), only 6 percent are registered as voters. And if the past is indicative of the future, an even smaller percentage will actually cast ballots.

Expect blame for this state of affairs to be laid on the people and their culture ('Chinese aren't used to voting') and on Beijing: Why bother to elect a third of a parliament? Britain and China will decide everything important before 1997, and China will decide everything after that.[28]

An alternative explanation is that most people in Hong Kong have been basically satisfied with the governing of the colony and take little interest in politics, focusing their time and energy on economic pursuits. It is also likely that the limited scope of democracy in Hong Kong has been a disincentive for local people to get involved in politics. The British signaled their intention to introduce some democratic procedures into the running of the colony before they depart by scheduling several local elections, beginning in 1991, to elect half of all Legislative Council seats by 1997.

This is precisely why Beijing's leaders have grown so concerned about the transitional period, for during more than 100 years of British colonial rule, the people of Hong Kong had virtually no rights to participate in the electoral process. Now Britain is pushing to give them these rights before the Chinese Communists take control. This would create a situation as of 1997 in which Beijing would be unable to exercise the same level of control over Hong Kong's people and political system as it does on the mainland. It would therefore mean that one part of the population, those living in Hong Kong, would enjoy rights that the rest of the Chinese population would not have. This situation could easily lead to pressure on Beijing to extend those rights to all Chinese.

Thus, concern that current efforts to develop a representative government in Hong Kong are really part of a conspiracy to use democracy to undercut China's rule in Hong Kong after 1997 has caused Beijing to resist further efforts at political reform in Hong Kong. China's leaders worry that political reform could, in fact, jeopardize Hong Kong's prosperity and stability by permitting special interests and political protest to flourish. They also are concerned that Hong Kong's social problems—narcotics, violence, gangs, prostitution, an underground economy—require that Hong Kong be controlled, not given autonomy. In fact, China has adopted a very status quo approach to Hong Kong. That is, Hong Kong's political system under British colonial control has been imposed from the outside. This system worked well and kept Hong Kong stable and prosperous. All Beijing wants to do is to replace the colonial ruler with a Chinese Communist Party ruler.[29]

Until Governor Patten came along, London seemed implicitly to accept this idea—pushing Beijing to allow further political reforms only to the point where Beijing said no. Those pressing for greater democratization have denounced the former British approach as giving precedence to Sino–British relations at the expense of Hong Kong's political liberalization.

Judiciary

Hong Kong's judiciary is independent. Once judges are appointed, the governor no longer has any control over them, and they remain in office until they are no longer able to function for mental or physical reasons. English common law, partly adapted to accommodate Chinese custom, is at the heart of the legal system. Much of the confidence of the international and local communities in Hong Kong as a good place to live and do business has been based on the reputation of its independent judiciary for integrity and competence, the stability of the legal and constitutional system, and Hong Kong's adherence to the rule of law.

Many of Beijing's concerns about Hong Kong after 1997 arise from the differences between the two political systems. China's legislative, executive, and judicial powers are not separate, and such legal concepts as habeas corpus, legal precedent, and the tradition of common law do not exist in China. As their own deeply embedded cultural traditions are antithetical to these, it is not surprising that "the Chinese people should have great respect for authority but little respect for law."[30]

China has promised to continue to allow Hong Kong's legal system to rely on common law precedents and not to subject it to the Politburo's guidelines for the rest of China. The problem is that there is no "bill of rights" to guarantee them. Rather, they exist because the British concept of legal right allows a person to act freely "until limited by statute." By contrast, in the Confucian and Marxist-Leninist traditions, rights do not exist until the government *confers* them.[31]

The Transition to 1997

Negotiations between the People's Republic of China and Great Britain over the future status of Hong Kong got off to a rocky start in 1982. British prime minister Margaret Thatcher set a contentious tone for the talks when she claimed after meeting with Chinese leaders in Beijing that the three nineteenth-century treaties that gave the United Kingdom control of Hong Kong were valid according to international law; and that China, like other nations, had an obligation to honor its treaty commitments. Thatcher's remarks infuriated China's leaders, since they consider the treaties to be the result of imperialist aggression that has no legitimacy in the contemporary world.

Nevertheless, negotiations did move forward. While both sides realized that Chinese sovereignty over Hong Kong would be reestablished in 1997, when the New Territories lease expired, they disagreed profoundly on what such sovereignty would mean in practice. The British claimed that they had a "moral commitment" to the people of Hong Kong to maintain the stability and prosperity of the colony. Both the British and the Hong Kong population hoped that Chinese sovereignty over Hong Kong might be more symbolic than substantive and that some arrangement could be worked out that would allow for continuing British participation in the administration of the area. The Chinese vehemently rejected any British role in Hong Kong affairs after 1997; national pride, they said, would prohibit them from allowing the continuation of what they termed "alien rule in Chinese territory." In the end, the Chinese insisted on sovereignty over

Hong Kong and ignored the economic value to China of a Hong Kong *not* under its administrative power.[32]

After several months of stalemate, both sides compromised enough to allow progress to be made in the talks. Britain agreed to end its administration of Hong Kong in 1997, while China agreed to work out a detailed and binding arrangement for how Hong Kong would be governed under Chinese sovereignty.

Negotiations speeded up after China declared that if no agreement were reached by mid-1984, it would cease negotiations and unilaterally announce its plans for Hong Kong's future. It was a threat, to be sure, but one that the British could not ignore, as a breakdown of the talks would seriously harm their relations with China and jeopardize the stability of Hong Kong.

The people of Hong Kong did not formally participate in the negotiations over the colony's fate. Both the British and the Chinese consulted various interested parties in the colony about their views on 1997 and beyond, but they simply ignored many of these viewpoints. China was particularly adamant that the people of Hong Kong were Chinese and that the government in Beijing represented *all Chinese* in talks with the British.

In September 1984 Great Britain and the People's Republic of China initialed the Joint Declaration on the Question of Hong Kong. The Joint Declaration states that as of July 1, 1997, Hong Kong will become a Special Administrative Region (SAR) of the People's Republic of China. The Sino–British Joint Liaison Group was created to oversee the transition to Chinese rule. Any changes in Hong Kong's laws made during the transition period, if they are expected to continue after 1997, must receive final approval from the Joint Liaison Group. If there is disagreement within the Group between the British and Chinese, they must talk until they reach agreement. This procedure gives China veto power over any proposed changes in Hong Kong's governance and laws proposed before 1997.[33]

The Basic Law is the crucial document that translates the spirit of the Joint Declaration drawn up between the British and the Chinese Communists into a legal code. It will function as a "mini-constitution" for Hong Kong to be governed as an SAR as of July 1, 1997. The British had no role in formulating it, as the Chinese considered it an internal, sovereign matter. China established a Basic Law Drafting Committee in 1985 under the direction of the National People's Congress (NPC). This Committee had 59 members, 36 from the mainland and 23 from Hong Kong. Of the latter, almost all were "prominent figures belonging to high and high-middle strata," with Hong Kong's economic elites at its core. In addition, China established a Consultative Committee in Hong Kong of 180 members. Its purpose was to function as a nonofficial representative organ of the people of Hong Kong from all walks of life, an organ that would channel their viewpoints to the Basic Law Drafting Committee. By so

(United Nations photo/M. Hayward)

The hundreds of thousands of refugees who have flocked to Hong Kong during the last few years have often ended up living in squatter settlements and on boats such as these in Aberdeen Harbor.

including Hong Kong's elite and a Hong Kong–wide civic representative organ in consultations about the Basic Law, China hoped to provide political legitimacy to the Basic Law.[34]

Once the Basic Law was approved in April 1990 by China's NPC, the final draft was promulgated. The Basic Law gives the Hong Kong SAR a high degree of autonomy after 1997, except in matters of foreign policy and defense, which will be under the direct control of Beijing. The SAR government will be made up of local inhabitants and headed by a nominated chief executive. They will be "elected by a broadly representative Election Committee in accordance with [the Basic] Law and appointed by the Central People's Government" (that is, the Standing Committee of the National People's Congress).[35]

The 800 members of the Election Committee will be drawn from the industrial, commercial, and financial sectors (200); the professions (200); labor, social service, religious, and other sectors (200); and members of the Legislative Council and other representative organs (200).[36] The chief executive will appoint key officials of the SAR (although they similarly must be approved by Beijing). Provisions were made to allow British and other foreign nationals to serve in the administration of the SAR, if such is the desire of the local government. An elected Legislature will be responsible for making the laws of the SAR.[37]

The maintenance of law and order will be the responsibility of the local authorities, but China has the right to station military forces in the SAR. The judicial and legal system in Hong Kong will remain basically unchanged, but China's NPC must approve of all laws written between 1990 and 1997.[38]

The Basic Law is critical to understanding China's anger in 1992 when Governor Patten proceeded to push for democratic reforms in Hong Kong without Beijing's agreement—particularly since his predecessor, David Wilson, always did consult Beijing and never pushed too hard. After numerous threats to tear up the Basic Law, Beijing simply stated in 1994 that it would nullify any efforts by the British to promote political liberalization that go beyond the Basic Law. Many observers feel, however, that it is Hong Kong's commercial value, not the Basic Law, that will protect it from a heavy-handed approach by the Chinese government.

In essence, the Joint Declaration and Basic Law bring Hong Kong under China's rule but allow it some measure of independence, such as continuing to control its own finances, budgeting, and revenue. In doing so, they commit China to preserving Hong Kong's "capitalist system and lifestyle" for 50 years. In other words, China has promised not to impose a socialist economic system on Hong Kong and to allow Hong Kong to remain a free port, with its own internationally convertible currency, over which China will not exercise authority (which may be a moot point by 1997, as China's own currency moves closer and closer to international convertibility). The free flow of capital will still be allowed, and Hong Kong will be able to enter into economic and cultural agreements with other nations, participate in relevant international organizations, and issue its own travel documents to citizens and visitors. The Basic Law states that all Hong Kong residents shall have freedom of speech, press, publication, association, assembly, procession, and demonstration, as well as the right to form and join trade unions and to strike. Freedom of religion, marriage, choice of occupation, and the right to social welfare are also protected by law.[39]

On political matters such as legislation, human rights, civil liberties, and freedom of the press, there remains considerable concern that the Basic Law is inadequate. For example, the Basic Law provides for China's Standing Committee of the NPC, not the Hong Kong SAR courts, to interpret the Basic Law and to determine whether future laws passed by the Hong Kong SAR Legislature conflict with the Basic Law. Nor will the Hong Kong courts be able to question whether China's political and administrative decisions are compatible with Hong Kong's Basic Law.

Furthermore, although Beijing had promised Hong Kong that executive authorities (ExCo) would be accountable to the Legislature (LegCo), the Basic Law states that the chief executive, to be appointed by China's NPC until at least the year 2012, will have the power to dissolve the Hong Kong Legislature and veto bills. Of even greater concern, Beijing has yet to state the relationship of Hong Kong's Basic Law to China's own constitution. It remains unclear whether, after 1997, Hong Kong will be required to recognize the leading role and authority of the Communist Party, as required in China's constitution. The fundamental incompatibility between the British tradition (in which the state's actions must not be in conflict with the laws) on the one hand, and China's practice of the state using law as a tool as well as conferring and withdrawing rights at will, on the other, is at the heart of the concern about future Chinese rule over Hong Kong.[40]

In short, the Basic Law does not actually protect the autonomy of Hong Kong as an SAR within China. When China promulgated the Basic Law in the spring of 1990, Hong Kong residents by the thousands took to the streets in protest, burning their copies of the Basic Law. As one quip went, "Basic Law for the poor; immigration law for the rich!" Hong Kong's population tends to see the British side as having repeatedly capitulated to China's opposition to plans for political reform in Hong Kong before 1997. They believe that the British have traded off Hong Kong's interests in favor of Great Britain's own interests in further trade and investment in China.

China's forceful crackdown on protesters in Beijing's Tiananmen Square on June 4, 1989, and subsequent repression traumatized the Hong Kong population. China's leadership warned that foreign agents might use such organizations as the Hong Kong Alliance in Support of the Patriotic Democratic Movement in China (a coalition of some 200 groups) to advance their intelligence activities on the mainland;[41] it even accused that group of "playing a subversive role by supporting the pro-democracy movement."[42]

Furthermore, China's foreign minister, Qian Qichen, commenting on the different histories, traditions, social system, social values, and lifestyles of China and Western countries, stated:

> Whether Western values are good or bad is one thing, but whether [they are] suitable for China is another. . . .[N]ow some people in Hongkong want to bring the capitalist systems and lifestyles into the mainland. This is not allowed.[43]

This form of verbal intimidation occurred again when Governor Patten began whipping up Hong Kong fervor for greater democratic reforms in 1992. China's statement in December 1992 that contracts that the enterprises or the government in Hong Kong signed with foreign companies would be invalid after 1997 sent shock waves throughout the colony. The Hang Sang stock exchange took a nosedive, for such a policy means that after 1997, China would in fact control Hong Kong's economy completely—a wholesale abrogation of the Basic Law.

Such statements have aroused fears that the Beijing regime might use force in Hong Kong after 1997 against politically motivated demonstrations. Beijing has, in fact, used subtle (and not so subtle) intimidation to discourage Hong Kong from supporting prodemocracy activities, suggesting that to do so would be "treasonous." The implication is that once China controls Hong Kong, these people might be accused of a political crime and punished for it, just as they would be in the rest of China. Were this to occur, few in Hong Kong believe that the Joint Declaration or the Basic Law would protect their rights.

What is more, as Beijing's feud with Governor Patten has made clear, China plans to obstruct Patten's efforts to move Hong Kong toward direct elections of the Executive and Legislative Councils; and it rejects Governor Patten's proposal to expand the franchise, first, by lowering the voting age to 18, and second, by extending it to all of Hong Kong's adult population (the electorate would be 3.7 million people) in time for the 1995 Legco elections. This would expand the

SHANGHAI: THE HONG KONG THAT MIGHT HAVE BEEN

Situated on China's eastern coast, Shanghai (pictured above) was China's major port before 1949. Various groups of foreigners lived there in areas called concessions, and, together with the Chinese, they built Shanghai into a bustling world port in the nineteenth and twentieth centuries. It was also a city of crime and vice, and large numbers of its citizens lived in terrible poverty.

Since 1949, both because China's former major trading partners joined the American embargo against trade with the People's Republic of China and because China itself at times pursued isolationist policies, Shanghai's role in international trade was eclipsed. The situation was aggravated by socialist policies that took trade out of the hands of independent trading corporations and placed it in the hands of a single state-run trading corporation. The state determined what was bought and sold, thus eliminating competition among Chinese companies. Some observers fear that Chinese control of Hong Kong after 1997 may rob it of its economic dynamism.

The 1980s' reforms in China and the opening of China to world trade did much to revive Shanghai's economy. Earlier in their rule, the Chinese Communists took steps to rid the city of notorious problems, like prostitution and drug dealing, and to establish a basic standard of welfare for most of its residents. Unfortunately, the return of the capitalist style to Shanghai has brought with it many of the problems that before 1949 had made it a "city of sin."

---

franchise beyond 1 percent of the population to all adults age 18 and over.

Governor Patten must formally present his proposals to the Legislative Council; but Hong Kong public opinion had by the end of 1992 already begun to turn against him because of concern that his democratization proposals might, by provoking retaliatory measures from China, destabilize the situation in Hong Kong. Many in Hong Kong (especially the businesspeople who have so much invested in both Hong Kong and China) wonder whether more democracy is worth the risks. Vincent Lo, who chairs the Hong Kong Business and Professionals Federation and is presumed to be the front-runner for Hong Kong's first chief executive after 1997, publicly stated the Federation's opposition to the Governor's political reform package: "The Federation, whose 159 members in-

clude some of Hong Kong's biggest companies, politely asked Mr. Patten to withdraw his proposals."[44]

As the British help prepare Hong Kong for a return to Chinese sovereignty in 1997, then, they are suddenly trying to turn over greater governmental power to local residents. Their commitment to quickening the pace of recruitment of Hong Kong Chinese into the higher levels of the government has angered Beijing. Governor Patten has clearly upset Beijing's dumpling cart with his insistence on greater democratization of Hong Kong before 1997 than the Basic Law called for. A way out of the impasse is possible only if Beijing chooses to negotiate, for the Joint Declaration requires that even a small increase in democracy must be agreed to by China. Thus, it is pointless for the British to insist on political reforms before 1997 if Beijing will not negotiate. To carry out reforms without Beijing's approval risks China's ripping up the Joint Declaration of 1984 and the Basic Law; and Beijing has announced that this is just what it plans to do.

THE FUTURE

Hong Kong's future is still clouded. China's leaders have stated that the post-1997 relationship between China and the Hong Kong SAR will be "one country, two systems." By this they mean that within one country, the capitalist system of Hong Kong may coexist alongside the socialist system of China. Yet China is changing so quickly—indeed, it is daily becoming more like Hong Kong in its commercial and economic features—that one has to wonder how much of China's socialist economic system will still exist by 1997. With China's commercial banks acting much the same as banks in any capitalist economy, a budding stockmarket, a currency whose value is no longer regulated by the state, and with even some of the remaining state-owned enterprises now wanting to opt out of a planned economy (because they simply cannot do well against all the privately owned enterprises), by 1997 China's economy may look much more like Hong Kong's than like a centrally planned socialist economy. China's 14th National Party Congress in October 1992 confirmed Deng Xiaoping's early 1992 proclamation of greater openness and experimentation.

The extraordinary economic boom since 1991 in southern China has made the Hong Kong population more optimistic than at any time since 1982. They see a new "dragon" emerging, one that combines Hong Kong's technology and skills with China's labor and resources. Yet for many, the major worry is that after 1997, China's bureaucracy and corruption may simply smother the economic vitality of Hong Kong unless appropriate political reforms are made.

Still, in the political realm, China is changing so profoundly that the two systems, which, just 15 years ago, seemed so far apart, are now far closer. China has itself been undertaking significant political liberalization, especially with respect to increasing electoral rights at the local level, permitting freedom in individual lifestyles, and according greater freedom to the mass media. And, because of the rapid growth of private property and business interests, China is undergoing major social changes, including the growth of numerous interest groups. Nevertheless, the legal safeguards of civil rights in Hong Kong are unmatched thus far on the mainland. The Chinese Communist Party has denounced calls for more democracy, especially multiparty democracy, as "bourgeois liberalization" and has reaffirmed its unchallengeable authority. It has repeatedly stated hostility to Western notions of democracy and has insisted that any political reforms in Hong Kong must be in line with China's own vision of political reform.

Because China has an important stake in having a successful takeover of Hong Kong, one that does not disrupt the economic sphere, it is concerned that Hong Kong's residents and the international business community believe in its future prosperity. China's rulers know that policies and events that were threatening to that confidence led in the 1980s to the loss of many of Hong Kong's most talented people, technological know-how, and investment. They do not want to risk losing even more. It is also in China's interest to maintain Hong Kong as a major free port and the regional center of trade, financing, shipping, and information. Finally, regardless of official denials by the government in Taiwan, Beijing's successful management of "one country, two systems" in Hong Kong will profoundly affect how Taiwan feels about its own peaceful integration with the mainland. As Beijing wants to regain control of Taiwan by peaceful means, it is critical that it handle Hong Kong well.

NOTES

1. R. G. Tiedemann, "Chasing the Dragon," *China Now,* No. 132 (February 1990,) p. 21.

2. Tiedemann, p. 22.

3. Jan S. Prybyla, "The Hong Kong Agreement and Its Impact on the World Economy," in Jurgen Domes and Yu-ming Shaw, (eds.) *Hong Kong: A Chinese and International Concern* (Boulder: Westview Special Studies on East Asia, 1988), p. 177.

4. Ambrose Y. C. King, "The Hong Kong Talks and Hong Kong Politics," in Domes and Shaw, p. 49.

5. Hungdah Chiu, Y. C. Jao, and Yual-li Wu, *The Future of Hong Kong: Toward 1997 and Beyond* (New York: Quorum Books, 1987), pp. 5–6.

6. Siu-kai Lau, "Hong Kong's 'Ungovernability' in the Twilight of Colonial Rule," in Lin Zhiling and Thomas W. Robinson, *The Chinese and Their Future: Beijing, Taipei, and Hong Kong* (Washington, D.C.: The American Enterprise Institute Press, 1994), pp. 288–290.

7. T. L. Tsim, "Introduction," in T. L. Tsim and Bernard H. K. Luk, *The Other Hong Kong Report* (Hong Kong: The Chinese University Press, 1989), p. xx.

8. See "Hong Kong," *Asia 1983 Yearbook* (Hong Kong: Far Eastern Economic Review, 1983), p. 146.

9. Siu-kai Lau, p. 300.

10. Charmian Suttill, "Chinese Culture in Hong Kong," *China Now,* No. 132 (February 1990) p. 14.

11. Tsim, in Tsim and Luk, p. xxi.

12. John Gordon Davies, "Introduction," *Hong Kong Through the Looking Glass* (Hong Kong: Kelly & Walsh, 1969).

13. Tsim, in Tsim and Luk, p. xix.

14. Jan S. Prybyla, "China's Economic Dynamos," *Current History* (September 1992), p. 263.

15. Tammy Tam, "Shenzhen Industrial Estate Developed to Boost Military Funds," *Hong Kong Standard* (September 5, 1989), p. 1.

16. Prybyla, "China's Economic Dynamos," p. 263.

17. Yun-wing Sung, "The Hong Kong Economy—To the 1997 Barrier and Beyond," in Zhiling Lin and Thomas W. Robinson, *The Chinese and Their Future: Beijing, Taipei, and Hong Kong* (Washington, D.C.: The American Enterprise Institute Press, 1994), pp. 319–323.

18. London's refusal to allow Hong Kong citizens to emigrate to the United Kingdom contributed to a sense of panic among the middle and upper classes in Hong Kong, those most worried about their economic and political future under Communist rule. Other countries have, however, been more than willing to accept these well-educated, wealthy immigrants, who come ready to make large deposits in their new host country's banks.

19. Yun-wing Sung, pp. 316–319.

20. *Ibid.,* pp. 45–46.

21. Siu-kai Lau, "Institutions Without Leaders: The Hong Kong Chinese View of Political Leadership," *Pacific Affairs,* Vol. 63, No. 2 (Summer 1990), p. 192.

22. *Ibid.,* pp. 196–197; and Siu-kai Lau, p. 302.

23. Siu-kai Lau, p. 306.

24. *Ibid.,* p. 205.

25. *Ibid.,* pp. 293, 304–305.

26. *Ibid.,* p. 294.

27. *Ibid.,* p. 294.

28. "Polls Apart," *Asiaweek* (September 28, 1990), p. 23.

29. King, in Domes and Shaw, pp. 51, 57.

30. Tsim, in Tsim and Luk, p. xvi.

31. Dennis Duncanson, "The Anglo-Chinese Negotiations," in Domes and Shaw, p. 39.

32. Tsim, in Tsim and Luk, p. xxv.

33. Norman J. Miners, "Constitution and Administration," in Tsim and Luk, p. 2

34. King, in Domes and Shaw, pp. 54–55.

35. Annex I, Nos. 1 and 4 of *The Basic Law of the Hong Kong Special Administrative Region of the People's Republic of China* (hereafter cited as *The Basic Law*). Printed in *Beijing Review*, Vol. 33, No. 18 (April 30–May 6, 1990), supplement. This document was adopted by the 7th National People's Congress on April 4, 1990.

36. Annex I, No. 2, *The Basic Law* (1990).

37. For specifics, see Annex II of *The Basic Law* (1990).

38. Article 14, *The Basic Law* (1990).

39. Articles 27, 32, 33, and 36 of *The Basic Law* (1990).

40. James L. Tyson, "Promises, Promises . . . ," *Christian Science Monitor*, April 20, 1989, p. 2.

41. Miu-wah Ma, "China Warns Against Political Ties Abroad," *Hong Kong Standard* (September 1, 1989), p. 4.

42. Viola Lee, "China 'Trying to Discourage HK People,' " *South China Morning Post* (August 21, 1989). The article, which originally appeared in an *RMRB* article in July, was elaborated upon in the August edition of *Outlook Weekly,* a mouthpiece of the CCP.

43. "Qian Accuses HK People of Interference," *South China Morning Post* (August 4, 1989).

44. "Sheriff Patten Comes to Town," *The Economist* (November 14, 1992), p. 35.

Annotated Table of Contents for Articles

PEOPLE'S REPUBLIC OF CHINA ARTICLES

Topic Guide to Articles

TOPIC AREA	TREATED IN	TOPIC AREA	TREATED IN
National Reunification	1. The China Puzzle 26. Asian Games: Taiwan Slowly Creeps Toward Nationhood	**Private Enterprise**	7. China's Communists: The Road from Tiananmen 11. China's Gilded Age 17. China's Rush to Riches
Natives	21. Two People, One Land 30. Vibrant, Popular Pantheon	**Religion**	9. Helmsman as Sage 24. Red Envelopes 29. Confucian Ritual in Modern Form 31. Every Number an Omen
Natural Resources	19. Taming the River Wild		
Peasants	14. Riddle of China 18. Cost of Growth: China's Environment 30. Vibrant, Popular Pantheon	**Repatriates**	16. Repatriates Transform Economy
		Rural Life	11. China's Gilded Age 18. Cost of Growth: China's Environment
Philosophy	9. Helmsman as Sage	**Social Reform**	10. China's Fragile Future 11. China's Gilded Age 12. Tightening the Screws on Dissent 13. China Sees "Market-Leninism" 14. Riddle of China 17. China's Rush to Riches 20. The Intellectual in China Today 23. China Goes Pop
Political Reform	5. The Muddle Kingdom? Bursting China's Bubble 6. The China Syndrome 7. China's Communists: The Road from Tiananmen 20. The Intellectual in China Today 27. The Moribund Rejuvenated 28. The First Modern Nation 32. One Servant, Two Masters		
Politics	2. Losing China Again 4. The China Deng Built 5. The Muddle Kingdom? Bursting China's Bubble 6. The China Syndrome 7. China's Communists: The Road from Tiananmen 8. China as a Regional Power 10. China's Fragile Future 12. Tightening the Screws on Dissent 17. China's Rush to Riches 25. Giving Taipei a Place at the Table 26. Asian Games: Taiwan Slowly Creeps Toward Nationhood 27. The Moribund Rejuvenated 28. The First Modern Nation 34. Hollow House	**Social Unrest**	6. The China Syndrome 13. China Sees "Market-Leninism" 14. Riddle of China 15. China's Women Demand Workplace Reform 20. The Intellectual in China Today
		Taiwan Independence	25. Giving Taipei a Place at the Table 26. Asian Games: Taiwan Slowly Creeps Toward Nationhood
		Tiananmen Square	3. "Mao Fever"—Why Now? 6. The China Syndrome 7. China's Communists: The Road from Tiananmen 20. The Intellectual in China Today
		Women	15. China's Women Demand Workplace Reform
		Youth	21. Two People, One Land

Articles from the World Press

PEOPLE'S REPUBLIC OF CHINA ARTICLES

Article 1   *The World Today*, August–September 1994

The China Puzzle

Peter K. C. Woo

The puzzle that is China can probably never be completely solved by the non-Chinese—or even the Chinese themselves. It can be compared to a glass of water, half filled: some would see it as half full, others as half empty. That perception will inevitably lead to different approaches and different policy formulations.

The China Puzzle is, in reality, a collection of puzzles but before looking at any of them, it is necessary to consider China's position in the world today. In the macro trade picture, China, Taiwan and Hong Kong can be considered as a trio. In world trade terms, this trio is surpassed only by the United States and Germany. That is a fact, not a puzzle. Together with Japan, we are talking about a 'T-4'.

With that in mind, let us consider the puzzle of China as an economic opportunity. It is a puzzle because of its sheer size, and as long as we look at China as one economic entity it will continue to be a puzzle. That is why I would argue that in economic terms there are more than 30 separate economic entities in China, not just one. An average-sized province has a population of 50m to 60m—about the size of the United Kingdom. Sichuan province alone tops 100m—if could be called the eighth largest economic entity in the world. Numerous cities have between 10m and 20m inhabitants and are thus larger than many states.

It might be helpful to imagine China as a collection of economic entities, comparable to the European Economic Community or the European Union—perhaps one might think of it as the Chinese Economic Community, the CEC, which would have the same market goals as the EEC or EU. The CEC is already in working order.

Most people looking at South-East Asia and East Asia see 10 countries: the five ASEAN countries, Japan, North and South Korea, Taiwan and China. But when I look at this region I see more than 40 economic entities. The growth in intra-regional trade among these 40-plus trading entities has reached 15 per cent compound. Because of the growth in trade and manufacturing activities in the past 10 years, huge employment opportunities have been created. As a result, wealth has been spread across a very broad base in Asia and new consumer markets have emerged. Their demands form the basis of the World Bank's estimate that East Asia imports $800bn worth of goods annually. That is more than all the imports into the United States—and the figure is growing at an annual rate of 15 per cent.

Against this background of regional trade and phenomenal growth, let me consider another puzzle: what are China's internal priorities today?

When I talk to the Chinese leaders during my visits to China, the first two issues to be raised are always whether China will have a good harvest and the problem of population growth, which each year adds another 18m mouths to feed (the equivalent of the entire population of Australia). The old methods cannot solve these problems. Today, the recognised solution to these problems is economic development and growth. Actually, there is no other choice, and if we accept that the economic solution is the only solution then we will understand why the direction in which China is moving today cannot and will not change.

Of course there are political pressures—they are bound to be felt in a country of 1.1bn people. But for every political idealist there may be 1,000 pragmatists who want real solutions to food shortages and overcrowding. The restriction of family size is, of course, against human rights—but for China or India a future without birth control is unimaginable.

Another priority is preventing the breakup of China. This is a favourite subject, but I myself do not see China breaking up. The history of China in the 100 years between 1850 and 1950 records a period when China was a country without a future, which had lost control of its own sovereignty. Today no Chinese, whether from the People's Republic of China (PRC) or elsewhere, wants to see the country break up. There is a strong collective will to see China as one and to see it succeed. This will should not be underestimated,

It is well known that when the present regime took power in 1949, past dynasties and their disintegration were very closely studied. From these studies valuable lessons were learnt about how to hold China together. Today, there is a four-dimensional system of political control from the centre to the provinces. These four dimensions are the Communist Party, the civil service, the army and national security—each representative of which comes from a different province to those of his colleagues serving in the same province. Economically, though, the control is looser.

Another puzzle to consider when evaluating China is the issue of succession. Even for the most knowledgeable China-watchers, this is still an exercise in crystal-ball gazing. For others, it is simply a fashionable diversion. The main questions are: will there be policy support from the army and will there be stability within the army? Also, will collective leadership continue? Central to the question of succession are three policy issues: the speed of economic growth; the relationship between the centre and the provinces; and the degree of central planning which will be retained.

I think, perhaps, that most people will be surprised at the answer to these questions. When the time comes, events may be less dramatic than expected. I see the possibility of two extreme scenarios after Deng Xiaoping. The first sees a new strong man emerge, which would bring about big changes in the senior leadership team. The current economic programme would be stopped and there would be a return to the old ways. The second scenario is that the senior leaders of today, who have already been in position for five years and are doing a credible job, stay in power. Under normal circumstances the administration has two five-year terms; it is therefore not inconceivable that the existing team continues for the next five years. Deng's contemporaries would have influence still, but their age would prevent domination.

A huge range of possibilities lies between the two extremes. I personally believe that the outcome will be closer to the second scenario than the first, In the 1990s we see more and more governments run by technocrats; I feel we may never again see the likes of the great dominant leaders of the post-1945 era. Take the situation in Japan, for example, which has had seven Prime Ministers in five years. The system is unforgiving of minor mistakes; it also leaves no room for greatness. It is most likely, therefore, that a corps of able technocrats will dominate—maybe less daring, maybe less risk-taking, but more than equal to the tasks of China's full agenda.

One of the principal items on that agenda is trade. What, then, about China's currency, the Renminbi (RMB), and the trade deficit—the next puzzle? Let me take the balance of trade first. To begin with, it must be remembered that the Chinese are savers—the savings rate is high. But what also needs to be stressed is the continuous and strict fiscal discipline which the government has maintained over the past 45 years.

China has no excessive debt—as a policy—so that external lenders can never prejudice China's internal policies and, therefore, its sovereignty. The situation faced by less developed countries (LDCs) in Latin America, burdened by huge trade deficits and a large foreign debt during the oil crisis, has no parallel here. Without long-term foreign debt to finance it, a large trade deficit was never a possibility. Cash-flow is the key to every transaction in China. China manages by cash-flow.

Now a look at the RMB. The adoption of one rate was the right move to make—a very bold move to be taken so quickly, and not without problems. It is no cure-all, but it is a necessary step. We know that the liquidity of the RMB is not adequate at this time. On a small scale, RMB exchange rate is manageable, but for large-scale transactions there are inadequacies.

There is no need to be alarmed by that. It helps to look at the current situation from an evolutionary angle and compare the situation of the RMB today with the Japanese yen in the late 1950s. That exchange rate was a hypothetical one, It was possible to exchange small amounts quite easily, but not large amounts, In those days a lot of business in Japan, such as the purchase of capital equipment, was done in dollars. A similar situation can be found in China today. If we take some practical references, the yen really became fully convertible as an international currency in the 1980s, more than 30 years after the Second World War. Exchange controls on the pound were abolished in 1980.

When one looks at the RMB issue, one naturally wonders about China's banking system. This is the most challenging issue for China today. The aim is to have a central bank, several policy banks such as EXIM and agriculture, and a commercial banking system. A Herculean leap forward will be needed to provide a sustainable and workable banking system necessary to take China to the next stage of its development.

With most-favoured nation (MFN) status no longer at issue, I believe there is a clear path to the General Agreement on Tariffs and Trade (GATT) for China at the end of 1994. I think almost everyone in the world (except one country) believes that China is ready. Going back to the T-4 idea I mentioned earlier, most people would agree that GATT membership makes a lot of sense for China. I would not be surprised, either, to see a fully convertible RMB sooner than the 10-year time-frame envisaged by many.

The next puzzle is the China-United States relationship. How will this key relationship evolve and how will it affect China internally and on the world stage? The relationship between the two countries started in 1972 with the Shanghai Communique: four years later, in 1976, President Carter agreed to MFN status. Between 1979 and 1989 a start was made on economic reforms, but there was little Western interest in the changes taking place in China. Then, from 1989 to 1994, huge advances were seen, both socially and economically, which led Ernest Stern, Managing Director of the World Bank, to remark: 'China has long been a centre of civilization. Now it is also being looked upon as a potential centre of economic gravity. It is thus time for China not just to respond to external conditions, but to help shape them.'

In May, China's MFN status was renewed by President Clinton—without linking it to human-rights issues. The China–United States relationship needs to be positive and there must be cooperation, for obvious reasons, between the two powers to ensure stability in the Asia-Pacific region. Each country has its own national interests at stake in this. The MFN announcement has set the tone for future cooperation.

Japan, as the third corner of a triangle, plays an important part in that relationship in the Pacific. Japan is interested in the resources and markets both in China and in the United States. It is one of the T-4. Over the next 50 years the China–America–Japan triangle will be at the centre of the most fascinating geopolitical, economic and military strategic game-play.

Finally, there is the puzzle of how China is doing generally. The end of the Cold War, the disintegration of the Soviet Union, the telecommunications revolution and the ease of cross-border transfer of technology have created a more favourable environment for China's development. Globally, trade is at the top of every country's agenda, and world competition will become even fiercer than it is today.

Currently, China has certain items on its agenda—energy, transport and telecommunications—which take priority over all others. When considering the China Puzzle, it is worth remembering that the Chinese rail system is equivalent to that of the United States 150 years ago; that the Yangtze River is 10 times the size of the Rhine but only carries 1 per cent of its tonnage; that 100 people share only 2 telephone lines; and that the per capita energy consumption of China is the equivalent of just 5 per cent of America's per capita consumption. Finally, it is worth remembering that as each of the massive power projects are completed in the next five years, their total output will be absorbed by demand on the first day of commission. According to figures published by the international Iron and Steel Institute, China's crude steel production during the first quarter of 1994 has just exceeded that of Japan, which makes it the leading crude steel producer in the world.

South China's economic success story is unparalleled, but even more significant than the opening up of South China was the awakening of Shanghai in 1992. When Shanghai is on the move, China is on the move. Shanghai and the Yangtze River Delta have an economic potential equivalent to that of Japan. There are 60m people in Guangdong province and 100m in the Shanghai-Yangtze River Delta region. There are other similar pockets of growth, such as the Chengdu and Chongqing region. These three pockets alone contain more than 180m people—they represent a trade base which is growing at a rate of more than 15 per cent annually.

Recent press reports allude to huge difficulties faced by China and the possibility of a hard landing. We have all read them, but to me it does not seem as if those pockets of growth are going to grind to a halt. They are already sizeable and successful. For them, this is perhaps the beginning of two decades of continuous development and growth. No U-turns need be expected.

Hong Kong, as a merchant city providing marketing and investment banking, has a key role to play in China's growth. Some 50m overseas Chinese, whose unofficial capital is Hong Kong, are the entrepreneurs and merchants who act as catalysts in this development. It is therefore not surprising that every Saturday the *South China Morning Post* in Hong Kong carries 200 pages of advertisements from companies looking for people to fill jobs.

Of course, the kind of growth we see in China cannot be achieved without inflation. China as a developing country has no monopoly on inflation, but recent economic indicators—money supply figures and the construction materials price index—suggest that a degree of progress is being made. It is also inevitable—and this is recognised by Beijing—that growth imbalances will appear: between rural and urban areas, between east and west, between the coastal areas and inland. Given sufficient cash-flow, however, cities, provinces and strategic industries will continue to grow, as grow they must. Fortunately, some relief from these imbalances is starting to become available as inland provinces begin to receive development investment from the more prosperous areas. Guangdong has been making such investments for several years.

In addition, there is a structural and sectoral adjustment taking place. Certain sectors will grow quickly, while others will not. There will be growth in some industries and contraction in others—notably the public sector and its state enterprises. Allowing this to happen is the right policy, as clearly nothing is really gained if China tries to bring everything down to the lowest common denominator.

In business terms we talk about 'stars', 'cash cows' and 'dogs'. Only China's own stars can assist its dogs. Without stars there will simply be more dogs. In the end, growing unevenly is better than the alternative—to contract across the board. Beijing learnt a very big lesson in 1988 and 1989 when a forced slowdown across the board led to social unrest. China cannot rely on outside help. It must count on its own stars to do the job. Hong Kong and South China and Shanghai and the Yangtze River Delta shine as China's superstars.

This rapid economic growth brings immense business opportunities, but it also presents huge challenges in terms of environmental quality and social development. In my association with the Business Leaders Forum, led by the Prince of Wales, we started in 1992 to promote the practice of good corporate citizenship and sustainable development in China and Hong Kong. It is a necessary and timely initiative in the light of the economic ambitions of the region.

All this is going to be very difficult. There will be numerous problems and many obstacles. But obstacles do not mean failure. There is great and rapid progress, driven by pent-up demand. In the final analysis we should take comfort from China's traditional fiscal discipline, which it has always exerted and will continue to exert in the future. That is the key stabilising factor. We should also take care not to underestimate China's iron determination and the momentum of change.

In conclusion I would like to say that the changes which have already taken place in China are irreversible. Continuation of the growth which has already begun is inevitable. The odds are good that the superstars will shine; some cash cows will become stars; and some of the dogs will become self sufficient. During this evolution there are great rewards to be won—by the Chinese themselves and by those who are willing to take the opportunities being offered.

Article 2

Commentary, April 1994

Losing China Again

Charles Horner

Charles Horner is president of the Madison Center in Washington, D.C. His article, "China on Our Minds," appeared in January, and he also contributed "China on the Rise" to our December 1992 issue.

During 1993, visitors to China began to notice the widespread appearance of trinkets, souvenirs, and other memorabilia of this century's most prominent Chinese leader, Mao Zedong (1893–1976). Though they were struck by something festive in the phenomenon, there was also speculation about darker implications. In particular, people remembered how portraits of Stalin began to pop up as the Soviet Union disintegrated, and how those were interpreted as nostalgic longing for iron-fisted good order, as an escape from freedom.

But China was not disintegrating; on the contrary, it was getting richer by the day. By some reckonings its open-market economy had become the third largest in the world, and businessmen everywhere were jostling to participate in its expansion. In 1993 alone, the Chinese government had approved almost 100,000 foreign-financed projects, representing commitments of some $110 billion *in toto*. The United States and China by themselves did about $30 billion in trade—$10 billion more than the preceding year. And there were other tabulations to show that, throughout the world, industrialists and financiers had been seized by a powerful Sinomania.

All this had resulted from decisions by China's government to allow capitalism an unprecedented sway throughout the country. Yet here was the same government planning and then putting on an old-style Communist spectacle for December 26, 1993, the 100th anniversary of Mao's birth, complete with the long-winded speeches, the giant portraits, and the almost forgotten phrases of Mao's own day. And after the ceremonies in the once-renowned Great Hall of the People in central Beijing, various dignitaries walked past Mao's embalmed body, still on Lenin-like display in a mausoleum at Tiananmen square.

For all this, however, there is little Maoism in today's China. Indeed, almost immediately upon Mao's death in 1976, his successors began to undo his work. In short order, his closest associates—to be immortalized as the "Gang of Four"—were neutralized, and his fearsome wife, Jiang Qing, later received a show trial. Not only that, but by 1977, the previously twice-purged Deng Xiaoping had returned from internal exile to become paramount leader. As against the imperial Mao, Deng strove to be taken for an ordinary bourgeois—a family man dandling his grandchildren, a bridge player, and even an audiophile with an expensive pair of high-end speakers for his home stereo system. But more importantly, Deng came armed with a plan for "four modernizations" and an "opening to the world" which has been at work full force ever since, and with spectacular success.

Moreover, it was as if the centenary celebrations were another way of marking the decline in Mao's historical standing, for both inside and outside the country there was no longer any denial that his reign had been marked by great failures and even greater atrocities. Everyone now acknowledged that one of his early inspirations, the "great leap forward" of the 1950's, had so battered rural areas that the ensuing famine eventually claimed as many as 30 million lives. The great proletarian cultural revolution, which proceeded in fits and starts in the decade prior to his death, was also now universally recognized to have been profoundly destructive. And as much as Mao had labored to become larger than life, in death he was becoming fodder for the tabloids. There were salacious accounts of the sexual adventures of his dotage, with more promised in the forthcoming memoirs of his long-time personal physician.

If Mao can be regarded as in some sense the last of the Chinese emperors, the posthumous pomp of his centenary was also devilishly exquisite in highlighting the country's positive reversal of fortune since his death. In nearby Japan, by contrast, there is still a very-much-alive emperor, and he traditionally greets his subjects on New Year's Day, as Akihito did on January 1, 1994. However, in Tokyo, unlike in Beijing, the end-of-the-year wrap-up was downbeat.

Japan, it was reported, was confronting "an awesome debacle." The country's financial system was threatened by losses in stock and property values of at least *$6 trillion*, losses which made the $350 billion squandered during America's savings-and-loan fiasco seem like spare change. The rising sun was beclouded and the economic miracle had ended. The vaunted Japanese bureaucrats had seriously bungled, and they now seemed far less intimidating—no longer the relentless policy-makers the world had been urged to emulate. Japan was descending into gloom and depression but, from the Chinese perspective, the turnaround was altogether natural. For centuries, they had disdained the Japanese and had especially resented them for becoming China's principal tormentor throughout the 20th century.Japan's defeat in 1945 had been a proper comeuppance; now, the prospect that Japan's postwar economic hegemony might also be waning was deeply satisfying to Chinese rulers old enough to remember Tokyo's past affronts. In the meantime China, as *Newsweek* put it, had become "the straw that stirs the Asian drink," and Boeing's largest customer to boot.

All these developments of the past fifteen years have revived old expectations. In the early 1950's, the "loss of China" became an emotional political issue in the United States. The establishment of a Communist regime in the world's most populous country—one which many Americans had assumed, in the 1940's, was somehow amenable to democracy, free enterprise, and even Protestantism—came as a great surprise, made ominous by the new China's alliance with the Soviet Union, and its increasingly bellicose stance toward the outer world. In addition to the bloody combat between the U.S. and China in the Korean war, there was the prospect of further Sino-American conflict over Taiwan and Indochina, and many other crises of greater or lesser severity—the Sino-Indian war of 1962, or Chinese ties to "national-liberation" movements in various places.

On the other hand, China's relations with the Soviet Union were deteriorating at an even faster rate, making possible a Sino-American diplomatic rapprochement in the early 1970's that went on to outlive the Soviet Union, which was its target. To the extent, then, that China had been "lost" in a strategic sense, it appeared to have been found again in only two decades.

Of course, China was still a Communist country and the Chinese were still convinced that their adoption of Communism had catapulted them out of their backwardness. But today the preferred way of 40 years ago is all but defunct in China, as it is defunct everywhere that matters. Far from placing a nation in the vanguard, Communism has become synonymous with the very condition of backwardness China still strives to overcome. It can certainly no longer serve as the foundation for a governing ideology; as the political scientists like to say, Chinese Communism has lost its legitimacy, or, as the Chinese themselves used to say, it has lost the mandate of heaven.

In this respect, the condition of the Communist-inspired system in China is not so very different from that of the last imperial dynasty in the late 19th century. Everyone knew that its days were numbered, though no one could forecast the precise day of its demise; it might take a decade or a century, but much as the dynasty might wiggle, squirm, and try to delay the inevitable, its doom was certain.

This sentiment, we may remember, was especially pronounced in 1989, at the height of China's democracy movement. The interest among China's best and brightest in Western parliamentarianism and human rights had reached unprecedented heights, and the recovery of China for Western-derived political values and institutions seemed at hand. In the grand sense, this would complete the process which had begun twenty years earlier with China's reintegration into the West's worldwide security system, and which had been followed by China's decision to become part of the West's worldwide trade and investment system. Even the now-famous Tiananmen massacre could be seen as mainly a temporary setback, not a strategic defeat. The window of opportunity opened by the collapse of the Soviet Union and the end of the cold war seemed larger than ever.

Yet now, less than five years later, these dynamics seem to be changing once again, and we may soon have cause to wonder about the loss of China for yet a second time in half a century.

Thus, Adrian Karatnycky, who coordinated this past year's Comparative Study of Freedom for Freedom House, reports that "the period of rapid democratic gains occasioned by the collapse of Soviet Communism appears to have ended," and that the "democratic renaissance that began in 1989" has of late suffered a dramatic blow. He notes how some repressive states—China among them—continue to get richer and more powerful and are therefore able to exert greater influence in what is becoming a strategic and philosophical global vacuum. What is perhaps more instructive is that many of these states have decided that their successes entitle—or at least enable—them to answer back against Western charges in the field of human rights. Money talks.

Last June, for example, the United Nations convened a World Conference on Human Rights, the first such it had sponsored since 1968. The Western representatives, expecting little more than to conduct ideological mopping-up operations in the wake of Communism's demise, were taken aback by the intensity of the resistance mounted by some traditional, albeit newly prosperous, states. China and Indonesia, not otherwise philosophical soulmates, were especially forceful in asserting the autonomy of their beliefs and practices.

Obviously, the Chinese do not wish to be called to account even before so weak a bar as the court of "world opinion." And even though they sometimes make concessions on human rights on a case-by-case basis, sufficient to deflect American pressures connected with trade policy, such adhoc accommodations are essentially "humanitarian," and do not imply an acceptance of our political principles.

Indeed, highly publicized agreements which purport to make the Chinese legal and penal systems more open to outside inspection can no doubt ameliorate harsh conditions of confinement for courageous political dissenters and may even cause the government to think twice before it moves against others. But such agreements are rooted in expediency on both sides. From the American point of view, some human rights are more politically correct than others: the Clinton administration has argued in federal court that Chinese seeking asylum here to escape forced sterilization at home should be deported; the Bush administration had favored the granting of asylum in such cases. And on the Chinese side, Beijing's occasional "flexibility" derives more from working the abacus than from any real change of heart.

The Chinese are apt to persist in doing their sums and in skillfully deflecting American entreaties as it becomes increasingly apparent that our heart is not much in it,

either—precisely because we follow the same arithmetic. For example, one influential Senate Democrat has said that if the President were to make good on his threat to withdraw China's trade benefits, it would be tantamount to dropping the economic and political equivalent of a nuclear bomb. As interpreted by the *New York Times*, this statement reflects a "new consensus . . . among Democrats." The idea is to secure Chinese cooperation—please, just this once, as it were—in return for our scrapping, "once and for all, the annual threat to withdraw preferred-trading status on the basis of China's human-rights record . . . [because] trade with China is now so economically important that . . . if Washington ever actually had to carry out its sanctions threat, the effects would be disastrous for both American business and Chinese reform." For America, about 180,000 jobs could be at stake.

For the Chinese, and beyond their workaday sense of how we now make our commercial and diplomatic calculations, there is also something deeper at work, even among those very closely identified with liberalization. Li Xianglu was a close adviser to Zhao Ziyang, China's reform-minded Prime Minister who openly sympathized with the Tiananmen protesters—for which he was placed under house arrest after the crackdown. Nevertheless Li, now in the United States, believes that there are viable, and indeed humane, alternatives to Western liberalism. In particular, an economically successful China could, he thinks, pose an alternative world view to American-style liberalism, especially because it will be aided by the fact that the East Asian countries all share a common value system."

Moreover, the case made by advocates of democracy, that it invariably promotes prosperity, is also under critical scrutiny. Professor Robert Barro of Harvard has assembled an array of data purporting to show, as he puts it, that "democracy has, at best, a mixed record as a contributor to improved standards of living," and that "the average effect of more democracy on economic growth is roughly zero."

Flourishing democracies, Barro argues, create powerful interest groups which generate policies that favor themselves but hamper economic growth overall. He compares China, with its "regime of political oppression and gradual economic liberalization" and its economic successes, with Russia, whose "sudden move to democracy" has not been rewarded with similar successes. And he concludes that "our pressure for enhanced political freedom in China may therefore be self-serving, but may not improve life for the Chinese people."

No doubt, the embrace of these points by the Chinese has its own self-serving aspect. But their real significance is that they reinforce the traditional Confucian critique of the West's unrestrained individualism and of how that individualism produces bad results for society as a whole.

Besides, the case that any Chinese can make for Western-style liberties inside his own country immediately encounters the visible evidence of the West's own civic decay and social pathology. If a nation can attain wealth and power and yet minimize its vulnerability to social instability and moral decadence, why take unnecessary risks?

For almost two centuries, intellectual and cultural commerce between China and the West has been seen as exclusively a seller's market. The products were of Western origin and the customer was invited to choose among socialism, Christianity, scientism, republicanism, existentialism, Marxism, social Darwinism, constitutional monarchism, Freudianism, vitalism, anarcho-syndicalism, pragmatism, hedonism—or any combination thereof. China's confidence in itself was so shaken that the country's older thinking was almost buried in ongoing debate about differing Western doctrines.

Yet there was also a lingering interest in searching for those things in China's own vast experience which might be mobilized in the nation's behalf. After all, Chinese culture had influenced more people, over a larger area, for a longer period, than anything else in the history of the world. Its ancient classics held sway for millennia. For but one example, China's "neo-Confucian" consensus, formulated about 1200 C.E., dominated political thought not only in China itself but in Japan, Korea, and Vietnam for the next several centuries. And Chinese achievements in every other realm of human endeavor were substantial and enduring.

So even in the early decades of this century, when China's problems continued apace, some Chinese still believed that there remained something in their cultural inheritance that might redeem the country, or perhaps unite with things Western to produce a new amalgamated world civilization; or that Chinese civilization's own presumed immutable, universal, and eternal truths might just win out in the end—that China would not be Westernized, but rather that the whole world would be Sinified.

This ambition is now gathering force once again, as China's formidable people become more and more involved in world intellectual and cultural life. Isolated for a long time now, first behind a screen of Confucian incomprehension, then behind a "bamboo curtain" of Maoist totalitarianism, the proverbial one-fourth of mankind has more than its fair share of smart people—if past history and present MIT enrollments are to be believed. And they are less and less inclined to try out Western-derived solutions to their problems. On the contrary, freed from the requirement to see their past as nothing but a preparation for Communism, they can now reclaim the riches of their own history as they search for new ways of living in the modern world. This process will certainly affect us in the West as well, and may even change our own sense of things.

A semblance of the new balance of intellectual and cultural trade is already discernible. Andrew Solomon draws the outlines of it in a lengthy and important discussion in the *New York Times Magazine* of China's exuberant artistic avantgarde. According to Solomon, these artists use Western styles, but for ends of their own. He also reports that, among these seeming subversives, there is an "ambivalent but incontrovertible" love for Chairman Mao because, as one of them puts it, misguided idealism is better than no idealism at all." Solomon is surprised when a performance artist—and a man imprisoned for leading pro-democracy demonstrations—tells him that his friends "arc nostalgic for the Cultural Revolution because it was so Chinese . . . [and] that no one at Tiananmen was interested in or understood the principle of free elections."

The ambivalence inherent in Chinese aping of Western artistic styles seems to crop up everywhere: imitation and rejection of the West are, in the best Chinese fashion, one and the same thing. The Western style reigns as a matter of chance, something these Chinese learned because they were born into a world wherein the West was at its zenith. But, as one explains, "the West is in a state of decline and China in a state of ascendancy." Western modernism, he thinks, may be the international language of art, but it is dominant in China only because of the current—and not necessarily permanent—international balance of political and economic power. In any event, it is far from obvious that the efforts of the Chinese avant-garde have as their objective the establishment of an American-style democracy.

After Mao proclaimed the People's Republic of China in 1949 and the United States decided to withhold diplomatic recognition, it fell to Dean Rusk to explain why. It was Rusk's misfortune to be Assistant Secretary of State for Far Eastern Affairs at that time, as it was his fate to be Secretary of State during the Kennedy and Johnson administrations, that is, during the Vietnam war. Rusk called the new Communist regime "a Slavic Manchukuo on a colossal scale." It was not, he said, the government of China, for it could not meet the first test: it was not Chinese.

At one time, Chinese Communism surely did mean an expansion of Soviet influence, but that did not last long and, besides, it never turned the Chinese into Russians. Similarly, China's course these past dozen years has certainly marked an expansion of American influence, and that will continue for a while also. But that influence has already peaked and it has not, in any event, turned the

Chinese into Americans; instead, it is now quietly bruited that it may turn the Chinese against Americans.

Indeed, even though we know little about current Chinese strategic thinking, American strategic analysis of the highest order has now begun to sense the stirrings of a coming Sino-American contest, probably not for world dominance, but more likely for paramountcy in Asia. To be sure, the sounds of this contest are still but the faint harmony to the far louder melody of commerce and capitalism, but they can be heard from time to time: the Chinese are hiring dispossessed Russian weapons ex-perts; the Chinese are buying ballistic-missile technology; the Chinese are abandoning territorial defense and equipping their forces for power-projection; the Chinese are still profoundly mistrustful of the United States.

These are, as they say, looming prospects and, given another decade or two, could become ugly ones. In that case, we will once again ask who lost China, wondering how it was that the ever-inscrutable Chinese could have become more like us and yet more like themselves at one and the same time.

Article 3   *World Monitor*, December 1992

Letter From China • 'X'

'Mao Fever'—Why Now?

An insider says China's masses are using a discredited Mao to warn his successors.

Author 'X' ("China's Sidelined Generation," WM July, 1991), who requests anonymity, works in a Beijing government ministry. He was a graduate student when he participated in 1989's democracy movement.

Ross Terrill ("Leaving Deng Behind," WM, November) translated and adapted this article from the Chinese. His latest book is "China in Our Time: From Mao to Tiananmen and Beyond."

At times in the past year, Mao Zedong has seemed so present in China that one felt he might come out of his crystal sarcophagus at any moment, wave his hand again before fanatical millions, and launch another earthshaking revolution.

It was in the winter of 1991–92 that the reborn public frenzy for Mao, founder of the People's Republic of China (PRC) and perhaps the most powerful leader in China's 4,000-year history, reached its peak. Foreign visitors to Beijing could hardly believe their eyes as books on Mao became best sellers, karaoke clubs echoed to songs in praise of Mao, taxis carried portraits of Mao hung by the steering wheel, and souvenir shops put Mao badges in their prime display cases.

Could it be that the Chinese people missed Mao and his disastrous socialist utopia? Were they unhappy with the departures from Maoism made under the leadership of Deng Xiaoping, patriarch of the Chinese Communists during the "reform era" that began in the late 1970s?

As a boy, I did not know what a god looked like, but I knew Mao was one.

"Mao fever," as it quickly became known, makes some people very pessimistic; it shows the hold of paternalism in China, they say. Others point the finger at the hardliners within the Chinese government, such as Premier Li Peng, and believe Mao fever is a result of their anti-reform manipulation. Yet others see Mao fever as a sign of grassroots dissatisfaction with Deng and his reforms.

The first thing to understand about Mao fever is that it is not the resurrection of Mao but of something else—the people's own picking up of lost memories.

It was four years ago, some months before the Tiananmen Square democracy movement, that Mao fever actually began, with readers snapping up lively writings on Mao the man. This was a different Mao from Mao the god or the awesome figure lying in state who will never speak again. Also different from the Mao of the Cultural Revolution who kept himself secluded from the people, offering only an occasional upraised arm in Tiananmen Square.

Let me tell a story here. As a boy, I did not know what a god looked like, but I knew that Mao was the god of our lives. When I was six, I accidentally broke a large porcelain Mao badge. Fear gripped me. In my life until that moment, the breaking of the badge seemed the worst thing I had ever done. Desperate to hide my crime, I took the pieces and threw them down a public toilet. For months I felt guilty. The shadow of the god still existed.

Pretty clearly, Mao fever annoyed and embarrassed Deng, yet he could not simply stamp out the remembrance of his predecessor. Recall how Deng handled the problem of Mao at the start of the reform era. In 1980, the Communist Party came out with an assessment of Mao's leadership of the PRC. Mao was

Pop Cultural revolution: Not Red Guards, but T-shirts are ubiquitous on China's urban thoroughfares. Beijing woman sports "I love Mao" shirt last summer in this the 100th year since Mao's birth.

carved into two parts: 70% good and 30% bad. The responsibility for most of the Cultural Revolution was shifted onto others, chiefly Jiang Qing, Mao's wife. This was Deng's method of laying the foundation for his own reign as Mao's successor. It left the 38-year marriage of Mao and Jiang as the strangest marital union in China's history, for the husband was "great," and the nation should toe the line of his Thought, yet his own wife was the rottenest egg in existence, and the nation was told to hate her.

During the Mao fever we Chinese people learned something of Mao the man. He had been lonely in the Forbidden City, and he showed emotion, crying in despair before his bodyguards, refusing to shake hands with actors who played the villain in a play. He was a common man in many of his tastes, for

example his fondness for hot peppers and pork braised in brown sauce. When he did not sleep well, he became ill-tempered.

Let me give another personal memory. In 1990, two decades after I broke the porcelain Mao badge, I was reading a book about Mao's life and work in the late 1950s, when suddenly I burst into loud laughter. On the page in front of me was an account of a provincial official who needed to consult with the leader on a hot afternoon. When he walked into the reception room, Mao was lying back in a chaise lounge, a cheap fan made from rushes in his hand, and his pink, callused bare feet pushed forward high in the air. In its coziness the scene seemed ridiculous. Surely this was an old farmer having a nap after coming in from the fields—not the supreme leader of the Chinese people!

Armed with all these new facts and stories, people found they came up with their own views on Mao. By no means was Deng's "70–30" evaluation the last word on the Mao question.

The new consideration of Mao from 1989 brought back the past and roused strong feelings. Then, after the crackdown against the Tiananmen Square democracy movement, Mao fever took on further life with badges, songs, more books, and even films and plays and TV dramas. The Chinese edition of "Mao," a biography by Ross Terrill [the translator of this article], has sold more than a million copies since 1989, and a pop music cassette "The Red Sun" (a Cultural Revolution appellation for Mao) has sold 6 million copies.

People twisted the fad in their own direction. Scholars came out with material on Mao that previously they had been unable to publish. Communist officials tried their best to tap Mao fever for the cause of China-first patriotism. Private businessmen took the opportunity to make money by selling Mao artifacts and cultural products. Ordinary folk simply looked at and listened to what they found interesting.

Outsiders may wonder why some sort of renewed attention to Mao did not come earlier. But the 1980s was a decade of collective amnesia. The arrival of the foreign world buttressed this. It was not that foreigners brought any direct message about the meaning of the Cultural Revolution. But the foreigners, with their superior products and higher standard of living, poked holes in the arrogance that had been bred in us by the Communist Party.

Remember, we were brought up on slogans like "Socialism advances from day to day, Imperialism grows more rotten from day to day." We actually came to believe the lie peddled to us by the Communist Party that the people on Taiwan were so poor they had to eat banana skins.

In the 1980s, what became clear in people's minds was that the imperialists were rich and China was poor. In the mood of the decade, money ruled, the future beckoned, and most people wanted to leave the dust of the past undisturbed. A popular slogan was "Time Is Money and Life." A hit song from the Special Economic Zone of Shenzhen near Hong Kong bore the title "What a Wonderful World Lies Outside." And a favorite novel was "If Only I Could Be Ten Years Younger."

People realized that telling lies in the Cultural Revolution had been harmful.

But, at the same time, they felt telling the truth now was too late to be useful. In the face of foreign superiority, why make the Chinese feel even worse by dissecting the Cultural Revolution?

But it is clear that the Deng reforms, focussing on economics, did not succeed in cutting the connection between present and past. There was Democracy Wall, with its political criticisms, in 1979—its hero, Wei Jingsheng, is still in prison for his writings at that time. There was the drive against "spiritual pollution" in 1983–84 and then another one against "bourgeois liberalism." Politics was always waiting in the wings, ready to bring back a stab of fear.

It is less uncomfortable to bring back the past as black humor than to confront it empirically as history. Looking back at Mao during 1989–92 was like opening an old scar while laughing loudly.

Deng's reforms were an effective means of curing the mental scars of the Chinese people. The introduction of some market forces and capitalist management methods raised growth rates and filled the shops with goods. The new stress on economic rationality had the effect of reducing government control over the lives of citizens. For example, we are far more mobile than in Mao's day. We can go from province to province, even abroad, whereas some years ago even a trip to visit my parents in another city required a letter from my work unit—or else I risked being arrested on the train.

The biggest fruit of Deng's policies, perhaps ironically, was in people's minds. No longer did we feel that our political performance was the great priority of our lives. We stopped wanting to join the Communist Party. We ceased to believe in our great and glorious leaders. We learned to observe and evaluate the world outside ourselves with our own eyes and minds.

Deng's policies brought about changes in Chinese society that probably deviated from his intentions. The green light to the private entrepreneur has led to the coming of a middle class.

The unpleasant emergence of "profiteering officials," who use their power to tap into the new money, is a revival of the *bureaucratism* of old China.

In the countryside, the rise of the "ten thousand yuan families" is essentially the return of *landlords*.

Those Chinese jumping in and out of cars with Western bosses, dressed in Western suits and speaking foreign languages, are the *compradors* (Chinese agents of foreign businesses) of yesterday.

Photo: Reuters/Bettmann

Crush for capitalism: More than a miilion would-be investors "queued up"—some for days—to buy shares at Shenzhen stock exchange last summer. In August a riot actually broke out.

Curiously, just before Mao fever came along, there occurred a revival of the excruciatingly boring "model operas" which Jiang Qing produced during the Cultural Revolution. Shows like "Taking Tiger Mountain by Strategy" and "Red Lantern," with magnificent heroes and horrible villains, ear-piercing, full of terror and glory. What was extraordinary was that people suddenly began to get fun out of these model operas.

After all, these shows were the alpha and omega of entertainment in those years of the 1960s. They formed the learning experience of children. Lovers would fondly remember dates at the theater when the program consisted of a model opera. Old people sat on stools in the lanes humming tunes from them. In the late '80s the charm of this music lay less in its intrinsic character than in recalling to mind what had been lost from one's mental life for years.

Had the propaganda contents of the operas made a fresh appeal, the reputation of Jiang Qing would also have revived. But this did not occur. When Mao's wife killed herself in the summer of 1991, not only did the government virtually ignore the event, but so, too, did most ordinary people. But the new pleasure taken in the model operas led directly into the Mao fever of 1989.

The most important point in all this cannot be completely comforting to Deng. Reform is not charity offered from on high by an enlightened Deng. Nor does he have a patent on it. There is something within the reform era that begins to return the initiative to the citizens. Mao fever may just indicate that the Chinese people are getting out from under a psychological burden, escaping from a historical vicious circle that has made them as passive as stuffed giraffes in a pantomime.

Mao himself said he accomplished two great things: the establishment of a "new China" and the unleashing of the Cultural Revolution. There indeed was a good period after the revolution of 1949, but it lasted only about five years. After wholesale collectivization came to the villages in 1956, people lost control of their lives and began to be buffeted by one political campaign after another. Because of Mao's megalomania, the time, wealth, and energy of the nation were drained away on the quest for "continuous revolution."

Just as Mao pointed to two achievements he was most proud of—the establishment of a "new China" and the unleashing of the Cultural Revolution—so Li Peng has spoken of Deng's two great achievements: his reassessment of Mao and his policies of economic reform and openness. Indeed, in both tasks Deng had to struggle against opposition, and he is to be praised for what he wrought.

Yet each achievement is flawed. The Tiananmen Square democracy movement and Mao fever have brought home these flaws. In the former, people stressed that economic reform cannot be sustained without a matching political reform—a step Deng has obstinately refused. In the latter, people began to reject the Communist Party's formalistic view of history and take a bit of history back into their own hands.

In the winter of 1992, as Mao fever reached its height and Deng's realization grew that reform needed a new start, he made his bold and astonishing trip to South China. He praised the Special Economic Zones (enclaves protected from the cruder political pressures, where capitalism roars ahead) and said the biggest political problem in China is hardline leftism.

A careful study of his remarks in Guangdong Province, Shanghai, and Shenzhen shows that he had been re-reading Mao. He adapted phrases of Mao's, talking of a new "leap" ahead and cursing the anti-reform folk as "old women tottering on bound feet." Hardly had Deng returned to Beijing than Mao fever began to vanish, and in its place a stock market fever took the nation by storm. People's attention is riveted by the two stock exchanges that now exist in China, and by stories and stratagems about getting rich by buying and selling stock. By giving more reform—at least in words—had Deng alleviated his Mao problem?

We all must be permitted our dreams. Formerly we wholeheartedly cried, "Long Live Chairman Mao!" and we dreamed his longevity would be our happiness. Now we would be bored out of our minds shouting "Long Live" anyone. And today's dreams are so different that communism itself seems nothing more than a dream. For we dream of a spacious apartment, of a pretty girl friend or boy friend, of having talented and healthy children, of winning big on that Shenzhen stock market.

At any rate, how fascinating it is that Deng must still dwell with Mao. Of course, in many ways Deng set out to be an anti-Mao. If Mao stressed ideology, Deng stressed economics. If Mao rose in a swirling personality cult, Deng declared himself a mere "son of the Chinese people." Deng has never made pilgrimages to his hometown in Sichuan Province, as Mao did to Shaoshan in Hunan Province. Deng seldom goes before the crowds to raise his arm in acknowledgment of the awe shown to power.

Yet I believe Deng's mind is controlled less by the people of China than by Mao.

If Deng were truly a son of the Chinese people, would he keep saying the reform policy won't be changed for so many decades, as if reform were his gift, patented, offered from on high?

Very often it seemed in China that a person's life could be bought for a dime.

Yet poverty makes me less afraid than the blind worship of a leader. In the vicious circle of poverty, the Chinese seemed to await a savior. Mao came along as one. In his day there were meetings to "recall past suffering and be aware of current happiness"—to reinforce the point. Likewise, in the Deng era, the Party has boasted that it has "held up the bowl of pork" for people to eat, but complained that two minutes later the satisfied diners "put down their chopsticks and criticize mother."

I believe that, taken together, the Tiananmen Square democracy movement and Mao fever prove something unexpected about the irreversibility of reform. Reform has changed the people. They know—and said so in 1989—that a new politics must come with a new society. They expressed in Mao fever the conviction that the past nightmare is *not* untouchable by all but Deng's Communist Party.

All through my lifetime the Chinese Communist Party has taught us to sing "The Internationale." In the Chinese version of that song there are the intriguing lines: "There never has been a savior. Nor should we rely upon gods and emperors. We will make a happy life in dependence on our own efforts." Only now, after decades of Communist tragedy, the Chinese people may be beginning to understand that oft-sung line.

Article 4

U.S. News & World Report, November 14, 1994

The China Deng built

leadership succession

The leader's reformist legacy is set. Now his country wants a bigger say throughout Asia

When leaders of three of the world's biggest economies and some of its fastest-growing ones sit down together in Indonesia next week, only one man can claim membership in both clubs: Jiang Zemin, China's president and chief of its Communist Party. Jiang will meet sepa-

rately with Bill Clinton amid talks on trade liberalization with the other members of the Asia-Pacific Economic Cooperation forum (APEC). Protocol may stop the American president from popping the question that will haunt the summit: Can China keep a steady course

at home and abroad once Deng Xiaoping, the ailing 90-year-old architect of China's reforms, leaves the scene?

The answer could determine whether the unprecedented peace and prosperity that Asia has enjoyed in recent years can continue—and whether China, Asia's

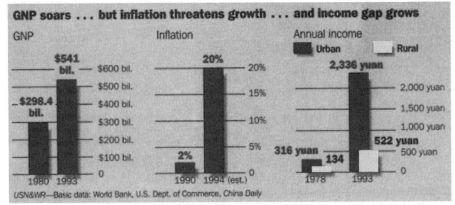

GNP soars ... but inflation threatens growth ... and income gap grows

GNP: $541 bil. (1993), $298.4 bil. (1980)

Inflation: 2% (1990), 20% (1994 est.)

Annual income — Urban / Rural: 316 yuan (1978), 134 yuan (1978 rural); 2,336 yuan (1993 urban), 522 yuan (1993 rural)

USN&WR—Basic data: World Bank, U.S. Dept. of Commerce, China Daily

USN&WR

emerging powerhouse, enters the 21st century as the United States' friend, foe or something in between.

Deng, who last appeared in public in February, is widely believed to be near death. The party line is that the paramount leader is in good health, but a senior official recently confirmed to an Asian diplomat that Deng has been hospitalized. As if to prepare for Deng's enshrinement in history, the first and second volumes of his selected works were republished last week. Citizens queued up to buy copies, and workplaces devoted seminars to the new volumes.

On China's National Day last month, Deng's colleagues used 40,000 flower pots to spell out their intention to stick to the Dengist path. They had to say that, of course, with or without flowers. But what gives their protestations credibility is that economic growth is now the main source of legitimacy for China's ruling Communist Party.

For 15 years, Deng's reforms have propelled the economy forward at a breakneck pace of 9 percent a year. Last year, China attracted $26 billion in foreign investment, second only to the United States.

This high-speed growth, translated into rapidly rising living standards, is what has kept China politically stable while other Communist regimes were disintegrating. But now China, too, is facing a host of potentially disruptive economic strains.

Prices began rising sharply in mid-1993 because of a frenzy of speculative property investment. Responding to consumer complaints, the government clamped price controls on major food items in August. But in September, consumer prices in China's 35 largest cities were 27.5 percent higher than a year earlier; food prices alone jumped 38.5 percent over the previous year. Bulletin boards in free markets around Beijing now list government-decreed prices and warn that vendors are allowed to charge no more than 10 percent extra. Analysts

IN THE WINGS

Politics after Deng: Receding waters and emerging stones

China's main evening news program recently devoted a full third of its airtime to a visit by Communist Party General Secretary Jiang Zemin to Sichuan province and communities along the Three Gorges of the Yangtze River. Reports of the trip dominated the front pages of national newspapers.

The blanket coverage was meant to reinforce the notion that the 68-year-old Jiang, paramount leader Deng Xiaoping's favored successor, is truly in charge in China. But five years after former Shanghai Party boss Jiang assumed the top party job, doubts remain that he can retain power after his patron's death.

Unimposing. Much has been made of Jiang's fondness for proverbs, Goethe and the Gettysburg Address. But Jiang, who also is China's president, rarely says anything substantive and is not identified with any major policy initiative. He doesn't threaten people notes a Western diplomat, and that may be his strongest qualification. Deng deserves some blame for his chosen successor's weakness: He has never bothered to explain publicly why Jiang deserved promotion. And two years ago, he undercut Jiang by not taking him along on a reform-touting trip to southern China.

Bill Clinton, on the other hand, boosted Jiang's authority last year when the two leaders met at the APEC summit in Seattle. The Chinese spin is that the two men established a personal bond that constitutes a foundation for improving Sino–U.S. relations. They are to meet again at next week's APEC summit.

Jiang's backing in the powerful military is narrow, although Defense Minister Chi Haotian is a supporter. One ally who is also seen as a potential challenger is Qiao Shi, 70, who heads China's lawmaking body, the National People's Congress. Qiao maintains close ties to the security apparatus but has a reputation as a liberal. An oft heard phrase in Beijing these days goes, "When the water recedes, the stone emerges." Jiang's name means "river." Qiao's given name, Shi, means "stone."

Premier Li Peng is likely to fade away in the post-Deng era. His term does not expire until 1998, but his association with the 1989 Tiananmen crackdown is a political liability, and a heart attack last year has visibly slowed him. For the long term, many eyes are on Hu Jintao, at 52 the youngest member of the Politburo Standing Committee, who holds a number of strategic party posts.

BY SUSAN V. LAWRENCE IN BEIJING

REGIONAL NEIGHBORS

Reaching out to the new China

Asian nations from Japan to Indonesia are watching with a mixture of hope and fear as Deng Xiaoping's reforms make China increasingly rich and powerful.

They are delighted by China's galloping integration into Asia's economic boom. The growing web of profitable trade and investment ties gives China a powerful interest to live peacefully with its neighbors. Asia has reached out to China through trade talks and in regional security symposiums that would have been unthinkable a few years ago. The aim is to convince Beijing that it has friends in the region and little to gain from bullying its neighbors.

Last year more than half of South Korea's Asian investment went to China. After hanging back for years, even cautious Japanese businessmen have China fever. Direct investment has risen nearly fivefold since 1990, reaching $1.69 billion last year. Uniformed Japanese military officials met with their Chinese counterparts in Beijing earlier this year for the first time since World War II.

Yet China's sheer size intimidates its neighbors, its political future is uncertain, and its foreign policy could be swayed by nationalist or military influence. China's claims to all of the South China Sea have brought it into dispute with most of Southeast Asia. The dispute is partly over oil, mineral and fishing rights, but no government in the region can afford politically to compromise on traditional claims of sovereignty.

Sea lanes. The biggest threat may be to Japan, which depends on free navigation through the area for nearly all its oil supplies. Any Chinese moves to enforce its claims to a cluster of islands, or to acquire the ships and aircraft to patrol the area, could provoke Japan to beef up its own military capabilities. That would accelerate the already booming arms trade in Asia. Chinese President Jiang Zemin will be pressed to clarify China's intentions during a scheduled swing this week through Southeast Asia.

So far the presence of some 100,000 U.S. military personnel in Asia has ensured stability and blocked an all-out arms race. Yet in spite of repeated assurances from Washington, few in Asia are convinced of America's long-term staying power. "Why are you still here?" asks a Southeast Asian diplomat, reflecting a growing worry in the region that with the cold war behind, the United States is not getting enough of a return on the money it spends to keep the 7th Fleet steaming through Pacific waters.

One upshot of these jitters is that President Clinton may get a sympathetic hearing next week when he asks APEC members to open the door to trade and investment. That runs against the desire of those countries that have thrived by controlling imports while targeting exports at the vast U.S. market. But amid uncertainty over China's real intentions, Asia is realizing that now is not the moment to risk alienating Washington.

BY STEVEN BUTLER IN TOKYO

---

say the administrative intervention will help lower the inflation rate, but only artificially—and only for a time.

Loose bank credit could fuel a further burst of inflation. In the first nine months of this year, China's banks issued 56 percent more money in loans than in the same period in 1993. Much of the credit has been pumped into unviable projects and subsidies for unprofitable state enterprises, drawing scarce resources away from efficient investment. But cutting state loans would be politically dangerous because it would swell ranks of disgruntled workers who are struggling to get by on small stipends or no money at all. Until an effective welfare net is put in place—and that isn't likely to happen soon—the state dares not give the go-ahead for bankruptcy. Officials in Chongqing told *U.S.*

News they had marked two factories for bankruptcy, but when managers begged for a reprieve, the city granted it.

Huge numbers of farmers continue to stream out of rural areas into big cities in search of work, despite a 45 percent hike in crop prices this past summer. The government estimates that 60 million have left the countryside for good, a scale of peacetime migration unprecedented anywhere in the world. In the cities, rural job seekers have contributed to soaring crime rates and to rising resentment.

Popular anger at official corruption—which along with inflation was a catalyst for the Tiananmen protests in 1989—is rising again. A recently opened exhibit on corruption at the military museum in Beijing has been drawing 10,000 visitors a day. The government admits that state-

sector woes have sparked some worker unrest, but so far there is no widespread interest in taking to the streets.

Without Deng's moral authority, China's next leaders (box, Page 99) will find painful economic decisions even harder to make. But while they may be divided about the pace of reform, all are convinced that growth not only bolsters their power at home but is also the surest path to the international respect that has eluded China since the humiliating Opium Wars a century and a half ago.

In recent years, China has improved ties with a long list of former adversaries, including Taiwan, Russia, Vietnam and South Korea. Jiang will cement a rapprochement with Vietnam when he visits Hanoi before the APEC summit. Last week, Premier Li Peng became the highest-ranking Chinese official to visit

Seoul since China and South Korea established diplomatic relations in 1992.

A threat? China's neighbors accept its claim to great power status (box, Page 100), but they are unsettled by its moves to modernize the world's largest army and enhance its ability to project its power outside China. The Chinese Air Force has bought 26 Su-27 fighter planes from Russia and has an order in for many dozens more. The Navy is acquiring a new generation of blue-water warships. Hong Kong-based military analyst Tai Ming Cheung says that China is also training 10 percent of its military for rapid deployment missions abroad. And Beijing continues to defy an international moratorium on nuclear weapons testing: It conducted its most recent underground test in October.

A worsening energy picture could also prompt China to adopt a more aggressive military posture. For the first time in nearly three decades, China became a net oil importer in January, and reliance on foreign oil is likely to grow.

Beijing dismisses what it derides as "a China threat theory," pointing out that while defense spending has risen in absolute terms, it has fallen as a percentage of gross national product. But at the same time, Chinese scholars are writing openly about a widening role for China in the region. "The United States is still the 'giant,' " scholars from the China Institute for Contemporary International Relations concede in an article, but China and the ASEAN, the Association of Southeast Asian Nations, are ascending powers. The think tank predicts that the United States and Japan will enter an "intensified" struggle for regional leadership and maintains that Sino-American relations have an uncertain future. The only relationship the institute views as "relatively stable" is that between China and Japan.

Unofficial publications go further in projecting China's future clout. An article this summer in Beijing's *Developing Zone Herald* outlined a three-stage scenario for Chinese leadership of Asia by the end of this century. The first step is the development of a "greater China circle," encompassing the mainland, Hong Kong and Taiwan. Next is the creation of a "middle triangle," linking China, South Korea and Southeast Asia, with overseas Chinese communities playing key roles. Last, China takes the dominant position in a triangle with the United States and Japan. Such predictions may be wildly premature, but they demonstrate the grand dreams China's economic success has inspired.

With the uncertainties of a post-Deng era looming, the Clinton administration has opted to engage China rather than confront it. "I know that some in China believe that the United States regards China as a threat, or at least a future threat," Defense Secretary William Perry told an audience of Chinese Army officers on a visit to China last month. "As secretary of defense of the United States, I can assure you that those who make these arguments don't understand American defense policy."

U.S. caution. While insisting otherwise in public, the administration is actively shying away from contentious issues with Beijing. During his visit, Perry did not raise American concerns about conventional Chinese arms sales to Myanmar and Iran, a subject high on the American agenda in the early 1990s. And when the defense secretary inaugurated a new bilateral commission on defense conversion last month, he demanded no safeguards against investment dollars being used to subsidize weapons production. "No company succeeds in commercial business by deflecting its profits off into another field," Perry assured reporters. Yet managers at the Jialing Industry Company, a Chongqing-based defense plant, told *U.S. News* that they rely on profits from nine foreign joint ventures and their civilian motorcycle production to pay for unprofitable military operations that the government will not let them close down. The firm also hands over nearly $6 million a year of commercial profits to its parent company, NORINCO, a major manufacturer and exporter of arms.

Human-rights groups charge that the United States has abandoned its human-rights crusade despite a renewed campaign against dissent since China secured renewal of its most-favored-nation status last spring. "The administra-

tion is doing the bare minimum to maintain Clinton's credibility," says Mike Jendrzejczyk of Human Rights Watch-Asia. "It is all form and no substance, as far as we can see."

Senior officials insist that Clinton will raise human-rights abuses, as well as proliferation and trade issues, in his meeting with Jiang. He will also follow up on Chinese Premier Li Peng's recent promise of assistance in enforcing the U.S. nuclear agreement with North Korea. The administration is hoping that China will take in North Korea's nuclear fuel rods when it is required to give them up.

Trade officials from the two countries will tackle America's trade deficit with China, which could reach $25 billion to $26 billion this year, up from $22.8 billion in 1993. But Topic A on the table will be China's application to join the General Agreement on Tariffs and Trade, the world trade body. China says that as a developing nation, it should not have to open its markets as far as demanded by Washington as a condition of membership. The administration counters that China's export sector is so sophisticated that it should not be treated as a developing country.

Nearby APEC countries have an even bigger stake in China's success. China's economic dynamo now drives Asia-Pacific economic growth. An unstable China could not only endanger enormous commercial interests, it would raise the specter of an exodus of tens—even hundreds—of millions of refugees. When the United States threatened to withdraw China's most-favored-nation status earlier this year, China's Asian neighbors sided with Beijing. At the APEC summit, they are likely to back China's entry into GATT. For all the anxiety China's neighbors may feel about an ascendent, assertive Beijing, they reason there is more to fear from China as an outlaw. That is perhaps the clearest indication that China's increasing influence really isn't a matter for discussion—the question is how that influence will manifest itself.

BY SUSAN V. LAWRENCE IN BEIJING WITH LOUISE LIEF AND BRUCE B. AUSTER

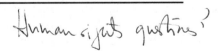

Article 5

Foreign Affairs, May/June 1994

The Muddle Kingdom?

Bursting China's Bubble

Richard Hornik

Richard Hornik, on leave from his post as Senior Correspondent for Time *magazine, is currently Journalist-in-Residence at the East-West Center in Honolulu. He was formerly* Time's *Bureau Chief in Beijing (1985–87) and Hong Kong (1991–93).*

BEIJING HAS FLUNKED THE FUNDAMENTALS

Part of the problem of analyzing China has long been that any critical view is seen as anti-Chinese. Simply to question the accomplishments of a 4,000-year-old civilization is taken as evidence of bias and, generally speaking, broad-gauge attacks on China's ancient political culture, particularly by foreigners, are dismissed out of hand. That said, even those most optimistic about the Chinese economic "miracle" should take a careful look at the present regime's track record before making sweeping predictions about China's future economic growth.

In the long debate over the best political and economic path to modernization, an East Asian "model" has seemingly emerged overnight. In the eyes of many, East Asia's success has proven that democracy, even pluralism, is a luxury to be indulged only after substantial economic progress has been made. Not only that, but economic progress itself is best guaranteed by a "soft" authoritarian regime. Only such a system, it is argued, can enforce the fiscal and monetary discipline that so often eludes democracies, which are forced to pander to public opinion or selfish interest groups. The benign intervention of wizened authoritarians can drive and direct economic growth, more easily allocate resources, push through austerity reforms that are beneficial in the long term but unpopular in the short, and all the while create an environment conducive to the growth of private enterprise.

The success of China's neighbors has provided the rationale behind grandiose projections about the Chinese economy becoming the world's largest in the year 2000, 2010, 2020—take your pick. This model is widely considered to provide grounds for the political legitimacy that Beijing will need if a new social contract is to be written with the Chinese people. East Asia's success is also the primary argument against efforts to force China

to liberalize its political system. Lee Kuan Yew, Singapore's senior minister, early last year warned the Clinton administration against meddling in China's domestic affairs, saying, "I would put that as the greatest error that could be made."

But much is overlooked in this analysis, about East Asia generally and China specifically. In its exhaustive study, *The East Asian Economic Miracle,* the World Bank recently concluded that while the benefits of specific policy interventions could be debated, "getting the fundamentals right was essential." In other words, key to the success of the East Asian economies are stable macroeconomic policies that emphasize fiscal and monetary stability. Yet, though it possesses a far harsher form of authoritarian rule than any of its successful neighbors, China's fiscal and monetary policies remain a shambles. Beijing, in other words, has the fundamentals wrong.

China's government appears no more capable of imposing fiscal and monetary discipline—the supposed advantage of authoritarianism—than a corrupt democracy. The present regime is more akin to the hyperinflationary Peronistas in Argentina than to the fiscally ascetic militarists who wrought South Korea's rise. Efforts to impose a modicum of financial discipline last summer resulted in but a brief pause before the credit taps once again gushed forth. Fearing a backlash from its urban proletariat and anxious to continue lining the pockets of friends and relatives, China's rulers will keep rolling the presses, printing an increasingly worthless currency to fuel a dangerously inflated bubble economy.

Bad macroeconomics is not the only reason that China's boom may be short-lived. Possessed of an admittedly rational fear that it is losing control over society, and convinced that entrepreneurs are politically subversive, the old guard in Beijing has proven incapable of permitting individual enterprise to flourish. Private businesses are kept on the margins of the economy and the law, subject to arbitrary enforcement of regulations, many of which are unpublished. China's periodic anticorruption campaigns, for example, invariably target even legitimate private entrepreneurs. At the same time, the central government's control over the provinces dwindles daily. Beijing is helpless to prevent interprovincial trade wars complete with tariffs and roadblocks. In the end, the limitations of Chinese political culture itself provoke the most profound skepticism about Beijing's ability to nurture sustained economic growth.

TOO HOT NOT TO COOL DOWN

Much of China's economic progress, so visible in its major cities, is ephemeral and based on hot money. Loose fiscal policies have spawned easy growth and fast profits, and a skeletal legal structure has allowed this money to accelerate through the economy as investors take advantage of rampant, unregulated and often illicit speculation. Profits are illegally siphoned off from quick-fix ventures, then injected into new speculative schemes or sent abroad, but always with the primary goal of hiding revenues from Beijing. This get-rich-quick risk-taking eschews the kinds of long-term projects that might nurture sustainable growth—precisely because few Chinese investors believe that the current boom can last.

Despite the risks, Chinese and foreign investors have fallen over themselves to make a quick killing in what many outside "experts" have proclaimed will soon be the biggest economy in Asia, if not the world. But far too often, there is less than meets the eye. Said a European diplomat who has witnessed the remarkable changes of the last few years: "The overall view of China seems so positive and yet every time you look closely at something it is a mess. There must be some missing link." A Western China watcher in Hong Kong, who lived in Beijing in the mid-1980s, said the problem is that the Chinese are good at creating a false impression: "It's like Hollywood. The buildings are very impressive from the front, but then you peek behind the facade and find there is nothing there."

By far the most worrisome element in the Chinese macroeconomy is the lack of fiscal and monetary discipline. Despite six years of efforts, macroeconomic levers to regulate rather than control the economy have yet to be put in place. Wu Xiaoling, deputy director of the Banking Reform Department of the People's Bank of China, admitted, "As far as the financial sector goes, the main instrument of control is still administrative." The root cause of the problem is a budget deficit that is spinning out of control. China's Finance Ministry expects the 1994 budget deficit to triple to $7.7 billion. The true deficit, however, will be $14.8 billion—over a fourth of government revenues—if one uses internationally accepted accounting rules and includes debt service payments and excludes "revenues" from bond sales to foreigners.

Last summer, with the renminbi having lost half its value in just months and the money supply up over 50 percent, China's newly minted economic czar, Vice Premier Zhu Rongji, launched an aggressive campaign to rein in the runaway growth of both the money and credit supplies. Zhu's policies met with heated resistance from

enterprises starved for funds and from investors who saw the price of real estate and stocks begin to fall. The squeeze particularly hurt the already shaky and over-manned state sector, threatening to put thousands if not millions of urban proletarians on the street. Provincial leaders with direct access to capital simply refused to cooperate with the austerity program.

The most worrisome element in the Chinese economy is the lack of fiscal and monetary discipline.

Zhu did manage to stabilize the currency and reduce inflation, although urban inflation in October remained above 20 percent. But under extreme pressure from special interests—provincial and local leaders, state enterprise managers, and friends and relatives with a vested interest in loose money—China's ruling gerontocrats blinked. At the Third Plenum of the 14th Party Central Committee in November, Zhu's Superiors declared victory over inflation and reopened the credit taps, which had already begun to flow in October when banks and other financial institutions extended $12 billion in new commercial credits. It is only a matter of time before credit and currency expansion spark inflation again.

The populace is sophisticated enough to realize that the value of its estimated $115 billion in individual savings accounts is being whittled away. The government's offer in early 1993 of three-year treasury notes at 11 percent interest had few voluntary takers—not surprising given the 20 percent urban inflation rate. Despite those difficulties, the Finance Ministry said in March that in 1994 it would sell bonds worth $11.5 billion, three times the amount issued last year.

Government economists argue that there is no danger of runaway inflation. Unlike in 1988 when, according to the *People's Daily*, 34.9 percent of urban households suffered a decline in real income, this time there are plenty of consumer goods around and thus less chance of the kind of panic buying that drives up prices. Nonetheless, the low yields offered by government bond sales reveal a dearth of inflation-proof investment vehicles. The result is the sort of asset inflation indicative of a bubble economy.

THE FLYING YUAN

Drive along the new four-lane highway from the airport into downtown Chengdu, capital of Sichuan, and practically every spare bit of land is fenced off behind a big sign proclaiming a new real estate development. But behind the fences very few have broken ground. That has not, however, stopped those companies from issuing shares. And the fact that the central authorities in Beijing refused to sanction a stock market in Chengdu did not prevent up to 30,000 people a day, seven days a week, from trading the shares of 50 companies, more than on either the Shenzhen or Shanghai exchanges. Nor did it prevent the city of Chengdu from providing an auditorium and collecting a three-yuan entrance fee from all-too-willing punters.

Such trading is haphazard, capitalism in its rawest form. But it is also quite dangerous. There is no auditing of the accounts of these companies. Often investors hardly know what they are buying, other than a piece of paper whose value is supposed to rise. Said a 34-year-old employee of a state industrial enterprise, "I bought a thousand shares at 5.50 yuan per share. When the price goes up in a few weeks I will sell them." But his shares could just as easily prove to be worthless, especially if the market bubble bursts, as has happened repeatedly in hot equity markets in Taiwan and Korea.

While some officials believe that this chaos is part of the maturation process, the mainland's more sophisticated investors are wary of the downside and prefer to invest their capital abroad. The biggest real estate deals in Hong Kong for the past two years have involved mainland investors. While actual foreign direct investment in China topped $15 billion in 1993, mainlanders were spending well over $1 billion on Hong Kong real estate alone. State-owned enterprises like China International Trust and Investment Corp., and China National Technical Import and Export Corp., are casting their nets farther afield with investments in North America and Southeast Asia. Says a Western economist in Beijing, "One wonders why foreigners are so desperate to invest here when the Chinese seem to be so desperate to invest overseas.

One obvious answer is that some of the money is hot. It is almost impossible to discover who the true investors are in many of these real estate deals. Several reportedly involve local and provincial government leaders trying to keep their hard currency earnings out of Beijing's hands or putting aside something for a rainy day. The easiest way to get one's money out is by double invoicing. A local authority or firm will buy a foreign piece of equipment for $1 million but receive an invoice for $1.2 million. The foreign firm then puts the difference in the Chinese partner's bank account. "This happens all the time," said one European businessman, "but now the Chinese have their own middlemen in Hong Kong to handle the double invoicing."

There are official ways of getting money out of the country as well, if one knows the right officials and has the right connections. According to official Chinese statistics, China's total capital outflow in 1992 ballooned to $30.5 billion, an $18.2 billion increase over 1991. Thanks to foreign investment, commercial bank loans and a foreign trade surplus, the country still ran a current account surplus of $6.4 billion. But that surplus was $6.9 billion less than in 1991. In 1993 China's trade deficit ballooned to more than $12 billion at the same time that Chinese investment overseas began to accelerate. As a result, the country's foreign exchange reserves are declining rapidly.

By far the most interesting official number in China's 1992 capital accounts was in the "errors and omissions" category, normally a catchall for odds and ends that don't fit elsewhere. International Monetary Fund experts were reportedly appalled when the Chinese claimed an unexplained outflow of over $6 billion for 1991. Eventually the IMF was satisfied that most of the money was legitimate foreign investment, which China's statisticians did not know how to account for. But in 1992, by which time the Chinese officials knew how to account for legal capital outflows, the total was over $8 billion. Taken together China's 1992 statistics raise serious questions about the health of its financial system and the economic sense of lending money to a country whose citizens seem to be aggressively moving capital abroad. Said Diane Yowell, director of Hongkong Bank China Services Ltd., "You could say that these numbers simply reflect the fact that China is becoming more of an open economy, but they also represent all of the elements of a capital flight scenario."

A DANGEROUS BOTTLENECK

China has gotten all the easy increments of economic growth that come from leaving individuals alone to make money. Now it must find ways to provide capital at all levels of the economy, particularly in the countryside. China's massive capital outflows could not come at a worse time. A capital shortage is already proving to be a potentially dangerous bottleneck to growth, stunting the creation of new jobs and casting vast migrant populations across the country in search of work. It has skewed economic growth by region and slowed the government's sale of unproductive enterprises. The tragedy is that there is plenty of capital in the country, but China's decrepit financial system—coupled with a sense of impending hyperinflation—prevents it from getting to productive enterprises.

The shortage of capital in the countryside has been most obvious in the past two years, as the government has been forced to pay some farmers with IOUS that they have not been able to redeem. A report last year by the official Xinhua news agency said the problem was shaking "the very foundation of agriculture." A veteran China-watching Western diplomat in Hong Kong put it this way: "It was clear that the one thing everyone agreed on [at the spring 1993 session of the National People's Congress] was that they are facing big problems in the countryside."

A Western economist working in Sichuan province put it more bluntly: "The agricultural economy is up against the wall. Incomes continue to rise but not real income, and the relative growth rates between agriculture and industry are diverging." Farmers' net incomes last year were about $87, compared with about $204 for urban workers. Meanwhile, although industrial output rose by 20 percent, agriculture grew by less than four percent. The only answer is more investment, but domestic capital is not heading for the countryside. In Fenghuang, a village 75 kilometers southwest of Chengdu, per capita incomes soared to $170 five years ago but have stagnated since. The village's hope now rests on possible Taiwanese investment in a stone-cutting enterprise.

The capital shortage is just as severe for urban enterprises. The fear of unrest has meant that efforts to trim staffs of state enterprises have foundered. In February, the New China News Agency quoted approvingly Zhou Yougui, director of the Fushun Petrochemical Factory: "We cannot lay off workers as in Western enterprises because this means putting a burden on society." Because money-losing state industries require so much money to keep them afloat, other businesses are crowded out or forced to pay exorbitant interest rates. Even the issuing of corporate bonds was suppressed because the government was unable to market its own paper. Many government officials—national, provincial and local—see foreign investment as their only salvation.

Certainly, foreign capital continues to flood into the region as investment gurus and self-described China "experts" like William Overholt of Bankers Trust continue to advise that China is a buy. But some foreign investors are beginning to have second thoughts about the Chinese gold rush. The legal system offers no protection from unscrupulous Chinese partners, and the incidence of work stoppages is increasing. In 1992, 18 strikes were reported in Guangdong province. Last March in the Zhuhai Special Economic Zone just across the border from Macao, 800 workers at a factory owned by Canon began a strike over pay and working conditions. The workers received about $69 a month, well above even the regional average. But they demanded increases of up to 50 percent plus company-supplied housing. Strikers cited the need for protection against inflation, raging at an estimated 30 percent a year in coastal regions of southern China. But privately they also mentioned that nearby state enterprises were paying higher wages. "China is definitely the place to be," says one Southeast Asian banker, "but we are not really putting our own

money in there. We prefer to act as a bridge for other investors because the risks are very high."

The net result of the capital shortage is a shortage of jobs and opportunities. Sichuan officials estimate that more than a million of their citizens have gone to coastal provinces seeking work. China's urban railroad stations are choked with blue-jacketed peasants who are careening around the country looking for jobs. By one government estimate, China's "floating" population of migrant workers is well over 50 million. Even residents of the more prosperous coastal regions want to migrate, as evidenced by the growing trade in smuggling Chinese into countries like the United States. In spite of the bright future that everyone else seems to see for China, these people are willing to indenture themselves for periods of four years or more in order to pay for passage.

Beijing has thus far followed the imperative for greater reform and increased economic freedom as a matter of simple economic and political survival. Said Richard Margolis, a former British diplomat now active in developing China's securities markets, "The leadership is driven by the simple mathematics of jobs versus job seekers." China has more than 150 million redundant rural workers and expects at least 50 million more by the end of the century. In addition, it adds 10 million new urban workers to the labor force every year. The prospect of mass unemployment and the potential for social unrest that would result has forced the old guard in Beijing to discard not only their vaguely held Marxist tenets, but also their innate fear of the chaos that can result in China whenever central controls are relaxed.

HAMMERING DOWN THE HIGHEST NAIL

While most experts have focused on China's explosive economic growth or its potential for a political explosion, by far the biggest change is its openness—not of the regime, perhaps, but of its citizens, and not just to foreigners. The Chinese people, if they are finally to succeed in modernizing their land, must not only open themselves to the outside world but also to each other in order to take advantage of the remarkable talents suppressed for at least a millennium by a succession of authoritarian regimes.

Analyses of China's potential invariably cite its 4,000-year-old civilization, with an aside to explain the country's lengthy stagnation and more recent crises. In fact, Mao's so-called communism was just the latest variant of an ancient social, political and economic structure that seems designed to throttle individual initiative and progress. Government is presumed to be interested only in the welfare of its people. Change is to be avoided because it might lead to chaos. And individuals must always take a back seat to the interests of the group. A fear of individualism is even ingrained in the language. The Chinese expression for "individual" has a pejorative connotation. Chinese children have drummed into them dozens of proverbs that warn of the dangers of being different—it's the long roof pole that is sawed off; it's the highest nail that gets hammered down; it's the first bird to take flight that is shot.

Economic freedom has encouraged a new openness among Chinese.

Thus despite burgeoning individual initiative, individuals themselves have few effective rights or powers. A successful commercial lawyer in Beijing says that the explosion in the registration of new companies is partly due to that very situation: "Everyone is setting up companies because as an individual you can do nothing but as a company you can do everything." But officially encouraged or not, individualism is the driving force in the country today. Explained Meng Peiyuan, a specialist in Confucianism at the Institute of Philosophy of the Chinese Academy of Social Sciences, "A market economy is a release of the energy of individuals, so any social value system today must be based on individuals."

In fact, economic freedom has encouraged a new openness among Chinese. In the old China, it was not so much the state who controlled people but rather their employer. Without a *danwei*, or work unit, you were nothing. Your *danwei* provided your housing, medical care, education for your children, your pension, your vacation spot, and most of the food you ate, for there was little to buy on the open market. If you lost your job, you were finished. Now there are many other ways to make money. Many private and collective enterprises as well as foreign ventures offer higher salaries but without providing any of the normal perks of a state enterprise. Said one Beijing resident, "It was always possible to quit your job if you were willing to suffer the consequences. Now people just don't care."

The new emphasis on the human spirit is not just an economic phenomenon. Part, too, is long-term fallout from the May–June 1989 uprisings, which touched practically every city in China. The violent crackdown succeeded in cauterizing public dissent, but it could not erase the general realization that millions of other Chinese felt just as strongly about the shortcomings of the regime. The openness takes different forms. Newspapers, for example, are now more likely to carry articles that

present more than one opinion on an important issue—like whether or not the economy is overheating—without endorsing one side or the other. In a March 1993 session at the Chinese Academy of Social Sciences, several of the forum's half-dozen philosophy researchers took public issue with each other on the role of Confucianism in creating a modern social value system.

This sense of liberation extends to all sectors of society. Artists and writers who used to worry about official acceptance so that they could join the Fine Arts Academy or the Writers' Union now thumb their noses at the cultural troglodytes who once arbitrarily anointed society's creative talents. In the countryside, freedom is more circumscribed and tends to follow the more traditional patterns of clan-based villages operating as independent units. Still, it is a start and a considerable one, since 73 percent of the population lives in the countryside. There are over six million communities in the countryside towns and villages—all operating independently.

Haunted by the sense that they are losing social and economic control, China's gerontocrats are trying to reassert political influence. In 1992 top government and party posts were recombined just six years after a formal decision for a split. All five members of the politburo's standing committee have been given top government jobs and responsibilities. The rejoining of party and government functions has reached down to the provincial level as well. Former provincial party secretaries have been made governors. In addition, according to Father Yves Nalet, a Jesuit Sinologist who heads China News Analysis, "They are putting in ideological and security people at all levels."

But the effort is probably too late. Almost daily, people are becoming more independent. A major influence is satellite TV, particularly STAR from Hong Kong. Although technically illegal, 500,000 satellite dishes were sold in China last year. It seems that every third or fourth apartment block in Chengdu has a dish on the roof. "This place has been global-villagized in a minute," says a Western diplomat in Chengdu. Even large towns in the countryside now have satellite dishes. Moreover, in Guangdong province an estimated six million homes watch Hong Kong TV on a regular basis without benefit of satellite dishes. That is more than in Hong Kong itself. There are even some products advertised on Hong Kong TV that are sold exclusively on the mainland.

The local authorities belatedly tried to control the proliferation of satellite dishes and instituted licensing regulations in late 1992. But one only has to say that the dish is needed to watch Gansu TV, and approval is forthcoming. The central government subsequently issued its own decree outlawing satellite dishes, but it has no way to enforce the ban outside the capital. Much of the central government's authority in the past came from control over purse strings. By cutting government offices at the local level adrift it has lost its call on their loyalty.

THE REGIME CANNOT REFORM

This opening up within China was not what Deng Xiaoping had in mind when he began his reforms more than a dozen years ago. Deng is first and foremost a social conservative. The spontaneity of the Cultural Revolution left its mark on him. The original reforms were based on the "household" responsibility system in which whole families contracted with the state to provide grain, produce or some service or handicraft. That provided a nice halfway house between the rigidity of a command economy and the chaos of a free market. To this day, Beijing insists that it is creating not a free-market economy but what is euphemistically called a socialist market economy.

In fact, Deng's limited reforms played themselves out rather quickly. By the mid-1980s the rural sector had achieved all of the gains that were to be had from simply eliminating counterproductive steps like forcing farmers to grow the wrong crops at the wrong times in the wrong places. It also helped to actually pay peasants to grow a crop. In addition, the urban economy had gotten nowhere because private entrepreneurs were completely hamstrung by bureaucratic restrictions and prejudices. What little progress was made came from the so-called collective or cooperative sector, many units of which were thinly disguised private enterprises. But by now, reform-induced prosperity is requisite for the legitimacy of Deng's successors, especially if they continue to interfere with individual initiative.

> *As long as it rulers insist on complete control, China is unlikely to replicate its neighbors' success.*

The noted political scientist Lucian Pye has written, "An ethical-moral dimension of the Confucian sense of legitimacy . . . seems to make the East Asian governments feel that they not only have the right to intervene in people's lives but that they have a definite obligation to do so if it can help improve the people's condition. At one time such interventions tended to be detrimental to economic growth, but that is no longer the case now that government officials know more about how economies grow.

Except in China. Even if the present rulers are not venal, they are certainly ignorant. Some members of the so-called Third Generation of leaders like Zhu Rongji may be better versed in economic theory, but that phalanx will not take over complete control any time soon. And the eventual paramount autocrat from within that group will probably not be someone foolish enough, as Zhu apparently was, to take on entrenched interest groups in the name of macroeconomic stability. Such political bravery, rare enough in stable periods, will be even less likely in the midst of a succession struggle, which has already begun.

China's immensely talented and motivated citizens clearly have the attributes necessary for their country to exceed even the rosiest predictions put forward by true experts on China and naive investment advisers alike. But that was also true in the late nineteenth and early twentieth centuries. The evidence available today suggests that, while chastened, the Chinese Communist Party is no more capable of harnessing the nation's productive potential for long-term development and growth than were its predecessors. But who will dare tell that truth to a "hard" authoritarian regime? More importantly, who could change it?

Both communist and latter-day Confucian states have always faced a dilemma when choosing public servants. In Stalin's day the choice was between "Red or expert." The Confucian conundrum has been between "virtue and merit." The collapse of the Soviet empire was due at least in part to the fact that Stalin and his successors invariably chose the Reds over the experts. Likewise, the success of modern Confucian economies has come in part because, as Pye has written, "In traditional Confucianism stress was placed mainly on the virtues of the upright man who embodied leadership. In recent times the idea of rule by an educated elite has meant the legitimization of technocrats in government." As long as China's rulers insist on complete political control, they will always choose loyalty over competence. As long as that is the case, it is difficult, given its present political structure, to argue that China will replicate the economic success of its neighbors.

Article 6   *Harvard International Review*, Winter 1992/93

The China Syndrome

Prospects for Democracy in the Middle Kingdom

Richard Baum

Richard Baum is a Professor of Political Science at the University of California at Los Angeles. He is currently working on a book on Chinese politics in the era of Deng Xiaoping.

When one million Chinese citizens poured into the streets of Beijing in May 1989, blocking convoys of government troops from entering the city to enforce martial law, they staged the most significant act of public defiance in the forty-year history of the People's Republic of China (PRC). To many on the scene, it appeared that the government of hard-line Premier Li Peng had lost the "Mandate of Heaven" and would soon be swept away in a paroxysm of "people power" similar to the one that engulfed Manila in February 1986.

> *By moving quickly to crush the incipient structures of civil society, the government effectively broke the back of the democracy movement.*

It was not to be. Far from empowering the people, the Beijing Spring turned into the Beijing Massacre. Within hours of the bloody June 4 crackdown the cries of "people power" were silenced. Within days leaders of the Tiananmen democracy movement were under arrest or on the run. Within weeks China's faction-ridden Communist Party leadership closed ranks around a rigid program of law-and-order conservatism. Within months a semblance of political "unity and stability" was restored. Within a year it was "business as usual" throughout the Middle Kingdom.

In view of the cascading collapse of communism in Eastern Europe and the USSR, the survival of China's Marxist-Leninist regime presents an ironic anomaly—ironic because it was in China that the tidal wave of anti-communist protest first crested in 1989 and anomalous because only in China did Leninist leaders succeed in resisting that tidal wave. Alone among communist countries, China seemingly defied the laws of contemporary political physics. (Cuba, North Korea and Vietnam also retain Leninist regimes, but due to relative geopolitical isolation and/or "closed door" economic policies, none of the three experienced significant popular political upheavals in 1989–91.)

Never more than a minor urban-intellectual current in a society consisting mainly of apolitical farmers, China's fledgling democracy movement was dealt a decisive blow on June 4, 1989. But did it die? Although most outside observers agree that communism is a cruel historical anachronism in China, as elsewhere, there is much disagreement over how and when Marxist-Leninist institutions and values will ultimately be replaced. Some still strongly believe that despite the temporary setback suffered by Chinese democracy in 1989, reform-driven forces of market competition, global information diffusion and attendant social changes will propel China from proletarian socialism to democratic capitalism via "peaceful evolution." Others foresee a more sudden, catalytic collapse of Chinese communism sparked by the death of "paramount leader" Deng Xiaoping or by a new inflation-driven, corruption-fed crisis.

While the expectation of sudden collapse once seemed "optimistic" in terms of China's prospects for an early democratic breakthrough, recent events in Eastern Europe and the former Soviet Union—from the catastrophic ethnic implosion of Yugoslavia to the remarkable electoral victory of Lithuania's resurgent Communist Party—have cast strong doubts upon the viability of democratic institutions and values in post-Leninist environments. The apocalyptic optimism of 1989 has given way to a more sober and restrained pessimism because of incipient political fragmentation, ethnic fragmentation and market chaos.

While expectations of a democratic breakthrough have decidedly dimmed, Chinese leaders paradoxically take comfort in the deepening national crises that have engulfed the former communist states of East-Central

Europe and the USSR. In the view of Deng Xiaoping and his elderly associates, the chaos that attended de-communization in Europe, Russia and Central Asia is directly attributable to Mikhail Gorbachev's unwillingness to deal firmly with emergent "bourgeois liberal" tendencies within the Soviet Bloc in the late 1980s. Proponents of democratic reform openly scorned such views as "reactionary" in 1989, but few scoff today. Deng's point is well—albeit grudgingly—taken: the expectation of post-communist democratic stability appears chimerical. Increasingly, the only viable alternative to the scylla of communism and the charybdis of chaos appears to be not pluralist democracy, but some form of post-Leninist neo-authoritarianism. Moreover, the factors that make such an outcome likely for China are precisely the same factors that help explain the failure of China's democracy movement to survive the 1989 Tiananmen crackdown. At least five such factors may be identified:

- Successful economic reform. In Eastern Europe and the Soviet Union, widespread economic distress and consumer despair contributed heavily to the collapse of communism as angry urban consumers joined dissident intellectuals and workers in a wave of anti-government protest. By contrast, a full decade of economic reform in China had served to raise the living standard of most citizens and provide a steady flow of consumer goods into urban markets. Although these gains were partially offset in the late 1980s by an overheated industrial economy and rapidly rising retail prices, the introduction of a government austerity program in the last half of 1988 successfully slowed the inflationary spiral and restored a measure of economic stability. Consequently, even at the height of the political unrest in 1989, there was little evidence of widespread consumer panic or revolt.

By the second half of 1990, China's economy had been successfully jump-started with assistance from burgeoning private and small-collective sectors. A healthy economy provided little incentive for renewed popular political mobilization by anti-government forces. In the southern Chinese province of Guangdong—where market reforms are furthest advanced and the people's standard of living has most dramatically improved—popular enthusiasm for democratic protest has been minimal, even at the height of the Beijing Spring.

- Communist Party unity. The presence of a powerful, legitimate state apparatus of coercion, coupled with widespread popular perceptions of intra-Party conflict and factional strife, contributed substantially to the escalation of student unrest in April and May of 1989. Pro-reform Party Chief Zhao Ziyang's signal of sympathy encouraged student demonstrators in Tiananmen Square to intensify their opposition to Party hard-liners. Zhao's actions enraged Deng Xiaoping,

who quickly removed Zhao and restored the appearance of Party unity. In the aftermath of the June crackdown, Party discipline was rigidly reimposed. All party members and cadres were required to denounce the "counterrevolutionary rebellion" and reaffirm their support for a conservative Party line. The public's perception of absolute, unwavering Party unity in support of the crackdown was a vitally important part of the attempt to discourage renewed protest.

- Military discipline. The dampening effects of a robust economy and a unified Communist Party were further reinforced by the generally high degree of political loyalty and discipline displayed by the Chinese People's Liberation Army (PLA) throughout the Tiananmen crisis. Despite numerous reports of military morale problems—including over 100 incidents involving army officers failing to obey orders—the PLA generally maintained discipline within its ranks throughout the May–June crackdown, averting the type of massive military defections that later sealed the fate of both the Ceausescu regime in Romania and the plotters of the abortive August 1991 Soviet coup attempt. Moreover, neither the PLA, with its long-standing guerilla tradition of cultivating close ties with civilians, nor the Chinese internal security forces (the People's Armed Police), has ever been a symbol of political oppression in China. Both of these factors—strong military discipline and a long tradition of civil-military harmony—clearly served to dampen popular enthusiasm for further revolt after the June crackdown.

- Absence of "civil society." Further reducing the mobilizational capacity of pro-democracy forces after June 4 was the virtual lack of any viable Chinese tradition or infrastructure of "civil society." The presence of a powerful, legitimate and coercive state apparatus, coupled with the near-total absence of autonomous, self-confident social forces—such as independent trade unions, churches, newspapers, student organizations or commercial associations—clearly contributed to the dearth of popular resistance to the June 4 crackdown. In contrast, Eastern European quasi-autonomous civic groups such as Charter 77, Civic Forum, Solidarity and the Catholic Church remained alive as focal points for the aggregation of social protest during the darkest days of communist regime repression.

In view of the important role played by civic associations in Eastern Europe, it is hardly accidental that the Chinese government attached highest priority during the June crackdown to the arrest of the leaders of newborn independent newspapers, student organizations and labor unions. By moving quickly to crush the incipient structures of civil society, the government effectively broke the back of the democracy movement. Once the initial shock of the June 4 massacre wore off, the most common attitude displayed by ordinary Chinese citizens was one of resignation and withdrawal—highly symptomatic of a politically atomized and inarticulate population.

- Fear of "chaos." Finally, the potential for renewed democratic protest was visibly diminished by pervasive popular fear of *luan* (chaos). This phobia, deeply ingrained in China's political culture, was played upon incessantly by regime propagandists in the months following the Tiananmen debacle. Reinforced by visible public anxiety over the effects of the Soviet political disintegration of 1991, the regime's propaganda campaign clearly produced the intended effect. Large numbers of ordinary Chinese citizens—including many erstwhile supporters of the 1989 democracy movement—began to cite "fear of chaos" as a primary reason for their lack of enthusiasm for renewed political demonstrations. Paradoxically, the Soviet collapse, far from accelerating the process of political change in China, had a powerfully conservative and retardant effect.

The Neo-Authoritarian Alternative

Although conditions in China appear manifestly unripe for an early, self-sustaining democratic breakthrough, there are abundant signs of change in the priorities and values of China's communist leaders. As the last surviving members of the original "Yenan generation" of socialist revolutionaries withdraw from politics and "prepare to meet Marx," their place is being taken by younger, better educated, more cosmopolitan cadres. While hardly qualifying as political liberals, most of these younger leaders—such as Politburo members Li Ruihuan, Tian Jiyun and Zhu Rongji—are less rigidly bound by Marxist-Leninist dogmas than their conservative predecessors. Generally in their fifties, most are firmly committed to pushing swiftly ahead with structural reforms in the Chinese economy. Advocating a combination of strong, centralized political leadership and dispersed market-driven economic decision making, these men are China's emerging "neo-authoritarians, or market Marxists."

The credo of neo-authoritarianism (*xin quanweizhuyi*) was first formally outlined by the now-disgraced Zhao Ziyang. In his report to the Thirteenth Party Congress in 1987, Zhao presented a blueprint for a highly centralized, non-dogmatic political system under a strong leader who would govern in consultation with bodies such as the Chinese People's Political Consultative Conference (CPPCC) under the nominal supervision of an indirectly elected National People's Congress.

In the absence of competitive political parties, direct legislative elections or a constitutional separation of powers, neo-authoritarian leaders would solicit "consent of the governed" through periodic plebiscites, opinion polls and the routinized articulation of group interests. There would be, however, little popular participation in the selection of leaders or policies. Incipient political discontent or opposition would be discouraged through strict controls on permissible speech and behavior.

Economic growth provides the key to the viability of neo-authoritarianism. Under a neo-authoritarian Chinese regime, the state would assume a vigorous entrepreneurial role, expanding the scope of free-market activity and promoting the country's global competitiveness through adoption of comprehensive industrial/trade policies. Several key institutions of Marxism-Leninism-Stalinism, including public ownership of industry and centralized state planning, would be eliminated. Under the technocratic ethos of neo-authoritarianism, strong pressures would be generated to reform the massive Chinese bureaucracy along merit-based civil service lines. Consequently, the role of the *nomenklatura*—the Communist Party's traditional system of politically-based personnel recruitment, promotion and dismissal—would be dramatically curtailed.

At best, a neo-authoritarian China might begin to converge with the much-publicized East Asian model of "soft authoritarianism" as practiced in Taiwan and South Korea between 1975–1987. That is, under conditions of sustained economic growth, a calm international environment, a politically quiescent citizenry and an entrepreneurial (rather than parasitic) political leadership, it is conceivable that China could begin to evolve, within one or two decades, into a proto-pluralistic East Asian NIC.

Two keys to such an optimistic outcome will be, first, the government's success in keeping rural birth rates low while developing programs to absorb almost two hundred million surplus farm workers into high-value-added, non-agricultural jobs; and second, the emergence of a basically articulate, self-confident urban middle class, capable eventually of acting as a restraint on one-party government.

Failing this, deepening demographic and socio-economic stresses could lead China toward a more regressive (and repressive) form of authoritarianism known as "neo-conservatism" (*xin baoshouzhuyi*). Currently favored by some members of China's so-called "Princes' Party"—the pampered offspring of Beijing's senior gerontocrats who currently occupy top positions in China's banking, finance and parastatal trading companies—neo-conservatism places substantially greater emphasis on gradualism and caution in economic reform and on continued state and/or Communist Party control over commodity production and distribution. It also calls for a renaissance in traditional, conservative Confucian culture and values to counteract the perceived threat of "peaceful evolution" and "bourgeois liberalization" from the West. Under a neo-conservative Chinese regime, substantially greater emphasis would be placed on political discipline, hierarchy and harmony while little scope would be allowed for autonomous socio-economic activity or the articulation/representation of group interests.

To its proponents, including Chen Yuan—deputy director of the People's Bank of China and son of communist patriarch Chen Yun—the neo-conservative agenda offers the hope of enhanced political stability and popular quiescence. To its detractors, who see in neo-conservatism a highly elitist ethos of state patrimonialism, there are ominous overtones of nascent fascism.

Pitfalls in Predicting the Future

Although the political outlook for China over the next decade is decidedly more authoritarian/conservative than democratic, there are a number of intervening variables that could dramatically alter the equation. While unlikely, a sudden collapse of the communist system is not out of the question. With economic graft, corruption, speculation and profiteering increasing at an alarming

rate; with traditional Marxist-Leninist visions and values demonstrably failing to inspire China's increasingly alienated, materialistic, money-oriented youth; with provincial and local governments increasingly asserting their economic muscle in defiance of central authority; and with ethnic tensions growing more volatile at the periphery, China's future political stability and integrity are by no means assured.

Currently the Fourteenth National Congress of the CCP is meeting to endorse Deng Xiaoping's plan to further accelerate China's economic reforms. According to informed reports, serious discussion of political reform has once again been postponed indefinitely. Reflecting the growing potency of China's middle-aged technocrats, the new Central Committee and Politburo selected by the Party Congress reportedly contained enlarged cohorts of neo-authoritarians and neo-conservatives. Just who among them—the "market Marxists" or the "pampered princes"—will prevail after Deng Xiaoping passes from the scene is far from clear. In either case, China is unlikely to provide fertile soil for the development of democratic pluralism any time soon.

Article 7

The Economist, June 4th 1994

CHINA'S COMMUNISTS

The road from Tiananmen

With the Tiananmen Square massacre five years ago, China's Communist Party saw off the latest serious challenge to its rule. The next challenge is coming from within, as the party's get-rich-quick policies breed corruption and regional rivalries that are tearing at its own fabric.

For a political organisation born supposedly of mass mobilisation and peasant revolution, the Chinese Communist Party has always set a lot of store by exclusivity. On the eve of China's "liberation" from the Nationalist government in 1949, only one person in a thousand in China was a Communist Party member, according to the late Lazlo Ladany, a Jesuit priest and China-watcher. Marshal Nie Rongzhen, who commanded Mao Zedong's forces in northern China, wrote in a memoir that there were just 3,000 party members and 5,000 collaborators in Beijing when the communist ar-

mies swept into the city. In Shanghai, a city of 9m people even in 1949, there were just 8,000 party members to orchestrate "the people's will". Hardly surprising that photographs of the PLA's triumphant entry into both cities show that the crowds lining the streets were wearing expressions of suspicion as often as of jubilation.

Once in government, the party has never allowed its membership to rise above 5% of China's population. The figure today is 4.3%, or 52m people, of whom 30m are cadres (full-time party officials or managers of state-owned

firms). A monopoly of political power over all China resides formally with this relative handful of people.

The formative years of organising illegally through underground cells and guerrilla units shaped the Communist Party into a force that was disciplined, motivated, loyal and obsessively secretive. It came to power convinced of the need to create socialism, determined to bend China to its will, and prepared to root out not merely those who were known to be its enemies but also anyone who it thought disposed to become an enemy in the future. Institutions that might have checked the party's power—the courts, for example—were devalued or destroyed. The state continued in name, but without any authority distinct from that of the Communist Party. Organisations of all kinds, including government ministries and large corporations, were run by the party committees planted within them.

Individuals were allowed no private life exempt from the scrutiny of officialdom, no freedom to choose where they lived or worked. Neighbourhood committees kept watch on local streets. Travel was impossible without a myriad of papers and permissions. The media were controlled by the party and used primarily for propaganda. Businesses were seized. In the towns, the party controlled all jobs. In the countryside, it bought all produce and owned all land. A person "belonged" in every sense of the word to his work-unit, which allocated housing, education and health care. By these means, and by the often savage punishment of resisters, the communist elite controlled a billion people.

As the years passed, however, so the memory of China's pre-revolutionary hardships began to fade. They were supplanted by memories of more recent hardships engineered by the Communist Party itself—such as the Great Leap Forward of 1958–61, an attempt at cottage-industrialisation which produced a famine that killed 30m–40m people; and the Cultural Revolution, which plunged the country into anarchy from 1966–69 with aftershocks well into the mid-1970s. After the death of Mao in 1976 and the chaotic interlude of the Gang of Four, a powerful section of the party leadership saw that China had been taken as far as it would go down the road of autarkic stagnation and political strife. If Mao Zedong had found little to inspire him in the notions of social calm and rising living standards, these were the things for which those who had been his subjects

now hungered. Deng Xiaoping, who rose to power in 1977–78, decided that economic growth had to take precedence over class-struggle politics. This crucial reversal, once it aid been accepted as party doctrine in late 1978, made possible the opening wide of China's economy to foreign trade and investment (see chart on this page), and with it an era of fabulous growth.

Heirs of the dogma

Today, 16 years after Deng Xiaoping's ascent, it is far from clear that even Mr Deng himself saw how far his programme of economic reform would eventually lead. Half of China's industrial output, and perhaps 75% of its total output, is now accounted for by private or "collective" firms; something drastic will have to be done with the half of industry that remains in state hands, for it is an all but insupportable drain on the national budget. And, while it is not quite true to claim—as even some of China's own communists now do—that economic reform has led the Communist Party to abandon ideology altogether, its policies and rhetoric are deeply confused.

Not even the most hard-line of Chinese communists now dares challenge the principles of Deng Xiaoping's reforms, even if some might secretly like to. But the party still numbers "Marxism-Leninism-Mao-Zedong-Thought" among its "four cardinal principles"; and even for the more progressive communists, decades of knee-jerk obedience to Marxist slogans have created habits of mind that are hard to shake off. The upshot is that, even while money-madness sweeps China, slogans which pay lip-service to socialist values are still popular.

In 1987, when Zhao Ziyang was at his zenith as Communist Party general secretary (he fell in disgrace during Tiananmen), the party settled on the notion that China was in a "primary stage of social-

ism". This was shorthand for the argument that socialism had to be built on a strong economy, and that non-socialist methods might be needed to achieve that strength. The reformers could thus get on with liberalising the economy while pretending that their long-term plan was still to build socialism.

Mr Zhao's slogan disappeared with him. Deng Xiaoping's own ingenious coinage, "socialism with Chinese characteristics" has proved more durable—perhaps because it is as much nationalist as it is socialist. Its precise meaning changes with each new policy: these days party members add "market" to the beginning of the phrase. Crustier communists prefer to stay close to the "four cardinal principles", which are (in addition to Marxism-Leninism-Mao-Zedong-Thought) the socialist road, the dictatorship of the proletariat, and the leadership of the Communist Party. With Mr Deng now 89 years old and failing, the interplay of slogans may reveal something of what one American China-watcher, Andrew Nathan of Columbia University, calls the "pre-post-Deng manoeuvrings". Supporters of Mr Deng's camp are now championing him as China's "Great Theorist"—elevating him, in effect, above Mao. Opponents are appealing even more than usual to the "four cardinal principles", a way to celebrate Mao but not Mr Deng. Jiang Zemin, whose positions as China's president and Communist Party general secretary give him a claim to be seen as Mr Deng's successor, is busy recommending the assiduous study of his patron's writings.

These internal and doctrinal arguments pale, however, beside the question of whether the party as a whole can preserve its grip on political power in the face of the economic liberalisations it has unleashed. The party survived the 1989 challenge to that power by ordering the massacre of people demonstrating in Beijing against its dictatorship. To judge from its internal panic, the leadership saw that event as a close-run thing. Now, five years later and despite a brief austerity drive in 1990–91, economic reform is running faster and further still, shrinking the party's power to plan the economy from the centre, strengthening the position of cities and provinces, and giving many more people previously unheard-of freedoms including the choice of where to live, work and spend money.

In 1979 there were—officially at least—no Chinese recorded as working in privately-owned businesses. Now, the official figure is 30m, and that is doubt-

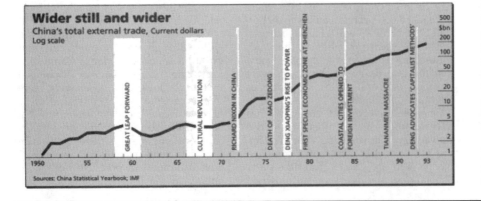

Wider still and wider
China's total external trade, Current dollars
Log scale

GREAT LEAP FORWARD
CULTURAL REVOLUTION
RICHARD NIXON IN CHINA
DEATH OF MAO ZEDONG
DENG XIAOPING'S RISE TO POWER
FIRST SPECIAL ECONOMIC ZONE AT SHENZHEN
COASTAL CITIES OPENED TO FOREIGN INVESTMENT
TIANANMEN MASSACRE
DENG ADVOCATES 'CAPITALIST METHODS'

500
$bn
200
100
50
20
10
5
2
1

1950   55   60   65   70   75   80   85   90   93

Sources: China Statistical Yearbook; IMF

less a substantial underestimate. "Township and village enterprises" (TVES)—light industrial groups with shared and often informal ownership—employ another 90m, and account for over a third of China's industrial output. The new mobility of labour has undermined the household registration system. Farmers, too, have been largely freed from the constraints of the state. To see how this hurts the party, start at ground level.

More equal than others

Its big cities aside, China is a vast country of 4m rural villages and 700m farmworkers. One of the Communist Party's strengths is, still, to be the nearest thing China has to a universal organisation; but its rural presence is decaying fast.

In the 1950s and 1960s, the hey-day of collectivisation, village cadres would transmit the orders from on high about how collectivisation should be carried out or carried further, what was to be grown, and what prices the government would pay for crops to feed the cities. But Mr Deng's "family responsibility system" abolished Mao's collective farms, restored households as the unit of production, and allowed part of the crop to be sold on the free market. As the countryside grew richer, prosperity lured some cadres back to the family farm or into private enterprise, leaving empty desks behind them. Others hung on to their authority simply in order to extort money from the villagers under their control. In the main, according to John Burns of the University of Hong Kong, who has studied village organisation in China, villages have returned to the kinship politics that prevailed before the communist revolution.

This loss of authority in the countryside might be less worrying for the Communist Party were it not that the countryside has at the same time been growing more restless. Rural incomes, which rose fast during the 1980s, are now stagnating. Farm prices are being capped again by the central government as an anti-inflation measure. Peasants who have remained on the land are growing envious of the much-flaunted new wealth of China's cities. Worse, some local governments have been paying for crops with IOUS that they cannot redeem; and remittances sent back to the farms by peasants who have migrated to work in the booming coastal provinces of Guangdong and Fujian appear to be drying up, or vanishing along the way. *Contemporary*, a Hong Kong China-watching journal, reports that 44 rural post offices have been ransacked in the past year by angry farmers.

The effect of stagnant incomes and increases in farm productivity is to drive people off the land at a growing pace. The World Bank estimates that there are 100m–150m displaced rural workers on the move in China, a huge and potentially volatile population. The great past challenges to authority in China—the Taiping rebellion of 1850–64, the communist revolution itself—came from the countryside. To judge from the urgency with which the Communist Party has been calling for rural "stability" this past year, it appears to be seriously worried that rural dissatisfaction might once again boil over into insurrection.

The problem would undoubtedly be more acute still, had the TVES not been so successful in soaking up labour. Their proliferation was encouraged by the party as a buffer between countryside and city that might absorb the shock of population movements. They have done that job well, but they have also proved so profitable that they have drifted almost entirely out of the party's control. In its place have come other groups including clans, syndicates of local businessmen and—particularly along the so-called "Gold Coast" of the maritime provinces—diverse extortionists, smugglers and criminal gangs, whose interest in paying taxes to or otherwise co-operating with the central government is minimal.

Breaking with Beijing

Relations between the central government on the one hand, and China's 22 provinces, three metropolitan areas and five "autonomous regions", on the other, are even more troubling for the party. The extreme case is Guangdong, which leads China in trade and inward investment and is largely self-financing. It pays little of its tax revenues to the central government and receives little central-government investment in return. This year, the central government is trying to bring China's growth rate down to 9% from 13% last year. Guangdong's response has been to thumb its nose at instructions and carry on profiting from its inflows of foreign investment and its synergies with Hong Kong. Shenzhen, the "special economic zone" next to Hong Kong, grew by 30% in real terms last year and has no plans to grow by a piffling 9% anytime soon. With Guangdong setting, to all intents and purposes, its own economic policy, the reality is a schism between at least one big provincial Communist Party and the central authorities in Beijing.

The central government is desperate to ensure that China's other economic powerhouses do not follow Guangdong towards de facto autonomy. Shanghai is only now being granted, slowly, the autonomy that Guangdong was given a decade ago. But the process of devolution, and the regional rivalries it has created, may already be too far advanced for the centre to regain its grip. Even poor and inaccessible provinces are setting up economic zones to mimic those of coastal provinces. Beggar-my-neighbour policies—tariffs and import controls at provincial borders, tax breaks for local businesses—are becoming a way of life. Provincial governments hungry for new revenues are neglecting investment in infrastructure while they speculate in property and invest in light industries and service businesses that they hope will bring quick returns. Taxes are handed over grudgingly, if at all; the ratio of central government revenue to GNP has dropped from more than 30% at the end of the 1970s to 19% today. It remains to be seen whether the national tax reforms enacted at the beginning of this year will succeed in giving more control over China's purse-strings back to the central authorities.

As dreams of wealth have gone to the heads of local governments, so they have gone to the heads of many individual Communist Party members. Corruption is widespread and flagrant at the township, county and even provincial level. An anti-corruption drive, reputedly the biggest in a decade, is now under way, with mass public trials and summary executions; a clutch of cadres was shot last month in Shenzhen. But while this may be enough to strike fear briefly into local cadres, the higher ranks of the party are still being left untouched. Official newspapers are sometimes directed to rail against the "big monkeys"; but China's senior officials have neither the will nor perhaps the means to go about purging their own.

The depth of corruption within the party is impossible to gauge but easy to guess at—just count the stolen limousines with smoked-glass windows that cruise the boulevards of China's cities. So completely has the culture of money saturated the party that anything done in the name of wealth-creation, save for the crudest bribe-taking, seems permissible. How, for example, to judge the minister who, ordered to live off a state-owned conglomerate, simply quits his government job after naming himself head of the company?

Few of the party's most senior members need to stoop to enriching themselves; they have families to do it. Entrepreneurs and bankers in China and Hong Kong will flock to bring foolproof deals to the son or daughter of a leader, hoping for favours in return. These "princelings" may be the children of provincial grandees, or central committee members, or even of Deng Xiaoping himself: the interests of one of Mr Deng's sons, Zhifang, include a private property company in Hong Kong that does business with mainland companies listed on the colony's stock exchange.

Big money from China, some of it hot and some of it not, is conspicuous in Hong Kong's property and share markets. Probably more than $20 billion of Chinese capital has flowed over the border into Hong Kong shell companies in recent years. Often, the money is channelled back into China as the "foreign investment" component of a joint venture project; this wins the tax and foreign-exchange privileges granted to such projects. In theory, this money may still belong to such-and-such a Chinese organisation; but in practice much of it has passed into the control of individuals who cannot be held to account.

When the party's over

Officially, the Communist Party professes itself aware of the need for vigilance and reform. It sees that economic liberalisation has raised people's expectations and it is trying hard to co-opt interests that might otherwise coalesce into rival centres of power. It is starting to champion consumer rights, workers' rights against foreign employers, even environmental concerns. It is wondering, too, how to streamline a central government that boasts 400 different ministries and bureaus, and it is circling again around an idea—once advocated by Mr Zhao—of developing a more professional civil service to give more backbone to the state. But these are all, essentially, refinements. It is still heresy to question the party's basic claim to control every lever of political power.

If it does worry privately about its future, the party may take comfort from its relatively steady relations with the army, despite a purge of fractious officers in 1992. Mao held that the "the party rules the gun"; in practice, the relationship has proved rather more ambivalent, the two hierarchies being scarcely separable. Every officer of the PLA is a party member; the army's interests are championed by a retired general, Liu Huaqing, who holds a seat on the Standing Committee of the Politburo, the apex of the party's command structure. The PLA's budget has been raised by a quarter this year. Many of its units are profiting from economic reform: they run private businesses on the side. By one estimate, the PLA now owns about 20,000 commercial companies, half of them in Guangdong.

There is little to suggest, therefore, that the army would not do again today what it did at Tiananmen Square in 1989, if the party were faced with another challenge to its monopoly of power. And that might be enough to secure the party's place, were history simply to repeat itself. But in the years since Tiananmen, the new dangers that face the party may have grown into more of a threat to it than idealistic students could ever hope to be. Its enemies now are corruption, fragmentation and loss of purpose. Against those, tanks can offer no defence.

Article 8   *Current History*, September 1992

China as a Regional Power

"Can a weak, oppressive state be expected to act asa responsible and peace-loving regional power? The once widely shared image of a China in disintegration and of a dragon rampant in Japan and Southeast Asia seems to be moving perilously close to reality."

Samuel S. Kim

Samuel S. Kim teaches at the Woodrow Wilson School of Public and International Affairs, Princeton University. He has written extensively on East Asian international relations and world order studies. His most recent book, coedited with Lowell Dittmer, is China's Quest for National Identity (Ithaca, N.Y.: Cornell University Press, 1993).

What can we say about China's status as a regional power in the post–cold war era? The question seems elementary yet defies an easy answer since, in international relations, the perception of power matters as much as the reality of it. In the Chinese case there persists the belief that China, by dint of its demographic weight or the greatness of its civilization, has a natural and inalienable right to great power status. The country's erratic shifts in foreign policy behavior over the years have been based on the conviction that China's strategic value can never be taken for granted by any external power, for it is both willing and able to play a decisive role in reshaping the structure of global high politics.

Yet while the cold war helped China project power well beyond the Asia-Pacific region, its end stripped away the veil of the China mystique and the semblance of Chinese influence in international life. The ending of the cold war has also shattered the illusion of a consensus on what constitutes a "superpower," made evident by the rise of Japan as a global power of a different kind (a one-dimensional global power), the sudden "third worldization" of the former Soviet Union, and America's heroic but ineffective claim of global leadership without bearing the costs and responsibilities.

Just as Japan is seen as a wallet in search of a global role, China has become an empty seat on the United Nations Security Council searching for a new national identity. Suddenly, Beijing is unsure of its place in a world no longer dominated by superpower rivalry and the country is in the grip of an unprecedented legitimacy-identity crisis. Not since the founding of the People's Republic in 1949 have the questions of internal and external legitimacy—catalyzed by the Tiananmen carnage and the collapse of global communism—been as conflated as in the past three years.

CHINA'S ASIAN IDENTITY

Handwritten: threat to other A. countries

The China threat—the image of a dragonrampant—looms large in the security calculus of every Asian state. Yet China's identity as a regional power is deeply problematic. Although most of the country's external relations pivot around the Asia-Pacific region, Beijing has yet to come up with any coherent definition of its place in Asian international relations.

The starting point for understanding China's awkward regional identity—and its inability to maintain any deep and enduring friendship with any Asian state, including North Korea—is to recognize that since the collapse of the traditional Sinocentric world order in the late nineteenth century, this proud and frustrated Asian giant has had enormous difficulty finding a comfortable place as an equal member state in the family of nation-states. During the cold war years the People's Republic succumbed to wild swings of identity, rotating through a series of roles: self-sacrificing junior partner in the Soviet-led socialist world; self-reliant hermit completely divorced from and fighting both superpowers; the revolutionary vanguard of an alternative United Nations; self-styled third world champion of a New International Economic Order; status quo-maintaining "partner" of NATO and favored recipient of largesse at the World Bank; and now, lone socialist global power in a postcommunist world.

None of these identities has much to do with Asian regional identity. The vast gap between being and becoming in the drive for status—and the contradiction between being a regional power and having global aspirations—have introduced a fundamental paradox in the prioritization of China's multiple identities: China as a socialist country; China as an anti-imperialist actor taking a radical system-transforming approach to world order; China as a poor developing country entitled to maximum preferential treatment in trade, investment, aid, and technology transfers; China as an irre-

Handwritten: What is it's identity?

dentist power flexing its military muscle power to defend its extensive territorial claims; China as a deft practitioner of *zhoubian* (good-neighbor) diplomacy; and China as a nuclear power, breaking the superpower nuclear duopoloy.

REGIONAL FOREIGN POLICY FACES

China's regional policy is Janus-faced, drawing on avariety of instrumentalities—force and diplomacy, positive and negative sanctions—in influencing its Asian neighbors. Caught between the twin pressures of globalism and unilateralism-cum-bilateralism, China has yet to define and proclaim a distinct regional role or a set of principles guiding its policy in Asia. China's regional policy seems no more than a blurred image of its changing definition of the world situation.

During much of the cold war, China's regional policy was a stepchild of its global superpower policy. All the turning points in Chinese foreign policy, though instantly reverberating throughout the entire region, concerned the United States and/or the Soviet Union. For example, in 1979 China justified its war against Vietnam in terms of global security imperatives, not as a matter of bilateral or even regional conflict. And until recently, even Beijing's Middle East policy could best be understood as a reaction to global events dominated by the superpowers rather than to indigenous conflicts in that region.

Since mid-1984, however, a significant readjustment has occurred in the form of a "world peace and development line" accompanied by a more positive view of an Asia-Pacific economic community. In mid-1985 the Central Military Commission directed the People's Liberation Army (PLA) to reorient its military strategy from the preparation for general nuclear war with the Soviet Union to the preparation for local and regional wars on China's periphery.

The most significant effect of these readjustments in Chinese thinking is the gradual process of decoupling local and regional conflicts from superpower rivalry. The ending of the cold war and the disintegration of the Soviet Union have accelerated this process. This does not mean that the center of gravity has shifted from hard globalism to soft regionalism. Instead, China's regional security policy has now become a function of its nationalism-unilateralism in bilateral clothing.

Despite the remarkable foreign policy achievements between 1978 and 1988,

and the recovery from the Western sanctions imposed after Tiananmen, China cannot be characterized as a satisfied status quo power. Post-Mao China redefined the central challenge to its foreign policy in terms of making the outside world safe for its born-again modernization drive. By May 1989 China had fully normalized relations with both superpowers, and was able to enjoy the best of both the first capitalist and second socialist worlds. And yet China's strategic behavior remained anchored in and driven by the holy trinity of state sovereignty, state status, and state security.

Handwritten margin: prioritization lay?

The challenge of transforming these multiple Chinas into a unified multinational state is another obstacle in the development of multilateral regionalism. In the wake of Tiananmen, the quest for national identity-cum-national unification may have suffered a lethal blow. At the same time China is an irredentist regional military power: China has more territorial disputes with its neighbors—including Japan—than any other major or middle-ranking power in the world. With its international reputation in collapse, its ideological appeal virtually nonexistent, its scientific and technological power obviously weak, and its strategic value marginalized in post–cold war world affairs, Beijing has taken on the role of becoming the dominant military power in East Asia. Thus, as part of its strategy to dominate the South China Sea, China has been building up its naval and air power. Official military spending this year is $6.8 billion, less than half of actual military spending but still up 52 percent from 1989. China has also been bargain-hunting in Russia and Ukraine for advanced weapons systems. It has bought 24 Su-27 fighter aircraft from Russia that are scheduled to be delivered in late 1992, and it is reportedly interested in buying an aircraft carrier, the *Varyag*, that Ukraine is building.

Handwritten margin: only mil. power tol.

The dogged determination to construct national identity in terms of sovereignty, status, and security stands in the way of responding positively to proposals for a regional collective security system. Soviet President Mikhail Gorbachev's initial overtures for a comprehensive security system for the entire Asia-Pacific region have been turned back to bilateral negotiations in order to exert pressure to meet China's three security demands, which China presents as the only way to renormalize relations. Beijing has also vetoed similar Australian, Canadian, and Japanese proposals for a multilateral Asia-Pacific security conference—a sort of Conference on Se-

C. not interested in regional mil. pacts, but bilateral agreements

curity and Cooperation in Asia. As Li Luye, director general of the China Centre for International Studies, put it: "Any attempt to copy Europe's model of collective security or to duplicate the pattern of integration of the two Germanies in Northeast Asia is not realistic and could by no means bring peace and stability to this area."[1]

Ex.

Chinese strategic analysts reject the notion that the seabed resources of disputed areas in the South China Sea should be jointly developed. China's resort to force in March 1988 in the Spratly (Nansha) Islands of the South China Sea served as a reminder of Beijing's growing naval power—and its willingness to use it if necessary—in a resource-rich area of more than 3.6 million square kilometers. The disputed Spratly and Paracel (Xisha) island groups in the South China Sea represent East Asia's most dangerous and contentious multilateral maritime issue. Seven Asia-Pacific states—Brunei, China, Indonesia, Malaysia, the Philippines, Taiwan, and Vietnam—have competing claims to the islands and have sometimes fought over the possibly oil-rich Spratly Islands.

(or huge $)

China, Taiwan, South Korea, and Japan are also locked in a dispute over the Diaoyu (Senkaku in Japanese) Islands farther north in the East China Sea. To possess the Diaoyu Islands, which comprise five islands some 166 kilometers northeast of Taiwan, is to have legal jurisdiction over about 21,645 square kilometers of continental shelf that is believed to hold up to 100 billion barrels of oil.

At the second international conference on "Joint Efforts for Development: Prevention of Conflicts," held in Bandung, Indonesia, in August 1991, Chinese officials strongly opposed both the establishment of a multilateral regime for handling territorial disputes and the intrusion of outside powers (that is, Japan, the United States, and the Soviet Union), maintaining that disputes should be resolved by the countries directly involved on a bilateral basis.

Against this backdrop, on February 25, 1992, the National People's Congress adopted "The Law of the People's Republic of China on Its Territorial Waters and Their Contiguous Areas," which, according to Article 1, will "enable the People's Republic of China to exercise its sovereignty over its territorial waters and its rights to exercise control over their adjacent areas, and to safeguard state security as well as its maritime rights and interests." Article 2 says China's territorial sovereignty includes

"the mainland and its offshore islands, Taiwan and the various affiliated islands including Diaoyu Islands, Penghu Islands, Dongsha Islands, Xisha Islands, Nansha Islands, and other islands that belong to the PRC."[2] The law gives the Chinese military the right to repel by force any foreign incursion into the stipulated islands and areas.

The law's promulgation provoked strong protests from Japan and several Association of Southeast Asian Nations members who had competing territorial claims to the islands. Tellingly, China's unilateral legislation came just before Communist party Secretary General Jiang Zemin's state visit to Japan to mark the twentieth anniversary of the restoration of diplomatic relations. The Chinese legislative strike sparked demonstrations by ultranationalist Japanese groups, marring Jiang's talks with Prime Minister Kiichi Miyazawa.

For China there is little room for compromise precisely because of the fusing of sovereignty, security, status, and economic issues. In domestic politics no Chinese leader can appear soft on the Japanese. Equally significant is the fact that the post–cold war strategic environment in this contested area presents a timely challenge and opportunity for China to strengthen its blue-water naval power.

The general silence and passivity on regional arms control and disarmament issues, in contrast to its activism in global arms control and disarmament (ACD) forums, bespeak Beijing's acute concern that the establishment of a multilateral arms control regime would cut too close to China's expansive regional security zone. Regional arms control processes would also pressure Beijing either to cooperate or defy them. Chinese behavior in arms control and disarmament talks follows a maxi-mini principle of maximizing narrowly construed security interests while minimizing normative costs by projecting China as part of the global solution.

This is a calculated, dual-track policy at work, giving moral and rhetorical support to global ACD programs—and free-riding off superpower arms control processes—while at the same time taking selective unilateral disarmament measures (for example, the demobilization of 1 million PLA troops). Regional arms control is not part of the policy. Since 1985 Beijing has been shifting from quantitative expansion to qualitative improvement with the aim of making its armed forces leaner and meaner. However, Chinese realpolitik is always at its

Machiavellian best in the behind-the-scenes bilateral negotiations, minimizing the danger of a true believer being suddenly caught in a red-light district.

REASSESSING CHINESE POWER

power is import

The Chinese concept of power is broad, dynamic, and shifting, fed by historical traditions and experiences. Reacting to the growth of the "decline" school in American studies of international relations, the new game nations now play is said to be a multidimensional notion of "comprehensive national strength" based on population, resources, economic power, science and technology, military affairs, culture, education, and diplomacy.

even stealing

Of this list, science and technology have become the master key for China in its intense drive toward the promised land of modernity. If China is to become a global power, it must beef up its national power, especially in high-technology industries. There is no escape from this high-tech rat race if China is ever to regain its proper place—"global citizenship" (qiuji)—in the emerging world order.

The government claims that science and technology do not have a class character; indeed, they are rationalized as a kind of global collective goods. Such a realpolitik—nationalistic technocracy dressed in hard globalism—is what is meant by "global citizenship." It also bespeaks the persistence of the nineteenth-century "ti-yong" dilemma—how to strengthen Chinese essence by using foreign technology.

Whether or not the party-state controls the guns, such technocratic realism gives the military a comparative advantage in shaping national policy. Without sufficient military power, according to China's strategic analysts, it will be impossible to preserve and enhance the country's status as a world power or play a decisive role in global politics. In the wake of America's high-tech military victory in the 1991 Persian Gulf war, Beijing decided to reorder its vaunted four modernizations, making science and technology a top priority before agriculture, industry, and defense. At the same time the PLA has been called on to take up a new mission at variance with the Maoist doctrine of protracted struggle: limited war to achieve a quick, decisive high-tech military victory in only a few days.

IS CHINA A GLOBAL POWER?

The sudden diminution of China's global status and influence threatens to take away the party-state's last remaining source of and claim to legitimacy: restoring China's great-power status in the post–cold war and postcommunist world.

Of course, there is no "scientific" way of assessing Chinese national power. In a rapidly changing international environment the very notion of "regional power" or "global power" is subject to continuing redefinition and reassessment. Elsewhere I have constructed a typology of Chinese power, comparing it against Japan, Germany, the United States, and the former Soviet Union and giving China's global ranking in 15 specific categories. Since the United States, the Soviet Union/Russia, Japan, Germany, and China are generally regarded as the world's great powers, China would have to be included in the top five global rankings to be regarded as a great power.[3]   pop - growth

Not surprisingly, China easily ranks among the top five in population, strategic nuclear warheads, and global arms trade. The Chinese would be first to admit that the burgeoning population (now at 1.2 billion) is a liability rather than an asset in the enhancement of comprehensive national strength. Since 1978, China's population has grown by nearly 200 million people, and in the 1990s at least another 150 million to 180 million will be added. The implications of these enormous numbers wanting to become rich, and the accompanying social, political, and economic pressures, are staggering, especially when placed in the context of industrial modernization and shrinking ecological capacity. China has already become an environmental giant of sorts, contributing to global warming faster than any other major country (China now releases 9.3 percent of global greenhouse-gas emissions, following the United States and the former Soviet Union but ahead of Japan, India, and Brazil).

When Chinese military power is measured quantitatively in terms of the number of strategic nuclear warheads, global arms trade (including global nuclear technology proliferation), and military manpower, China comes out as one of the world's five-largest military powers. However, mere numbers say little about the quality of the PLA or its performance in armed conflict.

China's economic power is mixed. In aggregate gross national product China ranks ninth in the world, but it is projected to become the world's fifth-largest economy by the year 2000. Sheer demographic size left China's per capita GNP at only $350 in 1989 (104th in the world),

and it is projected to reach about $800–$1,000 by 2000. Post-Mao China is a global economic power only in the sense of being a major source of cheap labor and a tempting cost-effective site for foreign toxic wastes and heavily polluting industries; indeed these are the defining features of China's place in the global economy. Although exports as a percentage of GNP increased from 4 percent to about 20 percent in the long Deng decade, China still has a long way to go to achieve the status of an important trading power.   but for W

Another category needs to be added in determining a country's global power position. East Asia emerged in the 1980s as the most dynamic region in the global economy with seemingly ever-expanding waves of regional economic integration. As the most important investor, trader, aid donor, and development model, Japan easily dominates the East Asian political economy. Japan's economic miracle demonstrates that a country's competitiveness in the global marketplace depends less and less on natural resource power and more and more on the brainpower needed for microelectronics, biotechnology, civilian aviation, telecommunications, robotics, computer hardware and software, and so forth.

China is extremely weak in this area. For example, China is not even included in the top fifteen in the category of issuing important patents. Revealingly, Chinese Foreign Economic Relations and Trade Minister Li Lanqing is reported to have proposed to Japanese Minister of International Trade and Industry Eiichi Nakao on March 22, 1991, a Sino-Japanese collaboration for the establishment of an "East-Asian Economic-Cooperation Sphere." The prospect of China emerging as the world's second- or third-largest economy by 2010, which was prognosticated in 1988 by the Commission on Integrated Long-Term Strategy, is rather dubious.

Where does China rank among states when its international reputation, cultural and ideological appeal, development model, and diplomatic leadership in the shaping of international decisions, norms, and treaties in international organizations are considered? Advertised or not, Maoist China commanded such appeal as an antihegemonic third world champion of the establishment of the New International Economic Order, which led many *dependencia* theorists to embrace Beijing as a model of self-reliant development. Mao's China stood out as the only third world country that gave

but never received any bilateral and multilateral aid. This alone vested Beijing with a measure of moral authority.

In 1978, all this changed when post-Mao China suddenly switched its national identity from a model of self-reliant socialist development to a poor global power actively seeking most-favored-nation trade treatment from the capitalist world. That same year also saw China's abrupt termination of its aid programs to Albania and Vietnam. The 1979 invasion of Vietnam was another reminder of the extent to which the post-Mao leadership was willing to bend the pledge never to act like a hegemonic power. These geopolitical and geoeconomic reversals, coupled with the harsh repression of the first wave of post-Mao democracy movements, began the decaying process of China's moral regime in global politics.

More than any event in modern Chinese history, the Tiananmen massacre, in a single stroke, dealt a severe blow to whatever credibility that was still retained by the make-believe moral regime. Almost overnight the People's Republic acquired a new national identity as an antipeople gerontocracy propped up by sheer repression. The worst was avoided because of a variety of geopolitical and geoeconomic reasons. Taking advantage of its permanent seat on the Security Council, Beijing once again demonstrated its negative power—and the Nixon/Kissinger/Haig/Bush line—that an engaged China is an irreducible prerequisite to any approach to world order. Beijing's bottom line seems clear enough: Ask not what China can do for a new world order; ask instead what every country, especially the lone superpower, can do to make China stable and strong in a sovereignty-centered international order.

The power China had as a "model" for the developing world has vanished in the post-Mao era. Not a single state in Asia or elsewhere looks up to Beijing as a development model. Nobody, not even the Chinese, knows what is meant by socialism with Chinese characteristics. That India and so many developing countries are now looking to Taiwan, not Russia, let alone China, as a model—or that this breakaway island country has recently surpassed Japan as the world's largest holder of foreign exchange reserves ($83 billion) must surely come as another blow to Beijing's national identity crisis. The born-again third world identity in the post-Tiananmen period seems hardly relevant to reestablishing a fit between tradition and modernity or for formulating the best strategies to make China the rich and powerful country that virtually all Chinese think is their due.

PERFORATED SOVEREIGNTY

Revolutionary power may grow from the barrels of guns, but no state—certainly not a huge multinational state—can be held together for long without a legitimizing value system, as was dramatically shown by the collapse of what was widely and wrongly perceived to be a strong state in the former Soviet Union. In at least one respect China is beyond compare. No country in our times has talked as much, launched as many ideological campaigns, succumbed to so many ideological mood swings, and accomplished so little in getting its ideological act together. Herein lies the ultimate tragedy of the Chinese Revolution.

To a startling degree, the post-Tiananmen government is paralyzed by a megacrisis—multiple and interlocking crises of authority, identity, motivation, and ideology. These have converged at a time when the center is fractured by another round of a deadly intraelite power struggle and is also facing challenges from an assertive civil society, peripheral but booming southern coastal provinces, and ethnonationalistic movements of non-Han minority peoples in the strategic borderlands of Tibet, Xinjiang, and Mongolia.

The extent to which China's legitimizing ideology has progressively decayed is captured in the common saying, "In the 1950s people helped people; in the 1960s people hurt people; in the 1970s people used people; in the 1980s and 1990s people eat people." For the majority of politically engaged intellectuals it is the Han Chinese nation, not the party-state, that has become the most significant referent for their individual and collective loyalty and identification, as found in the slogan, "We love our country, but we hate our government."

Viewed against the longstanding state-society and state-nation concordance and the Chinese intellectual tradition of dedication to serving the state, this represents a radical change in the conceptual evolution of China's intellectual community. The defining and differentiating feature of a weak state such as China today is the high level of internal threats to the government's security. External events are seen primarily in terms of how they affect the state's internal stability. The idea of national security, which refers to the defense of core national values against external threats, becomes subverted to the extent that the Chinese government is itself insecure.

China no longer has a legitimizing and unifying ideology of sufficient strength to do away with the large-scale repressive use of force in domestic life. As noted earlier, the post-Tiananmen government increased its defense budget by 52 percent in the last three years while China enjoys the best external environment in history and when outside security threats seem to have all but vanished. A renewed emphasis on political indoctrination of PLA members is reported to have taken up 60 to 70 percent of training time. More tellingly, the People's Armed Police has experienced unprecedented growth in personnel and equipment as a way of coping with growing internal security threats.

The great irony is that the center no longer fully controls the peripheries; Chinese state sovereignty is highly perforated. Well over half of China's economy has already escaped the control of central planners in Beijing. The center has lost control of tax collection, and even profit remittances from many of the state enterprises it owns. Virtually all the gains China has enjoyed since the early 1980s have come from nonstate industries with their share of industrial output zooming from less than 15 percent to a little over half today.

At the same time, the contemporary global information revolution has broken down the exclusive control over information that the center once enjoyed. This revolution has facilitated the rapid mobilization of people's demands, frustrations, and intolerance—indeed, it is the second "revolution of people power." Although its actual speed and magnitude in post-Tiananmen China are difficult to assess, the information revolution nonetheless undergirds the critical social forces and movements for change that are weighed down by the full repressive force of the weak and insecure state.

State sovereignty thus no longer provides the center with security or control, since it is constantly perforated by the forces of supranational globalization and local and regional fragmentation. Against such trends and pressures Chinese state sovereignty is a paper tiger. China is a weak, if not yet disintegrating, state. How can the wobbly edifice of the Chinese state survive the multiple threats from within? Can a weak, oppressive state be expected to act as a responsible and peace-loving regional power? The once widely shared image of a China in disintegration and of a dragon rampant in Japan and Southeast Asia seems to be moving perilously close to reality.

Notes

1. Li Luye, "The Current Situation in Northeast Asia: A Chinese View," Journal of Northeast Asian Studies, vol. 10, no. 1 (Spring 1991), pp. 78–81; the quotation is on p. 80.
2. Xinhua, February 25, 1992, in Foreign Broadcast Information Service, Daily Report: China (February 28, 1992), p. 2.
3. For a more detailed discussion, see Samuel S. Kim, China inand out of the Changing World Order (Center of International Studies, Princeton University, 1991), pp. 69–74.

Article 9   *ASIAWEEK*, April 6, 1994

Helmsman as Sage

Confucius Is Winning the Post-Maoist Battle for China's Soul

In the long chronicles of Chinese history, wave after wave of foreign influences have washed over the land and its culture. Alien armies and philosophies arrived to put what they thought was an indelible stamp on the Chinese psyche. But in the end they were all assimilated. Indian Buddhism crossed the Himalayas to capture the imaginations of the ruling classes two millennia ago. In a few generations the religion was transformed into something so Chinese that its roots could be recognized only by scholars. So too with the Mongols, whose conquering khans ended up as emperors epitomizing the Chineseness of China. A similar fate later awaited the Manchus.

In this century the most important foreign influence on China was the product of the minds of a German-Jewish thinker and a Slavic demagogue. But Marxism-Leninism, capable at first of moving millions, suffered in a few decades the fate of the others. Like Buddhism, it has survived only in its priesthood—communist cadres who chant the sacred tenets of dialectic materialism while pursuing capitalist money-making schemes for the state. Few true believers in the communist religion survive outside the propaganda bureaus of apparatchiks, who already sound faintly ridiculous to most Chinese. As their influence fades, what can fill the moral vacuum?

Even in its 1950s heyday, Chinese communism was quite unlike the regimes of Russia and eastern Europe. Huge portraits of Marx, Engels and Lenin were displayed like sacred icons in Tiananmen Square, but from the start Maoism reshaped the founders' doctrines. Chinese communism was, to begin with, a popular revolution from within. And that was transformed in the Cultural Revolution into something with no parallels abroad. This uniqueness was one reason it endured for half a century. The other was its embodiment in a larger-than-life human figure. While the Chairman's economic and social teachings have been utterly discredited, his God-like reputation lingers. Maoist memorabilia command a lively market price and much genuine feeling was invested last year in the centenary of his birth. His legend, like Genghis Khan's in Mongolia, has been divested of reality and recreated as myth.

Winston Churchill said of Lenin that it was Russia's greatest tragedy that he was born; and its second-greatest tragedy that he died. His untimely passing ushered in the excesses of Stalin and the horrors of collectivization. It could be said that it was China's tragedy that Mao died too late. Had he exited the stage in 1954 after he and his lieutenants had united China and founded the People's Republic, his position in history would today be untarnished by the untold misery of the shockingly misguided Great Leap Forward and the Cultural Revolution. But he lived 22 more years.

Chinese wrestle with their feelings about Mao Zedong. Was it better that he lived to free them from tyranny and give them dignity, or worse that he lived on to keep them poor? The Communist Party itself pronounced him 70% correct. Those who lived through the 1960s and 1970s will no doubt give him a lower score. But the image of the Great Helmsman never really died, and people are only now emotionally and psychologically reconciled to the god-emperor's place in their hearts and minds. That allows them to move on to a new phase in the life of their nation.

Many Chinese will never forgive Mao for the enforced communes and confiscations of property in the 1950s. However, most of those who cannot bring themselves to settle accounts probably live outside China. Now that time has passed and the emotional scars have healed, mainlanders are beginning to look back on the Mao era with a certain nostalgia. Taxi-drivers dangle his portrait as a talisman. Old and young dance to popular versions of the classic songs in praise of him. They certainly do not want a return to communism. It is more that they feel an emptiness they don't yet know how to fill. Mao restored China's pride after a century of abuse at the hands of Europeans and fellow Asians. He embodied many noble ideals, including service to the nation and struggle against oppressors. Many Chinese today feel a need to turn back in history and seek those same values in other figures from the past. That may explain the enormous popularity of the television series lauding the wisdom of Judge Bao Qingtian, the incorruptible Song Dynasty jurist who battled evil during one of the most corrupt times in China's history.

Capitalism's resurgence in China is bringing about the prosperity Mao's lieutenants dreamed of but could never achieve under communism. But at the same time it has left many adrift. The next series of economic reforms, which could include the breakup of state-owned enterprises, will be even more unsettling in terms of lost job security, inflation and corruption. Can economic progress alone damp the social tensions that will inevitably arise as an unwanted by-product of the transformation into a socialist-market economy? There is a source of wisdom more enduring, and perhaps even more persuasive, than Mao's. A resurgence of Confucian values could provide that necessary moral anchor.

Mao tried to suppress Confucianism as outdated and feudal. Red Guards desecrated shrines and destroyed classical texts. The vandalism has long since ended and most of the vilification dissipated. If the classics are not yet taught in schools, they are at least no longer suppressed. The sage's ancestral home is again well-tended and visited by tens of thousands every year. Of course, nothing need really be done to assert Confucianism. It is ingrained in the Chinese soul. In a way, its values were present even under Maoism. They will rise again of their own accord so long as nothing is done to push them down.

The Judge Bao series comes of course from Taiwan. As China seeks to catch up with the rest of the world, it is turning to its nearest neighbors. They are all fundamentally Confucian societies—Japanese, Koreans and Vietnamese in ways of their own, but Taiwan, Hong Kong, Macau and the immigrant communities of Southeast Asia in a way that China can directly relate to. Beijing's leaders find a model for managing bureaucracies in Tokyo. They find an example of an incorruptible civil service in Singapore. And for hard work, filial piety and nurturing family fortunes, there are any number of models in Taiwan and Hong Kong. At the moment the Mother Dragon looks to the Dragonlets for guidance. In time, the flow will reverse.

The return to Confucianism will not mean a retreat into the past. Confucianism has proved admirably adaptable and is as attuned to the modern age as any living philosophy. Its wisdoms have been applied to dynamic changing societies, as Singapore's Senior Minister Lee Kuan Yew constantly points out. But how can the Helmsman fit into this picture? Easily: it is the image, not the reality, that counts. Confucius is a saint only because those aspects of his teaching that suit the modern age are emphasized. The same thing will happen with the memory of Mao Zedong. There need be no moral void with the fall of communism. China has only to look inward to discover its soul.

Article 10

World Policy Journal, Fall 1994

China's Fragile Future

David Shambaugh

David Shambaugh is senior lecturer in Chinese politics at the School of Oriental and African Studies, University of London, and editor of the China Quarterly. *He recently edited* American Studies of Contemporary China (1993) *and* Chinese Foreign Policy: Theory and Practice.

At first glance, the People's Republic of China seems an unstoppable juggernaut. Possessing the world's fastest growing economy, largest population and standing army, and expansive industrial and resource endowment, China is no ordinary developing country. For the past 15 years, China's government and society have been engaged in a massive project to reform its stagnant, socialist economy and become a dynamic, modern nation. For over a decade, China's real GNP has grown by an average of almost 9 percent per year (13 percent in 1992 and 1993). If this growth persists, by some estimates China will overtake Japan around the turn of the century and the United States by 2010 to become the world's largest economy.

If one includes the increasingly integrated economies of Taiwan and Hong Kong—collectively referred to as Greater China—the aggregate size of the Chinese economy is even more stunning. Foreign trade and investment place Greater China among the world leaders. In 1993, the People's Republic of China absorbed an estimated $28 billion in actualized foreign direct investment, with an estimated $110 billion committed (although foreign direct investment has fallen off by about a third during the first half of 1994). Seventy-one percent of this "foreign" investment came from Hong Kong, Macao, and Taiwan. Indirect trade between Taiwan and the mainland (via Hong Kong) totaled $8.7 billion in 1993. An export-driven growth strategy has powered China's economic takeoff and has brought in substantial foreign exchange earnings. If Taiwan's $80 billion in foreign exchange is added to China's $21 billion and Hong Kong's $43 billion,[1] the foreign exchange reserves of Greater China dwarf those of other nations.

There are thus substantial reasons to be bullish about China. The People's Republic commands the world's attention by its sheer size, the magnitude of its market, and its growth potential. It is easy to conclude that Napoleon's prophesy of the awakened giant is being realized.

But the process of reform has not been smooth; nor is the horizon clear. China is an extremely fragile country with significant risks for foreign investors, traders, diplomatic interlocutors, and neighbors in Asia.

Overhauling an economy the size of China's without significant social and political dislocations is impossible. Many vested interests are tread upon and new ones created, expectations are raised and often go unfulfilled, the economy grows apace without adequate laws or infrastructure to support new growth, and strains are placed on the system at all levels. Nationwide protests over corruption, inflation, and democracy in 1989 were one such manifestation of the stresses but were hardly isolated events. Many of the factors that stimulated the outbreak of discontent in the spring of 1989 are still present in China today.

The economy is overheating with unrestrained capital expansion; inflation is running high, causing great dissatisfaction among consumers; infrastructure is strained past the breaking point; unemployment is mushrooming; huge internal migration pressures (more than 100 million rural migrants are on the move) are taxing urban governments; crime and corruption are rampant; social stability is breaking down; and demands are being made for greater political liberalization. How the Communist party and government handle these pressing problems will be decisive for both their own sustainability and in ensuring the future integrity of the nation-state. Adding to the current fragility is the looming succession to political patriarch Deng Xiaoping.

Succession Politics

On February 9, 1994, Chinese television viewers were given a 90-second glimpse of their de facto leader, Deng Xiaoping. What they witnessed was not reassuring. Appearing in public for the first time in more than a year, Deng's health had noticeably deteriorated. He appeared palsied, moved slowly with the assistance of aides, and stared blankly into space. In addition to his near-total deafness, 90-year-old Deng is widely rumored to be suffering from the effects of two strokes and pancreatic cancer. The television appearance was meant to reassure the public that the patriarch of Chinese politics remained at the helm, but it actually had the opposite effect. He appeared in control of neither his faculties nor the nation.

Communist political systems are notoriously poor at ensuring smooth and orderly political succession arrangements. Backroom maneuvering, vicious jockeying for power, midnight arrests, and purges are the norm. The best laid succession arrangements are often overturned, as anointed successors are frequently deposed following premature grabs for power. Deng Xiaoping has already disposed of two chosen successors—Hu Yaobang in 1987 and Zhao Ziyang in 1989.

Deng's most recent choice, Jiang Zemin, is generally seen as a weak transitional figure, although Jiang is working hard to cultivate constituencies among military and provincial leaders in order to sustain himself after Deng departs. Jiang may lack the requisite power bases in the military, party, or state bureaucracies to survive a rough succession struggle, but he is a nonthreatening compromise candidate whom various constituencies can support (and manipulate). He lacks the clientalistic and organizational networks of Gen. Zhang Zhen or Gen. Yang Shangkun in the People's Liberation Army, Premier Li Peng or Vice Premier Zhu Rongji in the State Council and provincial apparatus, or Qiao Shi in the security services. Without Deng Xiaoping's backing Jiang Zemin may be vulnerable, and one of these other figures may move to the fore. For the time being, however, Jiang is the first among equals in a collective leadership. The odds are that he will survive the initial transition and head a collective leadership for a period of time but that in the medium term he will be muscled aside by a more astute competitor (much as Deng Xiaoping muscled aside Mao's chosen successor, Hua Guofeng).

The party, state, and military leadership today is actually reasonably cohesive and collectivist. This was not the case following the 1989 Tiananmen Square massacre, or even a year and a half ago. But the sweeping personnel changes in the party and armed forces engineered by Deng and his allies at the Fourteenth Party Congress in October 1992 and subsequently have done much to reduce overt factionalism among the elite.

Ironically, the Chinese leadership is far more stable today than Chinese society—a reversal of most of the 45-year history of the People's Republic. To be sure, there exist differences of opinion among the elite over policies in several spheres, but they are not of a deeply divisive nature. Relative consensus exists. Personal animosities in the leadership are few. The elite polarization evident at the time of Mao's death or even in the aftermath of the Tiananmen massacre is not apparent today. All members of the leadership possess some vulnerabilities, but midnight arrests and sweeping purges do not appear in the offing if Deng passes from the scene soon. The legacy of the Tiananmen massacre continues to dog the regime, but unbeknownst to many a quiet shakeup has taken place. Personnel changes since 1992 have led to the removal of most of the individuals responsible for the massacre from the military High Command and ruling party Politburo. And in society at large the memory of the massacre has noticeably faded.

The succession to Deng will actually be less concerned with personalities than with competing institutional interests, central-local relations, the civil-military balance, and broader issues of socioeconomic change and stability. In each of these areas China remains fragile.

A Strained System

Communist party authority has eroded considerably in China. The party reigns but it does not rule. It is a hollow shell of an organization to which officials and citizens alike feign compliance at best and ignore in normal circumstances.

Corruption is rampant inside and outside the party and is a major source of resentment among the citizenry. As economic growth has accelerated, the number of privileges the party can provide its members has declined markedly. Membership has been declining steadily in recent years, and the party has few ideological adherents. It bases its legitimacy today almost entirely on economic growth, nationalism, and the remaining instruments of Leninist rule: the *nomenklatura* personnel system; control of paramilitary forces and the armed forces; and the internal security apparatus. It survives through its monopoly of political power; the suppression of dissent and lack of any organized political rival; by pushing economic growth; and by playing the nationalism card.

There exists a deep political vacuum in China today due to this atrophying of state authority.[2] In the absence of central control, local actors have filled the void. Beijing is having a difficult—if not impossible—time enforcing its will at the local level. Some observers refer to this phenomenon as "regionalism,"[3] but in fact it is localism. There are numerous indicators of localist independence. Beijing's much-vaunted economic austerity program of 1993 has proven ineffective because of resistance from the provincial leaders and the power of local capital. For example, in the first quarter of 1994 the State Council and State Planning Commission reportedly did not approve a single capital construction project, yet nationwide a reported 94,000 projects were approved locally with a total fixed asset investment of 1.8 trillion yuan.[4]

The central government cannot effectively control investment or collect taxes, with the result that inflationary pressures are growing rapidly and central government coffers are running dry. According to some reports, the central government only has enough cash on hand to pay state salaries for three months. The declining revenue base is probably the most pressing of a host of issues facing the government today. In late 1993 the government unveiled a new tax and revenue-sharing system, but this too is being resisted by the provinces and localities. The revenue collection problem is compounding a soaring budget deficit. The deficit for 1993 was $2.35 billion, four times that of 1992, and China's finance minister has warned that it will likely triple again in 1994.

The rising budget deficit did not, however, preclude another hefty increase in the military budget for 1994. For the sixth consecutive year, official military spending increased sharply (a 21 percent increase over 1993). Off-budget revenue and expenditures could total as much as five times the official figure of 52.4 billion yuan (approximately $6 billion).[5]

Overheating of the economy continues, although there are some signs that the government's tight credit policy is having an effect. Growth of GDP during the first half of 1994 "slowed" to 12 percent, while industrial output "dropped" to 19 percent. Nonetheless, it will be difficult to meet the targets of 9 percent GDP growth and 10 percent inflation for the year.

The Problems of Success

Beijing's social and political problems are born of economic success. Rising inflation is pinching urban incomes, and rural incomes have actually declined over the last three years. The potential for rural unrest has petrified the regime. In 1993, there were over 200 reported large-scale rural demonstrations, in which farmers stormed government offices and beat up officials to protest arbitrary levies imposed by local authorities, declining state grain purchase prices and payment in IOUs instead of cash for contracted output, and rural cadre despotism.

It is not only the countryside that concerns the government. Incidents of urban unrest have also increased sharply in 1994 due to the vast number of paralyzed state industries. Nearly two-thirds of China's 13,000 large and medium-sized state industries operate at a loss. The ballooning budget deficit is principally due to the subsidies paid by the central government to keep these socialist behemoths afloat. The People's Bank of China (the central bank) has earmarked 470 billion yuan in lending (subsidies) to state industries during 1994 (an approximately 20 percent increase over 1993). Nonetheless, production lines in most factories remain idle and worker absenteeism is high. Salaries are paid in a combination of cash and kind, if at all. Incidents of industrial action have sharply increased, particularly in the Manchurian "smokestack corridor." According to some reports, over 2,000 incidents of labor unrest occurred in the first quarter of 1994.[6] The problems in the state industrial sector offer a major challenge to the regime. The Communist party need not be told of the revolutionary potential of an aroused proletariat. It prefers to shoulder the burden of financial bailouts than risk the political and social fallout that would result from bankruptcies and privatization.

The government and citizenry are also deeply concerned about rising crime and corruption, both of which have become endemic. Despite widespread arrests and executions, law enforcement authorities appear to be losing the fight against both. In many cases, police and customs officials are themselves deeply involved in corruption and smuggling rings.

In addition to further demonstrations by rural farmers and urban workers, and the vast migrant "floating population" (estimated officially at 105 million), the government is concerned about pro-democracy activists and succession-minded ethnic minorities. In recent years there have been several incidents of armed ethnic uprisings in China's western "autonomous region" of Xinjing, where the desire to restore a Greater Turkestan with the newly independent Central Asian republics holds appeal among Muslim minorities. The Chinese military and People's Armed Police can be expected to continue to deal swiftly and harshly with further unrest, but at the same time sporadic incidents can be expected to reoccur so long as this region (like Tibet) exists under virtual Chinese occupation.

Thus, wherever the Chinese government looks internally it is confronted with unrest and disorder. This contrasts markedly with the relatively peaceful environment it enjoys externally.

The Insecurity of Security

For the first time in the history of the People's Republic, China knows no pressing threat to its national security. Of course, the crisis over North Korea is of concern to China, and territorial disputes in the South China Sea and elsewhere have potential to flare up, but on the whole adroit Chinese diplomacy should be credited with pacifying China's borders and normalizing relations with numerous former adversaries and neighbors.

This does not mean, on the other hand, that China is not seen as a potential threat to Asian security.[7] Changes in Chinese military doctrine that now emphasize low-intensity conflict scenarios around China's periphery, combined with China's assertive stance on territorial claims in the region, have many of its neighbors worried. The dramatic increases in China's official defense budget and the extensive amount of off-budget revenue that accrues to the military compound the concerns. The lack of transparency in China's military spending and force structure, and the military's reluctance to participate in multilateral security initiatives, increase the perception that China will be the principal threat to regional security in the years to come.

Fortunately, the armed forces' current weapons inventory should not be a cause for concern. Despite the military's desire to build rapid-deployment forces and a blue-water navy, and to generally improve its power-projection capacity, it will be a long time before it is able to do so. The current quality of weaponry remains 20 to 30 years behind the state of the art, and substantially behind the inventories of Russia, Japan, South Korea, Taiwan, and many Southeast Asian countries. Yet China's booming economy, its desire to become the predominant regional power, and recent trends in its military establishment suggest that a concerted buildup has begun.

The China Challenge

Whether China is seen as an economic powerhouse or a fragile country with high potential for instability, its impact on Asia and the world will be significant in the years to come. It is most likely that China's future will be characterized by both rapid growth *and* instability, the former producing the latter. The stresses and strains on the economy, and on the society, the polity, and the environment, are readily apparent in China today. No society in the world has undergone the magnitude of change that China has in the last decade. After three decades of socialist stagnation Chinese society has roared to life. Any government attempts to restrain growth and commerce will be met with overwhelming resistance, and in the future challenges to state power will only increase. Although China is not likely to break up or erupt in civil conflict, the sustainability of Communist party rule can no longer be taken for granted. The one certainty is that the genie is out of the bottle.

Notes

1. 1993 estimates.
2. See David Shambaugh, "Losing Control: The Erosion of State Authority in China," *Current History* 92 (September 1993), pp. 253–59.
3. See Gerald Segal, *China Changes Shape: Regionalism and Foreign Policy*, Adelphi Paper 287 (London: International Institute of Strategic Studies, 1994).
4. *China News Analysis* (Hong Kong), no. 1509 (1994), p. 4. China's local financial power is proving to be an important qualification to the much-heralded East Asian development model. The model—based largely on the experiences of Japan, South Korea, Taiwan, and Singapore—is known for the interventionist role of the central state economic planning apparatus. China's growth, on

the other hand, has been stimulated from below. It has come through a variety of forms of locally generated capital but also through direct foreign investment to localities.

5. See "World Military Expenditures: China," *SIPRI Yearbook: 1994* (Oxford: Oxford University Press, 1994).

6. Kathy Chen, "Facing Potentially Explosive Situation, China Moves to Aid State-Owned Firms," *Asian Wall Street Journal*, May 24, 1994, p. 1.

7. See David Shambaugh, "Growing Strong: China's Challenge to Asian Security," *Survival* 36 (Summer 1994), pp. 43–59.

Article 11   *The Atlantic Monthly,* April 1994

China's Gilded Age

A journey through a country bursting with new wealth but besotted by corruption and threatened by a split between its prosperous cities and its stagnant rural areas

Xiao-huang Yin

Xiao-huang Yin teaches at Occidental College, in Los Angeles. He is also an associate of the Fairbank Center for East Asian Research at Harvard University and a translator of Secret Speeches of Chairman Mao *(1989).*

Recently I took a six-week journey across China. It was my first trip back since I came to the United States to study, in 1985. In the course of my visit I saw—I felt—the perturbations of profound and chaotic social change. China's stunning hurtle from a centrally planned economy to a free market has set off an economic explosion and generated tremendous prosperity. Its economic growth was 13 percent in 1993, and average personal income in urban areas has doubled since 1985. With the state-owned sector accounting for less than 30 percent of total economic output, the socialist system is becoming an empty shell. Across China the lines between the state and private economies are blurring. At the largest national department store in Shanghai, a symbol of Chinese socialist business, customers now bargain for better prices.

The counters within the store have been contracted out to shop clerks, who decide the prices. Dual ownership has in essence turned this state enterprise into a private business. Asked if such a practice is an example of China's "socialist market economy," a professor of economics at Nanjing University, where I taught in the early 1980s, replied, "Nobody knows what the concept means. It

is only rhetoric, and it can mean anything but socialism."

With capitalism unleashed and investment from overseas stimulating the economy, China has become a land of opportunity. Rags-to-riches success stories fill people's conversation. Zhao Zhangguang, an herbalist whose "101" hair-stimulating lotion has sold extremely well around the world, has become one of China's richest men. In 1993 alone his net profits reached up to $50 million. Even some of my relatives have become millionaires. A distant cousin who was a high school teacher until 1986 told me modestly that he had made "a little money" by opening a factory that produces bristle brushes for export to America. He drove me to his new summer house in his new Mercedes-Benz 500SEL, one of his three luxury cars. "This is China's Gilded Age," a former colleague of mine commented sarcastically. "These Chinese Carnegies and Rockefellers are more successful than their American counterparts—they made more money within a shorter time."

To be sure, not everyone gets rich quick, but the economic boom has brought most urban Chinese a huge improvement in their standard of living. Color TV sets, refrigerators, and VCRs, considered luxuries when I lived in China, can be found in almost every working-class urban household—at least in the prosperous coastal cities. For the first time in my life I saw some overweight people in my home town of Yangzhou. With fax machines, satellite television, computer modems, and radio talk shows, the Chinese are well informed about events in the outside

world. They may even know as much as the average American about happenings in the United States. Hillary Clinton's health-insurance program, the gay-rights movement, and daily prices on the U.S. stock exchanges are familiar matters throughout China.

Of course, China is far from being an open and free society. Last August the government announced that it had sentenced a journalist, Wu Shishen, to life imprisonment in Beijing for his alleged selling of an "internal document" to a Hong Kong magazine for about $870. However, in other aspects of life the state has relaxed its control. In 1985, when I was last in China, the campaign against "spiritual pollution" was still under way, and it destroyed the careers of many intellectuals. One of my colleagues in Nanjing was sent to the countryside to receive "re-education" for his "unhealthy soul." He was accused of looking closely at the breasts of a woman student while he talked excitedly about graphic sexual portrayals in the fiction of Saul Bellow. Now the government seems to put fewer restrictions on popular culture and even risqué material from the West. In a hair salon a few blocks from my old home in Yangzhou glossy posters of naked girls cover the walls. Entering the shopping center of Jinling Hotel, in Nanjing, I was astounded to see a Playboy Bunny calendar welcoming customers. I was particularly struck by the sight because at Occidental College, where I have been teaching, there was a heated debate among students over whether the magazine should be removed from the college library.

Hearing my astonishment at the government's new tolerance of looser sexual mores, a friend of mine smiled. "The authorities now consider sex socially permissible and morally acceptable," he said. "It may be because the government feels that when people are interested in sex, they have less time to concern themselves with other issues."

I do not know how accurate my friend's comments are, but a recent study by the *Xinmin Evening News,* in Shanghai, indicates that the number of couples engaged in premarital or extramarital affairs in China is skyrocketing. Meanwhile, the quest for democracy has waned. Gone are the days when enthusiasm for political reform was the prevailing emotion in society. Having tasted the fruits of prosperity, ordinary Chinese are now more interested in making money. They fear that radical political reform may cost them their new wealth. A recent opinion poll conducted by the *Shenzhen Commercial Daily* discovered that 88 percent of residents in Beijing were concerned with inflation, and 81 percent with social stability. Only 42 percent showed some slight interest in politics. Perhaps the most obvious manifestation of this trend in social thought is the change in certain formalities. Until the end of the 1970s *"tongzhi"* ("comrade") was the standard form of address used by one Chinese to another. In the post-Mao 1980s the term *"xiansheng"* ("sir") gained popularity. Today *"laoban"* ("boss" or "manager") has become fashionable.

Similarly, the catchword *"canzheng"* ("participate in political reform") has been replaced by *"xiahai"* ("plunge into the sea"), which refers to going into business. Many of my former colleagues in Nanjing have plunged into the sea, hoping to make their fortunes. A friend of mine who was a classicist by training, and who liked to argue with me about the origins of parliamentary democracy, has become a cosmetics salesman—a job that I can hardly associate with his background and interests. When I mentioned this, he laughed. "Well, I have taken an indirect course to fight for democracy," he said, "because the growth of independent wealth, whether legitimate or ill-gotten, will surely erode the Party's control of the people." He may not be representative of China's educated elite, but many scholars seem to share his view that the most prudent course for intellectuals who champion the cause of democracy is to accommodate the economic demands of the masses.

Of course, people have not forgotten the Tiananmen Square crackdown of 1989, but they now believe that the best prospect for democracy in China is "peaceful evolution"—the Asian model, emphasizing social stability and economic prosperity rather than radical political changes, which many Chinese see as dangerously volatile. A restaurant owner who was sitting next to me in a train to Zhengjiang admitted that he had no intention of risking his good life by embracing the abstract notion of democracy. "You know, democracy is a luxury," he continued, after I bought him a bottle of Tsingtao beer. "Only people who have enough food on their dinner table can afford democracy. Look at the Russians: the root of their problem is that there is too much freedom but too little bread."

Indeed, the social upheaval and the rise of neo-Nazism as a result of unemployment and poverty in Russia—China's "Big Brother" in the 1950s—have caused great doubt about the wisdom of radical political change. Ordinary Chinese observe with dread that the Russian economy has sharply declined since the collapse of the old system, and that Russian society is violent and perpetually unstable. Horrible stories of Russian girls engaging in prostitution in China are widely circulated and reported in Chinese newspapers. In a crackdown last summer about a dozen Russian women in Guangzhou (Canton) were arrested for what a police spokesman called "doing pornographic business." The miserable experience of these Russian girls is recounted vividly by Cheng Naishan, a feminist writer in Shanghai. In her recent short story "White Russians, Red Russians," she tells how a daughter of a Russian aristocrat who fled to China after the Russian Revolution ended up as a prostitute in Shanghai. Now she is appalled to learn that a group of Russian girls, recruited by a posh hotel in Shanghai, have become the same kind of "Russian Miss" as was found in those pre-1949 days.

For many Chinese, the Russian lesson appears to be that only after a nation achieves a relatively high level of economic prosperity can it afford the fruit and the perils of democracy. The argument, which presumes that as prosperity rises the prospect of democracy expands, has been proved correct by what has happened in other East Asian nations. In the long run, as China's newly emerged middle class gains strength, it will demand more political power. When that happens, there will be a new enthusiasm for democracy.

However, the sybaritic ethos does not mean that there are no signs of political liberalization in China. The power of the National People's Congress—China's legislature—has increased significantly since the 1980s. The People's Congress was a rubber stamp in the Mao era, but its role expanded considerably when Peng Zhen, a former Beijing mayor and one of China's "Eight Elders," became its chairman, in 1983. Because government officials at all levels now have institutionalized nomination and tenure, the legislature has more say in decision-making. Official appointments at the local level must now be approved by a majority vote of the local people's congresses, giving rise to confrontations between the legislatures and the local government bureaucracies. In many cases local people's congresses vote down candidates nominated by the government. In my home town last year the nominee for director of the municipal energy bureau was rejected three times by the city's people's congress, because of his lack of professional training. The legislature and the municipal government were locked in a struggle for almost six months; finally the government changed its candidate. Since 1984 a dozen faculty members from Nanjing University have been elected to the local people's congress. Nostalgic for the days when the government was relatively incorrupt, these representatives are the most vocal critics of the tainted local Party bosses and the scandal-ridden government bureaucracy. They also care about issues that are linked with daily life, such as food prices, environmental protection, and traffic problems. Thus the people's congresses, at least those at the grassroots level, serve as a channel for ordinary Chinese to express their concerns.

Whereas enthusiasm for democracy has ebbed in China, corruption is flowing throughout the land. Financial scandals, which are widespread, highlight the chaos in Chinese society. Official statistics indicate that 30 percent of state enterprises, 60 percent of joint ventures, 80 percent of private businesses, and almost all shop owners regularly cheat on their taxes. Bank officials have embezzled billions of dollars in state funds and then fled overseas. It is an open secret that many government officials have deposits in foreign banks and own property abroad. It was widely rumored that not long ago a top-ranking Chinese official bought, through a relative, a multimillion-dollar mansion in Beverly

Hills—an impressive house even by Hollywood standards.

The proportion of Party members involved in bribery and embezzlement has reached levels that were inconceivable in the days when revolutionaries dominated the Communist Party. The government journal *Fortnight Chat* last July revealed that during the first three months of last year the number of cases of bribery and embezzlement involving more than a million yuan (at the time, about $175,000) had doubled from the previous year, with one Party member embezzling more than $6 million. Almost certainly with the assistance of Party cadres at the highest level, Shen Taifu, the general manager of the Great Wall Company, stole about $200 million from state funds and individual investors within five months. Rumor has it that members of Premier Li Peng's family were involved in the scandal.

The widespread corruption in China reflects a deep social, political, and psychological crisis in the nation. The gunshots at Tiananmen Square marked the end of the revolutionary phase of the Communist movement. Chinese leaders now openly acknowledge that the Party has changed from a "proletarian vanguard" into a ruling body. As a result the Party rank and file feel that they are no longer restrained by orthodox ethics. Many see the economic pluralism as providing them with an opportunity to loot. A fear that economic reform may falter at any time and a lack of confidence that the society will remain stable over the long term further impel the rush to get rich quick. Mao's slogan "Serve the people" has been thrown away, and the new motto for Party cadres is "Make the best use of power you can while still in office."

Recently the Chinese government has inaugurated a new anti-corruption campaign, but few people believe that this round will be any different from earlier ones. "This is the fifteenth time I've seen the government launch such a campaign since 1980," an old friend of mine told me cynically. "What they do is shoot a few small fliers [petty officials] but let the big tigers [senior cadres] run away." Others believe that since corruption is rampant and exists at every level of society, a complete cleanup is impossible—it would cause turmoil and upset the government's weak control over the pace and direction of economic growth. "The Party leaders simply cannot afford to have a real crackdown," a college professor remarked to me, "because it is too costly. They can stay in power only if

China has enough stability to guarantee economic progress."

There is some truth in these comments. Indeed, corruption has become an integral part of daily life in China. Graft and the loosening of controls allow the entrepreneurial spirit of those with ability to flourish. Moonlighting often brings people more income than their official pay. With their extra money ordinary Chinese can now display their personalities and reclaim their private lives. Perhaps this is why public outrage over corruption is not so strong as abroad I had heard it was. There is even a rather tolerant attitude toward graft, especially among the professionals who have benefited from the market economy. In their eyes, corruption is inevitable in the transition from totalitarianism to authoritarianism. "Corruption is a price that China has to pay for the changes from a centrally planned economy to a market system—it is the grease that can lubricate the political machine in a changing society," an economics professor in Nanjing preaches to his students. A popular ballad sums up the situation nicely: "Of the 1.2 billion [people], one billion are corrupted. We join forces to cheat the Party and government." A close friend of mine said, "As long as it brings along changes and prosperity, it is tolerable. In any case, I'd rather live in a corrupted but free and prosperous society than a purified but stifling and stagnant land."

Of course, not everyone would agree with his view. For those without skills or authority, it is infuriating to live in such a corrupt society. One of my relatives, a retired worker, had an operation last spring. Although she was fully covered by the state medical insurance, she had to pay bribes to virtually everyone involved in her treatment, from the surgeon to the cleaning woman. The bribes amounted to twice her monthly pension. Tourists in China often become victims of minor graft. For example, I was overcharged many times in restaurants, hotels, and shops. Even in my home town I was cheated by a taxi driver, who almost beat me up when I pointed out his dishonesty. The Chinese revolution of the fifties and sixties succeeded in breaking up the old agglomerations of power and wealth, and achieved a new way of distributing wealth—a social leveling—in a nation that historically had huge disparities between rich and poor. Until Deng Xiaoping's push for economic reform in late 1978, Chinese society was relatively egalitarian, although this goal

was met at the cost of intellectual freedom, individual aspiration, and economic growth. With prosperity, however, problems familiar from Chinese history have reappeared, old ways of viewing power and wealth are common once again, and traditional disparities are returning. Corruption and the widening income gap also spotlight a rising problem in Chinese society: rural poverty.

While personal income levels are rising rapidly in cities, the countryside, where 80 percent of China's population lives, is falling behind. A recent study of living standards in Shenzhen, Guangzhou, and Shanghai reports that the average annual income in the three cities has reached $1,200. But in Guizhou, a remote southwestern province, villagers earn only about $40 a year. Nationwide the average annual income of peasants is about $135.

I was struck by the gulf between the prosperity of urban centers and the poverty of rural areas when I took a bus along a winding dirt road to Xiao county, in North Anhui Plain. If coastal cities reflected China's stirring and optimistic mood, what I saw in North Anhui was just the opposite. What is the cause of rural poverty? Some villagers blame the corruption of local officials. But government officials in the major cities are just as greedy as those in the villages—perhaps more so, since the spoils are greater. The real problem is that the government has failed to raise the prices of farm products to keep up with those of manufactured goods. In the first half of 1993 the prices of fertilizer, fuel, and other farming necessities rose nearly twice as fast as those of farm commodities. Now the more grain a peasant produces, the less profit he makes. Villagers in coastal areas usually develop their land for fruits, vegetables, and other cash crops that cater to urban needs. They also make money in township mills, property speculation, and service industries. As a result, more than half of their annual income comes from nonagricultural sources. But peasants in inland areas are denied such advantages. Investment rarely comes in, because the lack of highways and railroads makes it difficult to transport goods produced inland to the great metropolises or to overseas markets. The various barriers will take years to remove, but they all contribute to the peasants' poverty and deepen the gulf between bustling urban China and depressed rural China.

To be sure, rural poverty is an old problem. But peasants now feel a more intense agony because they know that city life in coastal areas has improved, and they want to live better too. Grievances and jealousy are producing hatred, and the resentment felt by the have-nots can be striking. In August an explosion and a big fire occurred in Shenzhen, China's special economic zone across from Hong Kong. More than a dozen people were killed, and hundreds were wounded. "It served them right," I heard a migrant peasant worker from Henan say bitterly in a small restaurant near Shanghai. "These bastards have made too much money by exploiting us."

A more subtle manifestation of rural grievance is that many villagers now hang Mao's picture in their houses. When I asked if they really missed the Great Leader, an old woman hesitated and then said, "No one likes the old days." She quickly added in a louder voice, "But under his leadership at least we all lived the same kind of life. Chairman Mao put the interests of us villagers first. Now the leaders have forgotten us. We are no longer treated the same way as the town folks." At one time the Party was led by men who had all been born in rural families and had lived many years among villagers—and Mao did make peasants the centerpiece of his Marxist plan for revolution. The leaders of the current regime, however, have no roots in the countryside. As an educated and technocratic elite, they show neither concern for nor understanding of the grievances of peasants.

Surprisingly, I found growing prejudice among urban residents against peasants. A Shanghai taxi driver insisted that migrant peasant workers were all potential "criminals." In my home town peasant beggars from Anhui slept right on the sidewalks, but no one paid any attention to them. When I mentioned this to my friends, they shrugged and replied, "So what?" Some of them even argued that peasants in inland areas live in poverty because they waste money and because the lack of efficiency there turns diligent workers into layabouts.

The peasants are equally prejudiced against city people, especially the educated elite. To some extent their distrust is understandable. Throughout the brief history of the People's Republic, villagers have often suffered from the enthusiasm of urban intellectuals who used rural China for "grand experiments," betrayed its interests, disregarded its traditions, and treated peasants like stepping-stones toward more-ambitious goals. Under the nonsensical order of the Party cadres rice was planted in the cold, dry north and wheat was planted in the humid, warm south. The results were disastrous. In fact, it was the overweening confidence of urban intellectuals in their own particular abstractions that inflicted an enormous economic disaster on rural China during the Great Leap Forward at the end of the 1950s, resulting in the deaths of millions of peasants. Resentment still runs deep today.

The rural grievance has become more complicated as it mingles with the growing sentiment of the interior regions. During the past few years China's inland provinces saw the economic boom and the development clearly bypass them. As a petty cadre from Gansu, a poor northwestern province, complained to me, "You know, the relationship between us inlanders and you guys on the coast is just like that between underdeveloped countries and industrial nations. We supply you with raw materials and cheap migrant labor, but you turn around and sell us secondhand products at high prices. The gap bleeds us inland people of capital and resources. You robbed us of everything, from money to women!"

Such complaints are most alarming. Mixed with the rising tide of regionalism, rural grievances can be explosive. Rumors of peasant riots circulate widely. Indeed, the government confirmed that last June about 10,000 peasants rioted against the authorities in Renshou county, in Sichuan province. Rebellions have broken out in poverty-stricken inland regions throughout modern Chinese history, from the Taiping Rebellion to the Communist movement in Yan'an. Unrest in the remote countryside shook the foundations of the empire and brought down the old regime.

Themselves once organizers of the peasant revolution, old Party leaders are aware of the volatility of rural grievances. Wan Li, a former chairman of the National People's Congress and a close friend of China's paramount leader Deng, warned recently that if poverty persists among the peasants, another Chen Sheng–Wu Guang Rebellion will break out. He was referring to a famous peasant rebellion that took place some 200 years before the birth of Jesus. The rebellion triggered a series of civil wars and thus caused the collapse of the mighty Qin dynasty, founded by China's first Emperor, Qin Shihuang. Since historians often compare the Communist regime to the Qin dynasty and Mao to the whirlwind dictator Qin Shihuang, the parallel between rural unrest today and the peasant rebellion then presents an ominous lesson for the current regime.

The Party has taken action to soothe the peasants' wrath. Last summer it issued orders to reduce the taxes and fees levied on peasants. But there is no clear sign so far that these widely publicized policies differ from previous propaganda. Much depends on how determined the current regime is to solve rural problems and whether any real improvement occurs in the countryside. Unless the boom extends inland, China's long-term political stability and economic development will remain in doubt.

Despite the gloomy scene in the countryside, I made an encouraging discovery that is worth mentioning. The imbalance in the ratio of male to female babies in rural areas may not be as serious as people abroad have heard. Statistics show that China's sex imbalance at birth reached 114 males to 100 females in 1992. Most demographers believe that the disparity is caused by the ancient practice of female infanticide. But this does not seem to be the case. Stepped-up prosecution of infant killers and severe punishment have helped to curtail the practice. The disparity may, rather, have been caused by the underreporting of female births in villages. Chinese law requires the registration of births with local family-planning programs. To get around strict child quotas, villagers often fail to register the births of their daughters. They ship the girls off to be raised by relatives until a son is born. In a village near Baoying, in northern Jiangsu, I found seven such "ghost children." Their presence would have been unthinkable in the past, because the government controlled food distribution. But villagers now have their own land, so their livelihoods no longer depend on the state and they can afford to have more children.

What will happen after the eighty-nine-year-old Deng Xiaoping, China's de facto Emperor, dies? It is rumored that he is battling prostate cancer and suffering from Parkinson's disease. A widely circulated political joke says that now the most powerful person in China is not Deng but his daughter, because it is she who decides what her father is to know and to say.

How China after Deng's death can combine a capitalist economy with its legacy of communism is anybody's guess. Most Chinese agree that the economic reforms may continue and outlast Deng's political system. There is a great risk of chaos in the prospect, however, as indicated by a rising tide of regionalism, the widening gap between rich and poor, and the mutual distrust between the cities and the countryside. People wait in uneasy anticipation. The looming future may hold continued economic prosperity along with political freedom, but it may also hold an eruption of upheavals and disunity like that after the collapse of the Manchu Empire, in 1911. In any case, China's prospects are extremely uncertain.

When I asked about China's future at a party with my friends, no one answered. Obviously they didn't want to be bothered by such a question, at least not during our happy celebration. "Great disorder leads to great order," a historian finally said, murmuring a slogan of Mao's from the Cultural Revolution. After a long pause he added drily, "Let's hope for the best but prepare for the worst."

Article 12   *World Press Review*, December 1994

Tightening the Screws on Dissent

Hong Kong's "South China Morning Post" calls it a "great leap backward." Faced with economic and political problems, China's leaders are trying to tighten their grip on the country and create a personality cult around Paramount Leader Deng Xiaoping. Even as U.S.–China relations may be getting warmer, the already Herculean task of Chinese dissidents promises to get even harder. These three articles look at Chinese—at home and overseas—who have challenged their country's rulers. The news is not good.

Early in 1993, China's chronically divided democracy movement finally seemed to be getting its act together. Four years after the Tiananmen Square massacre, the two leading groups of political exiles met in Washington to form a single party. The activists' plans to set up modern China's first true opposition party doubtless set alarm bells ringing in Beijing. Since the Tiananmen massacre focused world attention on the struggle to bring democracy to China, many activists had been arguing that it was counterproductive to remain divided. But the unity conference broke down almost immediately over the selection of officers. By the end of the first day, there was not one but three organizations, each claiming the leadership of the movement.

Such chaotic infighting has become the rule rather than the exception among the political groups, foundations, magazines, and human-rights organizations that make up the overseas democracy movement. Most of the leading figures have dissipated their energies in factional struggles and an unending search for funding. And, with little prospect that cooperation will improve, the dissident movement seems set to become increasingly marginalized and irrelevant.

"With the enemy far away, they can only turn their fire on their comrades," says Gong Xiaoxia, an exuberant 20-year veteran of dissident political activities both in and, since 1987, out of China. She should know. Conversations in her tiny office at Harvard University are peppered with denunciations of other well-known figures in the movement—especially the young student leaders of the Tiananmen protests. "Our generation knew it was a vicious, brutal regime," she says, touching on the generational split that is the dissident movement's great divide. "But for them it was so easy to earn sudden fame, and the more irresponsible they became, the more famous."

Such squabbling is a far cry from the heady early days of the movement. For one or two years after Tiananmen, it was possible to regard the movement as a virtual shadow government awaiting the seemingly inevitable collapse of the Chinese Communist Party. The exiles' contact with key members of the U.S. Congress, human-rights lobbies, religious groups, and labor organizations helped keep the cause of human rights in China high on the U.S. political agenda. "Without [the exiles'] activities abroad, many things might perhaps have occurred [in China] without any notice by the international community," says Ding Xueliang, a lecturer at the Hong Kong University of Science and Technology. "This is their biggest achievement."

But the movement's more ambitious hopes have been shoved aside by the Chinese government's stubborn

Arresting Performances

On June 11, in the company of a few friends, Beijing artist Zhang Huan stripped himself naked and hung himself from the ceiling of the room. A doctor inserted two rubber tubes into his arms. For the next two hours, 200 cubic centimeters of Zhang's blood dripped slowly onto the floor. Zhang, a performance artist, escaped a police raid the following day and went into hiding outside Beijing.

The raid was part of the authorities' crackdown on experimental artists, whose performances, they allege, are not art but pornography. "Not a week passes without more artists being arrested," says Lao Li, a leading expert on China's avant-garde.

While not new in China, performance art—using one's own body as the artistic medium—is becoming increasingly popular. The police actions have raised the profile and credibility of the artists.

Ma Liuming, 24, staged gender-bending shows involving explicit sex acts. In his debut, a naked Ma masturbated while made up as a seductress. On June 12, Ma and another artist, Zhu Ming, were arrested. Zhu's performances have involved nothing more than blowing bubbles in a fish tank. Zhu and Ma have been kept incommunicado in a detention center.

What threats do such acts pose to the Chinese state? "The authorities always look at avant-garde art as antisocial and antigovernment," Lao Li says. He quotes the Chinese proverb: "killing the chicken to scare the monkey," or arresting two artists to prevent the emergence of a community outside state control.

Most performance artists used to live in a sleepy Beijing suburb known as the Eastern Village. Since the arrests, the Eastern Village has become a dusty ghost town. The artists' rooms have been sealed by police.

—*Matei Mihalca, "Eastern Express"*
liberal), Hong Kong.

---

strength and economic resilience. At the same time, the movement's ability to influence American policy toward China has steadily declined. That was never more apparent than in May, when President Bill Clinton formally declared that human-rights issues would not affect China's most-favored-nation (MFN) trading status with the U.S. With American and other foreign companies eager to tap into China's burgeoning market, the political weight of business lobbies simply overwhelmed those calling for a higher value to be placed on human rights.

The movement's ability to reach into China and influence events there is even more in doubt. "The only people in China I know who still care about what they [the leading dissidents] are doing overseas are their close friends or relatives and the state security people," says Ding.

A major factor limiting the exiles' influence in China is the very pace of the broad economic, social, and political changes sweeping the country. Untold numbers of businesspeople, freelance scholars, labor activists, and others are busily going about the work of creating a civil society without party permission.

In the face of such a process, the leading members of the 1980s generation of democratic elitists—most now living in the U.S.—become less relevant to the situation within China with each passing day. "The time has passed for that whole generation," says Merle Goldman, who teaches modern Chinese history at Boston University.

One result of such increasing irrelevance is the dwindling of any prospect that the exiles might eventually return to leadership positions in a future Chinese government. Says James Lilley, a former U.S. ambassador in Beijing who is now director of Asian studies at the American Enterprise Institute, "In the future, the power will belong to those who stayed and rose to positions of authority within the system, not to the ones outside China."

This dilemma of how to remain relevant is one of which the exiles themselves are painfully aware. "I never wanted to become a pitiful refugee, but I had no choice," says activist Wang Juntao. Wang's early-May release from prison was a final face-saving gift for Clinton in advance of the MFN decision. His jailers, says Wang, told him to leave the country or go back into prison. Facing the same choice, Chen Ziming, Wang's colleague at the privately funded Social and Economic Research Institute of Beijing, refused to leave and has since lived under virtual house arrest.

The exiles' movement lacks a single recognized leader, and Wang Juntao sometimes comes up as a candidate for the role. A key figure in the 1978–80 Democracy Wall movement, he had previously narrowly missed election in 1980 as a Beijing University representative to the Municipal People's Congress. A few years later, he helped Chen Ziming organize an independent think tank. Wang served as a senior adviser to the Tiananmen student leaders in 1989, though they rejected his counsel to leave the square.

At least for the record, Wang discounts the possibility that he could achieve overall leadership of the exile movement. Instead, he criticizes existing dissident groups for expending too much energy on internal power struggles. However, several days after delivering this critique, Wang showed up at the U.S. government-funded National Endowment for Democracy, looking for financial backing—to establish yet another organization.

Still, there is one ray of hope for exiled democrats. About 100 years ago, Sun Yat-sen rallied overseas Chinese opposition in the fight against the brittle and corrupt Qing Dynasty. Sun's years of struggle were crowned with success in 1912, when the Manchu regime collapsed, albeit largely from its own weight. Sun, who is revered by communists and nationalists as the father of modern China, was in Denver at the time of the revolution but went on to become president of the fledgling Republic of China.

—Carl Goldstein, "Far Eastern Economic Review"
(independent newsmagazine), Hong Kong.

Article 13   *The New York Times*, September 6, 1993

China Sees 'Market-Leninism' as Way to Future

Nicholas D. Kristof

The writer of this article recently completed nearly five years as chief of the Beijing bureau of The New York Times.

Ever since the Opium War erupted 150 years ago, China has been groping for a way to regain the edge over the West that it enjoyed for most of recorded history.

Now, in the 1990's, China's leaders seem to think that they have found the Way.

The plan is to jettison Communism—but not Communist Party rule—and move China's nearly 1.2 billion people into the East Asian tradition of free-market authoritarianism. Pioneered in the 1960's and 1970's by South Korea and Taiwan, this East Asian model combines harsh single-party rule with competition in the marketplace.

In short, dissidents are zapped with cattle prods and the economy is prodded with market incentives.

After Deng Xiaoping, China's current paramount leader, was purged in 1976, the People's Daily quoted Mao Zedong as saying that Mr. Deng "knows nothing of Marxism-Leninism." Mao may have been half-right, for the 89-year-old Mr. Deng has even advised visitors from developing countries not to bother with Marxism.

At the same time, Mr. Deng and other Chinese leaders retain a fondness for Leninism, in the sense of highly disciplined one-party rule with centralized decision-making. Their aim, in other words, is Market-Leninism.

In some ways, China already resembles Brezhnev's Soviet Union or Honecker's East Germany less than it does modern Indonesia: a nepotistic and corrupt dictatorship that presides over a booming market economy with both state and private sectors. Mao once talked of China's becoming another Soviet Union; Mr. Deng reserves his highest praise not for a socialist country but for that bastion of capitalism, Singapore.

Paramount Leader's Paradise

The attraction of Singapore is that it has achieved Western living standards without being infected by Western political standards. Singapore is a paramount leader's paradise, for it is populated by clean-cut, law-abiding citizens who obligingly use their ballots to keep their rulers in power.

"China's dream is to become another Singapore," a Western diplomat noted the other day. A few feet away, a foreign ambassador responded without a pause, "It'll never happen."

Whether China will succeed in transforming itself into another Singapore—or even Indonesia—is one of the fundamental international questions for the next decade or two.

If China can make that metamorphosis, a new superpower could emerge in the 21st century. If it fails to transform itself economically and politically, perhaps collapsing under popular resentments and ethnic and geographical divisions, then many Chinese officials believe that civil war and massive chaos are possible. In that case, more than one-fifth of humanity could be caught in the upheavals, new states with nuclear weapons could pop up in the center of Asia, and a tidal wave of tens of millions of boat people could engulf distant shores.

Police Sell Cattle Prods

But whatever the future holds, it is already pretty clear that China is no longer a Communist country in any meaningful sense.

No Communist country, at least, has ever so fully embraced stock markets, satellite television, private colleges, Avon ladies, music video and radio talk shows. The Communist Party is still in command, but its branches no longer devote much energy to controlling ideology. Instead, in the 1990's the business of the party is business.

The State Security Ministry runs a bakery, the Police Ministry sells electric cattle prods, and—until it was caught—the party's official women's organization ran a brothel.

Misleading Froth
THE UNDERSIDE OF A BOOM

The party's avarice and materialism tend to impress foreign visitors, who are dizzied by aggressive quasi-capitalism: the glitzy discos that keep everyone bopping until the wee hours, the 30 Rolls Royces sold so far this year in China, the luxury restaurants that sprinkle bits of 24-karat gold into their dishes because rich patrons think it is good for longevity.

Yet all this is froth, and misleading froth at that. When foreigners rave at the sight of all the gleaming new high-rises under construction in Beijing, local people sometimes respond with a cynical old folk saying: On the outside, even donkey droppings are shiny.

Visitors who travel only to major cities learn about as much about China as a foreigner would learn about the United States from a few days spent next to the pool of an elegant hotel in Beverly Hills. In the countryside, where three-quarters of the population lives, the peasants are far more likely to inhabit caves than discos, and for every Chinese who eats gold there are millions who cannot afford meat.

Just as important, this scramble to get rich may be undermining China's value system. Many Chinese worry that the social contract is collapsing, for the old glue that held society together—Communism—has lost its adhesive qualities. The Chinese have a saying: "yi fang, jiu luan"—as soon as control eases, there is chaos.

"All the time in Chinese history, when you don't have strong rule, you get chaos and warlords," said a military official in an extremely sensitive post. "If we try to get too much democracy, it'll all fall apart again. China will disintegrate, and it'll be worse than in the Soviet Union."

Selling Military Secrets
The official complained that social order is disintegrating because of an almost universal desire to make money, and he seemed to know something about that. His purpose in arranging the meeting was to try to sell a reporter top-secret information about Chinese missile sales to Pakistan.

His forehead glistening with sweat as he contemplated the executioner's bullet that would rip apart his skull if he were caught, he provided evidence of his role in the missile program. He said that

China was continuing to sell M-11 ballistic missiles to Pakistan, and he offered to provide the dates of shipments, quantities and other specific data in exchange for cash.

The United States formally concluded late last month that China was selling M-11 missile technology to Pakistan, in violation of international agreements, and imposed economic sanctions as a punishment. But the United States has not formally determined whether China has sold the complete missiles themselves to Pakistan.

Told that reporters do not pay for information, the military official asked for an introduction to an American diplomat who would pay. When that request was turned down as well, he declined to provide detailed information about M-11 shipments.

In the course of two lengthy meetings, in which a reporter tried to persuade him to give the information for free, and he continued to press for an introduction to a diplomat, the military official explained how he decided after months of agonizing to betray his country.

"If my neighbor's kid gets a toy, then my kid wants it too," he reflected during a tense meeting under a lamppost late one night. "Life's a competition now. Everybody's trying to make money. Everyone! Hey, I'm just trying to cash in on what I have."

The no-holds-barred capitalism shows in all kinds of ways. Children regularly die, for example, after drinking fake medicines that fly-by-night entrepreneurs churn out without regard to effectiveness or safety.

Restaurant owners in at least half a dozen provinces have been caught lacing their dishes with opium pods in an effort to make their food literally addictive. The Ministry of Public Security became so alarmed that it recently ordered a crackdown on the use of opium as a spice.

In the village of Haotou, in southern China's Guangdong Province, the peasants figured out an easy way to join the market economy. They began kidnapping girls and young women from other areas, hauling them back to the village and forcing them into prostitution. Many of the peasants turned their homes into brothels employing more than 100 sex slaves.

Corruption has grown to such huge proportions that President Jiang Zemin warned last month that it threatened to ruin the Communist Party itself. A few years ago, the problem was petty bribery of a few dollars; now officials steal millions or billions.

In June, the Agricultural Bank of China disclosed that officers of one of its branches had issued fraudulent letters of credit for $10 billion. The fraud was revealed only because the bank wanted to make clear that it would not honor the documents.

Minor graft has turned into Mafia-style organized crime. Particularly in coastal areas of southern China, local party and army officials have joined forces with criminal gangs in Hong Kong and in Chinatowns abroad to engage in massive smuggling and other rackets.

More than 90 percent of the videocassette recorders sold in China have been smuggled in, often with the help of the police, the army or border guards. In the first four months of this year, South Korea exported 26,000 cars to China, but only 166 were reported to Chinese customs officials so that duties could be paid.

Police officials in Beijing run a prostitution racket out of an army-owned hotel. Doctors routinely demand bribes of hundreds of dollars before performing major surgery, and journalists demand payoffs for attending corporate news conferences.

Failed Experiment
A CRISIS OF LEGITIMACY

"Corruption is much worse now than it ever was under the Nationalists," said an octogenarian former senior official, in a reference to the Government that the Communists overthrew in 1949. It is a bold statement, for corruption was so rampant under the Nationalists that the Government had virtually rotted away by the time the Communists overthrew it.

The old man was eating dinner in the spacious apartment that the Communist Government gave him as a reward for many decades of faithful service to the party. He has enjoyed all the perquisites of power in China and has even played bridge with Mr. Deng. But, largely because of the corruption, the party's esteem for him is not reciprocated.

"I'll tell you, in 1949, I hated the Nationalists," the old man said. "I went to welcome the Communists when they entered Beijing and I cheered for them. When a Communist soldier was shot, I went to get help for him. At a meeting in my office to discuss what to do, I was the first to speak out. I said we should support the Communist Party."

"Now, I would welcome the Nationalists back," he added bitterly. "In fact, I would go out and lead them into Beijing."

That sentiment is not unusual, particularly among intellectuals. Even many

Communist leaders are said to acknowledge privately that the grand experiment to which they have devoted their lives has in many respects been a failure.

In the United States, many college radicals of the 1960's have changed their views and become bankers. The thinking of many Chinese leaders appears to have undergone a parallel evolution, but it is always easier for members of a congregation to slip out than for the high priests to stand at the altar and admit to atheism.

"None of them really believe in Communism any more," said the child of one Politburo member. The widow of a top leader says: "He stopped believing all that long ago, but what could he do? The only person he could admit it to was me."

Some Chinese—including the old man who would welcome back the Nationalists—believe that the Communist Party is a collapsing dynasty, just like all the other dynasties that have disintegrated in the past. They point to the irrelevance of its ideology, just like that of Confucianism at the end of the Qing Dynasty a century ago.

Confronted with a crisis of legitimacy during a period of widespread alienation and corruption, the Qing rulers responded with the same combination of repression and reform that the Communist Party has repeatedly tried.

The New Revolution
ECONOMIC FORCES REMOLD
A NATION

There is a huge difference, however, between China at the end of the Qing Dynasty and China today: In the 1990's, China has the fastest growing economy in the world. Instead of disintegrating into floods and famines, the former sick man of Asia is enjoying the fruits of the world's latest economic miracle.

Prof. Thomas B. Gold, a sociologist at the University of California at Berkeley, agrees that China resembles a disintegrating dynasty, but he argues that the economic boom makes a crucial difference. It may have the momentum to keep the country going, he says.

"In many ways, what is happening in China today is more revolutionary than what the Communists did," Professor Gold said. He notes that change used to come from the top in China, dictated by political campaigns. But now it is the na-

tion's economic forces that are remolding the nation.

The emerging China, Professor Gold and other scholars suggest, will look increasingly like Taiwan and South Korea. On other continents, the parallels may be Spain under Franco in the 1960's or Chile under Gen. Augusto Pinochet in the 1970's.

Among the crucial changes in Taiwan, and in the other East Asian countries, were a rise in educational and income levels, greater interaction with the outside world and the emergence of a technocratic elite in the bureaucracy. The economic boom nurtured a growing urban middle class that was able, after the passing of the old guard, to demand what might be called stable change: far-reaching political and economic liberalization achieved without spilling too much blood.

The same processes are under way in China. It is an open question whether the Communists would allow them to work if it meant the party would be presiding over its own demise. Moreover, it is far more complicated to choreograph the transformation of a nation of 1.2 billion people—including minorities like Tibetans—than it is to transform a city-state like Singapore or an island like Taiwan.

The uncertainty about China's prospects reflects a long debate about whether a market for goods can flourish for long if there is no companion market for ideas. Particularly in the West, many people assume that China will be unable to liberalize its economy successfully if it does not liberalize its political system.

Yet in Asia, many people draw the opposite conclusion. They see democracies like the Philippines where economic growth is anemic and conclude that industry grows best in tightly controlled political greenhouses like China. The Soviet Union under Mikhail S. Gorbachev emphasized "glasnost" more than "perestroika"—openness more than economic restructuring—while China has churned up some impressive statistics by trying perestroika more than glasnost.

If China continues to thrive, it will offer a lesson to the third world that the West may find profoundly unsettling: Political repression is the grease that can lubricate an economic boom.

For students of the Soviet Union, one of the longest arguments was between those who foresaw the state's collapse and those who predicted convergence with the non-Communist world. In the

case of the Soviet Union, those who took the bleakest view were proved right.

Now the same argument is raging about China. One of the most talked-about books in China in recent years was a prediction of the collapse of the Communist world, written by Zbigniew Brzezinski in the 1980's and published in Chinese in a limited edition for senior officials.

Some young Chinese intellectuals worry that the Communist Party will survive the collapse of Communism, and that what the leadership is really trying to build is fascism. Mao himself was the first to warn of this risk.

"We are afraid that we will stop being a revolutionary country and will become a revisionist one," the Chairman said in 1963. "When that happens in a socialist country, it becomes worse than a capitalist coun- try. A Communist Party can turn into a fascist party."

And so, some argue, it has. There are parallels, for example, with Italy under Mussolini and especially with Spain under Franco, in the sense that China is an authoritarian, militarized and disciplined society in which state-controlled corporations compete in market conditions.

A Huge Improvement

Even if what is emerging in China is fascism, however, in practice it represents a huge improvement for most Chinese. The Government still smashes those who challenge it—the authorities sentenced a Chinese journalist to life in prison on Aug. 30 for leaking an official document—but it no longer tries to regulate every aspect of daily life.

When China had a redder tint, its people could not wear lipstick, listen to rock music, have foreign friends, dress in colorful clothes, or use "bourgeois" expressions like "Miss." Now Chinese have reclaimed their private lives from the Communist Party; once again, they can display personalities.

In short, China seems to be in an immensely important transition from totalitarianism to authoritarianism. Dissidents are still brutalized, but life for the average peasant or worker—who knows that politics, like explosives, are to be avoided—is relatively free.

It may be no more than the freedom of a bird cage. But most birds probably would prefer to be able to fly around in a cage than be skewered on a rotisserie, which is what life in China used to be like.

Article 14 The New York Times, September 7, 1993

Riddle of China: Repression As Standard of Living Soars

Nicholas D. Kristof

The writer of this article recently completed nearly five years as chief of the Beijing bureau of The New York Times.

What is intellectually irksome about China, for anyone who values human rights, is that a Communist Party that is often brutally repressive should be so stunningly successful in raising living standards.

The party torments many of the nation's bravest and boldest thinkers, sometimes locking them up in insane asylums or imprisoning them with criminals suffering from infectious diseases. Yet at the same time, the party is presiding over one of the greatest increases in living standards in the history of the world.

The Government fights leprosy as aggressively as it attacks dissent. It inoculates infants with the same fervor with which it arrests its critics. Partly as a result, a baby born in Shanghai now has a longer life expectancy than a baby born in New York City.

Annoying to Democrats

For those around the world who cherish democracy, China's success in generating prosperity and well-being is just a bit annoying—and certainly challenging to explain. It offends Western humanitarian values to think that a repressive Communist state can do more for its people than a democratic Government like India's.

Yet a Chinese woman is almost twice as likely to be literate as an Indian woman, and the risk of her baby's dying in the first year is less than half as much as in India. As a matter of priorities, many people would probably prefer a healthy baby to a meaningful vote.

"The first measure of any Government or administration is to ask, 'Is there any period in our previous history in which you would prefer to live,'" said David M. Lampton, the president of the National Committee on U.S.–China Relations. "And I think the answer for the

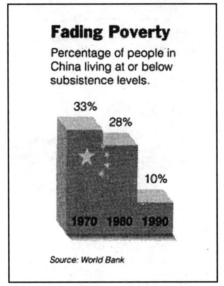

Fading Poverty

Percentage of people in China living at or below subsistence levels.

33%
28%
10%
1970 1980 1990

Source: World Bank

The New York Times

overwhelming majority of Chinese would probably be no."

This makes moral condemnations of China much trickier than denunciations of the former East bloc, which impoverished its citizens at the same time that it repressed them. The Clinton Administration periodically complains about the Chinese Government's abusing its citizens, yet there is no question that the Communist Party is overseeing a far greater rise in prosperity and general well-being than any Democratic or Republican administration has ever achieved in such a short time.

This is not to say that criticism of Communist repression is necessarily misguided.

"When Hitler held power, the German economy enjoyed a boom," Zhang Weiguo, a dissident journalist now living in California, noted drily. "And Japan grew very quickly during the militarist years before World War II. So we shouldn't regard economic development as our sole objective."

The point is simply that with China's economy the fastest-growing in the world, moral judgments about the Com-

munist Party's role become more complex. Particularly in the Chinese countryside, the issues sometimes seem more textured, the assessments more nuanced, than they do to casual observers abroad.

From afar, it sometimes seems as if the fundamental dynamic in China is brutal repression of dissent. In reality, political dissent plays an inconsequential role in most people's lives, particularly in the countryside. Three quarters of China's population of nearly 1.2 billion lives in the villages, and it is a world of its own.

ONE VILLAGE
Big Grievance Is Corruption

Take K. G. Sun's little village at the end of a winding dirt road in northern China. Chickens rush across the path, and a few cows and goats are tethered to the trees. It is a peaceful little place, although there was a bit of excitement in January when someone celebrated Chinese New Year by heaving a brick through the village chief's window.

Mr. Sun and the other peasants have their complaints, of course. Everyone hates the man in charge of enforcing restrictions on births, and eight different people reported him anonymously to the township when he tried to shield his son who was trying to have an extra baby.

A lean and muscular man in a ripped tank top, Mr. Sun seems to have stepped out of a painting by a Chinese Norman Rockwell. Asked his age, he says he was born in the Year of the Dog, 1958. As for his children: "I don't know which one's what age. I just know one's a 'dog,' and one's a 'pig.'"

For peasants like Mr. Sun, the big grievance is corruption, including the way the village and township cadres take bribes and squander public money to live it up.

"The big officials eat big, and the little officials eat a little," a middle-aged man said, using "eat" as slang for taking bribes or misusing public funds. "And if you're not an official, you don't eat."

The peasants knew enough to be suspicious when the village chief abruptly

Quality of Life: A Comparison

China's gains in improving its quality of life may dim in comparison with those of rich Western countries, but they far outpace those of the runner-up in population, India. Figures are current unless otherwise noted.

CHINA **INDIA**

LIFE EXPECTANCY

69 years
Life expectancy at birth

64 years
Median age at death

60 years
Life expectancy at birth

37 years
Median age at death

CHILDREN'S HEALTH

Children immunized for measles before age 1

96%

Child mortality rate (per 1,000 under age 5)

210
85
43
1960 1975 1990

Children immunized for measles before age 1

77%

Child mortality rate (per 1,000 under age 5)

235
195
127
1960 1975 1990

WEALTH AND KNOWLEDGE

7.8%
Average per-capita G.N.P. growth rate (1980-91)

Percentage of adults who are illiterate

27%

Average per-capita G.N.P. growth rate (1980-91)

3.2%

Percentage of adults who are illiterate

52%

CHINA INDIA

Source: The World Bank

took 12 acres of the village's best land out of production last fall and announced that a brick factory would be built on the site. The rest of the village's land was redivided so that everybody got a bit less.

Flurry of Protest Letters

The peasants protested, particularly when it became clear that the brick factory would be privately owned by the village chief, a police official from the county seat and a few other outsiders. The villagers wrote letters to everyone they could think of: to provincial leaders, to Prime Minister Li Peng, to People's Daily, even to The New York Times.

When an American showed up—the first Westerner ever to visit the village—the peasants delightedly poured out their complaints. Unfortunately, the village chief noticed and took his revenge.

The next day, the township police station summoned the peasants who had talked to the American and subjected them to a full day of grueling interrogation. They were told that it was illegal to make contact with foreigners and that in the old days they would have been beaten to death for the offense.

The police accused them of "leaking state secrets" and suggested that they were "counterrevolutionaries." The county police have summoned the peasants for interrogations in the county seat, and officials there apparently are still deciding how to punish the villagers.

Those peasants, in other words, have plenty of reasons to be furious at the authorities. And yet one of them, interviewed later in secret, has this to say of the mood in the village:

"Overall life has gotten much better. My family eats meat maybe four or five times a week now. Ten years ago, we never had meat."

"Now the peasants can go into the cities and earn 18 yuan a day doing odd jobs," he added, referring to the equivalent of about $3.15, a munificent sum in such places. "Of course the peasants are content."

In the Chinese countryside of the 1990's, Communist Party officials often bully and cheat the peasants, yet life is getting better so rapidly that many still support the system. Most Chinese say that if the Communist Party were suddenly to announce free elections, it could count on the votes of peasants to win overwhelmingly.

The New York Times

PROGRESS
Sufficient Food And Better Goods

The improvements are greatest in the most obscure sector of society: the poor mountain villages of central and western China where peasants still live in mud hovels and are lucky if they can send their children to elementary school for more than four or five years.

Life in those villages is still awful, but not so miserable as it used to be. Women may not give birth in clinics, but at least they are likely to have a trained midwife so that mother and infant alike have a fighting chance of surviving. Poor peasants may not be able to afford luxuries like brick houses or wrist watches or toilet paper, but at least they have enough rice so they do not have to choose which of their children to feed.

The World Bank reported in a study published this year that the proportion of Chinese living in absolute poverty—lacking decent food, housing and clothing—dropped from 220 million in 1980 to 100 million in 1990. In other words, a group of people equivalent to almost half the population of the United States can now potentially enjoy life instead of merely fight to subsist.

"What the peasants need above all is to fill their bellies," said a Chinese journalist who is often critical of the Government. "Only when they've got food to eat and a place to live will they start demanding political changes."

He cited an ancient Chinese proverb that only when men have enough to eat and a place to sleep do they run after women. The same, he said, holds for their desire for democracy.

Consumer Economy Emerges

One of the huge gains in the quality of life over the last 10 years is also the most difficult to quantify: the emergence of a consumer economy in which Chinese no longer have to stand in line everywhere, no longer have to wear shoes that pinch because the right sizes are unavailable, no longer have to put up with the scorn of rude shop clerks, no longer have to endure the indignity of pants that split or zippers that break.

"In a shortage economy, you always have to struggle for life; you have to struggle to get your daily necessities," said Huang Yasheng, a political scientist who grew up in Beijing and is now conducting research about China at Harvard. "It makes a tremendous difference if you can spend half an hour a day shopping instead of four or five hours."

Though Chinese no longer spend much time waiting in lines these days, no easy calculus is available to weigh that gain against the torture inflicted on Catholic priests. This reflects a broader issue. The improvements over which the Communist Party has presided tend to be in material and sometimes mundane areas, while the party's abuses touch directly upon issues of human dignity and freedom that the West says it cares most about.

The torture of a protester pressing for democracy arouses more empathy in the West than, say, the deaths of the 2,000 to 3,000 Chinese peasants who drown in floods in an average year.

THE PARTY
Publicizing Its Worst Side

One of the Communist Party's problems is a phenomenal incompetence in self-promotion. Not since coup leaders in Liberia, in West Africa, invited journalists to watch and photograph the execution of 13 ousted Cabinet ministers in 1980 has a Government shown off its worst side with such relish.

"They are incredibly inept at public relations," said John T. Kamm, a Hong Kong business consultant who has campaigned to free political prisoners.

On the other hand, what the party does well it does quietly. For instance, a comprehensive system of prenatal checkups and free maternal health care has sharply reduced the infant mortality rate over the last decade. In 1980, for every 1,000 live births, 56 babies died in their first year of life. Now only 38 die in every 1,000 live births.

That amounts to saving the lives of 378,000 babies each year. But that is a statistic, while the Government's repression is usually an anecdote—and sometimes a highly publicized one at that.

In a typical such anecdote, last month the authorities banned the country's most prominent independent labor leader, Han Dongfang, from returning to China. The authorities had earlier imprisoned him, tortured him by running a needle through his hand, and intentionally locked him up with tuberculosis patients until he became infected himself.

Which is the Real China?

So which is the real China? Is it the nation where police deliberately expose Mr. Han to the tuberculosis that almost kills him? Or is it the country that offers free prenatal checkups and infant inoculations?

For four decades, Westerners have been debating that question. But no sooner does a consensus emerge about which is the real China than the other one emerges to confuse everyone.

In fact, it is difficult to describe either vision of China as the fundamental one. Both exist side by side, the yin and yang of the China of the 1990's.

"Both faces of China are real ones," said a Chinese woman who has ties to the leadership and yet is privately critical of the party. "You can't pick out one element and say this is the important one."

All countries and all people contain some mix of good and bad, but in China the gulf between the two sides is particularly striking. To come up with a meaningful judgment is a bit like assessing Dr. Jekyll and Mr. Hyde.

Why is it that the party tries to destroy people the way it attacks disease?

Analyzing Deng Xiaoping

To answer that question, it helps to try to enter the mind of Deng Xiaoping and other Communist leaders. As far as anyone can make out, Mr. Deng, the paramount leader, is not just out for himself. He has genuine and profoundly held hopes for China, but these concern collective prosperity and national strength rather than individual freedom.

This is not surprising, for Chinese thinkers traditionally have emphasized the common good rather than individual rights. The expressions in Chinese for "democracy" and "freedom" were coined only 100 years ago, and terms like "human rights" have been used in a positive context by the Government for less than five years.

Mr. Deng has a desperate fear of chaos and conflict, inspired in part by his memories of the wars, famines and upheaval of the first part of this century. By some accounts Mr. Deng's father was beheaded by bandits in 1938, and two other family members were killed or driven to suicide during the Cultural Revolution that began in 1966—and that, to people like Mr. Deng, sums up the terrible price of disorder.

The combination of this mental orientation and practical experience is that Mr. Deng places a huge premium on order and that he is willing to destroy anyone who he believes might unravel it. Dissent, in his view, challenges not just the Communist Party but also China's best hope for modernization. In a talk to other leaders in 1987, he warned that if the proponents of democracy were not crushed, then China would again become simply a "dish of loose sand."

So if the price of saving China from disorder is that dissidents and their families are destroyed—or that demonstrators are mowed down by machine gun fire near Tiananmen Square—well, Mr. Deng has never been a squeamish man.

Still, many young Chinese believe that Mr. Deng is making a colossal miscalculation. They see his stability as that of a pressure cooker: when the top comes off, as it must some day, the explosion will be all the greater because the lid was so tight.

In any case, one open question is how much credit the Chinese Communist Party should get for the increase in living standards. One reason China is growing so rapidly is simply that it lagged in previous decades, and furthermore the boom seems to have more to do with private initiative than with public policy.

The problem of assaying virtue is not, of course, limited to China. Even child molesters can be polite and caring 99 percent of the time, as their mothers tearfully point out at sentencing. Iraq, Libya and the former Soviet Union all raised living standards for a time, yet non got much credit for it because they were simultaneously engaging in what much of the world regarded as repulsive behavior.

On the other hand, most of China's neighbors—Taiwan and South Korea,

among others—have also had their share of massacres and repression, yet the brutality gradually abated and a measure of democracy has begun to bloom in each place. In retrospect, one can make a case that the crucial historical process unfolding in each place a dozen years ago was not the torture of democracy campaigners but the emergence of a middle class that demanded and supported a more democratic system.

In the long run, then, recollections of China in the 1990's may depend on how the country develops in the coming years. If it manages to follow the East Asian model and transform itself into a prosperous and pluralistic nation along the lines of Taiwan or South Korea, then historians may regard the economic boom and the growth of a middle class as the crucial developments in China in the latter part of the 20th century.

On the other hand, if China collapses into chaos and civil war, historians are sure to find that this was predictable. They will argue that the biggest victim of the repression was ultimately the Communist Party itself, for in stifling criticism the party lost its bearings and its ability to correct itself.

Focusing on Repression

In that sense, repression may not be nearly as peripheral as it seems initially.

In the Soviet Union of the 1960's, for instance, dissidents were also on the fringe of society. Yet in retrospect, their voices turned out to be prophetic, and it was clearly worthwhile to focus attention on them instead of on infant mortality rates.

Repression is important in a larger sense as well: dictatorships are often more aggressive and militaristic than democracies. An authoritarian China might be more likely than a democratic one to try to "liberate" Taiwan, or "recover" Mongolia, or "secure" the South China Sea.

Mr. Zhang, the dissident journalist now living in California, suggests that in this respect the political repression, even if it directly involves only a small proportion of people, is still of crucial importance in understanding China. For all the economic strides of the last 15 years, Mr. Zhang said, the nation could lurch into chaos—or threaten its neighbors—unless the party opens up and turns to more democratic methods.

"If China develops its economy rapidly but fails to carry out political reform, there will also be a fundamental problem of safety to the international community," he warned. "In the past, we've seen the examples of Germany and Japan."

Article 15 *The Christian Science Monitor*, August 30, 1994

China's Women Demand Workplace Reform

Labor unrest is on the rise as Chinese women are kept from the benefits of the nation's economic success

Sheila Tefft

Staff writer of The Christian Science Monitor

FUZHOU, CHINA
Last November, 300 young women workers at the Taiwanese-owned Yongqi Footwear Company walked off their jobs for several days after a colleague was accused of stealing and was locked up in a doghouse for several hours.

The strike and the press uproar over the incident have brought some change for some 500 factory workers who left inland rural homes for jobs in the boom economy of coastal Fujian Province: Their overtime pay is one-third higher, food in the factory canteen has improved, and the Taiwanese managers no longer harass and search them for stolen goods.

The women say they are now forming a labor union, with Chinese government help, to press their case for an increase in their $40 monthly wage.

"Only after the big bosses from Taiwan came to investigate did the food get better and our overtime increased," says Ji Xiaolan, who only a year before worked in the fields of her native Jiangxi Province. "We're now setting up our own trade union organization."

As millions here prosper in China's boom times, women workers who fuel the economic engine are being left behind by the country's market reforms. Equality for women, once a cornerstone of Communist China, is eroding—within decrepit state enterprises as well as in glossy foreign ventures. Women workers are the first to get fired, the most widely exploited, and the most frequent victims in the industrial accidents that have hit China in the past year.

Western and Chinese analysts say that women anchor the growing underclass of Chinese jobless and rely on inadequate pensions and benefits that are often not paid. According to a 1993 survey of 1,230 state enterprises by the All-China Federation of Trade Unions, China's 50.6 million women workers make up 38 percent of the work force, but account for 60 percent of the 6 million officially unemployed, the official Economic Daily reports.

Despite gains for women during the more than four decades of Communist Party rule, "Chinese women have less opportunity to get educated, and this has resulted in lower employment status and [fewer] senior positions," says an analyst with China's official labor union.

> ## 'Only after the big bosses from Taiwan came to investigate did the food get better and our overtime increased.'
> ### —Ji Xiaolan, factory worker

Women also are at the center of a growing storm over worker treatment and safety in foreign-run ventures, many located in fast-growing eastern provinces such as Fujian. Hundreds of young women daily pour into this provincial capital from poor interior provinces, seeking jobs and alternatives to their dreary lives back home.

"Working in the factory in the city is fun. The food is better. And I can save 100 renminbi ($11) a month," Zhu Nianhua, a shoe factory worker, said as she sat in the dingy room with broken windows that she shares with three other young women.

"Living conditions are better than in rural areas. At home, we have to work in the fields and are exposed to

Bob Harbison – Staff

NO FRILLS: Ji Xiaolan and Zhu Nianhua, workers at the Yongqi Footwear Company, sit in their living quarters. Once a cornerstone of communist China, equality for women has eroded. Women workers are now the first to get fired, the most widely exploited, and the most frequent victims in industrial accidents.

the sun. But here we don't have to" do that kind of work, she added.

Fujian, a Chinese economic powerhouse with close links to nearby Taiwan, has 310,000 workers in more than 5,000 foreign-run enterprises, 58 percent of them women. In labor-intensive industries such as textiles, shoes, and garments, the percentage can go as high as 90 percent, reports Workers Daily newspaper.

But, Western and Chinese observers say the young women often have to work under appalling conditions: few safety measures; long, unbroken shifts; physical punishment; arbitrary firings; and wage embezzlement and deductions. Last year, dozens of women workers were killed in Fujian and neighboring Guangdong Province in fires in poorly maintained factories.

At fault are usually small and medium-sized factories run principally by Koreans, Japanese, and Chinese from Hong Kong and Taiwan, say the Chinese press and analysts. Mirroring the national picture, only about 20 percent of the foreign enterprises are unionized.

Worried that growing labor unrest in China could undermine its legitimacy, Communist officials have been forced to call for strengthening trade unions in foreign ventures, although they worry that such a move will scare away potential foreign investors and chances to make money.

"China doesn't have a sound legal system [or] labor law," says the trade union official. "Joint venture owners are oftentimes petty capitalists. They don't have much money, so they are against unions in their ventures."

Demands for more labor unions are increasing tensions among foreign businessmen who worry that union presence will only inject more official control rather than act as an honest intermediary in labor disputes. According to government figures, those disputes jumped 50 percent to more than 12,000 in 1993.

While admitting there are abuses, foreign factory managers also contend Chinese workers are often poor workers who steal and resent discipline and hard work. Chen Muchuan, factory director at the shoe factory, said that before the doghouse incident, business had been bad due to delayed deliveries of raw materials and that worker layoffs were in the offing.

"The workers simply don't know how to observe discipline. The factory rule is a fine of 10 yuan if a worker is caught spitting, but still they spit," he says, standing in a clean, properly lit workshop where workers stand around a stalled assembly line, chatting and reading.

"I pay a Chinese college graduate 500 yuan ($55) a month, but he still doesn't know how to supervise them," he adds.

Article 16   *The Christian Science Monitor, March 30, 1994*

Repatriates Transform Economy, Yet Endure Persistent Resentment

As millions returned to China in recent decades, their expectations collided with harsh realities. Now Beijing seeks to help returned Chinese find opportunities.

Sheila Tefft, staff

BEIJING

'Let me call again to the huaqiao *overseas Compatriots to the distant ends of the earth! Only because of the need to feed yourself Did you leave home to wander the seas.'*
—**Song of Revolution, early 20th century**

Liu Jinfeng is one of the tragedies of the Cultural Revolution.

After leaving her native Indonesia for schooling in China in the late 1950s, Ms. Liu hoped to study mathematics at one of Beijing's prestigious universities. But amid the political confusion and eco-

nomic disaster of China in the 1960s, her plans went awry.

As China reached out to foster ties with the developing world, Ms. Liu was assigned to study Turkish for a career in radio announcing at a broadcasting academy. "At the academy, the majority were mainlanders, so overseas ties became sensitive, first with the administrators and later with the students. Whenever we made mistakes, we were told we had 'bourgeois tails,' " she recalls, referring to the Cultural Revolution phrase meaning they were middle class. In 1966, Chairman Mao Zedong and his supporters launched the decade-long factional struggle known as the Cultural Revolution, which brought terror and chaos and rent families asunder.

Upon graduation, Liu was recruited to join the People's Liberation Army (PLA). But when she was identified as an overseas Chinese, or *huaqiao,* she was rejected and relegated to a foreign language publishing house where many with "problem" backgrounds were assigned. "The authorities said, 'She's huaqiao, how can she go to the PLA?' " Liu recalls.

In today's China, Ms. Liu and millions of other overseas Chinese no longer carry the stigma they once did.

As economic changes overshadow past disappointments, millions of overseas Chinese once again look homeward to China, lured by the riches of the robust economy and tugged sometimes by the deep emotions a reinvigorated China stirs.

Like modern China's founding fathers—Sun Yat-sen, Nationalist leader Chiang Kai-shek, and Mao—paramount leader Deng Xiaoping has galvanized prosperous overseas Chinese with a new vision of China.

By replacing Marxism with market reform, Mr. Deng has reaped billions of dollars in overseas Chinese investment and a flurry of new schools, hospitals, and other philanthropy. Accounting for 70 to 80 percent of foreign investment in China, overseas Chinese who were once persecuted for their foreign ties are now wooed by central and local officials across China.

Western and Asian observers contend the growing overseas Chinese presence in China, focused in booming coastal provinces, feeds the growing instability in China. Their secretive, backroom dealings fuel corruption in the Communist Party and the government. And their privileged status makes them targets of local resentment.

"Overseas Chinese are the engine behind the corruption and bribery rampant now in China," says an Asian banker in Beijing.

Still, in a country with nascent capital markets, rapid change, and no rule of law, the insider dealing and network of connections of overseas Chinese provide efficient channels for China's economic modernization. "Overseas connections are a good thing," Deng said in a goodwill pronouncement a few years ago.

In a gesture to right past wrongs and placate overseas investors, the government decided earlier this year to implement a controversial plan to aid returned overseas Chinese.

Although many were alienated by the excesses of the Cultural Revolution and fled, in a second exodus, to Hong Kong, Taiwan, and other countries, China still has about 30 million returned citizens and their relatives. About three-quarters came from Indonesia; they left after persecution during the 1950s and 1960s and were barred from returning.

The measures to aid overseas Chinese require local officials to help provide jobs, give priority in college enrollment and housing allotment, support their enterprises, end discrimination in conferring professional titles, and settle for houses confiscated in the past.

But local officials often oppose what they see as special treatment. Despite government goodwill, returned overseas Chinese say local Communist officials continue to restrict travel and discriminate in jobs.

The government admits that injustices of the past still have not been redressed.

In a recent speech, Xu Yongsheng, director of the Beijing overseas Chinese office, said that because prejudice remains, "returned overseas Chinese and their relatives still have lingering fears."

"Mainlanders think we're cutting into the cake. So if we leave, they will get a bigger share," Liu Jinfeng says.

Yanjing Overseas Chinese University, established in Beijing to expand educational opportunities, has difficulty placing its graduates because it lacks government accreditation. Unable to raise money in China, the university is building a new campus with the help of overseas Chinese from the Philippines and Indonesia and expects to get accreditation this year.

"It is hard to get jobs without a college education, and this is the problem that many children of returned overseas Chinese have," Yanjing provost Wu Yinshao says.

Recently, the official Outlook Weekly reported that an overseas Chinese woman in Guandong was dismissed for allegedly fabricating charges that her boss was steal-

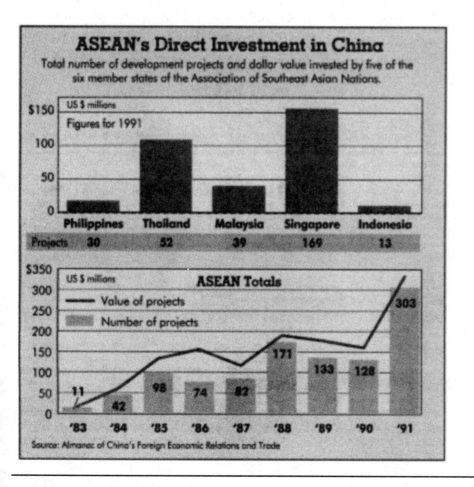

ASEAN's Direct Investment in China

Total number of development projects and dollar value invested by five of the six member states of the Association of Southeast Asian Nations.

US $ millions — Figures for 1991

	Philippines	Thailand	Malaysia	Singapore	Indonesia
Projects	30	52	39	169	13

ASEAN Totals (US $ millions) — Value of projects / Number of projects

'83: 11 (42) — '85: 98 — '86: 74 — '87: 82 — '88: 171 — '89: 133 — '90: 128 — '91: 303

Source: Almanac of China's Foreign Economic Relations and Trade

ing public funds. When she went to court demanding reinstatement, her case was dismissed after local officials interfered. The official Office of Overseas Chinese Affairs and the quasi-official All-China Federation of Returned Overseas Chinese refused interview requests.

"China regards overseas Chinese as dogs.... When the Nationalists came, the dog returned because of its attachment to the land. When the Nationalists wanted to kill the dog, it ran away again. When the Communists came, the same thing happened," says Lie Siong Tay, an Indonesian industrialist who fled to Jakarta when the Communists came to power in China in 1949. "Whenever the policy changes for the better, the dog returns."

Still, cynicism does not stop Mr. Lie from spending $10 million to open schools in his native Fujian Province, endowing a university, and planning joint-venture motorcycle production plants in three Chinese cities—Fuzhou, Guangzhou, and Shanghai.

For an oppressed Chinese minority in a country like Indonesia, donations and investment in China provide both self-esteem, which has been difficult to attain in their adoptive country, and inclusion in the vast Chinese family that needs and courts their money.

"I still feel rootless. I guess that's why I still feel attachment to the motherland," says Lie, who now goes by the Indonesian name Susanta Lyman.

Indonesian Chinese, who comprise the largest group of returnees, turned homeward during the 1950s and 1960s for education and refuge from tumult in Indonesia. In the early 1950s, Chinese were drawn not so much by patriotism as China's good universities.

Amid brutal anti-Chinese violence after Indonesia's abortive coup in 1965, many Chinese youths fled. But they found little refuge in a China plunging into the Cultural Revolution.

"They left Indonesia only to end up in the sheer chaos of China. They ended up in special zones in the south, coping with ... difficult circumstances," says Michael Godley, an Australian historian studying returned Indonesian Chinese.

Liu Jinfeng was part of a second wave of naively idealistic Chinese who left Indonesia amid anti-Chinese tensions in the late 1950s. Seasick and depressed during her voyage on a steamer carrying 3,000 Indonesian Chinese, Jinfeng and her younger sister, Quiping, survived on a vision.

"Illusions permeated the ship. We pictured life in China as so rosy," recalls Liu, a soft-spoken woman with a girlish giggle. But the sisters, who joined an older brother already in China, found nothing idyllic in hurly-burly Canton, their first stop. Life was more difficult and precarious than in Muslim Indonesia. Some of the goods their parents had given them for bartering were stolen.

Disillusionment grew as she was forced to do manual labor—digging a reservoir, building a government guest house, forging iron at a blast furnace—during the disastrous communization and mass mobilization campaign known as the Great Leap Forward.

"Food was scarce. I was hungry, but there was nothing to eat," she recalls.

In 1966, the Cultural Revolution erupted. As Liu found herself confined by her background in a job she didn't want, her life that year took another troubled turn. She married a Chinese soldier, a fellow student who she later believed worked as a military intelligence officer. The first of her two daughters was born later that year.

Liu's overseas ties, which almost prevented officials from sanctioning the marriage in the first place, became her husband's brutal weapon. He insisted on showing her letters to Indonesia to his bosses, so she stopped writing. When his application for Communist Party membership was held up due to her family background, he blamed her. "Once, after she bought a pottery set, "he chased me around the house, reading [Mao's] little red book."

Liu was barred from attending meetings at her workplace and isolated from her colleagues. When a school friend committed suicide, Red Guards implicated her. At her job and during several work stints in the countryside, she was the frequent target of "struggle sessions," at which people were brutally criticized to make them ideologically pure.

When her younger brother—who returned from Indonesia in the early 1960s—was sent to the countryside and decided to flee to Hong Kong, Liu and other family members intervened to keep him from going. They feared Liu's husband would take retribution against those who stayed behind.

As the Cultural Revolution ended and China's economic reforms took shape in the late 1970s, Liu's life also changed. She lost her job because China stopped exporting the revolution and the propaganda she translated.

Two years later, she divorced. Today, remarried and retired, she lives in Beijing in a small apartment with her husband, a college professor, and her youngest daughter. Just outside are the tattered suitcase and the old Dutch-made bicycle she brought from Indonesia.

"The overall policy may have changed, but in fact there is no fundamental change in the attitude to overseas Chinese.... No matter how hard the overseas Chinese tries, she won't be able to make it," she says.

Article 17   *The New York Times Magazine*, September 4, 1994

CHINA'S RUSH TO RICHES

Individuals like Ah Chang, not to mention whole Government agencies, are hustling their way to wealth on the primitive, crowded capitalist road.

Sheryl WuDunn

Before many more years go by, China is likely to surpass the United States as the world's biggest economy. It already is the fastest-growing economy, one of the consequences of a new Chinese revolution. Sheryl WuDunn and Nicholas D. Kristof watched that revolution from the inside as The Time's correspondents in Beijing from 1988 to 1993 and won a Pulitzer Prize for journalism in 1990.

In a new book, "China Wakes" (Times Books), they describe a society that is at once politically repressive and economically freewheeling. The regime still allows a prisoner to be asphyxiated by the fumes from his own uncollected excrement, turns the family members of imprisoned human rights campaigners out on the streets, forces young women to undergo sterilization and abortion. At the same time, the Government is overseeing a breathtaking transformation of individual lives and institutions that is rapidly making China richer than ever before. The following excerpts, written like their book in alternate chapters by the two authors, portray today's money-making frenzy—and China's future as a global economic giant.

The State Security Ministry secretly runs a dry-cleaning establishment that caters to foreigners in Beijing. Initially I was suspicious, thinking that this was a way to plant bugs in the suits of foreign diplomats and journalists. My Chinese friends laughed at my suspicions.

"Of course not," one said. "State Security just wants to make money."

For the same reason, State Security also ran a bakery, and the national police went into hotel management. The Army General Staff Department became part owner of one of China's best hotels, the Palace. For a time, a local army unit ran a travel service that operated a brothel. The army also runs scores of factories that make televisions, refrigerators, clocks and other products. The Public Security Ministry runs a fascinating pair of shops selling night sticks and electric cattle prods.

What happened is that Government offices felt that they had been left out of the money game. So they decided to go into business, often taking advantage of extra land, well-placed contacts or special skills. Even schools began to run their own factories or farm yards to raise extra money for chairs and textbooks and teacher salaries.

There's a downside to all of this, of course. Many school principals seem to devote more energy to their sideline businesses than to the curriculum. And when a liquor bureau runs a bar on the side, rival taverns may have reason to complain about the fairness of the regulations. Yet there's also a benefit: These companies give the bureaucrats a stake in the market economy. Officials at every level now depend for their personal incomes and benefits on the progress of the reforms and the economic system. Only a thriving market can satisfy their hunger.

Everyone in China, it seems, has gone into business or is moonlighting: waitressing at night, writing articles for popular magazines, teaching English or aerobics, consulting on computer programs or giving seminars on stocks and bonds. If they don't already have an evening job, Chinese intellectuals and officials are taking night classes to train for a second career. This way, they are able to triple or quadruple their salaries, and, at the same time, keep their "iron rice bowl"—with its job security, housing and health insurance.

China today is something of a cross between Dodge City and Dickensian England. It's a lawless place motivated by a strange mix of greed and apprehension that this wonderful money-making opportunity could end at any moment. China may not use little boys as chimney sweeps, but the textile and garment industries work children 14 hours a day, seven days a week, and often they sleep by their looms. If you lose your arm in the loom, you're fired. That may sound grim, but 19th-century capitalism is a big improvement over 18th-century feudalism.

Some people say China is not really moving toward Western-style capitalism because the capital still belongs to state-owned banks that assign it for noneconomic reasons. In other words, the price of capital in China isn't interest. It's a bribe. Or it's the work that has gone into cultivating guanxi, or connections, with the bankers and local officials. They are right, to some degree, but then again 19th-century capitalism didn't operate exactly by the book, either. Some of the vast fortunes were collected through monopolies, which in turn were frequently awarded because of bribes or connections in Washington or the state capitals.

The same kind of manipulation of economics and politics is happening today in China, and there is a strong sense throughout the country that now is the time in which the great financial empires will be made, before the system becomes more rigid and the opportunities fewer.

The analogy with the industrializing United States is also a reminder that a country can endure enormous shocks and turbulence at the same time it is enjoying economic growth. In the 19th century, Americans saw appalling inequity, gross manipulations of the political system, lynchings, bank collapses, brutal repression of labor and leftist activism.

A visitor to the United States in the 19th century might easily have been overwhelmed by the injustice and disorder. He could have interviewed penniless immigrants in the crime-plagued slums of Boss Tweed's New York, chatted with dispossessed farmers in the Great Plains during one of the several depressions, toured the cotton plantations of the South and the manufacturing cities of the Northeast and listened to the rage. And he could well have concluded that the center would never hold, that America would be swept by war and revolution. Instead, the history of the United States underscores how much abuse a country can absorb when it is growing economically.

China now enjoys that kind of economic growth, and perhaps it too will demonstrate this kind of resiliency. There is, however, one big difference. The United States had established a civil society and enjoyed a far more flexible political system, one that could respond to popular pressure without exploding. A free press had always flourished, and elections were regularly held everywhere, even if they were sometimes rigged. However inadequate the political and legal system was in the 19th century, it was far more responsive than China's is today. In China, the question remains: Will this era's emperors allow their system to evolve in similar ways?

A h Chang is a man in his early 30's, 5 foot 2, with thinning hair, a wrinkling smile and a thickening waistline. Nick and I met him through friends, and I looked him up whenever I visited his hometown of Guangzhou (Canton). Each time I dropped by, he was engaged in a different line of business. Each time he was richer.

Ah Chang, a nickname used by his Cantonese friends, never went to college. After he finished high school, he spent a year sawing boards and soldering wires in an electronics shop. From there, he was transferred to a job stoking a coal-burning furnace, where he shoveled coal all day long, breathing the moist dust each time he inhaled. When he came home, his hair and face clouded by a veil of black soot, his mother would look at him and cry.

He made his first fortune in the late 1980's as a restaurant owner. But he worried that the environment might change after Deng Xiaoping's death, and so he was looking for a way to move abroad. Then the 1989 Tiananmen movement gave him a chance. He was simply one of the millions of passive supporters of the Tiananmen movement, and he was in no danger of being arrested. Nevertheless, he had heard through the grapevine that America was giving political asylum to anyone who claimed involvement in the movement.

He sold his business and bought a false American passport for $20,000. The passport was a good forgery, but even so Ah Chang was worried about being caught. Instead of flying directly to the United States, he flew throughout Asia, stopping in Hong Kong, Singapore and Tokyo, where he stayed a few days before he made his way to San Francisco. Once he arrived in California, he thought he had made it. He destroyed his passport, because he was afraid of being caught with a forgery, and turned himself into the immigration authorities. He claimed political asylum.

The Immigration Service detained him for several months and then determined that he was not a genuine political refugee. It returned him to China. Once there, Ah Chang bribed and ingratiated his way out of trouble, but his money was gone—he had spent $30,000 on his passport, air tickets, bribes and other costs—and he had no business.

He started again from scratch, opening a small restaurant and bar in Guangdong, paying off the authorities so that he could run a cable from a satellite dish on a nearby roof. That enabled him to show Hong Kong television in his bar, and business improved. Even so, he wasn't making as much money as he wanted. His big break came when a major foreign developer wanted to buy out his restaurant and demolish it as part of a large construction project. The foreigners handed over $40,000 to Ah Chang.

"It wasn't a very good restaurant," he told me over dinner one evening. "I didn't manage it very well. I had all my friends over and they ate cheaply. But I had a good location. In a flash, I had $40,000."

Ah Chang took the money and bought a large apartment, which he furnished lavishly. His total assets were now about $70,000. He hardly cared about politics but he did like his freedom and he did want to travel. He had hooked up with a Hong Kong Da Laoban, or Big Boss, and was helping him hunt for property

deals. He had also begun trading shoes, contracting with factories and selling the shoes in other cities in China. He had his eye on a car and he had plunked down nearly $45,000 to buy a lakeside summer home.

Now is the time, many Chinese feel, when the great fortunes will be made, before the system becomes more rigid and opportunities fewer.

Ah Chang was always devising ways of making money, like selling medicines. He happened to befriend the factory manager of a large pharmaceutical manufacturer, and the manager agreed to supply him with one of the latest kinds of intravenous solutions.

"I've known the guy for an entire year," Ah Chang explained. "He calls me practically every day and I accompany him wherever he wants to go. I eat meals with him and run around and have fun with him. So he trusts me and I trust him. Then I took the purchaser at a hospital out to lunch, and he says he'll buy the medicine from me. I'll slip a little to him on the side."

"How much will you give him?" I asked.

"I'll give him 50 percent."

"How much will you give the factory manager?" I asked.

"I'll give him about 20 percent."

"But then all you have left is 30 percent," I said.

"But 30 percent isn't so bad. If I get 30 percent here, 30 percent there and 30 percent somewhere else, that's not so bad. There's really no other way. I have to give them a cut to make them happy. At least I make something. After all, the law doesn't allow individuals to trade in medicine, so I need a way to hook up with someone who has a license."

Ah Chang's newest moneymaking scheme is smuggling dogs into China. He is bringing in dogs as pets, not as food, which is how Cantonese traditionally viewed dogs. "In fact, this is good for society," he said. Chinese should stop looking at dogs as dishes and should start looking at them as companions, he added. There was a great demand for pets, but there was a rule against importing dogs: you simply couldn't bring them in for sale.

"Everyone smuggles, and I'm just a pea in the business," Ah Chang explained. "It may be against the law, but the law is ridiculous. You see, I'm not cheating anyone, really. I'm cheating the Government, but that's nothing. The Government has cheated the ordinary people for years, and it still cheats us because it doesn't let us import many things. Anyhow, I'm not smuggling drugs."

I was always curious how these smugglers operated. Were they the Chinese mafia? Were they an organized network of people who carried cellular phones and wore black suits? Ah Chang explained that a friend had introduced him to a maritime smuggler, a man who lives in a large multistoried brick house with lots of privacy. Most farmers use their land to grow rice or dig fish ponds. This man, an uneducated peasant who knew the sea but couldn't even write his name, had converted his plot of land into a nice lawn. His entire family had quit farming to work in the family smuggling business. No big networks. This guy fended for himself. His family owned two big boats that they kept hidden by the coast. Even Ah Chang didn't dare ask where the boats were.

"How does he actually smuggle the stuff into China?" I asked.

"I tell him what I want, where to get it, who to pick it up from in Hong Kong," Ah Chang said. "Then I give him a deposit, and when he brings the merchandise to me, I pay him the rest."

The whole family invited Ah Chang over to the house and then treated him to a fancy meal at a dimly lit restaurant with beautiful, and available, women.

"Each time we go out, he pays several thousand yuan," or hundreds of dollars, Ah Chang said. "He needs to find customers, too. Is this the underground mafia? Hmph! I don't know what this mafia is that everyone refers to. You call my small-time peasant fisherman the mafia? I don't think so. He just wants to make some money. Would you say I'm dealing with the mafia? I don't think so. What's the mafia, then? Maybe it's the people who smuggle heroin, maybe it's the pimps and prostitutes, the weapons dealers. Maybe that's it. In america, you know what's illegal. Your laws are clear. Not in China. In fact, in China, the policy, they're the worst of them all. They're linked to the smugglers, too. China is a crazy country now."

Organized crime seemed, in part, organized by the state. Everyone knew that the police and the customs officials were involved in smuggling and other illicit practices. There was Fangcheng, for instance.

Fangcheng, a small port in Guangxi Province, suddenly became one of the most popular harbors in China. The reason was that the local customs officials were involved in small sideline broker companies that offered to handle all the paper work for importing goods. These broker companies set up offices along a street near the port, and the importer simply handed shipping documents to the company, which then filled out all the customs forms, obtained the import licenses and ushered the goods through customs. For this the officials took a fat commission, but the buyer didn't feel the pinch. The customs officers never assessed the true substantial duties on goods handled by the sideline companies, so importers saved large sums on duties and the brokers could then skim some for themselves.

The central Government realized that something was up when cargoes destined for all parts of China lined up to use this one small port in Guangxi. There were huge delays for ships to get into the port, and hardly any duty was being paid. So the authorities investigated and temporarily closed the port in mid-1993.

The Government has had occasional successes like Fangcheng, but on a broader scale it is unable to come to grips with the country's rampant corruption. Rather, money and resources have gone into feeding the national obsession—the expansion of the economy. And this frenetic growth may be brokering a true revolution in China.

Nicholas D. Kristof

When the historians of the world gather 100 years from now, they may well conclude that the dominant trend of our age was the rise of China.

From the vantage point of someone with a long view, the ascendancy of the West is a recent phenomenon—dating from about 500 years ago. For much of history Chinese philosophy, poetry, science and government were more sophisticated than those of Europe, and China's standard of living may have been higher. If China can raise its standard of living and education, if it can squeeze out of its present ideological straitjacket, then—who knows what it may have in store for the world?

China's economic revolution is more significant than the Maoist revolution of the 1940's and 50's, and the best way to appreciate its magnitude is to squat in the fields in rural villages, chatting with peasants. The World Bank calculates that since the reform era began in 1978 a total of 170 million Chinese have risen from absolute poverty. That marks a 60 percent decline in the number of the destitute in China—impressive by any standard. In the Philippines, the number of absolutely poor people in 1990, 13 million, is the same as in 1970.

Xing Yisheng's life offers a window into the scope of the change for the poorest Chinese. I met him in a mud-brick village on the edge of the Gobi Desert in northwestern Gansu Province. Xing, 74, was wearing a much-patched and faded Mao suit. He was hobbling down a rutted dirt path, and he invited me into his shack a few doors away.

The shack had two rooms, each dominated by a kang, a platform bed with a fireplace underneath. The dirt floor was swept clean and the furniture consisted of three rickety wooden chairs set around a crude wooden table. The mud walls were papered with newspapers, with pictures from old calendars providing a bit of color. Xing grandly commanded a daughter-in-law to bring tea, which she carefully poured into a couple of cracked cups.

"Before Liberation," he recalled, referring to the Communist takeover in 1949, "I was just a farmhand, working for the landlords, because I didn't have any land. I had two sons then, but I had to sell them because I didn't have any money. I was ill with typhoid. So I sold my two boys for 400 pounds of rice each. I never saw them again.

"There's a huge difference between life now and the way it was then," Xing added. A grown son—one of four children born after 1949—sat quietly a few feet away, looking bored, as if he had heard it all before. "Our life today is better than a landlord's life in the past. But

I tell this to young people and they don't want to hear. They say, Go away! They don't know about the old life."

Xing pointed reproachfully at his son, who appeared to be in his late 30's. "Young man," Xing declared, his voice rising, "now you're living in heaven! You dress well, you eat well." Xing turned back to me and waved dismissively at his son. "Why, last year this young man wanted to buy a stereo cassette recorder for 700 yuan [about $80 at the unofficial exchange rate]. I said: 'No, that's too much. We should buy a mule.' A mule can work. It's useful. A stereo isn't. And a mule is so big, while a stereo is so small."

It was clear who had won the argument. A nice stereo occupied the place of honor in the middle of the room. Despite Xing's misgivings, the family was doing more than subsist; it was beginning to enjoy a bit of leisure. A similar change is unfolding in most of the million-odd villages in China.

Since Deng Xiaoping took over in 1978, the Chinese economy has enjoyed an annual average growth rate of a bit more than 9 percent. That is triple the average growth rate of the United States in that period, and about 70 percent more than the growth rate in India or Indonesia.

China is now the biggest producer in the world of coal, cement, grain, cotton, meat and fish. It ranks third in steel production, after Japan and the United States and fifth in crude oil output, after the United States, Saudi Arabia, Russia and Iran.

To get a sense of the giddy pace of change in China, just consider the process of industrialization around the world. Britain was the first country to enjoy an industrial revolution, beginning in the late 18th century, and it then took 58 years for per capita British gross domestic product to double. The American Industrial revolution was a bit faster, with per capita output doubling in 47 years from 1839. Beginning in 1885, Japan doubled its per capita gross domestic product in 34 years.

Now, in the late 20th century, China is roaring along with its own industrial revolution, doubling its per capita output every 10 years. The "Four Dragons"—Taiwan, Hong Kong, Singapore and South Korea—managed similar growth rates, or even slightly higher ones, in peak periods of their development, but together they are no more than the size of a Chinese province. For such growth rates in such a huge country as China, there's been nothing like it in history.

Last year, the World Bank published a major study on East Asia, concluding that there was only one chance in 10,000 that so many economic miracles would be located so close to one another. There are some important common threads among the region's success stories, and they may shed some light on China's prospects.

Like its neighbors, China began its reform program with an effort to boost agricultural incentives. Japan, Taiwan and South Korea also underwent a land redistribution in the aftermath of World War II, and the relative equality seems to have been a factor in their growth. Again, like its neighbors, China has opened itself up to foreign investment, and its export drive in the coastal provinces has forced it to compete with other manufacturers around the world.

The high saving rate in today's East Asia is particularly striking. China has a personal saving rate that ranges between 35 and 40 percent, compared with about 5 percent in the United States. These savings generate the capital for new factories, roads and shops that, in turn, boost economic growth.

The other kind of capital necessary for sustained growth is human capital—a healthy, educated work force that can run assembly lines and figure out how to do things better and faster. The Communists have done well in primary education, and nearly all children get at least a few years of elementary school. Perhaps 95 percent of all children start school and more than 80 percent graduate from elementary school. Because of the Communist Party's traditional suspicion of intellectuals, China has a low university enrollment, only 1.7 percent. But even there China manages to focus its training on the specialties it needs; every year it manages to graduate more than 200,000 engineers, nearly twice as many as the United States.

Literacy is still low, but it is much higher than ever before. Wang Chigang, a 76-year-old peasant in central Anhui Province, typifies the country's many illiterates. He grew up as a landless peasant and beggar, never went to school and still cannot write his name. "I don't like the city," he said, sipping a cup of dark tea in his shack. "Too crowded. Nobody has time for you. And it's embarrassing when I have to go to the toilet—I don't know which is which. Since I don't know the characters for 'man' and 'woman,' I have to ask for help finding the right one." Yet Wang's children and his grandchildren have all gone to school. Pointing to a grandson who finished high school, Wang boasted, "He can write really well."

While some local governments ignore the illiteracy problem, others are actively campaigning to teach people to read and write. In the villages of Xiping County in Henan Province in central China, students stop visitors and ask them to read a few characters on a blackboard. Any visitor who cannot read the characters is not allowed to enter the village. This means that illiterates are effectively grounded, and in frustration many have joined the special reading classes offered in each village. Now in Xiping County, according to local officials, only 1.7 percent of those between the ages of 20 and 40 are illiterate.

The other crucial kind of human capital in which the Communists have invested is public health care. The Chinese medical system is in many ways a model for developing countries. While China spends less than 4 percent of gross national product on medical care (compared with 15 percent in the United States), its health statistics are comparable to those of much richer nations. And in the cities, health statistics are as good as those of American urban areas. In Shanghai, for example, the most recent figure shows that 9.9 out of every 1,000 infants die in their first year of life. In New York City the infant mortality rate is 10.2 per 1,000. A baby in Shanghai can expect to live 76 years, while average life expectancy in New York is 73.8 years.

To get a better sense of how Chinese doctors achieve such health statistics, I spent a day with the perpetually sorrowful Dr. Su Ke in the villages of Xishuangbanna District, a tropical region near Vietnam. A 46-year-old with a graying crew cut, Dr. Su works out of a rural clinic but regularly hikes with the other doctors into the mountains to see the peasants who don't believe in doctors. As we drove into the mountains in my hired car, he explained the difficulties.

"When we go out and try to inoculate babies, some of the peasants are very frightened and hide their kids," Dr. Su said. "Or they turn their dogs on us to bite us and drive us away." Even if Dr. Su manages to get his needle into the derrière of a local child—a task made easier because none of them wear pants—he is likely to get in trouble. "We give them injections against measles, and then the kid gets a cold. So the parents come and complain. They say, 'You promised that my child wouldn't get sick!'"

We stopped the car by a roadside one-room clinic operated by an 18-year-old peasant who had just opened up shop as a doctor. The peasant was trying to pull the abscessed tooth of a teen-age girl, but he wasn't making much headway. Blood was all over, and knives and pliers were scattered about, and both the doctor and the patient looked a bit discouraged. There was no Novocain, but the young woman was using some Chinese medicine that seemed to deaden the pain pretty well. Dr. Su took over the pair of pliers, rapped away with a chisel, and after about five minutes the tooth came out.

Instead of allocating resources for dental offices or complex procedures like coronary operations or dialysis, China has channeled its money to basic care—an approach that is far more cost-effective. For example, basic treatment for leukemia costs about $5,000 and on average adds a bit more than a month to a patient's life. The same $5,000, used to buy vitamin A supplements for children, adds a total of 10,000 years of life expectancy.

What do these improvements in health, education and living standards add up to? For all the brutality of the Chinese regime, it is presiding over an economic revolution that is scarcely fathomable. Never before in human history have so many people—or even such a large share of humanity—risen from poverty so rapidly.

China's economic gains are mirrored in a broader phenomenon: the rise of a "Greater China" as an increasingly integrated economic entity. Greater China consists of China, Hong Kong and Taiwan; despite their political differences, their economies are being melded into one. Taiwanese companies have moved entire assembly lines across the Taiwan Strait into southern China. Most of the Taiwan shoemaking industry has relocated to Guangdong and Fujian Provinces; much of the garment and sportswear industries have moved as well. Once Taiwan allows direct flights across the strait, that air route from China to Taiwan may well become one of the busiest in the world, the Asian equivalent of the Boston–New York–Washington corridor.

The global economy is sometimes said to be tripolar, revolving around the United States, Japan and the European Community. But Greater China is rapidly becoming a fourth pole, a new pillar of the international economy. According to World Bank projections using comparable international prices, Greater China in the year 2002 is projected to have a gross domestic product of $9.8 trillion, compared with $9.7 trillion in the same year for the United States. If those forecasts hold, Greater China would not just be another economic pole. It would be the biggest of them all.

It is possible that China will fall apart during the succession struggles after the death of Deng Xiaoping. But, for all the risks, there is a strong chance China will succeed over the coming decades in sustaining an economic boom. If so, the ramifications would not only be economic; the global diplomatic, political and military balance may also have to be recalibrated.

Continued economic growth also means that China will demand far more of the world's energy resources. It will add substantially to the world's problems with acid rain, chlorofluorocarbons and other environmental hazards. China may come to dominate a number of sports and sweep the medals chart in every Olympics. Already China has the largest army in the world and the most rapidly increasing military budget.

Some would argue that China's Government cannot sustain its economic revolution because it is so despotic. But that is probably faulty thinking. In determining economic growth, repression may matter, but savings rates matter more. There is a historical parallel that underscores how one can harbor hopes for China while retaining an antipathy for the present leadership.

The dynasty in Chinese history most like the present one is the Qin, founded in 221 B.C. by an emperor who was a brilliant military leader and a cruel tyrant. The Qin emperor burned books and buried scholars alive, but he also unified the country and linked border fortifications to create the Great Wall. Mao Zedong himself acknowledged (and was flattered by) the similarities in vision and ruthlessness between him and the Qin emperor.

Partly because the Qin emperor was so harsh his dynasty lasted just a few years after his death. Yet the Qin emperor laid a foundation that served China well. The next dynasty was the Han, which lasted more than four centuries and was a golden era—a flourishing age for the arts and scholarship as well as for the economy.

The Communist dynasty, like the Qin, may well have inadvertently laid a foundation for the next dynasty. The Communists' brutality and incompetence killed tens of millions of Chinese, and torture continues today in prisons around the country. But the party also united China, redistributed land and wealth, and destroyed the special interests that were stifling economic growth. China now has a chance to grow and prosper and become a major international power, perhaps eventually a superpower such as the world has never known.

Article 18   *The Wall Street Journal,* July 25, 1994

Cost of Growth

China's Environment Is Severely Stressed As Its Industry Surges

Beijing Seeks Foreign Help In Addressing a Problem With Global Implications

Role for Western Companies

Marcus W. Brauchli

Staff Reporter of The Wall Street Journal

TANGXI, China—The slow, hot days of summer are here, and sun-fed algae is starting to clot the milky surface of Chao Lake. Soon a living scum will carpet a patch the size of New York City. It will quickly blacken and rot—and the 4,000 residents of this lakeside village will face another summer of misery.

Fish will be scarce, and fresh water rife with biological toxins. But that isn't what residents dread most. "The smell is so terrible you cannot describe it," says Xu Jiajiao, a retired farmer who still remembers the bountiful fishing in China's fifth-biggest lake before it was choked by algae-breeding pollutants. In the city of Hefei, where a million people get putrid lake water from their taps each summer, a scientist named Zhang Zhiyuan declares: "This problem must be solved."

The question is, by whom?

Canada and Australia have lent money for water-treatment facilities. The European Union is funding a study of the problems. So is the Asian Development Bank, which may be asked to provide a $100 million loan next year. The government of surrounding Anhui Province last year sent a delegation to the U.S., in part to seek American assistance in the cleanup. Total estimated cost: $200 million-plus.

Common Pattern

"I can't say we have enough capability to solve all our problems without some foreign help," admits Wang Yuqing, deputy administrator of China's National Environmental Protection Agency. "But we are committed."

The mess at Chao Lake, which lies about 200 miles west of Shanghai, is an oft-repeated pattern these days in China. Rapid development has transformed big tracts of this ancient nation into environmental wasteland. Acid rain nibbles at the Great Wall; the Grand Canal in places resembles an open sewer; part of Shanghai is slowly sinking as its water table is depleted; and Benxi, in Manchuria, is so thick with air pollution the city doesn't appear in satellite pictures. Yet though Beijing pledges often and loudly to clean up the proliferating messes, it depends heavily on foreigners to finance, supply and even manage cleanup efforts.

For aid agencies and governments, the ecological calamities resulting from China's 10% average annual growth over the last decade and a half present tremendous need. No major economy is growing faster—and nowhere are environmental stresses greater. Japan fears that sulfurous rain clouds drifting over from China will blemish its own cleanup efforts.

Foreign Aid

Motivated by such worries, the World Bank now channels as much as $500 million a year into environmental programs in China. Japan, Europe, Canada and Australia are offering hundreds of millions more in loans, technical assistance and equipment. The U.S., which is barred under sanctions imposed after a crackdown on democracy demonstrations in 1989 from giving direct support to environmental programs, is considering regulations that would encourage American companies to help China clean up.

Environmental companies are circling. "There could be big opportunities," says Thomas G. Smith, who heads the Asian operation of global waste concern WMX Technologies Inc., of Oak Brook, Ill. (formerly known as Waste Management Inc.), which is gathering data on China's myriad messes.

Adds California Lt. Gov. Leo McCarthy, who has led several successful environmental trade missions to China and plans to do more after he retires this year: "No country needs environmental technology as badly as China. "This isn't abstract."

Enormous Scope

By its sheer dimensions—nearly one in every four people lives in China, on less arable land per capita than any other country save Egypt or Bangladesh—China seems foreordained to be an environmental burden on the world. Vaclav Smil, a professor at the University of Manitoba in Canada, figures that if China's economy putters along at an average real growth rate of only 2% a year—a fraction of its explosive 13.4% growth last year—arable land lost to development between now and the year 2000 will equal all the cultivated land in Vietnam; China's particulate emissions will leap by an amount equal to what the U.S. spewed out in 1990; and output of acid-rain-causing sulfur dioxide will rise by an amount equal to Germany's.

"If anybody's economic development is unsustainable, it's China's," frets Prof. Smil. "Many people in the top leadership are aware that it's bad to develop and let the environment slip. But their hearts aren't in it."

But China is determined to prove the Cassandras wrong. The State Council has declared the environment a top priority, along with controlling the growth of the population, now nearing 1.2 billion. Officials link the two: "Family planning is in charge of the people who aren't born, environmental protection is responsible for dealing with those who are," jokes Pan Tiansheng, a deputy director of the Anhui Environmental Protection Bureau, who was hospitalized for two years earlier in his life because of industrial pollution. The provincial capital of Hefei symbolizes the problem: When the Communist Party came to power in 1949, it was a rural outpost of 20,000; today, its population of more than one million spews 300,000 tons a day of untreated waste water and sewage.

Alarmed by such statistics, China's environmental agencies are trying to clamp down, threatening tough measures, including jail, for violating environmental laws. Shanghai shut down 10 factories last year, while Guangdong Province, just north of Hong Kong, ordered 12 heavily polluting factories out of cities in 1992 and banned the use of coal in the coastal zone of Zhuhai. The reason: Four of every 10 rainfalls in the province were acidic.

Regulators also assess fines—though some local environmental offices are chary of cracking down too well on polluters, because fines are a main source of regulators' revenue. "They can't really afford for everyone to comply" with environmental laws, says a specialist who has worked with the Chinese agencies. That reluctance has spawned some unusual approaches in this tightly controlled, nominally Communist state. Journalists sometimes are invited to "expose" polluters, and Beijing quietly has allowed nongovernmental organizations to work on the environment.

Air and Water

Beijing says its efforts are paying off. Waste-water discharges declined 3% last year to 35.5 billion tons—still the equivalent of all the water that flowed through the Yellow River that year. But air pollution worsened—though the government won't quantify it—and deaths by lung cancer, the leading cause of death in China, rose to 34 per 100,000 people; that is an increase of 18.5% in five years.

In spite of China's pledge to clean up, foreign companies in China often find they are pioneers in ecological awareness. When H. B. Fuller Co., a Minneapolis-based adhesives company, put in water-treatment equipment at its factory in a gritty industrial zone outside Guangzhou, "our Chinese competitors thought we were crazy," says William E. O'Brien, Fuller's general manager. His rivals were accustomed to using and dumping water untreated. But having seen Western companies such as Fuller, Coca-Cola Co. and PepsiCo Inc. putting in the latest equipment, Chinese companies are starting to follow suit—in part to avoid penalties.

'Rich Is Glorious'

That could prove a commercial bonanza for environmental companies, which are just starting to scavenge for opportunities. "There is so much work to be done in China," says Li Daotang, a Shanghai professor who runs Hua Au Biotechnology & Wastewater Treatment Co., a rapidly growing firm partly owned by Australia's Broken Hill Proprietary Co. Still, adds Mr. Smith of WMX Technologies: "You can see a great need, but need doesn't always translate to business."

The big drawback is financing. Chinese officials say they are concerned about the environment, but projected environmental expenditures of 83 billion yuan (about $950 million) between 1991 and 1995 are less than 0.7% of gross domestic product. In early July, Beijing said it would drastically increase spending to a total of $23 billion by the year 2000, but that sum includes money used on dams, clean energy projects and related industries—not just on cleaning up. When it comes to spending money, most Chinese would rather invest in a new factory than clean up an existing one. "One should not give up eating for fear of choking," goes a saying. Financing for wastewater projects is sometimes siphoned off to build power plants.

Blame the spirit of paramount leader Deng Xiaoping's maxim, "To get rich is glorious." Entrepreneurs, says Li Yihui, vice director of the Guangdong Province environmental bureau, "don't understand the relationship between environmental protection and economic growth." David Braga, managing director of Energy & Environmental Technologies Ltd., a Hong Kong company, moans: "The story is always the same: 'We'd love to do it. Can you lend us the money?' Then the guy gets into his Mercedes and drives off."

When Canada's government last year arranged a trade mission for environmental companies to visit six cities in eastern China, their hosts all wanted concessional loans to finance environmental purchases. "This is China's biggest problem," says Richard Belliveau, Canada's consul-general in Shanghai: "Finding enough money to do what they need desperately to do."

Multinationals Go To Work

Environmental companies that find a way to pry open a cash box get work. "If you can find a way to bring the money in, they welcome you," says Peter F. Walley, business manager of Binnie Consultants Ltd., an environmental company based in the U.K. Binnie stumbled in the mid-1980s when it first targeted China's worsening environment for cleanup; it put two full-time engineers in China, who encountered considerable interest in Western technology but little funding. Now it has revised its strategy, going in with foreign companies, which have the money.

"Multinationals are more interested in projecting a green image, especially in China," notes Martin D. McMillan, Binnie's managing director in Hong Kong. "They're people who appreciate what we can actually do."

And many foreigners care about the Chinese problems. Marc Brody, president of a private U.S. group called the China Environment Fund, has been appointed an agent for the highly polluted northern industrial city of Shenyang. His mission: to get money for environmental projects. He faces a big problem. Beijing, trying to contain the credit fueling China's frenetic economic boom, won't permit Shenyang to borrow more than $30 million a year. He would like direct aid from international agencies. He says the World Bank, the Asian Development Bank and other agencies now provide less than 5% of the $40 billion or so that Asia as a whole is estimated to need *each year* for environmental cleanup. "Unless private capital comes forward and says, 'Here's a chance to get a return,' [China's] industrialization will be very, very damaging," Mr. Brody says.

Some in Congress are trying to pry capital loose for China. The Senate Energy and natural Resources Committee is considering whether U.S. companies should be allowed to count reductions they achieve in China of so-called greenhouse gases toward targets imposed on them in the U.S. "A billion dollars spent in the U.S. on equipment or technology would get you only a fraction of the progress you'd get with $1 billion in a country like China," a committee staffer says.

"And China is producing more and more of them."

The Clinton administration says it is concerned about China's environmental problems. "This enormous economic growth going on in China . . . [is] going to run full speed into an environmental wall of unsustainability," U.S. Undersecretary of State Timothy E. Wirth warned earlier this month. "And the Chinese are desperate for help, because they see that wall coming and they also want to change."

For a country sensitive to suggestions that it requires help, China's dependence on foreign environmental help may seem odd. But the country has benefited from foreign expertise before, as officials are quick to point out. In 1949, China

could support only seven of its citizens on a hectare of land, about 2.47 acres. Thanks to the advent of Western-developed fertilizers, it now can support 12 people on that amount of land.

But it is those same nitrogen-based fertilizers that are behind the toxic algae infestation of Anhui's Chao Lake. Now, the West is being asked for tens of millions of dollars more to clean it up. Local officials aren't optimistic. As he stands in the prow of a poured-cement boat chugging across the shallow lake, Wang Yinxiang, director of water processing at the lake, is circumspect. "China has too many people to preserve its nature," he says. "After another 1,000 years, I don't think this lake will even exist."

Article 19   *Time*, December 19, 1994

Taming the River Wild

The world's largest dam is under way in China, but it won't solve the country's giant energy problems

Sandra Burton

YICHANG

Midway between its icy source in Tibet and the fertile delta at its mouth in Shanghai, 3,900 miles to the east, China's Yangtze River hurtles through a series of sheer chasms known as the Three Gorges. Legend has it that the scenic channel was carved in stone by the goddess Yao Ji as a way of diverting the river around the petrified remains of a dozen dragons she had slain for harassing the peasants. Over the centuries painters and poets have idealized the canyons as a mist-shrouded wilderness. While that may have once been true, the region lost much of its majesty in modern times, as demolition teams blasted rocky obstructions from the river's course, and the bucolic villages on its banks gave way to grim new factory towns.

Now both visions of the Three Gorges—the ideal and the real—are about to be consigned to a watery grave. Later this month, Chinese Premier Li Peng will preside over the symbolic first pouring of concrete in what is intended to be the world's largest hydroelectric dam. Already, mammoth earthworks on

both banks of the construction site have begun to constrict the flow of the river where it gushes forth from the Xiling Gorge. Over the next 14 years, if all goes as planned, first an earthen coffer dam and then a 200-yd-high concrete spillway and adjacent set of ship-lifting locks will block the swirling channel, transforming the Three Gorges into a single deep and currentless reservoir. Covering everything from ancient temples to contemporary slag heaps, the water will flood 28,000 acres of farmland and 20 towns and drive 1.4 million people from their homes.

The gigantic Three Gorges project has inspired awe and opposition ever since it was first proposed 75 years ago by modern China's founding father, Sun Yat-sen. During the 1980s the dam plan became a favorite target of pro-democracy dissidents. It was not until 1992, three years after the critics were brutally silenced in Tiananmen Square, that the communist rulers rammed the project through the National People's Congress. Even today, as construction finally gets rolling, the dam still draws fire from environmentalists around the world. To opponents, it is a symbol of mankind's monstrous interventions in nature, an

enterprise that will not only displace people but also devastate wildlife and alter the landscape forever.

Powerless to block Three Gorges, critics hope it will be at least slowed by inadequate financing. They are urging governments and private investors to withhold the $3 billion in foreign loans and investments that the Chinese are seeking to help build the $30 billion dam. Says Dai Qing, a Chinese opponent of the dam who won a Goldman Environmental Prize last year, and is now a visiting scholar at the Australian National University: "I hope that people all over the world who love the environment and who love China will band together to stop this disastrous project."

Chinese leaders argue just as vehemently that Three Gorges is vital to their country's future—and actually good for the environment as a whole. They say it will prevent the periodic flooding that has claimed 500,000 lives in this century. More important, its production of clean hydroelectric power will reduce China's reliance on coal, the dirtiest of all fossil fuels, which now supplies 75% of the country's energy needs. The burning of coal has cast a pall of pollution over major Chinese cities and helped make pulmonary disease the nation's leading cause of death.

The issue is how a rapidly growing nation of 1.2 billion people, all of whom would like refrigerators and other conveniences, can promote economic development without wrecking its environment. For the Chinese government, hydropower in general and Three Gorges in particular are a big part of the solution. "The advantages outweigh the disadvantages," contends He Gong, vice president of the China Yangtze Three Gorges Project Development Corp.

How China meets its energy needs has an impact far beyond its boundaries. Sulfurous emissions from Chinese power plants and factories blow eastward and fall as acid rain on Japan and Korea. In fact, the pollution has planetwide implications: China is the world's second-largest producer of carbon dioxide and other greenhouse gases that are collecting in the atmosphere and may, many scientists believe, lead to global warming. If China maintains its annual economic growth rate of 11%, the country will need to add 17,000 megawatts of electrical generating capacity each year for the rest of the decade. Within 10 years, that would be as much new power as the U.S. generates overall today. If China uses mostly coal to produce that power, the greenhouse effect could be catastrophic.

Many opponents of Three Gorges have no quarrel with the effort to move away from coal toward hydropower. But they argue that for a lower price, numerous smaller dams could produce more power and greater flood-control benefits. They fear that a dam so large on the notoriously muddy Yangtze will lead to dangerous buildups of silt in some parts of the river, creating new obstacles to navigation and causing floods upstream. Chinese officials respond that both big and small dams are needed. Indeed, 10 projects smaller than Three Gorges, with a total capacity of nearly 12,000 megawatts, are under construction on the upper reaches of the Yangtze and its tributaries.

Whether or not Three Gorges is ever finished, hydropower can never meet the bulk of China's energy needs. Part of the problem is that most of the potential dam sites are in the less populated southwestern part of the country, making it expensive to transmit electricity to the industrial north and east. Experts say hydropower will account for no more than 20% of China's electricity generation by 2010.

Nuclear plants are another clean power source, at least in terms of air pollution but splitting the atom won't solve China's energy problems either. The government's controls on electricity prices and its failure to adopt international nuclear-safety standards have discouraged foreign investors from helping China build commercial reactors. Only two nuclear plants are in operation, and one of those was built to supply electricity mainly to Hong Kong at rates five times as high as what can be charged in China. Jiang Xinxiong, president of the China Nuclear Industry Corp., predicts that 20 more atom plants will be on line by 2020, but even so, nuclear power would meet less than 10% of China's energy needs.

That leaves no way around a heavy dependence on coal. The best China can hope for, say experts, is to cut coal's portion of the energy mix from 75% to 60% by 2010. The imperative, then, is to find cleaner, more efficient ways to burn the plentiful fossil fuel, reducing emissions of carbon dioxide, sulfur compounds and the incompletely combusted particles that form soot.

To begin with, the Chinese have mounted a successful campaign to equip major coal-burning factories and power plants with devices that wash the fuel. That has reduced the soot pouring out of the largest smokestacks but has hardly begun to clear the air. Reason: the main sources of pollution are millions of small factory boilers and household stoves burning unwashed coal. While the government hopes that as much as half the urban population can eventually be supplied with clean natural gas for cooking, rising prices and short supplies may undercut that effort.

One of the most costly—and crucial—steps in cleaning up coal boilers is curbing sulfur emissions. They combine with water in the atmosphere to create sulfuric acid and thus produce acid rain. Yet only one Chinese power plant boasts desulfurization equipment. China Huaneng Group, the market-oriented Chinese company that built the plant, was able to cover the cost of installing the antipollution devices only because the government agreed to raise electricity rates to users, according to Huaneng president Wang Chuanjian.

Even if coal is burned cleanly and efficiently, it produces large amounts of carbon dioxide, the most common greenhouse gas. To help ease the threat of global warming, China might use new technology to convert a portion of its coal reserves to natural gas, which delivers much more energy for the amount of CO_2 released. The process, though, is expensive. The U.S. Department of Energy asked Congress this year for a $50 million grant that would be earmarked to help China build a demonstration coal-gasification power plant, but the appropriation has not been approved. By contrast, Japan is underwriting an environmental center in Beijing as a showcase for antipollution technology.

Clearly, China needs a great deal more financial help to develop clean energy sources. Mou Guangfeng, a deputy director in the National Environmental Protection Bureau, estimates that the country needs $300 billion just for antipollution equipment. Yet the usual sources of aid, foreign governments and international lending agencies, are running dry: the World Bank alone has poured $20 billion into all sorts of China projects and can't do much more.

The only solution may be to bring in private capital from abroad by floating stocks and bonds, and Western bankers are ready to help. Says Ray Spitzley, executive director of Morgan Stanley Asia in Hong Kong: "China has evolved into a credit-worthy country that can tap world markets." Maybe so, but the poor showing of the few stocks traded internationally has made investors skittish. Eager to make their securities more attractive, Chinese officials are talking with the World Bank about setting up a Chinese National Power and Development Fund that would sell bonds backed by the bank to private investors.

While foreigners may be justifiably reluctant to help finance a project as audacious and controversial as Three Gorges, many indisputably worthy ventures, form coal gasification to experiments with solar power, are also begging for funds. Governments and investors naturally wonder if they can afford to gamble on China. But as the most populous nation threatens to pollute the entire planet, can the rest of the world afford to turn its back?

—With reporting by Jaime A. FlorCruz and Mia Turner/Beijing

Article 20   *The World & I*, December 1994

The Intellectual in China Today

Li Honglin

False Confessions and Their Legacy

Li Honglin, a social scientist, has been one of the leading intellectuals in the People's Republic of China for many years. He was demoted and ostracized several times for his free thinking and jailed for one year for his sympathy for the Tiananmen Square protesters. He is currently a visiting scholar at Columbia University.

Recently I saw a couplet on the wall of the apartment of a well-known intellectual. It read: "Nothing is more important than the fate of the nation; the hardest thing is to be a mere observer." This has been the typical mentality of Chinese intellectuals for centuries, up to this very day; they always assume responsibility for the rise and fall of the nation. Despite the ideological twists and turns throughout history, from Confucius in the sixth century B.C. to the students in Tiananmen Square in 1989, the intellectuals' sense of responsibility has remained firm.

After the June 4, 1989, crackdown on the prodemocracy movement, many leading intellectuals and students were arrested and imprisoned. However, according to the official account, not one of all the people charged by the government has pleaded guilty or admitted any wrongdoing. As an example, the recently released student leader, Wang Dan, refused to "confess" to the authorities.

The arrests and trials did not end the June 4 crackdown; rather, it merely marked the beginning of nationwide persecutions, euphemistically called a "screening and shuffling movement." At both the central and local levels, those cadres who were "soft" on the prodemocracy movement were removed. In the "screening and shuffling movement," intellectuals were not only forced to make self-confessions but also to report on the wrongdoings of others to help the government track down more "counterrevolutionaries." This movement also required public support of the 1989 military crackdown.

According to official propaganda, the "screening and shuffling movement" has been a great success; as a result, numerous cadres and members of the Chinese Communist Party (CCP) have been disciplined. All dissenting voices disappeared. The entire nation stood together on the same side with the party"—and stability was restored.

But such a conclusion may be premature.

Ever since the communists took power in 1949, Chinese intellectuals have been coerced to make false confessions, to advocate principles they do not accept, and to struggle against their loved ones. Not surprisingly, after each such episode, despite the tremendous pressure, the intellectuals were overcome with a sense of guilt. Over the years, this became a commonplace occurrence—there was no longer anything extraordinary about it. Gradually, Chinese intellectuals developed a "conscience buffer" to mitigate their pain. But the 1989 massacre ultimately destroyed this buffer; the endurance level of the Chinese intellectuals against the abuse of the authorities had reached a breaking point: They were now being coerced to show their support for the killings in the square. This unbearable violation of their basic human conscience and dignity was something they could no longer swallow.

Since June 4, 1989, the major focus of the CCP has been the restoration of "stability as the highest priority." In almost every policy statement about national affairs, the phrase "political stability" repeatedly appears. It is true that "stability" is in the common interest of all Chinese people as well as that of the entire international community, including the so-called counterrevolutionaries within China and the "imperialists" abroad. However, the CCP's use of the phrase "political stability" implies that the majority of the Chinese people are denied political participation. As a result, the prevalent cynicism among the people has been expressed in their apathy toward politics. This attitude, ironically, is one of the major factors contributing to the maintenance of the CCP's so-called political stability.

However, this political apathy is really quite superficial. If we go beneath the surface, for example, to private parties or nonpublic gatherings, we would overhear many active and animated discussions about politics. This is especially true among intellectuals. In China today, ordinary citizens, including intellectuals, can only passively "participate" in politics, such as by studying and supporting official documents; active participation, such as policy debates and engaging in decision making, is completely out of the question. The result has been that the people have invented their own ways to become involved: by exchanging "rumors" and second-guessing what goes on at the higher echelons of power. One of the hot topics, of course, is the personal lives of the top officials, such as the health of paramount leader Deng Xiaoping.

The general consensus at these unofficial gatherings is a hope for a smooth evolution of political power from the current ideologically driven, hard-line policies to a moderate, more tolerant stance. That is, the sentiment of Chinese intellectuals today is that China should pursue political democratization in conjunction with its economic liberalization, against a backdrop of political stability But this line of thinking is unacceptable to the hard-liners, who negatively label it as promotion of "liberalization" and "peaceful evolution."

Jumping into the Sea

The events of June 1989 affected every segment of Chinese society; the effect was especially acute among intellectuals. For instance, since 1989, there has been a big wave of "jumping into the sea" throughout the country. "Jumping into the sea" refers to those people who quit their tenured state jobs to go into business on their own. Some intellectuals also joined this bandwagon, partly because of the temptation to make more money and partly for political reasons. In the current political environment, serious research in the social sciences involves great political risks. Going into business, on the other hand, does not entail such risks. And if one is lucky, one may end up making a fortune. Business ventures still face many unreasonable government restrictions as well as flagrant corruption, but if one is willing to pay all the "fees," these difficulties can be overcome relatively easily.

> *The events of June 1989 affected every segment of Chinese society; the effect was especially acute among intellectuals.*

Of course, not everyone is meant for business. The majority of intellectuals have stuck to what they know best: their own research. Politically sensitive topics are off-limits. But some areas that are not politically sensitive have produced reasonable and, in certain areas, impressive progress. Surprisingly, the field of literature has even flourished. Since 1989, many literary scholars have not had much to do, so they have focused their energy on writing novels. As a result, many novels of high quality have been published. The recent years have also witnessed some progress in the social sciences. Positivism is no longer banned and has, in fact, been adopted by researchers. Sociologists have accumulated vast amounts of empirical data.

Most of all, economics has developed swiftly because the authorities recognize its importance to the reforms. Political economy, which formerly was the only officially sanctioned branch of economics, no longer dominates the scene; instead, Western microeconomics, econometrics, accounting, management, and marketing sciences are all hot topics pursued by both researchers and practitioners.

Progress can also be seen in the area of CCP history, an area that prior to the opening up was extremely sensitive. For example, before the 1980s, the authorities allowed only the publication of largely altered, "correct" official versions of CCP history. The role and title of every historical figure (including who was to be referred to as "comrade" and who could be called "great") as well as every event were officially decided at the highest levels, and even deviations in tone were not permitted. But now, the official version of party history seems to have disappeared; there are no restrictions or limits in terms of how to write about historical figures, including Mao Zedong and Chiang Kai-shek. Much has been published about their private lives, and the authorities appear to be rather tolerant of this. Of course, if one wants to write about party leaders who are still alive, one must still be careful and exercise a certain amount of self-censorship; if such writings come under official scrutiny after publication, it is too late.

More evidence of liberalization is the current mushrooming of publications. The number of newspapers and magazines has exploded, as well as the number of publishing houses. Almost every entity in China has its own publishing house: from government organs, social organizations, and universities to local governments. An interesting development following the rapid growth of publications is that although virtually all the publishing houses are state owned, they cannot afford to follow only the official ideological line. Economic incentives and intense competition have forced them to publish what the market demands. In this sense, economic liberalization has become a catalyst for a greater degree of political tolerance—but still falling short of full democratization.

'Antispiritual Pollution'

Still, the CCP periodically launches "antispiritual pollution campaigns" to crack down on undesirable publications. According to communist doctrine, there are two-types of spiritual pollution: the first is anything that is anticommunist party or antisocialist; the second is anything that can be labeled pornographic. For a long time, the CCP could not differentiate between serious studies of sex-related subjects and pornography, so everything that dealt with sex was condemned as pornography. Before 1989, great efforts were made to ban both types of pollution. But after June 1989, the authorities appear to be less concerned about pornography; the subject of sex can be publicly discussed—although the sex life of China's leaders is still inappropriate, as the BBC learned from the official criticism of its TV documentary on Mao Zedong to commemorate the 100th anniversary of his birthday in December 1993.

> *For a long time, the CCP could not differentiate between serious studies of sex-related subjects and pornography, so everything that dealt with sex was condemned as pornography.*

There are two obvious reasons for this apparent loosening up with respect to pornography: In fact it is harmless to political rule—actually it may help divert the people's attention away from politics; and the demand for it is great. Now novels dealing with intimate sexual relations are common, and explicit sex in movies is not rare. Although no one can predict the profound effects of this belated "sex revolution" in China, for better or for worse, the sex revolution has helped break the gray monotony of the former ideologically oriented entertainment that was strictly guided by the party line.

However, the fate of the other source of pollution, politically sensitive publications, has not been as fortunate. These works are still officially banned. But, as mentioned earlier, social science topics that are not politically sensitive have expanded substantially, and quite a few good books in these fields have been published.

In general, then, the early 1990s witnessed an uneven development in the social sciences, in literature, and in the arts. The topics that have been neglected due to political reasons have been compensated for by overdevelopment in other subject areas. This must be an example of the realization of the "principle of the conservation of mass-energy" in a social sense; intellectuals are bound to create despite all obstacles—their creativity cannot be suppressed for long. When they are restrained in one direction, they will compensate for this by turning their creativity in another direction.

The Legacy of Suppression

According to a Chinese adage, "If the river is frozen up to three feet, the weather must have been cold for more than one day." The current status of intellectuals in China reflects a legacy of more than a half century of suppression of the free press. As early as the 1930s, Chinese intellectuals were suppressed by the Nationalist Party. This made them more positively inclined toward the CCP. But, oddly enough, under the CCP intellectuals were viewed as outsiders. This is probably the root cause for their ill fate under the communist regime. Even the top leaders of the CCP have come to realize this. Hu Yaobang, the late general secretary of the CCP admitted: "Reviewing the history of our party, it was always the case that the cadres of working-class backgrounds purged the intellectuals. Intellectuals were always treated unfairly."

Mao Zedong wrote that "the philosophy of the communist party is the philosophy of struggle." The essence of life of the party is to continue to fight. The mission of the party is to divide people into classes and to carry on the class struggle between the people. Marx believed in this, and Stalin practiced this. Because Marx and the other communist fathers, such as Lenin, identified themselves as intellectuals, even though intellectuals were struggled against like other "class enemies," there was nothing particularly evil about them. However, when communism was imported into China, the CCP inherited this tradition of struggle, but it created a new target that has been the focus of every struggle at every stage of the revolution: the intellectuals. Some analysts have attributed the terrible treatment of intellectuals in China to Mao Zedong, whose early dreams of becoming an intellectual were tarnished by his mediocre academic performance. The intellectual establishment of the early 1920s denied him acceptance, and their successors have paid the price for this in the following decades!

The CCP'S Targeting of Intellectuals

As early as 1942, seven years before the CCP assumed power, it launched a "movement of shaking up," in which intellectuals were targeted for persecution. Intellectuals became the object of ridicule and contempt. There were four charges brought against them: first, they did not know how to farm; second, they could not operate machines; third, they were incapable of fighting; and fourth, they simply could not do anything right. Those who were adept in these four areas—namely, farmers, workers, soldiers, and party members—were superior to intellectuals and were mobilized to attack the intellectuals. At first, the movement was limited to seminars and debates; later on, it went out of control. Secret investigations were conducted, and many intellectuals were accused of being "agents of the Nationalist Party." Wang Shiwei, an eminent leftist intellectual who was very outspoken at the time and had criticized the strict hierarchy of the CCP, was executed.

> *As early as 1942, seven years before the CCP assumed power, it launched a "movement of shaking up," in which intellectuals were targeted for persecution.*

After it took power in 1949, the Communist Party launched a series of movements similar to the 1942 rectification movement. Intellectuals were repeatedly singled out for attack. Similar to the law of the "negation of negatives" in dialectics (where events evolve spirally, repeating themselves at a next higher level), before 1949, the revolution was a "democratic" revolution, and intellectuals were labeled the petty bourgeoisie who had to be reformed, but basically they were allied with the revolution. But after 1949, the revolution was upgraded to a "socialist" revolution, and, correspondingly, the intellectuals became "bourgeois intellectuals."

As expected, the intellectuals were not only offended by this appellation but also very worried. All of the "bourgeois intellectuals," from elementary school teachers to university professors and from technicians to renowned scholars, wanted to rid themselves of this title as quickly as possible. They wanted to become allied with the "proletarian class." But this was not possible. By party standards, they were unfit to be members of the worker and peasant classes, the classes that the party claimed to represent. There was no way for the intellectuals to escape the forthcoming struggles against them.

Up until 1954, such struggles remained verbal, or "criticism of thoughts." The major target then was Hu

Shi, the founder of modern Chinese literature. A series of struggle sessions were carried out to cleanse the thoughts of the intellectuals and to help rid them of their "bourgeois" ideology

By 1955, the struggles became more serious. Hu Feng (unrelated to Hu Shi), a well-known writer, was charged as a "counterrevolutionary," resulting in deadly consequences. This charge was based on the contents of his private letters to friends, which were completely misinterpreted. His conviction set a precedent whereby millions suffered and some were even executed solely on the basis of private thoughts. After Hu Feng was imprisoned, seventy-eight people connected to him were also persecuted. Later, during the 1957 Anti-Rightist Movement, about 5.5 million people, most of them intellectuals, were systematically purged. Ten years later, in 1966, Mao launched the Great Proletarian Cultural Revolution (1966–1976). During that period, intellectuals experienced mental and physical abuse on an unprecedented scale, leading many to suicide. At least ten people I knew took their own lives, and many more became permanently mentally ill due to the constant persecutions.

> *Since Mao's death in 1976, the lot of the intellectual in China has substantially improved with the launching of the reform period.*

The Cultural Revolution and Capital Punishment

It can be said that before the Cultural Revolution "thought crimes" did not warrant capital punishment. But during the Cultural Revolution, even "thought crimes" were subject to execution. Zhang Zhixin, a young woman who expressed her dissenting views to a colleague, was sentenced to death and was executed at a struggle rally attended by thousands of "revolutionary masses." On the day of her execution, the authorities slashed her throat, lest she shout further "counterrevolutionary" slogans before her death. Many intellectuals, like Zhang, who had been able to retain some independent thought were eliminated during those ten years of madness.

Since Mao's death in 1976, the lot of the intellectual in China has substantially improved with the launching of the reform period.

The Deng era brought China out of the shadow of Mao as it embarked on the road of modernization. Modernization must rely on science, advanced technology and contemporary management techniques—all of which can be translated into productivity. Above all, modernization requires familiarity with modern economics. This requirement needed the help of the intellectuals. Deng Xiaoping was the first Communist Party leader to promote "respect for knowledge, respect for human talent." At the same time, he removed the label of "bourgeois" from the intellectuals and formally declared that the intellectuals were "part of the working class." This was perhaps the highest honor that could ever be bestowed on intellectuals in a communist society.

Deng's New Policy

Deng's new policy brought great expectations to the intellectuals at a time when their living situations could not have been worse. They were encouraged to participate in research and development, business management, finance, and other areas of economic and technical development. For the first time in the history of communist China, intellectuals were able to apply what they knew toward the enhancement and well-being of society. Human resources are the ultimate resource to reach these goals. The successful mobilization of the intellectuals has been one of the major factors contributing to China's rapid economic development since the late 1970s.

As a result, intellectuals with professions that are in demand, such as applied scientists and financial and marketing analysts, substantially improved their income and living standards. Other intellectuals, such as celebrated artists and writers of best-selling books, also benefited a great deal from the reforms.

But the rest of the intellectual class were not as fortunate. It is true that they no longer have to submit to political humiliation or reeducation as they did during the Mao period. In a sense, they are now left alone by the communist political machine. But they have also been forgotten by the economic boom. Scholars such as historians, philosophers, or literary critics do not possess skills that are readily applicable to, for example, the prediction of trends in the stock market. Their income is limited to the fixed salaries they draw from the state, which nowadays can hardly keep pace with the high rate of inflation (about 15 percent annually). For the more fortunate segments of the intellectual class, fixed salaries account for only 50–60 percent of their total income.

The above phenomenon means a sad but inevitable displacement for the intellectual class. Mao had a wrong and quite cruel anti-intellectual policy. When Deng came to power and brought about positive change, intellectuals hoped for a new policy that would confer respect as well as economic benefits. The intellectuals do not view themselves as independent; they are rather heavily, if not entirely, dependent on how the state treats them. Of course, given the nature of China's political economy before the reforms (where the state was the sole provider), there is a good reason for this mentality. But what is paradoxical is that even if the state now wants to treat the intellectuals well economically, it no longer has the resources to do so. One of the direct results of the reforms is that the state has become weaker and cannot satisfy every segment of the society

So the state has called on intellectuals to take advantage of the economic boom and make their own money in the market economy. But how can a Hegelian scholar or an expert on Das Kapital use these skills to go out and make money? What's more, because of so many years' emphasis on philosophy and political economy, all the best talents were drawn to these fields, and China has now accumulated a huge army of people in these professions.

But the fate of those intellectuals whose knowledge is not directly linked to the market economy is not the worst. Those who specialize in politically sensitive areas such as political science, political philosophy, or any field that could be labeled "bourgeois spiritual pollution" face an even worse lot. They are not allowed to publish, let alone conduct their own research. Although they are a relatively small group, their attitude and behavior directly influence the political situation in China. To a great extent, they affect political opinions in Chinese society; naturally, they are closely monitored by the state.

Immediately after Mao's death in 1976, there was overwhelming sentiment for change in China. As this momentum picked up, China underwent a brief period of an ideological thaw, which was called "liberalization of thought." Deng Xiaoping and Hu Yaobang were the first patrons of this liberalization movement. With their support, a great number of social scientists began to criticize the ultraleftist theory and practice of Mao Zedong. This liberalization movement directly challenged the legitimacy of Mao's designated heir, Hua Guofeng. Hua was later removed from leadership, and the Deng era formally began in 1979. However, after Deng consolidated his power, he had no need to continue the liberalization movement, lest it ultimately challenge the legitimacy of communist rule. Thus, instead of liberalization of thought, the theme evolved into "maintaining the same tone as the party"

The brief thaw had given intellectuals a taste of freedom of press—although limited and often self-censored. So the intellectuals were no longer satisfied "maintaining the same tone as the party." Clashes with the party became inevitable. In 1983 the CCP launched the "antispiritual pollution" campaign, and, four years later, it started the "anti-bourgeois liberalization" campaign to purge those intellectuals who "deviated from the party line."

> *The hope for Chinese intellectuals is that one day we will no longer be "mere observers" but instead we will become active participants in the political process.*

Of course, compared to the Mao era, the recent purges have been more humane. In Mao's day, most intellectuals who were purged were removed from their posts and *xiafang* (sent down) to the countryside to engage in manual labor. Many were left to work in the fields for as long as twenty years!

Under Deng, *xiafang* has been eliminated. Dissidents have been arrested and sentenced (some sentences are very heavy), but their number is much smaller than during the days of Mao. In most cases, those who have been purged have simply been expelled from the party. They still have most of their rights as citizens, and some even have the right to travel abroad. This would have been unthinkable under Mao. Thus, we are beginning to see the emergence of a civil society in China.

The biggest setback since the late 1970s was the June 4, 1989, crackdown. This event has carved a permanent scar in the hearts of the Chinese people. Intellectuals were particularly hard hit by this crackdown. But even this did not tarnish their sense of mission for a better China. Whether they have just recently been released from prison or have recently "jumped into the sea" of business, they are all keeping a close eye on political developments in China.

As conventional wisdom says, "The only thing that is certain about China is its uncertainty." When the Old Guard exits from the political stage, there will be changes and even the risk of turmoil. But, for the first time since the 1949 revolution, the Chinese people are enjoying economic freedom and modest prosperity with limited political freedoms. One thing is quite certain: The people will never want to return to the old days of communist China. Any setbacks after Deng's death—if they do occur—will be short-lived. The long-term trend for China's political and economic development is toward a market economy and political pluralism.

We are beginning to see the light at the end of the tunnel. The hope for Chinese intellectuals is that one day we will no longer be "mere observers" but instead we will become active participants in the political process.

Article 21

U.S. News & World Report, June 7, 1993

Two people, one land

A rare look at how Chinese capitalism is exacerbating tensions in Tibet

Two long-haired teenagers from Sichuan are doing a brisk business in Lhasa's Barkhor market selling a hot item that officially is still contraband: portraits of Tibet's exiled spiritual and political leader, the Dalai Lama. A large photo in a frame costs 15 yuan ($2.70), a palm-size photo 18 cents. One of the hottest sellers is a picture of the Dalai Lama in a 1991 meeting with George Bush that enraged Beijing.

The Barkhor, which circles the ancient Jokhang temple in the center of Tibet's capital, is full of vendors from the Chinese interior selling cheap goods that their counterparts in Beijing have long since abandoned in favor of silk blouses and hand-held video games. A man from Gansu hawks toilet paper, matches, gloves and toothpaste. A handful of Tibetan traders have stalls in the market, too, selling fabric for Tibetan robes, Buddhist money and the colorful prayer flags that fly above every Tibetan home. But most Tibetans in the Barkhor are either praying or begging. An old man in crimson robes sits on a low stool chanting prayers, with a shoe box to collect alms. Other similarly clad Tibetans ring bells and bang drums while pilgrims from the countryside do aerobic prostrations in front of the temple.

When the worst protests in four years broke out in Lhasa last week, prompting Chinese police to fire tear gas for two hours, foreign witnesses reported that demonstrators shouted "Chinese out of Tibet" along with various slogans protesting price rises and rent increases. Tibetan advocacy groups claim the influx of Han Chinese is the root cause of the Tibetans' discontent. The Dalai Lama calls the phenomenon "cultural genocide" and is believed to have raised the issue when he met President Clinton in April.

Some members of the U.S. Congress have sought to end Han migration by linking it to the extension of most-favored-nation trading status for China. Instead, President Clinton last week tied renewal of MFN in 1994 to China making "significant progress" toward "protecting Tibet's distinctive religious and cultural heritage."

The Han Chinese who are flooding into Tibet today are not part of a government effort to colonize Tibet, however. Rather, the young fortune seekers who brave days and nights on dangerous mountain roads to start new lives in Tibet are a reflection of the reduced role of the government in people's lives. With the state no longer dictating where people may live and work, more and more Chinese are seeking economic opportunities in new frontiers such as booming Guangdong province—and Tibet.

Local Tibetan factories produce so few manufactured goods that almost anything imported from the interior will sell, even at a hefty markup. Tibet's service sector is so rudimentary that almost any restaurant, photo stand or bicycle repair shop is guaranteed instant success. Economic official Xiang Yang boasts that thanks to the migrants, "The vegetable market in Lhasa is almost as good as in Beijing."

The opportunism of these migrants coincides with Beijing's interest in promoting economic development in a bid to reduce political disaffection. The Chinese government pours more money per capita into Tibet than any other region. (Beijing's annual subsidies in recent years have averaged $175 million.) But last week's turmoil suggests that economic development cannot make the Tibetans forget the grievances that have accumulated since China invaded their land in 1950. Indeed, opening Tibet to enterprising Han Chinese appears to be fomenting tension rather than easing it because so few of the profits are trickling down to Tibetans, who appear noticeably poorer than Chinese in the streets of Lhasa.

Wrongheaded. Phunkhang Goranangpa, a Tibetan with Chinese citizenship who lives in Beijing, cites the building of Lhasa's leading hotel, now managed by Holiday Inn, as an example of wrongheaded development. A construction team from Jiangsu built the hotel, bringing in not only architects, engineers and technical workers but also unskilled laborers. It even used Jiangsu cement, though Tibet produces its own, and it imported Jiangsu marble although Tibetan marble is superior. "If they had used Tibetan laborers, we would have our own construction workers by now," says Goranangpa. Still, he sees an expansion of tourism as offering the best prospect of jobs for Tibetans.

Xiang Yang, the director of Tibet's Planning and Economy Committee, says that 50,000 of Lhasa's 60,000 registered private businessmen are from China proper. Although migrants are supposed to apply for residence permits and business licenses, Xiang concedes that, "Some do, some don't."

A Sichuanese restaurateur reckons there are 100,000 of his fellow provincials in Lhasa and that they run 90 percent of the city's eateries. He earns 10 times as much in Tibet as he did as a cook back home. On the wall behind him is the Han answer to the ubiquitous Dalai Lama pictures: a laminated portrait of Mao Zedong.

Beijing is seeking foreign aid and loans and offering incentives for foreigners and Chinese to set up the kind of rural industries that have produced the world's highest growth rates along China's southeast coast. Tibetan authorities seek investments in processing local products such as yak meat, butter and leather; cashmere wool; barley, and minerals.

But attracting investment is not easy. Tibet's links with the outside world are grossly inadequate. The only overland route is over treacherous mountain roads. Flights through Chengdu, the capital of Sichuan, are expensive and heavily booked. The most accessible Chinese port is Tianjin, more than 3,100 miles away. Opening another border post with India could provide access to a closer port in Calcutta, but closer means 750 miles away.

To make matters worse, Tibet offers minimal labor skills and high wages. Local officials admit that even if a projected light industrial zone in Lhasa gets going and creates tens of thousands of jobs, few of them will go to Tibetans because of their low literacy rate and low levels of technical training. New factories will simply suck in more workers from outside.

The most ambitious project in Tibet today is "One River, Two Streams," a hydropower scheme for Tibet's largest river. Electricity from the project is expected to spur local textile ventures; improved irrigation should raise grain and vegetable yields, encouraging Tibetans to move beyond subsistence farming. Eventually the project will affect some 800,000 people, more than a third of the registered population. But so far its beneficiaries—skilled workmen and scientists—are almost all non-Tibetan.

Some people fear that Chinese-led development—with its accompanying karaoke bars, discothèques and pop idol posters—threatens Tibet's traditional culture. Han cadres have tried to get Tibetans more involved in the market economy. But the gap in values leaves them frustrated. "If a Tibetan has a single cake of yak butter, he will take it to the temple rather than use it himself," one Han official says uncomprehendingly. When the official tried to help some Tibetans sell their produce, the villagers asked in shocked tones, "Isn't that doing business?" The cadre says he reassured them that "Deng Xiaoping says it's all right to do business."

Buddhist market. One Tibetan institution that has been driven to the market is the lamasery. Despite generous handouts from the government for printing holy texts and restoring religious buildings—including some $11 million for the exiled Dalai Lama's Potala Palace alone—lamaseries have found it increasingly hard to support their monks. Now, the Drepung Lamasery outside Lhasa sells Dalai Lama portraits, fountain pens, hard candies, cigarettes and Pabst Blue Ribbon beer. There are no restrictions on how the lamasery spends the store's $1,000-a-month profit.

Despite China's subsidies, its efforts to stimulate investment in Tibet and its crackdowns on dissent, some Tibetans still proclaim their devotion to the Dalai Lama, who fled after an abortive uprising in 1959, by wearing plastic buttons with his picture and hanging his portrait in their homes. Lamaseries display Dalai Lama likenesses in every nook and cranny. Beijing says it will negotiate with the Dalai Lama only if he will "give up his divisive stand and recognize that Tibet is an inalienable part of China."

The Han rulers of Tibet have few illusions about the loyalty of the Tibetans. Last year, when Chinese were studying the pro-capitalist speeches of Deng Xiaoping, Tibet launched a four-month-long "socialist education" campaign. Some officials interpreted their brief as teaching remote villagers how to make money. But in most of Tibet, the central themes of the campaign were "love the motherland and love socialism."

A blackboard in Lhasa's Planning Committee building reminds the staff to set aside three afternoons a week for free political study. Workplaces in the Chinese interior now hold political study sessions once a week if at all. "When I go to visit my father in Xi'an," says a Han cadre working in Lhasa, "I realize that he is living in a capitalist world while I am still living in a socialist world." But even making Tibet part of the capitalist world may not succeed in making Tibetans think of their land as part of China.

By Susan V. Lawrence in Lhasa

Article 22

The World & I, October 1989

Script Reform in China

Victor H. Mair

Victor H. Mair is professor of Chinese in the Department of Oriental Studies at the University of Pennsylvania. He is a specialist on early vernacular texts and Sino-Indian cultural relations. Among his publications are Tung-huang Popular Narratives *(Cambridge, 1983).* Painting and Performance: Chinese Picture Recitation and Its Indian Genesis *(Hawaii, 1988), and* T'ang Transformation Texts: A Study of the Buddhist Contribution to the Rise of Vernacular Fiction and Drama in China *(Harvard, 1989).*

Nearly everyone who has seen Chinese characters is deeply impressed by them. Even without being able to read a single graph, one is struck by their longevity, beauty, complexity, and numerousness. Indeed, all these qualities are true of the Chinese writing system and account for the strong feelings it evokes. These emotions are particularly intense for those who consider the script to be one of the primary symbols of Chinese cultural identity. There is a great fear that, without this distinctive set of graphs, Chinese civilization as such would cease to exist.

Yet, during the past century, there have been persistent and equally urgent calls for radical changes in the script—including its abolition—from other segments of society. The traditionalists strive to maintain a proud and unique heritage that goes back over three millennia. The reformers worry that, unless their country modernizes its cumbersome, out-of-date script, everything—including the script itself—will be lost in an unsuccessful race to keep up with the rest of the world. A dispassionate look at the history and nature of writing in

Samples of complicated or full forms of the tetragraphs on the top line, with the simplified modern forms on the bottom line.

戰	獨	龍	舊	國	難
战	独	龙	旧	国	难
Battle	Solitary	Dragon	Old	Nation	Disaster or Difficulty

China may help to reconcile these two contradictory attitudes.

The Chinese writing system first occurs in virtually full-blown form around 1200 B.C. in the oracle bone inscriptions of the Shang dynasty. Scholars are perplexed by the suddenness with which the script appears; prior to the oracle bone inscriptions, there were only a few isolated and still undecipherable marks on pottery and occasionally on other objects. Hence the origins of the Chinese script remain a mystery. Its basic characteristics, however, do not. From its very inception as a tool for recording facts and ideas, the same fundamental principles have governed both the shape and the function of the individual graphs. In spite of widespread belief to the contrary, there seems never to have been a purely pictographic or ideographic state of full writing in China. The earliest connected texts contain sizable proportions of signs that communicate meaning through sound (the so-called "cyclical stems and branches," the graph for "all"

[*xian*], the graph for "come" [*lai*], and so forth).

John DeFrancis and others have convincingly shown that it is actually impossible to record all the nuances of speech without substantial recourse to phonetic indicators. Certainly, for at least the last twenty-five hundred years, by far the largest proportion of Chinese characters was made up of a component that conveys meaning and another component that conveys sound, though neither does so with precision alone. Since these components are gathered together in a consistently quadrilateral configuration, Chinese refer to them as tetragraphs (*fangkuaizi*, literally "square graphs" [a cluster of four successive letters in cryptography]).

REASONS FOR LANGUAGE REFORM

Perhaps the single most outstanding dissimilarity between the Chinese writing system and alphabets is the vast quantity of separate units in the former compared to the strictly limited elements of the latter. In contrast to the 26 letters of the English alphabet, for example, there are over 60,000 discrete tetragraphs in the Chinese script, and new ones are being added continually. Mastery of such an enormous assemblage of individual shapes is beyond the ability of any mortal. For practical purposes, literacy in Chinese requires the passive recognition of approximately 2,000 tetragraphs and the active ability to write about 1,000 of them. Even the most learned persons are rarely able to read more than 5,000 tetragraphs and can reproduce only about half that amount without the aid of a dictionary. The other 50,000-plus tetragraphs consist largely of obscure variants, shapes whose sound or meaning (or both) is not known, and classical terms seldom or never used in modern parlance. Unfortunately, once a tetragraph has entered the lexicon, it becomes embedded there permanently. Typesetters, teachers, and translators must be prepared to cope with all 60,000 of them when the occasion demands.

Such large figures immediately lead to one of the most difficult questions about the tetragraphs: how to order them. It is easy to store and retrieve information in languages using an alphabetical script. The systematic nature of straightforward alphabetical ordering is one of the hallmarks of modern civilization. The case is entirely different with the tetragraphs. There is a large variety of traditional ways for arranging them, and they are very hard to control. The most common method is to break down each of the tetragraphs into a semantic classifier (also popularly called a radical or key) and a number of residual strokes. There are still several problems: The semantic cluster is not always readily identifiable, counting the residual strokes is both time-consuming and fraught with error, and the exact sequence of the semantic classifiers (usually 214) can be memorized only with tremendous effort.

Another complaint of the script reform advocates is the excessive amount of time and energy students have to spend in their early years to acquire minimum reading and writing skills. Several steps have already been taken to alleviate the burden placed upon young schoolchildren during the first few grades of their studies. In Taiwan, the National Phonetic Alphabet is used as an auxiliary to help beginners remember the sounds of the tetragraphs, and in the People's Republic of China, the initial lessons are given in Pinyin (romanized

spelling). An increasing number of children's books written entirely in the National Phonetic Alphabet or in Pinyin are made available for students in elementary grades. Wide-scale experimental projects in Pinyin only or Pinyin mixed with tetragraphs for elementary education have been initiated in China. Results thus far show unmistakably that students learn to read much more quickly through Pinyin than when they are exposed to the tetragraphs alone.

Even more dramatic is the drastic reduction of the strokes in many tetragraphs and the limitations on the total number of tetragraphs officially accepted by the government of the People's Republic. These steps, particularly the former, fall under the rubric of "simplification." By 1964, altogether 2,238 tetragraphs, most of those that are frequently used, had been simplified. Nearly another 900 were scheduled for simplification in 1977, but the scheme was withdrawn when it met with stiff opposition from those who asserted that it would lead to intolerable confusion. Because of the disparity between the original, complicated forms used in Taiwan and the simplified forms employed on the mainland, there now exist, in essence, two sets of tetragraphs. This has caused some obstacles to communication between peoples from the two areas.

Another very important sphere of language reform activity in China centers on efforts to increase familiarity with the national language, Modern Standard Mandarin, and to diminish reliance upon regional languages such as Cantonese, Taiwanese, and Shanghainese. The latter are often referred to erroneously as "dialects," but this is due to misinterpretation of the Chinese term *fangyan* ("topolect" [speech pattern of a place]) as well as to certain nonlinguistic, political constraints. Even within the Han or Sinitic group, there are dozens of mutually unintelligible tongues, most of which have never been written down. This is not to mention the non-Sinitic languages such as Mongolian, Tibetan, Uighur, Zhuang, Yi, and the like, many of which have their own alphabets or syllabaries. The linguistic map of China is thus quite complicated. Statements to the effect that there are a billion speakers of "Chinese" are therefore as misleading as to say that there are a billion speakers of "European" worldwide or a billion speakers of "Indic." Pinyin has played a vital role in attempts to unify the pronunciation, vocabulary, and grammar of the various Han languages, but there is still a tremendous amount of work that

This is the cover of volume eleven of the Mandarian language text used in the six-year elementary school curriculum of the People's Republic of China. Note the use of Pinyin.

needs to be done before someone from Peking will be able to converse with someone from Amoy, Swatow, or Fuchow.

The governmental organ charged with overseeing language reform in China is the Script Reform Committee (Wenzi Gaige Weiyuanhui), whose name, significantly, has recently been changed to the State Language Committee (Guojia Yuyan Wenzi Gongzuo Weiyuanhui). The new name may be interpreted as reflecting either decreasing government involvement in script reform or a resolve to broaden the committee's work. Judging from discussions with ranking members, it would seem that the chief aim of the reconstituted body is to transfer reform initiatives to the private sector, leaving the committee to act merely in an oversight capacity.

RESISTANCE TO TAMPERING WITH THE SCRIPT

The government was prompted to downplay its championing of language reform because of the strong opposition to it from certain circles of society. Particularly during the period of liberalization that began after the close of the Cultural Revolution, the hostility toward

The Vertical message in Canton is an exhortation to the people in Canton to remember those who worked hard and overcame many struggles in the oil fields. For political messages, the Chinese prefer simplified characters, which ably lend themselves to the horizontal widening that has become commonplace for such purposes. The first and fourth characters are the same as in the past; the remaining ones are simplified and originally contained from six to twelve additional character strokes. Although one of the reasons for using these simplified characters was to save ink (and paint) and to ease comprehension, many Chinese actually have greater difficulty in distinguishing the meaning of look-alike character sets or their elements. Note, for example, the similarities between the fourth and fifth character.

officially sponsored changes in the script became more vociferous and more determined. It is curious that the most outspoken adversaries of language reform are to be found among the overseas communities. Living in countries where they are a minority, these émigrés keenly feel the need to assert their cultural identity. The tetragraphic script, as one of the most remarkable attributes of Chinese civilization, makes an excellent vehicle for the expression of nationalistic sentiments. Overseas spokesmen against language reform have contributed sizable sums of money toward the campaign to prevent further erosion of their cherished script. They are regularly given ample opportunity to express their opinions in such prominent newspapers as the *Peoples' Daily* and the *Guangming Daily*. By contrast, proponents of additional modifications of the script no longer have a nationwide forum in which to air their views. Instead, they work in small semiofficial or unofficial groups at the city or, at best, provincial level.

Echoing the overseas opponents to script reform are classicists and other conservative factions within China proper. They decry the publication of ancient texts in simplified characters, pointing out that such practices often lead to ambiguity and distortion. There are, as well, those who propose a return to more ancient styles of writing and the reintroduction of more classical materials in the curriculum. The nearest paral-

lel that can be imagined for the West would be the restitution of Greek and Latin as a requirement for all pupils.

Whether living abroad or within the homeland, critics of language reform declare that further adjustments to the script will only serve to cut young Chinese off from their past even more decisively than they already are. Although all middle and high school students are minimally acquainted with ancient Chinese through exposure to set passages, much as we might learn a few lines of *Beowulf* or Chaucer in the original, only highly trained specialists can read the Confucian *Analects* or a T'ang essay with any degree of facility. The gap between Classical Chinese and Modern Standard Mandarin is at least as great as that between Sanskrit and Hindi or between Latin and Italian. If additional changes are imposed upon the Chinese script, traditionalists argue that it will be impossible for all but paleographers to make any sense whatsoever of the old texts.

The antireformers are also alarmed by the flood of vernacular translations of classical texts issued in Taiwan, China, Hong Kong, and Singapore. This tendency is tantamount to admission that Chinese can no longer read the original texts anyway and only adds fuel to the fires of those who demand a complete revamping of the script. In truth, the trend toward greater use of the written vernacular at the expense of the classical goes back over one thousand years and would appear to be irreversible. With the final collapse of the imperial structure of government in 1911 and the abandonment of the examination system that went hand in hand with it, the demise of Classical Chinese as the officially sanctioned written medium was inevitable. This has naturally had a huge impact on the status of the tetragraphs, which are so perfectly well suited to Classical Chinese but are demonstrably less congenial to the vernaculars.

PROSPECTS FOR THE FUTURE

The principles governing the operation of the Chinese tetragraphs are almost identical to those on which the ancient Sumerian, Egyptian, and Hittite scripts were based. All four writing systems relied heavily on a mixture of phonophoric (i.e., "sound-bearing") components and semantic classifiers to convey meaning. It is no wonder that the Chinese people are experiencing hardship in trying to make their archaic writing system compatible with modern information procession technology, which is geared to phonetic scripts. Here lies the real source of the debate over the future of the tetragraphs: Can technology bend to accommodate the tetragraphs, or must the tetragraphs make concessions to technology?

Their affection for the beloved tetragraphs notwithstanding, the Chinese people as a whole have already permitted Pinyin to displace the traditional script in many applications, simply because it is more convenient and efficient. Hotel and hospital registration, Chinese braille and semaphore, book indices, library catalogs, and dozens of other instances could be cited. It is particularly revealing that both the Modern Standard Mandarin translation of the *Encyclopaedia Britannica* and the new *Great Chinese Encyclopedia* (*Zhongguo Da Baikequanshu*) have selected the Pinyin alphabetic order for their entries. This choice is sure to have a deep influence on the way Chinese view Pinyin vis-à-vis the characters. Above all, it is the computer that is pushing China further and further down the path to phoneticization. For modern word processing, the most user-friendly inputting methods, such as those devised by Tianma, Great Wall, and Xerox, all use Pinyin entry by word (not by syllable) and automatic conversion to tetragraphs. The danger, of course, is that there is but a short step from Pinyin in and tetragraphs out to Pinyin in and Pinyin out.

It is highly unlikely that China will ever legislate the romanization of its national language in the sweeping manner adopted by the Turks on January 1, 1929. Instead, there will undoubtedly be a gradual spread of Pinyin in those areas where it is warranted for strictly economic reasons. For example, international Chinese telegraphy is largely carried out in Pinyin because it is much cheaper than paying operators to memorize and transmit accurately the arbitrary code consisting of 10,000 numbers that has hitherto been used to send tetragraphic telegrams within China. Alphabetic telegraphy has already begun to make inroads in China proper. Pinyin has also been used for more than twenty years in experimental attempts at machine translation.

At present, there in only one romanized journal, *Xin Tang*, published in China. Yet nearly all Chinese journals give their titles in Pinyin and in tetragraphs. Barring unforeseen political upheavals, it will not be long before other scattered Pinyin magazines spring up in various parts of China. A few mostly independent, locally financed newspapers

子貢問 曰有一言而終身行之者乎子曰其恕乎 己所不欲勿施於人

Original Classical Chinese text written in the full (i.e., complicated) forms of the tetragraphs.

子贡问,"有可以一辈子奉行的一句话吗?" 孔子说,"就是宽大吧!自己不喜欢的事儿, 也不加在别人的身上."

Translation of the above into Modern Standard Mandarin and written in simplified tetragraphs.

Zigong wen, "You keyi yi beizi fengxing de yi ju hua ma?" Kongzi shuo, "Jiushi 'kuanda' ba! Ziji bu xihuan de shir, ye bu jiazai bieren shen shang." Romanized Modern Standard Mandarin.

[The disciple] Zigong asked, "Is there a motto which one can follow all one's life?" Confucius said, "How about 'generosity?' Do not do unto others what you yourself do not like." English translation.

employing a mixture of Pinyin and tetragraphs have begun to appear in the past few years. Educational authorities in the province of Honan have stressed Pinyin heavily in grade schools, and many parents, along with their children, are learning it enthusiastically.

A momentous step toward romanization was quietly taken in August 1988 when the rules for Pinyin orthography were promulgated without fanfare in *Language Construction*, the official organ of the State Language Commission. With these rules, word boundaries were established, punctuation was regularized, and grammatical usage defined. Pinyin now has the potential to become a fully functioning alphabetical script. Whether it does or not depends on many factors, including the extent to which English is used instead of Pinyin Mandarin in international networks and other instances where an alphabetical script is deemed superior to the tetragraphs. The most likely scenario is a long period, at least fifty to a hundred years, of digraphs in which the tetragraphic script and Pinyin coexist. During this period of digraphs, use of the tetragraphs and Pinyin will probably be restricted to those applica-

tions for which they are best suited—Pinyin for science, technology, commerce, and industry; the tetragraphs for calligraphy, classical studies, and literature.

The fate of Chinese characters has yet to be decided. Vietnam and North Korea have outlawed them, South Korea spurns them for most general purposes, and Japan restricts their number severely in favor of its two syllabaries (*katakana, hiragana*) and *romaji* (romanization). Only in the land of their birth, China, do the tetragraphs still hold sway. Even there, however, these extraordinary signs have come under attack. They have been simplified, reduced in number, phonetically annotated, analyzed, decomposed, put in sequence according to hundreds of different finding methods, and otherwise abused by reformers whose sole purpose is to make them more amenable to the needs of modern society. However, the tetragraphs will not fade from the scene without a struggle. Regarded even by illiterates with utmost veneration, their disappearance would constitute a mortal blow against what many hold to be the very soul of Chinese civilization. It is a gross understatement to say that traditional Chinese intellectuals have a large stake in maintaining their tetragraphic writing system intact for as long as possible. On the other hand, China's most celebrated writer of the twentieth century, Lu Hsün, is reported to have declared that "if Chinese characters are not annihilated, China will perish."

Where the tetragraphs are concerned, emotions run high both among those who want to reform them out of existence and among those who wish to preserve them eternally. Both sides are earnestly committed to their cause and honestly believe they have China's best interest at heart. Ultimately though, one side will lose. Regardless of the outcome, China is undergoing a painful process of self-discovery. The tumultuous events that have recently wrecked China are part of a continuous adjust-

ment to modernity. At the vortex of these struggles may be found the Chinese script and all that it represents.

ADDITIONAL READING

John DeFrancis, The Chinese Language: Fact and Fantasy, University of Hawaii Press, Honolulu, 1984.

—, Nationalism and Language Reform in China, Princeton University Press, Princeton, 1950; reprint: Octagon, New York, 1972.

—, Visible Speech: The Diverse Oneness of Writing Systems, University of Hawaii Press, Honolulu, 1989.

I. J. Gelb, A Study of Writing, University of Chicago Press, Chicago, 1963, revised edition.

William Hannas, The Simplification of Chinese Character-Based Writing, University of Pennsylvania Ph.D. dissertation, 1988.

Robert K. Logan, The Alphabet Effect: The Impact of the Phonetic Alphabet on the Devel-

opment of Western Civilization, William Morrow, New York, 1986.

Tom McArthur, Worlds of Reference: Lexicography, Learning and Language from the Clay Tablet to the Computer, Cambridge University Press, Cambridge, 1986.

Victor H. Mair, "The Need for an Alphabetically Arranged General Usage Dictionary of Mandarin Chinese: A Review Article of Some Recent Dictionaries and Current Lexicographical Projects," Sino-Platonic Papers, 1 (November 1986).

Jerry Norman, Chinese, Cambridge University Press, Cambridge, 1988.

S. Robert Ramsey, The Languages of China, Princeton University Press, Princeton, 1987.

Robert Sanders, "The Four Languages of 'Mandarin,'" Sino-Platonic Papers, 4 (November 1987).

James Unger, The Fifth Generation Fallacy: Why Japan Is Betting Its Future on Artificial Intelligence, Oxford University Press, Oxford, 1987.

Article 23   *The Nation*, March 21, 1994

Communism Lite in Beijing

China Goes Pop; Mao Meets Muzak

Jianying Zha

Jianying Zha is a Chicago-based writer who has published fiction in China. A version of this article will appear in her book on Chinese culture and politics, published by The New Press in 1995.

Beijing

A little more than a year ago, *China Culture Gazette*, official organ of China's Ministry of Culture, was transformed. For years *C.C.G.* had been an infamous stronghold of the hard-line apparatchiks, choking with dull, harsh Communist Party propaganda. With a new issue of its *Cultural Weekend* edition, the paper changed color overnight: from red to yellow.

The pictures did the trick. On that day, the four-page *Cultural Weekend* displayed many nude and half-nude photographs (mostly of busty Western women in languidly seductive poses); instantly it became known as "the coolest paper in Beijing." It also ran a front-page

interview on the subject of nudity with Liu Xiaoqing, China's brash movie queen. The issue sold like hot cakes.

The Ministry of Propaganda was furious. The Ministry of Culture wasn't happy about it, either. Rumor had it that Communist Party General Secretary Jiang Zemin, who has a propensity for showing off his "high-culture" taste, happened to pick up a copy of *C.C.G.* at a subway station. The General Secretary couldn't believe what he saw, and afterward expressed grave concern about the moral health of Chinese society.

Graver concerns these days center around economics. Considered to be on the front line of ideological battles, Chinese print media have always been both financially dependent on the party and under its tight control. For the past four decades the basic axiom taught in all Chinese journalism departments was "news is the party's throat and tongue." Every newspaper had—and still has—a party secretary, who would often take the post of chief editor as well, and who would report not so much to his readers but directly to his party boss.

But with the economic reform and a mushrooming of new papers and journals competing with the old ones, the situation has changed significantly in the past five years or so. *C.C.G.* had been in the red politically and financially. In fact, the paper was so deeply mired in debt it was on the brink of folding. Everyone on the staff knew that the party was not going to bail them out: As inflation continued and the price of paper climbed, the government ladled out the same meager subsidy.

Fortunately, just around this time, Deng Xiaoping, China's de facto emperor, issued his call for wider and deeper marketization. Following Deng's orders, the State General Press and Publishing Administration announced new guidelines: Publishers were given more decision-making power over matters such as printing erotic material and kung fu novels; the previous ban on printing pictures of young women in bikinis, foreign movie stars and pop singers on Chinese calendars was lifted; publishers in specialized fields could now cross over to general subjects to help sales.

So when Zhang Zuomin, a short, urchinlike former Red Guard, took charge of *Cultural Weekend*, he was given a free hand to make it profitable, and he knew exactly in what direction and how far he was to exercise that freedom. What was remarkable was that *C.C.G.*'s hard-line chief editor stood firmly behind Zhang when the nudity scandal broke. The wily old apparatchik even snapped at his grumbling superiors at the ministries. "Are we no longer 'marching toward the market'?" he demanded, employing a party slogan currently in fashion. "If not, I quit."

Readers are tired of 'hard news' found in the official print media.

Such a rationale could not be questioned for the moment, so the muttering stopped. Circulation of *Cultural Weekend* soared to 260,000—not as high as some of China's most popular papers and magazines with their half-million or more circulations, but breaking *C.C.G.*'s old record by far. Thanks to a steady outpouring of front-page reports on women, sex and the pop culture scene, written by Zhang Zuomin himself, *Cultural Weekend* soon became one of "the four little dragons of the Beijing press," and Zhang the newspaperman whom all others love to hate. Some dismiss him as the scumbag of the profession, while others acknowledge grudgingly that he may be a journalist for his times.

Zhang himself seems to delight in his notoriety, taking pride in all the irreverent pranks he has gotten away with in his life. "I'm making a name now, so I need to shake things up a bit, to send some shock waves to the market," he told me. "In any event, I believe we must smash open Chinese culture, and apply 'the great fearless spirit' to our newspaper work." He was lapsing into Red Guard jargon! Indeed, it was during the lawless period of the Cultural Revolution that it dawned on Zhang that a newspaper could be a profitable venture. He and some young comrades once printed a small propaganda sheet with a stolen mimeograph machine, and Zhang pocketed the profit they made from selling the first batch. Another "fearless" act Zhang proudly recounted to me was that in 1987 he had worn plastic sandals while covering a high-level state function. "The chairman of China was present!" Zhang bragged. "I'm sure I was the one and only person who did that."

All the same, Zhang knows what lines he cannot cross. "I will not run anything antiparty in my paper," Zhang told me emphatically. "And I will not run pornography." He went into an absurdly meticulous explanation about how the degree of bodily exposure in the nude photos he printed was well within the prescribed rules of decorum. This is a particularly Chinese technique among the professional orders: the art of creatively interpreting party policies to protect and advance your own interests, while in the course of it portraying yourself as engaged in a nobly subversive cause.

In their pursuit of the average reader, many other papers are testing the new boundaries the government has staked out. The average reader is apparently tired of "hard news"—the kind of stories found in the official print media that go on and on about party congresses, production rates and ideological education while remaining silent about political oppression and abuses of power. How much more inviting is gossip about movie stars and millionaires! Look at those colorful photos, sensational titles, lurid tales! Readers are sure to gulp it down. With the new formula, the papers have begun to support themselves, attract advertisements and relieve government of its financial burden, but only at the expense of the official papers. Once-dominant journals are being ignored by readers. Papers like *People's Daily* and *Guangming Daily* still arrive in the offices of all state enterprises, but few look to them for interesting coverage of popular events. They can't compete with what's on the newsstands.

Some frown at the vulgarity of it all, some criticize the degrading fact that most Chinese journalists nowadays take fees or bribes from the people they report on and still others think that all this "soft news" is the new opium for the masses, designed to distract them from harsh realities. "I'm deeply disappointed by our reporters," said the prominent dissident journalist Dai Qing. "They are totally corrupted by commercialization." Another noted magazine editor hissed, "All these noises they've made, and you can't find even one paper of a quality and weight that's comparable to *World Economic Herald*." The *Herald* was a Shanghai-based reformist paper that closed in response to government censorship around the time of Tiananmen Square. (A good number of other dissident journals that had been quietly building up semi-autonomous bases within or on the margin of the official press were also either suspended or purged. Dai Qing herself was jailed for a year, and her reporting is still banned in China.)

Chen Xilin, the young director of the weekend edition of the sober and serious *China Business Times*, is impatient with such criticism. "Don't talk to me about Tiananmen; it gives me a headache. Those elites have done a good job of enlightening us. They taught us a lesson. But their time is over. Tragic, yes, but that's history. The new elite is a lot smarter, and one thing is certain about the future of China: It belongs to smart people."

With his reputation of having created the first Chinese paper for white-collar professionals, Chen is typical of China's post-Tiananmen elite; he works hard and plays hard. He edits by day, frequents expensive restaurants and *karaoke* bars in the evening with visiting Hong Kong and Taiwan colleagues (who pay the bill), and stays up late with pots of coffee to draw editorial cartoons for his paper and to dash out short essays that bring him extra income. By shunning harsh political propaganda and focusing on the economy and life style, his paper embodies a brand of journalism that is smart, slick and politically moderate.

Chen's sarcasm toward papers like *Cultural Weekend* is thinly veiled: "It's O.K. But I wouldn't call it journalism." On the whole, though, he is optimistic about Chinese media: "After a while, some of these small, gossipy papers will fold, some will remain. The society always needs this sort of reading, but not so much of it. They play an important role in the eventual freeing of the press: They've broken up the official news language, shifted the concerns from the government and state affairs to ordinary people and social lives. They are already affecting the big papers, forcing them to loosen up a bit, to compete, to be more attractive to readers. Isn't this a victory in itself?"

A lot of people in the profession echo this sentiment. Many people I meet in Beijing these days have changed their minds about Tiananmen. They see direct confrontation with the state as hopeless and politically immature, Western democracy as unfit for Chinese circumstances. Four years ago, Deng Xiaoping was widely cursed as the butcher of his own people; today many talk about him as the wise patriarch who knows the only right way to handle the messy transitions China

is going through. "It's like getting a hard punch in the face from your father," said a media reporter who had been deeply involved with the Tiananmen protests. "Very hard to get over. Only by and by do you realize he's your father after all. And there is nothing you can do but slowly chip away at that hard socialist wall." Heroism is dropped; pragmatism is embraced. This surge of what the Chinese call "new conservatism" recalls the ancient Taoist wisdom: Water is the strongest thing in the world.

Is this all a matter of self-delusion, an easy rhetoric to absolve the speakers of moral irresponsibility in treacherous circumstances? What's clear is that ponderous questions of this sort are out of keeping with the tenor of the times. Today the national mood favors News Lite. Culture Lite. Communism Lite. Old taboos are being broken, new frontiers crossed, but the transgressors often wear a sly grin, ready to duck or backtrack at the first sign of danger. Gone is the kind of romantic uplift with which the 1980s Chinese cultural scene was imbued.

Tiananmen was a turning point, though the direction the country has taken in the wake of the tanks and blood caught many by surprise. As the engine of economic reform has shifted into overdrive, the largest nation on earth has set off on a frantic race for material wealth. Popular culture is shifting gears too. Political lectures are out, elite sentiments are ignored and ordinary people, particularly younger ones, are demanding services long overdue: soft rock, kung fu videos, late night radio talk shows, sitcoms, variety shows, *karaoke* bars. As they chase after money and a merrier life style, Deng's subjects are also losing the stoic patience Mao's people once displayed.

"Serve the people" was once Mao's famous slogan; now it is having a second, speedier life, in which even the Chairman himself is repackaged and served up. One of the best-selling audiocassettes in China these days is *Red Sun*, a tape that adapted old hymns to Mao to soft rock rhythms with electronic synthesizers. The vogue spread quickly. All sorts of revolutionary songs were dug up and adapted to the beat of the new time. Mao meets Muzak and MTV.

The scene has changed so quickly, and often so absurdly, that for those who labor in the culture industry, adaptability has become a quality both valuable and suspect. There is a generational split too. Those who stick to the good old socialist habit of taking the long view and sitting things out watch with growing apprehension. These tend to be people over 45. Those who seize the moment with entrepreneurial flair see a different vista and have different stories to tell. These tend to be people in their 20s and 30s. "It's like watching a bunch of monkeys turning somersaults," a Beijing movie director coolly remarked to me. "Energetic, fun, agile, but oh the dust! So much dust is kicked up."

The king of these agile monkeys is Wang Shuo, the 35-year-old Beijing "hooligan writer" with a knack for turning culture into a commodity. A colorful character with a roguish sense of humor, Wang started out as a fiction writer, then moved on to writing scripts for movies and television, all as a freelancer and all with sweeping success. He has helped create three of the most-talked-about television series in recent years. The latest one, a soap opera called *No Choice in Loving You,* set a precedent: Instead of producing the series in-house, CCTV, China's official television network, had to pay a handsome price to buy it. Wang has a publicist's knack for attracting media exposure. He advertises himself the way celebrities do, talks about fame and money with open bravado. The tabloids love him, and he never fails to supply them with a punchy quote or two. He is the first writer in the post-Mao era to publish a four-volume *Selected Works.* The last one was Mao himself.

Wang admits that his commercial instincts were honed from his early days as a hustling small-business man: "I learned to watch what my customers need." Posing as a writer for common folks, he uses his home-grown, sardonic wit to mock both the Communist ideologues and the elite intellectuals. But the latter are really his favorite target. One of Wang's famous epigrams goes: "Before you die, have your high!" And one of Wang Shuo's highs is to let his cynical, smartass hooligan antiheroes poke fun at everything holy and serious. "I can't stand people with a sense of mission," he declares.

Wang remains a controversial figure in spite—or because—of his immense popularity in the pop culture scene. People are passionately divided over what "the Wang Shuo phenomenon" means. For some, it is an alarming sign of the nihilism among the young generation. One of the famous lines in *No Choice in Loving You,* for instance, is what a young man told his girlfriend: "Although my feelings for you don't add up to love, they are more than enough for marriage." Citing this, a noted young Shanghai literary critic, Wang Xiaoming, wrote:

Here is the currently trendy Beijing youth culture, and Wang Shuo's works are its artistic expression:

To be cool is to mock everything. It results from disillusionment and a sense of powerlessness; it's a logical spasm of a withering Chinese spirit that has been under oppression for half a century. It mocks a dated official ideology that has long lost its grip over the public; more deadly, it dissolves all that might form the foundation of any new spiritual belief, including reason, passion for rebellion, and even certain basic values such as sincerity, steadfastness, respect for others. In fact it has already been acquiesced in by the authorities, becoming a part of the new ruling ideology. What's amusing is that the trend thinks of itself as having something in common with postmodernism in the West. There is nothing more laughable than this.

Wang's fans, however, defend him ardently. China's educated elite have been alienated from the ordinary people, they argue, and there was always something hypocritical and hollow about their timid idealism and oppositional posturing, since they themselves were politically and economically dependent on the state. Wang, on the other hand, is a true independent spirit: He earns a living on his own and refuses to participate in any political game. He cares about ordinary readers and is refreshingly candid about matters like money and success. Some contend his cynicism is long overdue. One of Wang's avid readers is Fang Lijun, a young Beijing painter known for his large canvas portraits of merry, dopey-looking urban street people, which he has successfully marketed to foreign patrons. Fang echoes Wang Shuo this way: "We prefer to be called the lost, bored, crises-ridden, bewildered hoodlums, but we will not be cheated again. Don't think about educating us with old methods, for we shall put 10,000 question marks across all dogmas, then negate them and toss them on the trash heap." Fang's combination of defiance, disillusionment and determination is a sentiment increasingly common in today's China. As he concludes cheerfully, "Only a jackass would fall into a trap after having fallen into it a hundred times."

Article 24

Sinorama, January 1992

Red Envelopes: It's the Thought that Counts

Melody Hsieh

Past or present, in China or abroad, it is unlikely you could find a gift like the "red envelope," which in Chinese society has the capability of ascending to heaven or plumbing the depths of hell.

To attach a piece of red paper to a sacrificial offering depicts sending a red envelope to the deity, symbolizing a request for expelling evil or granting of good fortune. On Ghost Festival (the fifteenth day of the seventh month on the lunar calendar), you may burn some paper money wrapped in red paper to bribe the "good brothers" (ghosts), in hopes that they will be satiated and do no more mischief.

In the corporeal world, the red envelope is even more versatile: as a congratulatory gift for all manner of auspicious events, as a New Year's gift given by adults to children, as a "small consideration to the doctor before surgery or the birth of a child, as an expression of a boss's appreciation to his employees. ... For whatever the giver may desire, the red envelope is just the thing to build up personal sentiment in the receiver.

In fairy tales, the fairy godmother can wave her magic wand and turn stone into gold or a pumpkin into a luxurious carriage. But calling it a magic wand is not so good as seeing it as a wand of hope for all mankind.

The red envelope is like the Chinese wand of hope, and it often carries limitless desires. To give a red envelope at a happy occasion is like embroidering a flower on a quilt; when meeting misfortune, to receive a red envelope is a psychological palliative which just might change your luck.

Whether it be congratulations, encouragement, sympathy, gratitude, compensation ... just give a red envelope, and not only will the sentiment he expressed, substantive help will also have arrived.

The fact that the red envelope opens so many doors and is so versatile today also naturally has practical advantages. For marriages, funerals, birthdays and illness, send a gift. But choosing a gift is an art in itself, and you can wrack your brains and spend a whole day shopping, and you still won't know if the other person will like it or need it. That's not nearly as good as wrapping money in red paper, which on the one hand saves work and on the other is useful, so everybody's happy. Compared with the way Westerners give gifts, giving a red envelope may be lacking in commemorative sentiment, but it's a lot more practical.

Nevertheless, Chinese haven't always been so substantive." In fact, it is only in the last few decades that red envelopes have become so commonly used.

A Brilliant Fire Neutralizing the Year: Kuo Licheng, a specialist in popular culture who is today an advisor to *ECHO* magazine, points out that traditionally Chinese did not present gifts of money. For example, when a child reached one month old, friends and family would send a gold locket; when visiting a sick person, people would bring Chinese medicine; upon meeting for the first time, people would exchange rings or jade from their person as a greeting gift. ... None of these carry, as the Chinese say, the "unpleasant odor of brass," implying penny-pinching greed.

No one knows when money began to replace these traditional gifts. The only certain continuous tradition of using money to express sentiment—perhaps the origin of the practice of combining usefulness and sentiment, material and spiritual—is the tradition of the "age neutralizing money" (cash given on New Year's day to children), which has been carried down to this day.

"In the past, the New Year's money was simply a piece of red paper attached to a gold yuan, or the use of a red twine to string together cash. When eating New Year's dinner, the money would be pressed beneath the stove, representing 'a brilliant fire, abundant wealth;' only after dinner would it be pulled out and handed out to the small children. The meaning is that, after undergoing a baptism of fire, it was hoped that it could expel evil and resolve dangers, so that the children could put the past behind them ("neutralize" the past) and grow up strong and healthy," says Juan Chang-juei, director of the Anthropology Committee of the Provincial Museum, laughing that in fact "age neutralizing money" should be called "age extension money.

The writer Hsiao Min lived in Peking before 1938. At that time she was just a little sprite of less than ten years old, but because the New Year is quite different today from what it was in the past, she has a very deep impression of the New Year's money.

She recalls that it was not easy to get the "age neutralizing money" in those days. The children had to kneel on the floor and kowtow, and your forehead had to touch the floor, and it would only count if it was hard enough to make a sound. "In the past, floors were made of rough concrete, and we kids often had to kneel until our knees hurt and knock our heads until we were dizzy, before we could get our New Year's money."

It was only with the spread of paper currency that the New Year's money became paper cash wrapped in red envelopes. The reason why the paper is red, or why in early days red thread was used, rather than white, green, or black, is from religious rituals.

Better Red Than Dread: Juan Chang-juei suggests that in primitive times, when man would see a bright red flower in a green field, he would find it quite eye-catching and delightful. so maybe this is why red is an "auspicious" color.

Further, red is the same as the color of blood, and since a sacrifice of blood has a lucky effect, red came to be ordained as having the meaning of avoiding ill-fortune.

"Before the red envelope form appeared, people 'carried red' to represent auspiciousness and evading evil," says Juan. He says that in previous generations people would attach a piece of red paper to a religious offering or to a wedding dress, in both cases having this meaning. It was only after cut-paper techniques had been invented that the red piece of paper was changed to the "double-happiness" character. Before paper was invented, perhaps they used red cloth or painted on some red pigment instead.

Juan Chang-juei reminds us that because red symbolizes the vitality of life, and all mankind in early times had their magic ways to expel evil, it was by no means unique to China, and in the distant past Westerners also considered red to represent auspiciousness.

For example, shortly after Columbus landed in America, he gave the local natives red cloth to wrap around their heads to show celebration. For this reason, in the past red was always the color used to wrap presents in the West, and only later did it evolve that many colors were used.

But Chinese are relatively more concerned about colors, as Confucius has said: "I hate the way purple spoils vermilion," Colors are divided into "appropriate" colors and "deviant" colors. Red in this sense is the orthodox representation for good fortune, which cannot be altered lightly.

A Not Unreasonable Perquisite: As for using red envelopes as a small consideration in order to get the other person to do something on your behalf, very early on there was the "gratuity" for servants.

Kuo Li-cheng indicates that in novels like *The Golden Lotus,* you can often see in old style banquets that when the chef serves the main course the guest of honor must give the cook a "gratuity," using silver wrapped in red paper, to express appreciation to the host.

Or, family or friends might dispatch a servant to deliver a gift to your door. For the person giving the gift, it's only natural that they would send a servant, but for the person receiving the gift, the emissary is performing an unusual service, "so the recipient always had to ask the servant to bring back a letter of thanks,

and to give a red envelope, which was called a *li* [strength] or *ching-shih* [respect for the emissary], to express gratitude for his legwork and provide transportation expenses." Kuo Li-cheng adds that the *ching-shih* was usually about 1/20th the value of the original gift, so this kind of red envelope was a reasonable perk as far as the servant was concerned.

"The ching-shih was originally a gift of money replete with sentiment, and it's only because modern people use it erroneously that the significance of the red envelope has become muddled," notes Kuo, who cannot help but lament that today "sending a red envelope" is synonymous with giving a bribe.

Some Chinese have adapted to circumstances, and since a red envelope can bribe a living, breathing human being, the effect should be no less in sucking up to the ghosts of the nether world. Today, in some rural townships in south and central Taiwan, especially at Ghost Festival, people wrap up the spirit money in red paper and burn it as an offering to the "good brothers" (spirits), hoping that after they get a red envelope and become a local god of wealth, they will no longer tamper with the affairs of men.

Juan Chang-juei says that in the past there was by no means the custom of sending red envelopes to ghosts, and this is a product of circumstance invented by Chinese in recent years.

Evangelical Red Envelopes: "The red envelope in and of itself is not to blame, and originally it was just to express a friendly intent, a symbol of sentiment," states Juan. Those who can afford to give red envelopes are always the older generation or the boss or the leader. He raises an example, noting that over the New Year's holiday in 1991, the Provincial Museum sponsored an opera appreciation activity for children. The day work began, the museum curator gave

every one of the people who worked on it with him a red envelope, to thank his colleagues for giving up their holiday to work for the museum.

Hsiao Min also believes that there have also been some positive changes in the red envelope as it has evolved.

"In the past, the red envelope was just a simple red packet, without any characters printed on it. Today a lot of organizations, like restaurants or hotels, will imprint relevant auspicious phrases, and will give a set of red stationery to customers as a small gift at New Year's, to add a little more human feeling." For example, the Lai Lai Sheraton prints "May good fortune come, May wealth come, May happiness come" on its red envelopes, a play on the word lai (to come) in its name; steakhouses may print a golden bull, to make a deeper impression on their customers.

It's worth noting that even evangelical organizations cannot underestimate the attraction of a red envelope. Hsiao Min, a Christian, says that every time the passage to a new year approaches, churches will print their own red envelopes, which congregants can use at no charge. Because propitious proverbs from the Bible have been imprinted on the set, they are very popular among the congregants, so that supply can't keep up with demand. Since they integrate traditional customs, they can also help the evangelical church spread and adapt to local conditions.

"However, no matter how much money is in the red packet, how can a few pieces of paper currency take the place of or outweigh the feeling in one's heart?" says Hsiao Min. She concluded, that a small gift given with a big heart, the act of giving and receiving, and mutual affection are the real meanings of giving a red envelope.

TAIWAN ARTICLES

Article 25   *Foreign Affairs*, November/December 1994

Giving Taipei a Place at the Table

Ross H. Munro

Ross H. Munro is Director of the Asia Program at the Foreign Policy Research Institute. He was a correspondent in Asia for Time magazine, and The Globe and Mail during the 1970s and 1980s.

LET TWO CHINAS BLOOM

What in the world is Taiwan up to? More than two decades ago, the Republic of China on Taiwan was forced out of the United Nations when a majority of U.N. members voted to seat the People's Republic of China. At that time Taiwan adamantly refused to endorse any formula that might have allowed it to retain its U.N. membership alongside the P.R.C., which was being given the Security Council seat. Now Taiwan is pressing for a role in the United Nations under almost any conditions. Launched in mid-1993, Taiwan's all-out campaign to return to the United Nations is being widely dismissed even by some of its friends as quixotic at best. Nevertheless, it merits serious attention in Washington, and even more so in Beijing, because it is emblematic of the rapid democratization of Taiwan's politics that is transforming its foreign policy, particularly toward the P.R.C.

The rationale for Taiwan's U.N. stance is that, while the Republic of China (R.O.C.) remains committed to the idea of one China and thus theoretically to the eventual reunification with the mainland, a separate government has ruled the island and its now 21 million residents continuously since 1949. And it has ruled well: Taiwan boasts a modern economy that provides a good living standard for the vast majority of its citizens and a political system that has virtually completed the transition to democracy. Today Taiwan outstrips most U.N. members in GNP (with the world's twentieth-largest economy), trade volume (the world's thirteenth-largest), and population (larger than that of two-thirds of the U.N. membership). Following the precedent set by Germany and Korea of dual representation for divided nations, the Republic of China on Taiwan clearly deserves a place in the U.N. system.

CHINA'S HOLLOW VICTORY

Despite the strong case made by Taiwan for U.N. membership on historical, legal, economic, and ethical grounds, its first attempt to put the issue before the United Nations in the fall of 1993 was an embarrassing failure. Only a few countries—most of them small, poor Caribbean Basin nations that receive economic assistance from Taiwan—spoke out on its behalf. The explanation for Taipei's failure was simple: Beijing fervently opposes any role in the United Nations for what it still portrays as a renegade province with an illegitimate government. With China's burgeoning economic and military power making it second in importance only to the United States in many nations' eyes, Beijing had little trouble ensuring that few would speak on Taiwan's behalf. In pragmatic terms, even U.N. members enjoying good ties with Taiwan faced an easy, expedient choice: to incur Beijing's wrath by openly supporting Taiwan's apparently hopeless quest, or to remain silent while the issue was buried in committee.

And buried in committee the issue might remain. As long as the Beijing government presides over a strong and reasonably united People's Republic, it can easily wield enough power to frustrate Taiwan's effort to reenter the United Nations. But in doing so, Beijing is hurting its own interests and retarding the cause of Chinese reunification.

Because Taiwan's U.N. prospects seem so bleak, even many of Taiwan's friends abroad have been unsettled by its U.N. campaign. Some observers have dismissed it as a product of domestic Taiwan politics. But that is precisely why Taiwan's U.N. campaign is so significant. The people of Taiwan are speaking out and, now that democracy has arrived, the government is listening carefully. At the center of Taiwan's democratic politics today is the emotional issue of Taiwan's international identity—

whether to seek an independent Taiwan or some form of reunification with China, and since neither seems immediately attainable, how best to manage the ambiguity of Taiwan's current status. Although this debate is far from resolved and often conducted in veiled language, the people of newly democratic Taiwan are determined to be heard on the issue of their island's future. Indeed, the Kuomintang (KMT, or Nationalist Party) government launched its U.N. campaign, with great reluctance, only after concluding that the Taiwanese people, whatever their political allegiance, had overwhelmingly supported the main opposition party's call for U.N. membership.

So Beijing should not rest on its easy victory against Taipei at the United Nations; easy victories often prove hollow. Beijing instead could serve its own interests by trying to understand the factors, chief among them the democratic process, that drove Taiwan's government to seek U.N. membership despite the overwhelming odds against it. So far it seems that the leaders of the People's Republic of China fear but do not understand the new politics of Taiwan.

THE NEW TAIWAN

In January 1988, Lee Teng-hui became president of the R.O.C. on Taiwan and immediately made flexibility and pragmatism the official hallmarks of his foreign policy. Underlying this approach was a radical new principle that became official Taiwan policy in 1991: one China, two political entities. It asserts that in China today there are two governments, the R.O.C. and the P.R.C., each legitimately ruling the area it controls. The logical extension of this argument is that both governments deserve to be represented abroad, which might strike some as obvious. But it represents a sharp break from the previous position of the R.O.C. on Taiwan: that there is only one China, and it can have only one legitimate government. This is still the position taken by the P.R.C., which has been unrelentingly attacking the R.O.C. for shifting its stance.

The leaders of the P.R.C. fear but do not understand the new politics of Taiwan.

Under President Lee's new policies, Taiwan began pressing vigorously for admission to international organizations. It returned in 1988 to Asian Development Bank meetings, accepting the designation it had spurned

two years before. In 1990, Taiwan applied for membership in the General Agreement on Tariffs and Trade as the "Customs Territory of Taiwan, Penghu, Kin-men, and Matsu." Taiwan's GATT nomenclature paid implicit tribute to the idea of one China while reflecting the reality that Taiwan was governed separately, but Beijing refused to recognize the conciliatory gesture. In 1991, Taiwan was admitted to the Asia-Pacific Economic Cooperation forum's meetings.

Even more impressive was Taipei's drive to develop intergovernmental relations with countries that had diplomatic relations with Beijing. By mid-1994 the R.O.C. government had set up "administrative" or "representative" offices, performing many functions of a typical embassy, in about 60 countries. In another 30 countries where Taiwan was forced to adopt a lower profile, it maintained some sort of agency, such as a business office or travel bureau, as a point of contact.

In the late 1980s and early 1990s, Taiwan's unofficial relations with the United States continued to improve. In September 1992 President George Bush approved a $6 billion sale of 150 F-16 fighters to Taiwan, partly to restore a military balance of power that had been disturbed by the P.R.C.'s purchase of Su-27 bomber aircraft from Russia. Within days U.S. authorities also announced the sale of 12 SH-2F helicopters to Taiwan for $161 million. This year Congress passed legislation that effectively overturned the Reagan administration's agreement to reduce arms sales to Taiwan, declaring that the commitment of the 1979 Taiwan Relations Act to ensure that Taiwan has sufficient self-defense capability takes precedence. In September the Clinton administration announced that it was modestly expanding its official ties with Taiwan and allowing its offices in Washington and other cities to be renamed the Taipei Economic and Cultural Representative Office in the United States. A senior State Department officer, however, said visits by Taiwan's top officials would still be barred.

Taiwan has also developed extensive unofficial ties with communist and formerly communist countries. Taiwan succeeded in setting up de facto government offices throughout Central Europe, where its presence was once negligible. In Asia, Taiwan's greatest success was establishing ties with Vietnam in 1988; by 1994 Taiwan was Vietnam's leading foreign investor.

Taipei even enjoyed some minor victories in its longstanding competition with Beijing over formal diplomatic ties. Between 1989 and 1992 Taiwan convinced seven Caribbean and African nations that had diplomatic relations with Beijing to establish formal ties with Taipei. Taipei was clearly hoping that Beijing would not automatically break off relations with the countries concerned, but in every case it did, even when ties stopped short of full diplomatic relations. After Latvia decided in

January 1992 to upgrade relations with Taiwan to the consulate-general level, Beijing continued to protest the arrangement until Latvia retreated this year.

CHINA OUTBIDS TAIWAN

The 1988–92 period may well have been the heyday of Taiwan's pragmatic diplomacy. Taiwan undoubtedly benefited from the temporary decline in Beijing's international standing after the Chinese leadership ordered tanks into Tiananmen Square in June 1989 to suppress anti-regime demonstrators. When China's economic growth then temporarily slowed, Taiwan clearly drew advantage from its burgeoning economy and huge foreign exchange reserves, then the largest in the world. Taiwan's economic strength, relative to the mainland's, probably reached its zenith during this period.

But by mid-1992 China's market-oriented economic reformers were back in control, with Deng Xiaoping at the vanguard, and the mainland economy had resumed its hyper-rapid growth. Eager to profit from what promised to be the biggest economic takeoff in history, the world's business leaders were beating a path to Beijing's door, and the political leaders of many industrial nations were not far behind.

With its economic, military, and political power growing rapidly, China had the resources to outbid the R.O.C. in the international arena. In August 1992 China's burgeoning economy and international trade helped lead South Korea to forsake its old and deep friendship with Taiwan and establish diplomatic ties with Beijing. France agreed to end arms sales to Taiwan after the P.R.C. made it clear that French companies would be punished if such sales continued and rewarded if they stopped. Although in 1994 the Republic of China on Taiwan still maintained formal diplomatic relations with 29 countries, only one of them, South Africa, could be classified by size, wealth, or population as large.

China now enjoys enormous power in the world community. It can prevent many things from happening or make efforts difficult for other major powers, including the United States. The P.R.C.'s veto in the Security Council is the most obvious manifestation of this fact; its ability to make or break an embargo of North Korea is another.

Taiwan's leading policymakers, who are acutely sensitive to every shift in their environment, understood that, no matter how prosperous and modern Taiwan's economy might be, it cannot directly match the international leverage inherent in a Chinese economy of enormous size growing at more than ten percent a year. Taiwan's authorities had to conclude that the rapid increase since the mid-1980s in the number and substance of its quasi-

diplomatic ties with foreign countries was not necessarily going to continue indefinitely.

THE SOUTHERN STRATEGY

Even more troubling to Taiwan's political leaders was the extent to which Taiwanese businesses were being drawn to the mainland. Taiwan's businessmen, eager to escape the high land and labor costs that were crimping the profits of their labor-intensive, export-oriented industries such as toys and footwear, had begun shifting production to the mainland in the mid-1980s.

Ironically, the shift sharply accelerated soon after the Tiananmen incident and has continued to increase every year. Taiwanese businessmen shrewdly recognized that Beijing was desperate for investors when most countries hesitated to sink additional capital into the P.R.C. By 1992, according to the R.O.C. Central Bank, the mainland was absorbing 45 percent of Taiwan's capital outflow. By mid-1993 Taiwanese companies had made investment commitments on the mainland of $14.2 billion, of which more than $10 billion had already been expended. Unofficial estimates of current Taiwanese investment on the mainland run as high as $30 billion. Eyeing these trends, the leaders in Taipei realized that most of Taiwan's overseas investment capital would be sunk into mainland enterprises within a few years. This means that the P.R.C. would enjoy overwhelming leverage over Taiwan's business community and thus considerable influence over the R.O.C. government.

Taiwan's fears were anything but fanciful. After the December 1992 elections, which saw an upsurge in the strength of the pro-independence opposition, the Democratic Progressive Party (DPP), Beijing apparently realized that it was blocked politically in its drive for assimilation of Taiwan. It began emphasizing economic and trade relations over political issues, with the intent of diffusing Taiwan's independence movement through economic integration. Taiwan's leaders saw the same picture, prompting them to seek countervailing international connections to offset the risk of being absorbed economically and politically by the mainland.

This set the stage for the launching of Taiwan's U.N. campaign the following spring. The Taiwanese government also urged business leaders to slow the pace of investment on the mainland and look at investment Opportunities elsewhere. Officials announced a "southern strategy" aimed at strengthening Taiwan's ties with Southeast Asia by encouraging Taiwan's businesses to invest more in that region. Until about 1990, Taiwan's investment in Southeast Asia had increased rapidly. But by then China was beckoning, and annual new investment by Taiwanese companies in Southeast Asia plummeted. By 1994 it was less than one-fifth, and possibly just one-tenth, of 1990 levels. While Taiwan's total investment in Southeast Asia is currently about $16.7 billion, that figure will soon be overtaken by investment on the Chinese mainland, if it has not been already.

Taiwan's leaders realize that they and their Southeast Asian counterparts have a strong mutual interest in Steering Taiwanese investment to that region. Particularly in Indonesia, Malaysia, Singapore, and the Philippines, concern about China's economic power and military intentions is high. Their leaders are anxious about potential investors, both domestic and foreign (that is, Taiwan), being lured away by the China boom. Taiwanese authorities have been working with several Southeast Asian governments to offer incentives to Taiwanese investors, and in the Philippines and Vietnam they have helped sponsor industrial development zones aimed at attracting Taiwanese capital.

A LITTLE RESPECT

The people of Taiwan are proud of what their island nation has accomplished economically, socially, and politically. That pride is mixed with increasing resentment over their nation's international outcast status, which they consider unfair, unjust, and insulting. These feelings connect with a growing consciousness of a Taiwanese identity and a growing wariness of the mainland. These sentiments are shared by those who hope that Taiwan can one day be a separate and independent country and those still committed, however abstractly, to the ultimate goal of one China. They transcend party lines and the increasingly fuzzy division between mainlander and Taiwanese families. One aspect of this is the desire for respect, "face," or standing—call it what you will—for Taiwan in the international community.

> *Taiwan understands that the road to the U.N. ultimately goes through Beijing.*

The DPP tapped into such sentiments years ago. When the opposition DPP was founded in the fall of 1986, the party called for U.N. membership for Taiwan. It proved to be a political masterstroke and a no-lose issue for the DPP. The demand struck a sympathetic chord throughout the population. Of course, the pro-independence DPP expected the P.R.C. to fiercely oppose its U.N. plank, but this served the DPP's interest in portraying the P.R.C. as hostile to Taiwan. And as long as the DPP harped on the need for U.N. membership, it helped divert public attention from the substantial foreign policy achievements of President Lee and the KMT government.

The DPP's U.N. plank hurt the KMT not just because it won widespread popular support but also because it threatened to change the terms of political debate in Taiwan. The DPP's position made it clear that a DPP government would apply for U.N. membership as "Taiwan," a new state. In other words, the DPP's popular call for U.N. membership amounted to a backdoor endorsement of Taiwan independence. So the KMT, whose historic identity stems in part from its commitment, however abstract, to the eventual reunification of China, felt compelled to take the U.N. issue away from the DPP and redefine it as a legitimate demand that both parts of a divided nation be represented in the United Nations. The alternative for the KMT was to remain on the political defensive and risk relinquishing its dominance of the central political debate over Taiwan's identity and future.

When Taiwanese officials launched their U.N. campaign in mid-1993, their initial goal was merely to "participate" in the United Nations; they carefully avoided making their demands more explicit. They also signaled their willingness to participate initially only in peripheral U.N. organizations. Given the flexibility Taiwan's authorities have displayed over the form and legal basis of their participation in the United Nations, the P.R.C. seems once again to have missed an opportunity to advance its interests as well as the cause of reunification. If the Foreign Ministry in Beijing had been sufficiently shrewd and creative to offer Taiwan some sort of subordinate participatory role in the United Nations, it might have created a painful dilemma for Taipei. If it accepted, it could be construed as acknowledging Beijing's power to determine its international status. If it refused, its U.N. campaign would be fatally undermined, and it would appear rigid while Beijing appeared accommodating.

Unfortunately, all of this remains speculation. Beijing responded to Taiwan's U.N. initiative on September 1, 1993, with a white paper that made clear Beijing's renewed determination to block the participation of the R.O.C. in the international community, including the United Nations. Once again the P.R.C. refused to acknowledge that a legitimate, democratic government exists on the island. According to the white paper, "the sole legal government representing the entire Chinese people" is in Beijing.

While it is doubtful that any diplomat was won over by the white paper's arguments per se, it served its purpose. It reminded the world's envoys and foreign policy makers that the P.R.C. would treat as a hostile act even the mildest manifestation of support or sympathy for

Taiwan's plea to participate in the United Nations. Little more needed to be said. The P.R.C. had demonstrated its willingness to punish countries economically if they maintained ties with Taiwan. The P.R.C.'s version of dollar diplomacy aside, it also enjoyed the advantages of the defender. It was not asking other countries to do anything except to ensure that the Taiwan participation issue be quietly buried by inaction—a request that undoubtedly appeals to cautious diplomats.

Certainly one could infer that Taiwan had many timid, silent sympathizers when the question of its participation in the United Nations was raised at a meeting of the U.N. General Committee on September 24, 1993. The question was simply whether to put the issue on the committee agenda. Of those committee members in attendance, three countries with whom the R.O.C. maintains diplomatic relations spoke in favor of Taiwan. Eleven countries spoke against. The majority—24—said nothing. No formal vote was taken and, as far as that year at the United Nations was concerned, the issue was moot.

Since that setback, Taiwan has not ceased promoting its case. The KMT government still seems completely committed to the U.N. campaign, even though some of the pressures that precipitated the decision to launch the campaign have eased. The slowdown in new Taiwanese investment in the mainland that began in 1993 is continuing, and since the December 1992 election, the DPP has not fared quite as well. Even so, by early this summer, Taipei's worldwide campaign for the 1994–95 U.N. season was in high gear.

THROUGH THE BACK DOOR

Some friends of Taiwan have been promoting the idea of entering the United Nations through the back door, that is, by participating in the work of the specialized U.N. agencies. Taiwan has repeatedly offered substantial financial contributions to U.N. organizations that allow it to participate. That way Taiwan would gain legal or de facto membership in the specialized agencies and could gradually enlist a two-thirds majority of U.N. members to support its application for membership.

Such suggestions seem to imply that China is economically weak or diplomatically inept. It is neither. The reality is that the P.R.C.'s diplomats are already quite aware of this proposed gradualist strategy—and are primed to react to any evidence that Taiwan is adopting it. In addition, the foundation of this strategy—using Taiwan's economic clout to make offers to U.N. agencies too generous to be refused-is flawed. Taiwan's relative economic strength vis-à-vis the P.R.C. has probably peaked; Taiwan's strong and expanding economy is no match for the sheer volume of growth generated by China's economic takeoff This means that the P.R.C. has

sufficient economic resources to prevail, directly or indirectly, in any bidding war at the United Nations. In short, the P.R.C. today has the economic clout and the diplomatic savvy to stymie a Taiwanese effort to enter the United Nations through the back door—or, for that matter, the front door.

Although they cannot publicly acknowledge it, Taiwan's top officials undoubtedly understand that the road to the United Nations ultimately goes through Beijing. Taiwan has been sending a subtle message to the P.R.C. that is part threat and part promise. The threat is that if Beijing continues to isolate and humiliate Taiwan internationally, especially by blocking its participation in the United Nations and other intergovernmental Organizations, then it will foster pro-independence sentiments in Taiwan that the KMT will be unable to counter. Alternatively, Taipei officials seem to be saying, they are ready to enter serious talks aimed at eventual reunification once Beijing gives Taiwan "face" and endorses its participation in the United Nations. Taiwanese officials must measure their words carefully here because of the great wariness of the mainland that prevails in Taiwan.

Nevertheless, several Taiwanese officials have said in recent months that Beijing could promote the goal of reunification by endorsing Taiwan's U.N. bid. Given that Taipei has repeatedly made clear that the terms of its participation in the United Nations are negotiable, Beijing should recognize the opening that is being presented.

A SYMBOLIC UNION

The P.R.C. must first come to grips with the reality of a democratic Taiwan. Beijing has long acted as if its goal was to browbeat or inveigle a ruling clique on Taiwan into agreeing to peaceful reunification. That window, if it was ever open, has now closed forever. When Beijing treats the elected government of Taiwan as an illegitimate entity ruling a renegade province, it insults the people of Taiwan, including those who did not vote for the ruling party. Such tactics only promote pro-independence sentiment.

Beijing must also rid itself of the comforting delusion that Taiwan's campaign to participate in the United Nations is a concoction of Taiwan's political elite and unnamed villains in the United States, something the P.R.C. media regularly suggests. Instead, Beijing must see the U.N. campaign as a product of Taiwan's democratic process.

The P.R.C. has only one realistic option if it wants to achieve even a symbolic reunification with Taiwan, and that is to woo the people and leaders of Taiwan. Beijing has never made clear how its formula for reunification—one country, two systems—would work in Taiwan. While Hong Kong will begin operating under that formula in 1997, the transition from British rule so far has not provided a reassuring precedent for Taiwan residents. Even the director of the Institute of Taiwan Studies in Beijing acknowledges pervasive "misgivings" about one country, two systems, and the existence of public opinion polls showing that few Taiwanese support it.

Serious wooing by Beijing would mean making a creative and conciliatory proposal to Taiwan that, without surrendering the principle of one China, would respect and acknowledge Taiwan's legitimacy as a separate political entity. Any realistic arrangement would acknowledge Taiwan's right to play a role in the international community, including the United Nations. In return, Taiwan would have to join with the P.R.C. in reinvigorating the idea of one China, giving it some institutional reality, however symbolic. There are many ideas about how to accomplish that, but they will remain so much smoke until Beijing makes a genuine and generous overture to Taiwan.

Such an overture will have to wait until a younger and more flexible leadership consolidates control in the post-Deng era. A reading of the communist media in Beijing and Hong Kong suggests that Deng's rigid position on Taiwan issues is still the key factor in the P.R.C.'s Taiwan policies. Nevertheless, it is not too early for Beijing's younger leaders to contemplate the political trends in Taiwan that indicate time is not on their side.

ALL FOR ONE

What role should the United States play in all this? The short answer is, a wary but sympathetic one. While the State Department's current position is that it does not support U.N. membership for Taiwan, it should at least declare that it favors any agreement between Taiwan and the P.R.C. that would allow Taiwan to participate in the United Nations. A senior State Department official committed the United States in September to increased efforts to support Taiwan's attempts to gain admission to international organizations like GATT that do not require members to be nation-states. Beyond that, the United

States must exercise caution, because Washington has a strong interest in upholding the principle of one China. The U.S. government has repeatedly acknowledged this principle ever since President Richard Nixon's joint communiqué with Premier Zhou Enlai in 1972. If the United States were to endorse a U.N. role for Taiwan in the face of P.R.C. opposition, Beijing could then attack Washington for violating the one-China principle.

The one-China principle has gained renewed importance in light of the possibility that the DPP could gain power in Taiwan sometime in the future. The DPP's promotion of Taiwan's independence ultimately rests on an irresponsible gamble—that it could get away with provoking Beijing by declaring de facto independence because the United States would come to Taiwan's defense.

It is true that the Taiwan Relations Act declares U.S. opposition to any attempt by the P.R.C. to use force against Taiwan. Although it stops short of an explicit commitment, the act morally obliges the United States to come to Taiwan's aid if the P.R.C. attacks it. But that obligation was made in the context of the U.S. commitment to one China. The U.S. commitment to defend Taiwan would no longer be clear once a pro-independence government took power in Taiwan and repudiated the principle of one China.

Chinese military action against Taiwan would prompt a bitter debate in the United States, with some arguing that America's commitment to a democratic Taiwan was undiluted and others that the United States should not risk all-out war with China because of a rash act by Taiwan. Thus Washington has a strong interest in continuing to support the principle of one China.

The best thing Washington can do is to remind Beijing of the mutual interest of the United States and the P.R.C. in avoiding the crisis that would become inevitable if Taiwan declared independence. But responsibility for avoiding such a development is not mutual. It is up to Beijing to propose a new formula that will preserve the idea of one China while accepting Taiwan's right to a respected place in the world.

Article 26

The Wall Street Journal, October 3, 1994

Asian Games

Taiwan Slowly Creeps Toward Nationhood, To China's Annoyance

Islanders Are Losing Interest In Reunification, Moving Ahead With Democracy

Diplomatic Trouble for U.S.

Marcus W. Brauchli and Jeremy Mark

Staff Reporters of The Wall Street Journal

TAIPEI, Taiwan—A dawn mist cloaked eastern China's scenic Qiandao Lake when the charred pleasure boat was found. In its hold was a gruesome cargo: 32 bodies, including those of 24 Taiwanese tourists, robbed of their valuables.

The March 31 incident stunned Taiwan. The murders were horrible, but more shocking to many here was the aftermath: Chinese authorities tried to cover them up, refusing to return remains for autopsies, harassing Taiwanese relatives and journalists who came to China, and executing three men for the crime after a brief, poorly documented trial.

"It was barbaric," says Tien Hungmao, a University of Wisconsin professor who heads a research institute in Taipei. For the first time since civil war severed this island from the mainland in 1949, many Taiwanese saw China not as their once and future motherland but as a remote and alien culture. Polls since the killings show that the vast majority now oppose reunification with China—and that support for full independence of Taiwan has reached an all-time high of 27%.

Collision Course

Wary of China and emboldened by prosperity, Taiwan is creeping toward nationhood. The shift is still subtle, but the implications are enormous: As prospects for a German-style merger recede, Taipei risks a collision with Beijing and its insistence on reunifying, by force if need be. For other nations, the challenge is to accommodate this Asian dynamo's emerging ambition for an international identity without provoking the giant next door.

That makes for a delicate minuet. Taiwan already has the attributes of a prosperous country: 21 million people, the world's 14th-largest trading economy and $90 billion in foreign-exchange reserves—more cash on hand than any other government except Japan's. Taiwan also is turning into a democracy. By 1996, it will have elections for all public offices, including the presidency.

Yet Taiwan is stuck in geopolitical limbo. Its constitution is that of the "Republic of China," but only 29 aid-hungry countries still forgo relations with the 1.2 billion people of China to maintain ties with Taiwan. Last month, only a handful of governments stood up for Taiwan at the United Nations in its bid to rejoin the organization, which it quit in 1972 when China joined.

A Diplomatic Problem

To other countries, Taiwan remains a diplomatic problem. Washington, its closest friend, has just revamped the awkward rules governing their "unofficial" relationship for the first time since recognizing Beijing in 1979. The Clinton administration will allow Taiwan's representative office in Washington, long called the Coordination Council for North American Affairs, to use the name Taipei—but not Taiwan. US. and Taiwanese officials can meet more freely, though not at the State Department.

The U.S. intends to keep Taiwan at arm's length to avoid harming relations with China, which last month warned of "chaos" if the U.S. lends support to Taiwanese independence. Assistant Secretary of State Winston Lord told a Senate panel Washington would continue to maintain a "balance" in relations with Beijing and Taipei. It is a balance that is sometimes peculiar: Diplomats assigned to Taiwan must officially "resign" when they move to Taipei and "rejoin" the State Department when their tours end.

"The U.S. policy is illogical," says a senior Western observer in Taipei. But because it maintains access to both sides, "It works."

Who's in First?

Perhaps, but will it continue to? The answer will become clearer soon, as Taipei vies with China in the global credibility sweepstakes. Both Taipei and Beijing are racing to become founding members of the World Trade Organization, the successor to the General Agreement on Tariffs and Trade. Trade experts say China is unlikely to qualify for entry by the WTO's launch next year; Taiwan is far closer to meeting the market-opening criteria. GATT members have agreed that China should enter the WTO first, but nothing is certain. "Would other GATT members be willing to block a qualified applicant from joining because of political pressure from Beijing?" a foreign observer in Taiwan asks.

China hopes so. It does what it can to keep Taiwan from gaining global legs. It wants Taiwan's international telephone dialing code change from 886 to 86, the same as China's. When President Clinton hosted the Asia Pacific Economic Cooperation summit in Seattle last year, Chinese President Jiang Zemin agreed to attend only if Taiwan President Lee Teng-hui wasn't invited. Mr. Lee won't be asked to this year's meeting in Indonesia, either.

Although Beijing fears that each Taiwanese bid for diplomatic breathing room leads toward independence, President Lee himself says China is mistaken. "The ultimate goal of the Republic of China is unification," the 71-year-old head of state says in an interview. "But until conditions [in China] become more mature, we won't talk. If the Chinese Communists continue to behave like they do, then the people of Taiwan will be apprehensive." He adds that it isn't likely Taiwan and China can reunify until China is "free and democratic and the people of the mainland enjoy prosperity."

Japan knows how nettlesome an ambitious Taiwan can be. The international organizing committee for this month's Asian Games in Hiroshima startled Tokyo recently by inviting President Lee to attend the opening ceremony. President Lee, Japanese-educated and longing to visit Japan, set off alarms in Beijing when he accepted. It took pressure from both China and Japan to get the organizers to rescind the invitation. But Tokyo, perhaps mindful of the nearly $25 billion a year in Japanese exports to Taiwan, still said Taiwan's vice premier could attend. And China, despite loud rhetoric against Tokyo, said it would participate in the games.

"This is really a very confused era, when a lot of things are in a state of flux," notes Taiwan's Justice Minister, Ma Ying-jeou. "Our relations with the mainland are uncertain and our international relations are uncertain."

Taiwan's economic stature is not. Some of its high-tech companies, such as computer maker Acer Inc. and chip maker United Microelectronics Corp., are world leaders. Many of its officials have studied in the U.S. or Japan, as about 40,000 Taiwanese do yearly. Taipei is a modern, traffic-shackled capital that has more in common with Tokyo than

with developing China, where per capita income is a tenth of Taiwan's $11,000 a year.

Ordinary Taiwanese are increasingly aware of the gap between their cozy, cable-TV-wired island and the vast, nominally Communist realm across the water. Anne Chang, a 38-year-old teacher whose parents were born on the mainland, was stunned by what she saw on a trip to her father's ancestral village in northern China. Her relatives had an eight-month-old baby who had never been bathed.

"Our opportunities have been greater than theirs because we are free," Ms. Chang says. She wants to keep those opportunities, even if doing so requires abandoning reunification. Her parents also have revised their dreams; they now want to be buried in Taiwan, not in the family plot in China.

Slowly Shedding Ties

Taiwanese have been shedding their ties to China for years. Over 90% of them were born here. "I'd always considered myself Chinese because that's what I was taught," says Tsai Fu-hai, a 46-year-old fish farmer. "But I was born in Taiwan, not China. How could I have been so stupid? I'm Taiwanese."

That realization has become a potent political force. Shao Tza-lin, a fiery opposition-party activist, says Taiwan must be prepared for a "bloody revolution" to ensure nationhood. Tsai Shih-yuan, a more cautious opposition leader, says: "If a politician advocates reunification with China, he is doomed. The people want an independent Taiwan."

So, up to a point, do Taiwan's leaders. In July, the government issued a historic white paper aimed at ending two decades of tightening diplomatic isolation and staking out carefully circumscribed independence. Its officials, sensitive to public opinion, say they want Taiwan acknowledged as a "sovereign political entity" that can join international organizations. Some even muse about a formal name change, saying such a move doesn't preclude future unification and might facilitate it, if China achieves the economic and political development that would make unification logical. But, in what once would have been heresy, some officials hint that that day may never come.

"We didn't work 40 years to be a colony," declares Su Chi, 45-year-old vice chairman of the cabinet-level Mainland Affairs Council. He says he considers China's claim to Taiwan "ridiculous."

Political Reforms

Such open talk, especially by senior government officials, reflects a new political reality in this once-authoritarian state. Political reforms were set in motion in the late 1980s by Chiang Ching-kuo, the son of the late dictator Chiang Kai-shek. But the country was under martial law until 1987, and it was President Lee—a Taiwanese native who has never set foot on the mainland—who energized the reforms after the younger Chiang died in 1988.

And only in 1991 did President Lee renounce the claim to sovereignty over China. For decades, Taiwanese had no choice but to accept that they were part of China and deny their own cultural heritage. All opposition to the official dogma was crushed; children were punished just for speaking Taiwanese in school.

The memories of that period, which President Lee has called "the sorrow of the Taiwanese," have been permitted to surface openly only in recent years. Tsai Hsin-yi, a 77-year-old eel farmer in the southern port of Putai, recalls friends disappearing after speaking out for independence early in Chiang Kai-shek's China-obsessed rule.

Today, nonchalance has replaced paranoia. At an army outpost near Putai, where battle-worn soldiers once scanned the sea for Communist Chinese invaders, Taiwanese draftees placidly guard commercial oyster beds and try to stay out of the sun. A pimply 21-year-old serving two years of national service sees no threat from China: "I don't think they'll ever come."

Taiwan now focuses on domestic politics. When Taipei shut unlicensed opposition radio stations in August, hundreds of Taipei taxi rivers and other loyal listeners rioted, throwing bricks and destroying cars before police rushed in with batons. "You see?" yelled Pastor William J. K. Lo, a 53-year-old Presbyterian standing defiantly under a plume of black smoke. "They still oppress us."

But while the mainland is still led by a single party dominated by octogenarians, Taiwan is experimenting with a new and raucous political system. It goes far beyond the film clips, often shown on U.S. TV news, of brawls in the legislature. Most elected politicians are Taiwanese, and office holders who are the children of mainland exiles are learning the local dialect and proclaiming their local roots.

The new pluralism has breathed life into Taiwan's craving for an independent identity just as Taiwan and China have developed a complex web of contacts. While Taiwanese focus on the possibility of a Chinese invasion, the real assault has been in the other direction; Taiwanese companies have invested at least $15 billion in mainland factories, real estate and karaoke bars. Taiwanese tourists have spent billions of dollars in China, and the government warns of the danger of economic dependence on the mainland.

But to many Taiwanese, all this contact makes Taiwan and China seem even farther apart. Talks that began in 1993 over fishing disputes, plane hijackings and other issues—far from being a prologue to unification—underscore differences.

"Maybe we haven't understood until now that our ideology isn't the same, the thinking isn't the same," says David Tzeng, a 43-year-old owner of an acrylic factory in Tainan. He first visited China in 1989, when pro-democracy protesters were gathering in Beijing. "It was incredibly exciting," he recalls. After the crackdown, he slowly grew more disillusioned. In four subsequent visits to the mainland, he invested $180,000 to open a restaurant in the eastern city of Hangzhou, then closed it because of harassment by Chinese officials and local gangsters. "Now I have no feeling for China," he says.

Even some veterans of China's civil war who came over to Taiwan as peasant soldiers half a century ago are losing their emotional links. Many married Taiwanese and watched their children grow up as part of the "Taiwan Miracle." They have visited the impoverished villages they left behind and learned that they are usually valued back home for little more than the money they bring. Some men who long nurtured the hope of returning to China as liberators are rethinking their ideas.

"I've been back to China, and I was saddened by what I saw," says Chen Hsiu-jen, a 66-year-old retiree who was drafted into Chiang Kai-shek's army when just 15. "Now, I think we are already independent. Just maybe we shouldn't say it openly and make Beijing angry."

Article 27   *Free China Review,* March 1994

The Moribund Rejuvenated

It would be wrong to assume that showmanship in the Legislative Yuan will continue to overshadow workmanship.

The Legislative Yuan, the ROC's highest legislative body, has in recent years earned an unenviable reputation at home and abroad because its parliamentary debates have all too frequently deteriorated into histrionics and fisticuffs. But the ripped-out microphones, spray-painted desks, torn clothes, and multiple bruises are just surface manifestations of deeper and more important currents in Taiwan's political development. The past five years have seen the beginnings of a more equitable balance of power between the Executive Yuan and the Legislative Yuan, the rise of a much more competitive multiparty environment, and an expanding media role in politics. These changes are proving to be anything but smooth.

From 1949 to 1991, the powers granted by the ROC Constitution to the Legislative Yuan were circumscribed by special provisions adopted by the National Assembly because of the civil war with the Chinese Communists. These provisions greatly enhanced the power of the president and the Executive Yuan. As a result, the Legislature became a moribund rubber stamp, relegated for the most part to giving its imprimatur to bills submitted by the Executive Yuan for ratification, not deliberation.

But the Legislature has been overhauled. In December 1992, the public elected a whole new Legislature. The voters not only gave new life to the body, they also elected a substantial number of opposition party candidates. Soon, new political battle lines were drawn between the Legislative Yuan and the Executive Yuan, between the political parties in the Legislature, and between legislators in the same party. The result: during its first years of real power, the Legislature has expended a vast amount of energy on acrimony.

One reason for the high level of friction is that the Legislature has had trouble adjusting to its new role of actually deliberating on bills, whether submitted for consideration by the Executive Yuan or by its own members. Genuine analysis of potential legislation requires knowledge, and legislators have found that they lack the institutional back-up available to democratic parliaments elsewhere. Basic sources of information are either missing or wholly inadequate. Although there is a small legislative library and a Legislative Research Service, both have inadequate holdings, facilities, and professionalism.

Moreover, the system of personal and committee staff aides is a new phenomenon. Although several legislators have hired large staffs, most find themselves reinventing the wheel—neither legislators nor their aides can draw on tradition. Everyone is learning that responsiveness to voter demands is a complex task.

The absence of institutional and professional support has put legislators at a disadvantage when trying to assess legislation proposed by the Executive Yuan. The two sides are unequal. Executive Yuan agencies have huge staff support and powerful research arms compared to the Legislative Yuan. So what are legislators to do when confronted with a bill they don't like? The frequently selected tactic has been to yell, scream, and holler at the premier and other government officials appearing in the Legislature.

But it would be wrong to assume that showmanship will continue to overshadow workmanship. Personal legislative aides are already learning the ropes, helping their bosses deal with constituents as well as research bills. And some steps are being taken to build and computerize library holdings and expand research services. Nevertheless, overcoming the Legislature's reputation for slow processing of bills will require more.

Disputes between political parties will have to be raised to a higher plane. Throwing documents and colleagues to the floor are not good methods for reaching the sorts of legislative compromises that make democratic governments work. The Kuomintang (KMT), for four decades the ruling party, is still learning how to be a majority party that must deal with a vocal and popular opposition. At the same time, the Democratic Progressive Party (DPP) and the Chinese New Party (CNP), which recently broke away from the KMT, are both still trying to pull together a sensible approach to opposition politics. And while all parties call for laying down

clearer rules of the game governing their interactions, many legislators seem to forget there are any rules at all when they appear in committees and on the floor.

One reason for this is a lack of political party cohesion. Ideally, party members work together, hammer out differences, and unite to support legislation that is in line with their party platform. But this is difficult, especially because so many legislators are not beholden to their party leadership. When they ran for office, they raised their own campaign money (much of it personal or family funds), hired their own media people, and planned their own campaigns. They may have received party endorsement, and a few party leaders may have made campaign appearances now and then, but most candidates ran their own show, and their obligations are often greater to

special interest groups than to their party.

This explains another reason for the scenes of legislative mayhem on the evening news. Legislators have to show the voters they are active—and what better way than to be on television? The problem with TV reporting is that sound bites are also thought bites. There is tinsel, but little substance. Positions are truncated and ideas are trivialized. But since putting on a good show scores points with the voters, the pressure is on legislators to attract cameras, not minds.

The rejuvenation of the Legislative Yuan has obviously raised a host of problems, many of them not much different from those found in other democratic societies. But if the ROC's highest legislative body is to gain greater power and respectability, its members will have to craft their own solutions.

Article 28　　　　　　　　　　　　　*Far Eastern Economic Review*, December 15, 1994

The First Modern Nation

Taiwan's voters pick trade over politics

Sometimes how you do something is more important than what you do. Take Taiwan. In the wake of its just-ended elections, the pundits have hailed the island as a triumph of democracy, not least democracy in Asia. We wouldn't argue with that. But Taiwan's significance lies much deeper than the way it chooses its leaders: For all the electioneering and politicking that attended these elections, diplomatically isolated Taiwan has created a society where politics takes a back seat to economics. And in this, Taiwan may be the world's first thoroughly modern nation.

This is not to say that politics has no role in Taiwan. To the contrary, with each election the Kuomintang faces a fresh referendum on its 45-year-long rule. President Lee Teng-hui—himself a native Taiwanese—can take some satisfaction that Taiwanese have apparently endorsed his ruling party once again, electing its incumbent as provincial governor and leaving it with majorities in the provincial assembly and the city council of Kaohsiung. But Taiwanese also proved they want no monopolies by electing the Democratic Progressive Party's charismatic

Chen Shui-bian as mayor of Taipei and denying the KMT a majority in the Taipei city council.

Although Mayor-elect Chen is well-known for his pro-independence views, he campaigned chiefly as an honest man of the people who would put an end to the cosy relationship between the KMT and city contractors. This willingness to put bread-and-butter issues ahead of political ones represents great progress. What it suggests is that Taiwanese are having more and more control of their day-to-day lives; nobody talked about sewerage systems and mass-transit systems in Chiang Kai-shek's day. The point is that today politicians can no longer win by resorting to easy slogans and scare tactics. Were Mr. Chen and his DPP colleagues to drop independence altogether, the party would probably win many more elections.

The wild card here, of course, remains China. Although Beijing and KMT officials are both committed to unification, China's belligerence makes this less likely with every passing day. To the contrary, what pro-independence feelings there are in Taiwan are only encouraged by China's bullying. One post-election poll showed

and legitimacy

that 70% of Taiwan's population believes China might invade, which helps explain why even the ruling party feels under pressure to gain greater recognition of its de facto independence. Indeed, were China to offer the olive branch rather than the fist, these same Taiwanese leaders would probably find themselves under public pressure to show a little accommodation themselves.

Yet whatever the question mark over Taiwan's political future, it has already given us the answers to some very modern dilemmas. Above all it has shown that diplomatic pariah status is no obstacle to development—and that people can live without immediate answers to intractable problems. Our guess is that in a post-Gatt world where politics involves more of the nitty gritty and less of the absolute, more countries, at least the more successful ones, will look like Taiwan. It will be worth remembering who got there first.

Article 29

Free China Review, January 1988

CONFUCIAN RITUAL IN MODERN FORM

Pei-Jung Fu

Dr. Pei-jung Fu is an associate professor in the Department of Philosophy, National Taiwan University.

Confucianism is a philosophy with a religious function. As a system of philosophy, its earliest principles were initiated by Confucius (551–479 B.C.) and further developed by Mencius (371–289 B.C.). It focuses on the correct way of human existence, which presupposes an understanding of human nature, and seeks the blissful state of human perfection, that is, the union of Heaven and man. Confucianism thus emphasizes both moral cultivation and ultimate concerns.

The religious function of Confucianism comes from its inheritance of the ancient Chinese religion which centers on worship, sacrifice, and ritual. In fact, Confucianism is still regarded by the Chinese of today as one of the three religions of China (the *san jiao*), the other two being Taoism and Buddhism. Confucianism is very often described as a ritual religion, a characterization that can be clarified by examining in turn the ritual aspect of Confucianism, the three kinds of worship maintained by the Confucian tradition, the Confucian concept of man, and the place of Confucianism in the modern world.

Ritual

Etymologically, the ideograph for ritual (*li*) is composed of two parts: the right half of the character signifies anything related to spiritual beings, while the left symbolizes a vessel with two pieces of jade used in sacrificial services. Hsu Shen of the Eastern Han Dynasty (25–220 A.D.) defined ritual as "following" or "treading," i.e., the step or act whereby spiritual beings are properly served and human happiness obtained. In other words, ritual originally meant "a religious sacrifice," and such sacrifice can be traced back to the earliest times of man.

Thus, in ancient China man can be defined as a "ritual being." For example, the ancient classical text of history and philosophy called the *Tso Chuan* says: "Ritual determines the relations of high and low; it is the warp and woof of Heaven and Earth; it is the life of people." Elsewhere it adds, "Ritual (is found in) the regular procedure of Heaven, the right phenomena of Earth, and the actions of men."

Defined as sacrificial rites, ritual is primarily religious although its connotation goes beyond the reach of purely religious matters. The Duke of Chou (ca. 1180–1082 B.C.) first made explicit the political and ethical implications contained in ritual. For example, concerning politics he is credited with saying, "It is ritual which governs State and clans, gives settlement to the tutelary altars, secures the order of the people, and provides for the good of one's future heirs." And furthermore: "Ritual is that by which a ruler maintains his State, carries out his governmental orders, and does not lose his people."

In ethics, it is necessary "that the ruler order and the subject obey, the father be kind and the son dutiful, the elder brother loving and the younger respectful, the husband be harmonious and the wife gentle, the mother-in-law obedient—these are things in ritual." In sum, "Ritual is that through which we can see loyalty, faithfulness, benevolence, and righteousness."

By the time of Confucius, however, the ritual tradition so richly described by the *Tso Chuan* was in a state of collapse, primarily because of the religious import of ritual was being neglected. With the loss of their religious dimension, the ceremonies came to be used by the ruler as a means "to awe his officials so that they will not transgress the laws," and to ensure that through their use "the unity of the people is strengthened."

These crass interpretations deprived ritual of its original significance, its role as an instrument of moral perfection; instead the performance of ritual turned out to be not much more than a formalistic activity. This was the real breakdown of meaning and function that worried Confucius so much.

In the field of politics, Confucius emphasizes that ritual is the best way of governing a state. He says, "It is by ritual (or the rites) that a state is administered" (This and all subsequent quotes come from the Analects unless otherwise indicated). "When those above love ritual, none of the common people will dare be irreverent;" "Guide them by virtue, keep them in line with ritual, and they will, besides having a sense of shame, reform themselves."

In the domain of ethics, Confucius construes ritual as the criterion of such virtues as "respectfulness, carefulness, courage, and forthrightness." When asked what constitutes a complete man, he answers that in addition to virtues like knowledge, courage, and freedom from covetousness, ritual and music are still required to realize the complete man. Ritual is the designated ground on which a man can stand firm. Confucius teaches his own son, "Unless you study ritual, you will be ill-equipped to take your stand."

This idea is expressed in other cases with the same reference to the "establishment" of a man. Confucius says of himself: "At 30, I took my stand." Here, "taking a stand" implies that his character is already established in the ritual that he has diligently studied and learned.

To Confucius, it seems that the religious essence of ritual has died out. People perform sacrifices only as a routine, without believing in the presence of spirits. A statement in the *Analects* reading, "Sacrifice as if present" is taken to mean "sacrifice to the gods as if the gods were present." Scholars usually take this sentence as evidence to argue that Confucius is an agnostic with regard to knowledge of spirits, or that he claims an "as if" philosophy in this respect.

This is not necessarily the case, because it is still uncertain who actually said the above statement. What Confucius really said is the subsequent sentence, "I do not agree with those who sacrifice as if not doing sacrifice." Other relevant sayings in the *Analects* never tell if Confucius denied the existence of spiritual beings or not.

Whatever the case, it is clear that Confucius never forsook the ritual tradition; rather, he tried to revive this tradition by emphasizing that proper dispositions should accompany all ritual performances. He says, "What can a man do with ritual who is not benevolent? What can a man do with music who is not be-

nevolent?" Ritual is therefore rooted in the nature of man and plays an important role in bringing man to perfection.

Before examining the Confucian concept of man, it will be helpful first to review the three kinds of worship or sacrifice maintained by Confucianism, for these best express the essence of the so-called ritual religion.

Worship

The religious dimension of Confucianism can be easily perceived by its emphasis on sacrifice and worship. Three kinds of sacrifice have been observed by the Confucian tradition: sacrifices to Heaven, to ancestors, and to the sages. Heaven is worshipped because it is believed to be the source of all things; ancestors are worshipped because they are the fountain-head of the present human being; and the sages are worshipped because they exemplify the perfect personality and are models of the best rulers and teachers of proper behavior.

The worship of Heaven is sometimes understood as worshipping all of nature. However, Heaven never signifies mere nature in Confucianism. Heaven for Confucius not only makes "the four seasons go around and the hundred things come into being," but is also concerned with the transmission of culture. It thus confers a unique mission on Confucius, making him "the wooden tongue for a bell," which means to teach people on behalf of Heaven.

According to Mencius (as recorded in the classic book *Mencius*), Heaven does not speak, "but reveals itself through its acts and deeds." Moreover, its revelation is universalized in the reflection of man's heart. Every man has the presence of Heaven in his heart which always reveals correct guidance for action. Therefore, if a man fully searches his heart, he will understand his nature; and if he knows his own nature, he will know Heaven.

Meanwhile, Mencius claims that the proper way to serve Heaven is for man to retain his heart and nurture his nature. Far from being mere hypothesis, Heaven manifests itself in the functioning of the heart. The heart, being the microcosm of Heaven, is the representative of transcendence in the realm of immanence. The opening statement of *The Golden Mean*—one of the four basic classics of Confucianism along with the *Analects*, the *Mencius*, and *The Great Learning*—reads, "What Heaven has conferred is called the (human) nature." Human nature is ordained by Heaven.

Thus, the text continues, the perfection of man cannot depart from the revelation of Heaven: "Being sincere is the way of Heaven; becoming sincere is the way of man."

Obviously, the close relation between Heaven and man would be incomprehensible without an understanding of how Confucians view the nature of man.

Nature of Man

Early Confucians view human nature as tending toward goodness. This is not a proper place to present all the necessary arguments, but the consequences of this theory which are accepted by all Confucians can be stated as follows:

First, no one is incapable of becoming a gentleman. Confucius said that he never met anyone whose strength was insufficient for practising benevolence. Mencius expressly insisted that all men can become a sage like Yao or Shun.

Second, all men are obliged to become gentlemen. To be genuinely human is to become virtuous; and to be virtuous is simply to fulfill completely the nature of man which tends toward goodness. Man's natural life is for the purpose of realizing his moral potency. The obligation here is a categorical one. Confucius held that man should sacrifice his life for the sake of benevolence, and Mencius claimed that he would rather have righteousness than life. Hsun Tzu, a later Confucianist (ca. 310–230 B.C.), also declared, "A gentleman, though worrying about danger and misery, does not avoid to die for the sake of righteousness."

Third, all men, while becoming gentlemen, are responsible for bringing others to attain their perfect state. A famous saying of Confucius reads, "A benevolent man helps others to take their stand in so far as he himself wishes to take his stand, and gets others there in so far as he himself wishes to get there."

This passage discloses the essence of Confucian humanism which lays stress of human potentiality, moral education, and mutual responsibility. More significantly, this humanism is open ended, that is, open to Heaven, which is the source of all that exists. This open humanism leads Confucians to take the "union of Heaven and man," which is equivalent to the state of sagehood, as their highest possible goal in this life.

Confucianism Today

Confucianism has attracted increasing numbers of contemporary scholars to search for the reason why it is regarded as the main ethical factor in the success of East Asian modernization. Max Weber (1864–1920), the great theorist of modernization, argued that Confucianism was a "this-worldly religion, but not one which embodies ascetic values." He concluded that it was unable to bring forth modern capitalism, and consequently, would fail to produce modernization. The facts of today now speak for themselves, and they give a much different answer.

It is useful to investigate the way Confucians apply their theory of man to actual situations. To begin with, to affirm human nature as tending toward goodness is to maintain that man is born with moral potentiality which is to be actualized in the whole process of his life. That is to say, man's obligation to renew his virtue or to perfect himself is present as long as he lives. Thus, the path for a man to follow in his life—the way of man—becomes obvious: "to choose what is good and firmly hold it fast," as *The Golden Mean* states.

A key question arises: What is good according to Confucianism? The answer to this provides a clue to understanding the Confucian influence on Chinese society.

For Confucians, goodness is not an objective entity, nor is it a purely subjective attribute. Rather, goodness is the natural and spontaneous tendency of man properly embodied in human relationships. Goodness in isolation is incomprehensible or even meaning-

less. Thus, the close and hence inevitable relations between men become a necessary condition for a man to be good or to fulfill his nature.

The so-called "five relationships" that form the main structure of traditional ethics are those between sovereign and minister, father and son, husband and wife, elder brother and younger, and between friends. They are regarded in *The Golden Mean* as "five ways of bringing man to goodness." Influenced by this ethical doctrine, Chinese people are inclined to obey the properly exercised authority, to regard family as the birthplace of crucial virtues, and to emphasize the mutual benefit of friendship in terms of moral cultivation. Without these relationships, "the way of man" is merely an empty phrase. It is in this context that Confucian humanism shows its compatibility with the spirit of asceticism.

Confucians are supposed to be very considerate of other people. The golden rule of Confucianism found in the *Analects* reads, "Do not impose on others what you yourself do not desire." Confucius advises further, "To set strict standards for oneself and make allowances for others when making demands on them." Self-restraint is also strongly emphasized. One passage occurs several times in the *Analects:* "A gentleman does not forget what is right at the sight of gain."

This attitude toward self and others can be understood as a moderate asceticism. That is to say, it demands a strict

self-discipline but with no feeling of bitterness, because it also anticipates the fulfillment of human nature. Confucian asceticism is therefore accompanied with a sense of joy.

Following this line of thought, Mencius proclaims that "all the ten thousand things are there in me. There is no greater joy for me than to find, on self-examination, that I am true to myself. Try your best to treat others as you would wish to be treated yourself, and you will find that this is the shortest way to benevolence."

Thus, an understanding of the Confucian theory of man demonstrates that the previously alleged incompatibility between this-worldliness and asceticism proves to be a false conception. Besides, in the place of the concept of "calling" which motivates and impels Protestantism in the direction of modernization, Confucianism believes that man is born with a judge in his heart which reveals the will of Heaven, the ultimate source of all that exists.

The heart as judge is to be understood as a mission conferred on every man by Heaven, one that manifests a spirit of man which makes him in but not of this world. Following this line of thought, it can be argued that Weber's interpretation of Confucianism can be safely abandoned while accepting his insights regarding the emergence of modernization. Furthermore, it can be affirmed that Confucianism has indeed provided a working ethic for modernization.

Article 30   *Free China Review,* January 1988

Vibrant, Popular Pantheon

Tong Fung-wan

Dr. Tong Fung-wan is academic dean and an associate professor in the history of religion at Taiwan Theological Seminary.

Traditionally every agricultural society has a polytheistic view of God, and this is seen as well in the Taiwanese religious experience. The Taiwanese pantheon originated in Southern China, especially the provinces of Fukien and Kwangtung, and came to the island with Chinese immigrant believers over a 300 year period. Today, it is clear that different members of the pantheon have taken root in different localities throughout Taiwan.

Nowadays, the Taiwanese, 85 percent of whom are descendants of those original immigrants from Fukien and Kwangtung, rely on this pantheon as they seek secular security, set their ideals, and earn their living. Such religious phenomena are an integral part of Chinese tradition and culture. As such, the pantheon offers an insight into the thought and activity of contemporary Chinese on Taiwan.

The Taiwanese pantheon exhibits the characteristics of anthropomorphism, geographical relatedness, efficacy, and laissez-faire.

Anthropomorphism

All kinds of objects can be anthropomorphized as personal gods or goddesses. For instance, there are the gods or goddesses of *heaven,* such as the heavens themselves, the five directions of the firmament, and those of the sun, moon, and stars, and of lightning, thunder, rain, and wind; of *earth,* including the earth itself, the five directions of the earth's foundation, the seas, waters (rivers, lakes), mountains, stones, and plants; of *animals,* especially the dragon, phoenix, turtle, snake, tiger, lion, pig, dog, and cat; plus *fetishes,* such as bones of the dead, packages of incense, idols, icons, written spells, and magic tools; and *spirits of the dead,* including those of ancestors, sages and heroes, wandering spirits, and fierce ghosts.

Moreover, there are social levels in the kingdom of the pantheon, just as there

Ching Shui Tsu Shih—Protective God of Anshi people from Fukien Province.

are in human society, and the members must have their needs provided for; this is made easier by assigning them titles like those in the mundane world.

Titles fall into two general categories, official and familial. The former include the following: Emperor (or more specifically, the Jade Emperor); King (King Hsieh); General (General Fan); and Commander-in-Chief (Commander-in-Chief Kang). These are all gods.

There are also high-ranking goddesses: Queen (Queen Tien); Princess (The Princess of the Jade Emperor); and Madam (Madam Cheng Huang).

The latter category of family includes the male god, Grandfather (Grandfather Earth), and Grandmother (Grandmother Wenchou, who is a local Matsu); and Maiden (Maiden Seven Stars).

Gods, like humans, require a home. Thus, geographical positioning and maintenance of temples is a key part of Taiwanese folk religion.

Temples are the houses of gods and goddesses. More correctly stated, they are actually their palaces or courts.

Birthdays for the gods or goddesses are an explicit result of anthropomorphism. Examples are the 9th day of the 1st month for Grandfather Tien, the 23rd day of the 3rd month for Matsu, the double 7th for Maiden Seven Stars, and the double 9th for King Chung Yang. Almost every day of the year as reckoned by the lunar calendar is the birthday of some member of the Taiwanese pantheon.

Offerings are important to the pantheonic society. Like humans, the gods and goddesses need food, clothing, and money for their daily existence. Generally people offer pigs and goats to the pantheon when the most important festivals are underway. Considerable quantities of delicious Chinese food are first offered to the pantheon, then the worshippers eat what remains. Moreover, large amounts of paper money are burned for their use; sometimes there are even offerings of new clothes decorated with old-fashioned gold medals for the gods.

Family, according to tradition, is also a key heavenly institution. The gods may have their wives and children living together in a joyful family atmosphere. People give their children the titles of princes or princesses, and call their wives "madam." Unfortunately a god always has many wives, such as Madam Cheng Huang No. 1 and No. 4. It is unclear whether or not family quarrels and divorce often occur in the polygamous society of the gods.

Clearly, pantheonic society is a copy of human society. People follow their own ideals when constructing their pan-

theonic kingdom. And people's needs and customs are reflected in the pantheon as well. Nevertheless, the traditional ideology still remains in place. So far the gods of the pantheon have not become Westernized to the extent of wearing Western jackets and neckties; they continue wearing the old-fashioned robes of officials. In addition, worshippers do not offer Western food or U.S. dollars to the Taiwanese pantheon—they are as much strangers to the intricacies of knives and forks as they are to the customs of George Washington and Abraham Lincoln.

Geographical Relatedness

Taiwanese people have a strong sense of being related to their own locality. Such a tendency also expresses itself in worship objects, especially the so-called local protective pantheon. Generally the local protective gods are connected with the immigrants' homelands in Fukien and Kwangtung. People worship them as an expression of community identity as

they seek to earn their living. Some especially popular local protective gods are as follows:

People and their locality
Chuanchou people, Fukien
Changchou people, Fukien
Anshi people, Fukien
Hakka people, Kwangtung

Protective gods
Kuang Tse Tsun Wang
Kai Chang Sheng Wang
Ching Shui Tsu Shih
San Shan Kuo Wang

Efficacy

Taiwanese go to temples looking for security. They explicitly require efficacy from their gods. Any god that gives people the blessings they want earns great quantities of "burning incense." On the other hand, if the god they approach cannot help them (or so the worshippers feel), he is left alone so that only a spider's web keeps him company in his temple.

To such a tendency as this, Max Mueller gave the term "kathenotheism," for people choose their worship objects according to their own likes and dislikes. "Matsu could not help me, so I went to ask Grandfather Earth, but when I doubted his efficacy I prayed to the Tiger God." Everyone seeks his gods or goddesses according to how he feels at the time. So this kind of kathenotheistic current causes people to fall into superstition—the members of the pantheon are their servants, seemingly like the genie in the Arabian Nights whom people urge to do what they want. Obviously, the relationship between gods and men is upside down: the gods are the servants and men are the lords of the pantheon.

Laissez-Faire or "Doing Your Own Thing"

There is a Taiwanese saying: "It is better to believe in something than not to believe in anything." This attitude makes Taiwanese believe in all kinds of gods. For instance: Buddhas, bodhisattvas, and arhats in Buddhism; Confucius in Confucianism; Lao Tzu and the pantheon in Taoism; even Jesus and Mohammed have been accepted as their protective gods.

In olden times, people talked about three religions (Confucianism, Taoism and Buddhism) in one, but today it is five or six (the previous three, plus Christianity, Islam, and Shintoism) in

Lin Bor-liang
Kuanyin, Goddess of Mercy, is immensely popular in Taiwan, with over 450 temples in her honor.

one. Even now, new gods or goddesses are freely coming into being all the time. All divine beings, even dead spirits or demons, may be worshipped if they can help people live in peace.

About 15 years ago a serious flood occurred in the central part of Taiwan, causing many deaths. Among the dead was a young girl, whose body was washed down Chuohsui River and found by villagers. They were afraid that her spirit would harm them, because according to traditional beliefs, it was thought that due to her unnatural death her spirit would be exceptionally malevolent. So they began worshipping her as a goddess called Chang Yu Koo. Through the propaganda of shamans and sorcerers, the place suddenly became a sacred spot and attracted many pilgrims from all over the island. This extraordinary religious phenomenon lasted for several years until it finally ended in police intervention.

Furthermore, people in Taiwan also believe in the pantheon that comes from Chinese classical histories and fiction. This includes figures from *The Legend of Deification*, *Pilgrims to the West* also known as *The Adventures of Monkey*, and *The Romance of the Three Kingdoms*.

So far, for example, the Prince of No Cha in *The Legend of Deification*, Sun Wu Kung or the Great Monkey in *Pilgrims to the West*, and Kuan Kung in *The Romance of the Three Kingdoms* are among the most important gods in Taiwan. No Cha and Sun Wu Kung are both fictional characters, only Kuan Kung is an historical figure from the Three Kingdoms era (220–265 A.D.).

From these examples we can clearly see how Taiwanese do as they please in religious beliefs.

Social Structures in the Taiwanese Pantheon

Before considering the social structures in the Taiwanese pantheon, it would be useful to examine two diagrams that illustrate the external expression of Taiwanese folk beliefs. These will help put the following analysis into more understandable form:

Diagram One

Diagram One. The inner circle represents the three major religions found in Taiwan: Taoism, Confucianism, and Buddhism. these make up the core of folk belief, but Taoism occupies half of the circle to demonstrate its stronger influence on folk religion generally speaking.

The outer circle in the first diagram is labeled "animism." This represents an operational hypothesis to describe folk beliefs, including all the elements of primitive religious phenomena. These include, for example, nature worship, ancestor worship, fetishism, and magic.

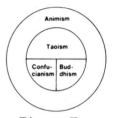

Diagram Two

Diagram Two. The innermost circle has five key objects of worship:

A. Grandfather Heaven
B. Grandfather Earth
C. The Sea Goddess, Matsu
D. The Healing God, Ta Tao Kung
E. The Pestilence God, Wang Yeh

The second circle from the center in Diagram Two represents the next echelon of 12 important gods and goddesses in Taiwan:

The Gods of Confucianism: (1) Confucius, (2) Kuan Kung, and (3) Koxinga;

The Gods of Buddhism: (4) Buddhas (Trinity Buddhas), (5) Bodhisattvas (Kuanyin and Ti Tsang), (6) Ching Shui Tsu Shih (who is the protective god of Anshi people in Fukien Province) and 18 Arhats;

The Gods of Taoism: (7) Lu Tung Pin, (8) San Chieh Kung, (9) Hsuan Tien Shang Ti, (10) Shen Nung Ta Ti, (11) Prince No Cha, and (12) Wang Mu Niang Niang.

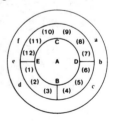

Tong Fung-wan

The Ti Tsang Bodhisattva is a civil administrator commanding 10 courts in hell.

Tong Fung-wan
Tai Tzu Yeh belongs to the third level of military command in the pantheon.

The third, outer circle of the second diagram represents various categories of popular worship in Taiwan;

(a) Ancestor worship or filial piety;

(b) Animism, which includes the four major sub-categories of: Nature worship (sun, moon, stars; the five directions of both heaven and earth; thunder, lightning, storm, and wind; mountains and the waters of the four seas; and animals, vegetables, stones, and the earth); Worship of the Dead (demons, unnatural dead, hungry ghosts, malevolent spirits, dead relatives, historical heroes, and sages); Fetishism (natural fetishes such as dead bones and turtle shells, and artificial fetishes such as idols and magic tools); and Magic (shamans, exorcists, spells, and charms);

(c) Local protecting gods and goddesses;

(d) Gods and goddesses protecting various occupations;

(e) Gods and goddesses from myths and legends; and

(f) Foreign gods and goddesses.

Both diagrams present a summary of Taiwanese folk beliefs. The first indicates their syncretic religious content; the second expresses the totality of worshipped objects.

The latter diagram has especially deep implications for Taiwanese religious life. The innermost circle represents the core of folk beliefs. Grandfather Heaven is the highest god, expressing Taiwanese dependence upon Heaven for earning a living. Grandfather Earth is a production god, for Taiwanese work very hard and have an intimate relationship with the soil. The Sea Goddess, Matsu, is a sacred Mother of the Taiwanese people, reflecting the adventurous spirit of their ancestors who crossed the terrible Taiwan Straits. The Healing God, Ta Tao Kung, is a Preserver of the Taiwanese, reflecting the need of the people for security. The Pestilence God, Wang Yeh, is a Destroyer—so people hold a great festival every three years to humor him and prevent pestilence.

The second circle contains 12 gods and goddesses in three groups belonging to Confucianism, Buddhism and Taoism. Among them, the members of the Taoist pantheon are greater in number than those of the other two. It is easy to find very strong sectarian Taoist influence in Taiwanese folk religion.

The outer circle shows the popular pantheon in Taiwan. Clearly the pantheon in this circle has religious phenomena which are psychologically primitive, traditional, and syncretic. It may even be called a new pantheon in the making, for today Jesus, Mohammed, Sun Yat-sen, and Chiang Kai-shek are all accepted as new gods in Taiwanese folk beliefs. This shows the unrestricted laissez-faire nature of local religious attitudes.

The Hierarchy of the Taiwanese Pantheon

At the apex of the Taiwanese pantheon is Grandfather Heaven, also known as the Jade Emperor. Next in power and importance are two gods who sit at either hand, the God of Life (The Southern Star God) who is Left Prime Minister of Heaven, and the God of Death (The Northern Star God) who is Right Prime Minister of Heaven.

Next there is a trinity of officials (San Chieh Kung): the God of Blessing (Shang Yuan or Heaven Official), the God of Forgiving (Chung Yuan or Earth Official, and the God of Saving (Hsia Yuan or Water Official).

On a lower level of power and importance come the *Gods judging certain localities*. These include Cheng Huang, who is the city god; the Lord of Area, Grandfather Earth, and Wang Yeh.

Next come *Gods protecting various occupations and special groups*, who are so important to the daily life of Taiwanese:

Gods protecting people from certain localities

Kai Tai Sheng Wang	Taiwan
Kai Chang Sheng Wang	Changchou, Fukien
Kuang Tse Tsun Wang	Chuanchou, Fukien
Ching Shui Tsu Shih	Anshi, Fukien
San Shan Kuo Wang	Hakka people, Kwangtung

Other categories of gods are listed below to give a sense of the diversity of the Taiwanese pantheon. These are still but a portion of the virtually uncounted total:

God	Occupation
Shen Nung	Agriculture, Medicine
Kuan Ti	Commerce
Lu Tung Pin	Barbers
Ching Shui Tsu Shih	Butchers
Hsi Chin Wang Yeh	Musicians
Tien Tu Yuan Shuai	Actors
Husan Tien Shang Ti	Exorcists
Shui Hsien Tsun Wang	Seamen
Matsu	Voyagers
Tai Tzu Yeh	Shamans
San Nai Fu Jen	Mediums
Special Groups	
Chi Hsing Niang Niang	Children
Chu Sheng Niang Niang	Women
Kuanyin	Children, mothers
Tu Ti Kung	Fertility

The gods judging in hell are the Ti Tsang Bodhisattva, Tung Yueh Ta Ti, and an additional Ten Gods of the Courts in Hell. These are served by various other gods, such as the Assistant gods (one who holds the seal on the left side, and another who holds the sword on the right side); Assistants to the judge gods (the secretary god who sits on the left side, and the god of punishment on the right side; and Matsu's assistant gods (the god with thousand mile eyes, and the god with radio-like ears).

The civil organization of the gods is matched with a military one that is once again a copy of the organization found in the mundane world:

These social and military structures in the Taiwanese pantheon are copied from ancient Chinese society, and therefore their organized systems can never be changed. Today Taiwanese still keep this traditional ideology as part of their beliefs, for they satisfy such areas as mysticism.

In spite of scientific developments, Taiwanese steadfastly believe in a trichotomous view of the cosmos: the Heavenly World, the Earthly World, and the World of Dead Spirits. Each world has its ruler and officers, and its organization and specific activities, but the whole cosmos is controlled by the highest God, the Heavenly Grandfather. The kingdom of the pantheon always faces its rivals—demons, evil spirits, malevolent ghosts, and wandering devils, for example, so it needs military forces to exorcize them and keep the people at peace.

Conclusion

It may be wondered why Taiwanese people still worship such a pantheon in

The Military Organization of the Taiwanese Pantheon

	5 Heavenly Gods		Blue Emperor (E. Heaven) Red Emperor (S. Heaven) White Emperor (W. Heaven) Black Emperor (N. Heaven) Yellow Emperor (Middle Heaven)
Jade Emperor (Commander- in-Chief)	Wang Yeh (Com- mander)	26 Heavenly Hosts	
		72 Earthly armies	
		5 generals	Eastern legion Southern legion Western legion Northern legion Center legion (No Cha)
		8 officers	Wen and Wu judges Ox and Horse police Chia Yeh and Suo Yeh Day & Night watchers (7th Yeh and 8th Yeh)
	4 Great Ching Kang		1. Feng (風) 2. Tiao (調) 3. Yu (雨) 4. Shun (順)

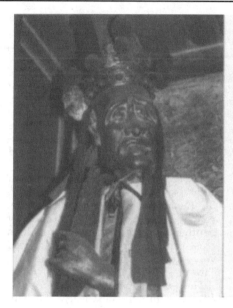

Tong Fung-wan

King Hsieh (left) and General Fan (right) serve as adjuncts to Commander Cheng Huang.

this civilized era. The answers lie in the realization that folk beliefs have their cultural essence and also their historical background. It is unjust to call this religious phenomenon superstition, for it is a true religious experience among Taiwanese people. For example, though many people are converted in their hearts to more institutionalized religions such as Christianity, and appear to have forsaken traditional worship, they still cannot forsake the old ideology. As a result, some Taiwanese Christians may be described as "folk religion Christians" because they seek security in Jesus Christ and the Holy Spirit and look to God the Creator as a benevolent old man—an Earthly Grandpa—while praying to Jesus as a healing god.

This can be illustrated by the Christian church elder who asked his dying father to protect his family during the funeral. How natural Christian ancestor worship is! If every kind of religious experience is true, it is very difficult to say these kinds of religious expression are superstitious.

Polytheistic beliefs are a necessary tendency of an agricultural society because the cultural situation supports people in this way of thinking. Obviously it cannot be denied that folk beliefs include superstitions, especially laissez-faire religious attitudes such as living in fear of demons, believing in shamanic therapy, and control by unknown divine beings. But these beliefs are the contemporary manifestations of a lengthy, and continuing, tradition.

Article 31

Sinorama, November 1992

Every Number an Omen—Chinese Lucky Numbers

Congratulations! Mr. Chang, today is your 80th birthday, and is also a good day to bring a daughter-in-law into the house. Let me calculate for a minute here and get you a good expression. To celebrate: Living in harmony as one group, The coming of two happinesses to your door, The Mutual support among three generations, All as you wish for the four seasons, The approach of the five fortunes, Six-six everything goes smoothly, Seven sons and eight sons-in-law,

Many things through the nine wishes, and Perfection ten times over.

There is a set of famous streets in Kaohsiung City in Taiwan, which all begin with numbers. They are Yihsin (One Heart), Ersheng (Two Sacreds), Santo (Three Mores), Ssuwei (Four Upholds), Wufu (Five Fortunes), Liuho (Six Realms), Chihsien (Seven Virtues), Pateh (Eight Moral Precepts), Chiuju (Nine

Wishes), and Shihchuan (Perfect Ten) Streets. This sequence of auspicious street names gives people a warm feeling when they hear it, and brings more than a little luck to the residents.

Many foreign visitors can't help but exclaim that the Chinese are really creative, and can line numbers up so "auspiciously."

Chinese not only use numbers to appeal for good fortune, they also bring them out to chew people out: "You 250 [fool], you do things neither three nor four [without any order or out of touch], and still you dare to say that I'm 13 points [stupid] and 3–8 [scatterbrained]."

Although it isn't really possible to know where these came from, one thing is for sure: numbers are intimately related to the daily life of Chinese!

Origins in the *Book of Changes:* In antiquity, people kept tallies by tying knots in ropes, and only employed numbers and words later on.

From natural phenomena and life experience, people gradually came to recognize the signs of change in a particular matter. For example, there was the ancients' saying that "If the moon has a halo it will be windy, and a damp plinth foretells rain." It is inevitable that there will be misfortune in life, so people began to adopt ways to attract the auspicious and expel the malicious. Add to this that people have psychological activity and the ability to link things together in their minds, and a whole set of auspiciousness-attracting and evil-expelling habits took shape.

The *I Ching* or *Book of Changes* is a compilation which records the experience of people in ancient times with luck and divination. In the *Book of Changes,* each number has some significance: one is the *tai-chi* or "great supreme," two is the "two rituals," three is for the "three powers," four for the "four directions," five is for the "five pathways," six stands for the "six realms," seven for the "seven rules of government," eight means the "eight trigrams," nine is for the "nine chains," and ten is the "ten depictions."

We often say "three *yang* make good fortune" to describe the hope that misfortune will be held at bay and good luck will follow. It is a saying often used at the New Year and symbolizes a new beginning and finds its origins in the *Book of Changes.* *Yang* is the positive force in the universe, and there is enormous *yang* and very weak *yin* (negative force) in the first, second, and third of the ninth trigrams. So the three *yang* are very positive.

Li Heng-lih, chairman of the International Taoism Scholarly Foundation, who feels that numbers have no connection with fortune good or ill, says that the only significance numbers have is what people ascribe to them. Trying to say that a given number is either auspicious or ominous is mere superstition.

Still, unlike the western sensitivity to the number 13, Chinese have a whole philosophy built up around numbers, which is spread or experienced in real life.

年畫「三陽開泰」
New Year's painting: "Three yang bring good fortune."

年畫「一團和氣」
New Year's painting: "Harmonious as one unit."

年畫「五福迎春」
New Year's painting: "Five fortunes welcome the coming of spring."

年畫「百子千孫」
New Year's painting: "One hundred sons and one thousand grandsons."

Courtesy of the Council for Cultural Planning and Development

Yuan Chang-rue, head of the Anthropology Section at the Taiwan Provincial Museum, raises the theory of "identity supernaturalism." He states that Chinese people believe that similar sounds can produce similar outcomes, so that "identity of pronunciation" has become the foundation of many allegedly beneficent numbers.

The vast influence of identical pronunciation: For example, in Cantonese the pronunciations of "eight" and "success" are very close, which makes the number significant for Cantonese. But for Fukienese it has no function.

Taiwanese have many taboos around the similarity of the sounds for "four" and "death," but Hakkanese couldn't seem to care less.

The study of names and the nine-boxed-paper, a very widespread belief among ordinary people, involves surmising a person's personality and fate according to the number of strokes of the pen in the three characters of the name. In the West and Japan, a type of fortune-telling has been developed based on adding together the numbers of the year, month, and day of one's birth, and using it to assess the person's fate. Others are able to roughly guess a person's personality from their favorite numbers.

The popularity of auspicious or lucky numbers is related to the idea of the pursuit of harmony in names by, for instance, using the radical or character for "metal" to compensate for apparent lack of "metal" in the person, or using the "water" radical to make up for a deficiency of same. Li Heng-lih points out that numbers can be divided into *sheng* and *cheng* types, the former being one through five and the latter being six through ten. In this scheme, one and six are for water; two and seven are for fire; three and eight belong to wood; four and nine signify metal; and five and ten are for earth. If you divide them up by *yin* and *yang*, the negative and positive forces, one, three, five, seven, and nine are all *yang*, and two, four, six, eight, and ten are *yin*.

If a person's celestial branch or stem as determined by their date and time of birth (the *pa-tzu* or "eight character horoscope") come under "wood," then it is necessary to add "water" to feed the wood. So one could choose one or six as lucky numbers. Which one would be better? If the person comes under *yin* wood, then it would be better to choose the number one, which symbolizes both *yang* and water.

Gods can be alone, but people cannot: One is the number marking the beginning, and also has the meaning of "independent" or "alone."

Tong Fung-wan, a professor of theology at Taiwan Theological Seminary, points out that in Taiwan people prefer even numbers which symbolize "fortune comes in pairs." They are more wary of one, three, five, seven, and nine. Because the character for "odd" in Chinese (*tan*) also means "alone," people are not very fond of it. But although people like even numbers, the gods can be alone. Thus in odd-numbered months holidays have been stipulated to help people get by, from New Years (first day of the first month on the lunar calendar) and Tomb Sweeping Day (third day of the third month) to Dragon Boat Festival (fifth of the fifth), Chinese Valentine's Day (seventh of the seventh), and Old People's Day (ninth day of the ninth month in the lunar calendar).

At weddings, when Chinese people give "red envelopes" with gifts of cash, they only send even amounts, like 1,200 or 3,600. Because the pronunciation of "four" is close to that of "death" in Taiwanese, if you send 4,400 to the bride and groom, people won't be grateful and might even criticize you behind your back for failing to understand basic manners. At funerals, on the other hand, people usually give offerings with the last digit being odd, so as to avoid ill fortune not coming "alone."

Happiness comes in pairs: In the book *Popular Chinese Customs* Professor Lou Tzu-kuang notes that when people got married in ancient times, betrothal gifts would include a document recording all the details of the accompanying gifts. The writing style was rather meticulous. Thus, for example, chickens or ducks would be written as "Four wings of poultry." Gold bracelets would be written "Gold bracelets becoming a pair." Candles would be written as "Festive candles with double glow." No place would odd numbers be allowed.

When inquiring into the other's name and the "eight character horoscope" of the other party, it would be written for instance: "The groom [or bride] is in the beginning of the sixth month of his [her] twentieth year, having been born at such-and-such an hour. . . ." The number of characters in the Chinese text would always have to add up to an even number; if they were short one then an "auspicious" character would be added.

The writer Hsiao Min adds that because the character for "odd" also means "incomplete," when she was in her old home in Peking, they would always

make sure that the number of steamed rolls made for New Year's was even in order to make a good beginning.

Chuang Po-ho, a scholar of folk traditions, argues that Chinese have always been rather inclined to the number three. Just open up a Chinese dictionary and there are sayings using three or multiples thereof sprinkled everywhere. They are even more numerous in local sayings and slang.

He points out that one reason Chinese like three is that it stands for "many." In *Lao Tzu* it is said that "Tao gave birth to the one, the one gave birth to the two, two gave birth to three, and three gave birth to the ten thousand things." From nothing to something, or something to infinity, "three" plays a critical role.

Huai Nan Tzu points out that in making offerings to the dead, three bowls of rice was considered in accordance with ritual; and in expressing an offering three gestures were appropriate.

"In the hopes of Chinese people in their lives, 'more' is considered to have an auspicious meaning, so the term 'three mores' naturally arose," says Chuang Po-ho. In widespread folk depictions, the "three mores" are the three fruits including the bergamot orange, the peach, and the pomegranate, signifying "more fortune, more years of life, and more sons." Buddhists, on the other hand, describe the three mores as "more closely associating with friends who will be good for you," "more inhaling of mild fragrance from prayer incense," and "more self-cultivation to correct bad habits."

Elevators without fourth floors: The scholar Su Hsueh-lin has written that in ancient China the numbers four and 72 were perhaps both mysterious numbers, and moreover that "four" was a symbol for the great earth.

But in Taiwan four is not especially well looked-upon. Hospitals and hotels normally have no fourth floor, and the numbers in the elevator just skip right from three to five. It's probably only in places where Chinese people live that this type of facility is necessary. Also, the price of an apartment on the fourth floor is usually cheaper.

In general, Chinese assign little good or bad significance to "five."

"May the five fortunes approach your door" is a saying often seen at festive occasions. The five fortunes are long life, wealth, health, an ethical life, and a peaceful death.

Besides this, the five elements (metal, wood, water, fire, earth) provided a framework for people at former times to classify natural phenomena. Confucianism also says that five implies the concept of "the mean."

The writer on geomancy Li Jen-kuei points out that Confucians believe that five is very close to the path of the golden mean of "adopting the middle between two extremes," and also promotes the thought of the "five pathways." As a number, five has two at the front and two behind, with one in the middle. "This middle figure has two assistants on each side, and is unbiased in the middle. Thus five fits in well with the idea of the 'mean' always promoted by Confucian scholars," he has written.

Leaving aside for the moment the question of how accurate this is, few people ever suspect anything bad about the number five. The only exception is that in playing the Taiwan drinking game of guess-fingers, the probability of five coming up is higher than for any other number, so there is a slight "taboo" that rules that one cannot call out this number.

One six eight, on the way to success: Where did "66 everything goes smoothly" come from? Lin Mao-hsien, executive secretary of the Chinese Customs and Handicrafts Foundation, contends that it might have something to do with playing dice. Six is the largest number on a die, so wouldn't one win by coming up with two sixes?

According to informal statistics, not many people take seven to be a lucky number. According to the old text *Yu Hsiao Ling Yin*, when someone first dies the mourning period should be seven days. "Doing the sevens" is the custom at funerals in Fukienese areas. For the first seven days after someone passes away, to the seventh seven days, there are appropriate rituals for each. Some people, because the number seven can easily bring to mind "doing the sevens," plus the fact that the seventh month of the lunar year is "ghost month," don't like it. In Taiwanese "3–7" refers to the 30–70 division of money between a prostitute and her pimp, so it cannot be lightly employed.

The fondness for "eight" comes, most people would say, from the Cantonese. In Cantonese, eight and "success" are similar in sound. And in North China, there is the saying that "if you want to succeed, don't stray from eight."

Hongkong, where most of the population is Cantonese, is perhaps the place where faith in numbers is strongest. Li Heng-lih analyzes that it is a very crowded, very competitive industrial metropolis. Businessmen are especially obsessed with success or failure, so they have to include auspiciousness in consideration of any affair like opening a factory or signing a contract. If they can choose a day with eight in it, then they have a "successful" beginning. Nine symbolizes smoothness and endurance, while six, as noted, is for "66 everything goes smoothly."

In the 1980's, lucky numbers went from Hongkong into Kwangtung Province in mainland China, as this trend began to spread from south to north.

Liu Cheng-feng, columnist for the *China Times*, noted in one report that the last four digits of the phone number of the Canton Hotel are 8168, a homophone for "success and yet more success." Most of the shoe stores in the Lungfu Building in Peking use "auspicious" prices on their tags. One of the fastest movers is one whose tag is 168, which symbolizes "the road to success." And when businessmen stay in hotels, they like to stay in rooms 518, 688, or 816. One hotel in Canton even has a higher price on rooms with lucky numbers.

Mainland numbers fever in Taiwan: When the stock market was all the rage, the Jihsheng Securities Company spent NT$600,000 (over US$23,000) to buy the license plate ending in "8888." Now that the stock market is bullish no longer, during bidding for license plates for personal cars this fall, the highest price fetched by "8888" and "6666" was only NT$55,000.

In mainland China, the first time the city of Chungking auctioned off telephone numbers, a mobile phone number of 900-8888 drew a bid of RMB50,000. In the auction held in Shanghai in March of this year, the starting price of numbers ending in 8888 was RMB30,000, and one sold for RMB46,000. A number ending in 2222 was bought for RMB37,000, because in Shanghai dialect it sounds like "come, come, come, come." The record was set on May 18 (the numerical date of which, 5-18, is a homophone for "I will succeed"), when a Hangchow mobile phone number 901-688 was sold for RMB129,000 (over US$25,000).

At the auction of telephone numbers in Peking in August of this year, in just one morning 48 numbers were auctioned off for a total amount of RMB1.04 million. That's about 400 years' salary for the average worker earning about RMB200 a month.

Believe it or not, its up to you: Nine generally refers to a great majority or large number. In former times people often used nine to say "a great many."

Because nine is an extreme number, Chinese have the saying that it is inauspicious to run across nine. Especially for older men, the 69th and 79th birthdays are celebrated as the 70th and 80th instead. Many people also believe that a young man of 29 is at the decisive point in life.

When people use lucky numbers to symbolize wealth and fortune, or peace and benevolence, any number can be explained in such a way as to make it fit. Aren't "everything starts with one and comes around again," "seven generations living together," and "wealth flowing across the four seas" all pleasing to the ears?

Although that's easy enough for us to say, there are still plenty of people who play the lotteries or play the ponies, running near and far, burning incense to the gods, looking for a lucky number that belongs only to them!

Sunny Hsiao/photos courtesy of the Council for Cultural Planning and Development/tr. by Phil Newell)

HONG KONG ARTICLES

Article 32   *Harvard International Review,* Summer 1994

One Servant, Two Masters

The Economics of Hong Kong's Transition

Hugh Eakin

Hugh Eakin is a Staff Writer for the Harvard International Review.

Cosmopolites eager for a piece of history have begun making hotel reservations in Hong Kong for June 30, 1997. The British colony, which has become the most popular destination in Asia in recent years, has attracted the attention of the international community on the eve of its 1997 transition to Chinese rule. While other Pacific Rim countries and the West have found new reason to pay attention to Hong Kong, much more is at stake than just Hong Kong's flourishing tourism industry, especially for the People's Republic of China (PRC) and Great Britain.

Hong Kong has achieved the distinction of serving concomitantly as the PRC's "catalyst" for economic transformation and as the West's principal access to the PRC's expanding market. Western interest in China has exploded in the past two years; foreign investors contracted to spend US$83 billion in the PRC in the first nine months of 1993 alone. Accounting for an estimated 55 percent of China's foreign investment, Hong Kong plays a pivotal role in channeling this capital from the West into the mainland.

The colony's economic ties to both the PRC and the West and its political status as a soon-to-be-relinquished Crown possession have made Hong Kong the trump card in Sino-British relations. Diplomacy between the two countries has remained off-balance since the British colony gave mass support to the student protesters in the 1989 Tiananmen Square massacre. More recently, Beijing has caustically denounced Hong Kong Governor Christopher Patten's electoral reform proposals, announced in October 1992.

The political rift threatens to create serious turbulence in the upcoming transition to Chinese rule. Even as Britain hopes to protect Hong Kong's free trade status, it may jeopardize its economic relations with the PRC by endorsing the Patten legislation. China is now the world's third largest and fastest-growing market, and while Western powerhouses such as Germany, which landed US$2.8 billion worth of contracts after Chancellor Helmut Kohl's recent visit to Beijing, have begun large-scale ventures on the mainland, Hong Kong's legislative proposals have locked Great Britain into a stalemate with China. The precarious political situation will not only color future Sino-British economic relations, but also may decide Hong Kong's role in the global economic community after 1997.

Hong Kong's New Prosperity

The influx of Western capital that has fueled China's high-octane economy has been intricately linked with Hong Kong. As Hong Kong's nearest mainland neighbor, the Chinese province of Guangdong has led the way in drawing foreign investment to China. While the PRC's annual real Gross National Product (GNP) growth averaged 13 percent in 1992 and 1993, nearly four percentage points ahead of its nearest Asian competitor, Guangdong province alone has maintained a comparable level of growth every year since 1979, not including its 19.5 percent growth in 1992. Capital and technological investment from Hong Kong have played an enormous role in this growth; as the political scientist William H. Overholt argues in his recent book *The Rise of China,* "[Guangdong's] spectacular growth is not the fruit of Guangdong's effort alone, but rather the result of a gigantic

joint venture between Hong Kong and Guangdong."

While China has served as an almost unlimited source of inexpensive labor for Hong Kong, the colony has provided China with the industrial technology, global market knowledge and leadership in capitalist management necessary for economic transformation. More than 80 percent of Hong Kong's manufacturers currently have mainland branches employing an estimated 3 million PRC Chinese, and over 50,000 Hong Kong professionals commute to and from Guangdong daily. Beijing, in turn, has taken a variety of measures to facilitate this "joint venture"; the PRC-designed Shenzen (an urban-industrial complex in a designated "special economic zone" on the Guangdong-Hong Kong border), for instance, will serve as an intermediary between the province, still relatively backward, and the hyper-developed international trading port.

Hong Kong's international commerce has profited enormously from the colony's relationship with Guangdong. Since Hong Kong first entered the mainland market after China opened up in 1979, its World Trade Rank has risen from 20th to 10th globally, while its GDP has nearly quadrupled from US$21.6 billion to US$81.6 billion; nearly 35 percent of China's international trade currently passes through the colony.

While the colony has flourished for over a decade from its relationship with Guangdong, Western corporations, including many British firms in Hong Kong, have only recently discovered the positive economic value of development and investment in China. While British officials continue to dominate the *political* scene today, British control over the colony's *economic* sector has steadily declined since the early 1970s, when entrepreneurial Hong Kong natives began to replace the British capitalist tycoons in the leadership of many of the powerful "hongs" or trading companies. In the early and mid-1980s, these entrepreneurs began to establish ties in China, aided by personal connections, or *guanxi*, and their method of working around the system from the local level. In contrast, Western venture capitalists, including the British, achieved little success in their attempts to initiate Western-style "official" business relations in China. At that time, foreign investors in the colony's market regarded the nearby presence of the expansive, underdeveloped mainland as a hindrance to the port city's economic growth.

Amidst this growth of native Hong Kong firms, the interests of many of the remaining British-run hongs have been marginalized. The Hong Kong firms have recently been joined by German, American and Japanese investors in the profitable Chinese market. Great Britain, however, which has just begun to emerge from its recent recession (output growth rebounded to 2.1 percent in 1993), has lacked the financial resources to back the expansion of its colonial firms on the mainland. Some of the old-guard hongs continue to struggle on the mainland today in the wake of their better-connected and more firmly established competitors. Jardine Matheson, the oldest of the extant British hongs, has upset China by supporting Patten's proposed reforms, perhaps at the expense of the firm's further expansion in China.

With the PRC's rapid economic expansion driving the Hong Kong economy, why are so many investors continuing to channel funds through Hong Kong rather than directly into China? While the experimental mainland stock exchanges in Shanghai and Shenzen have experienced considerable success, neither one currently has a securities law, a securities trading law or a national company law. Many of the oversized and decaying regional administrations have attempted to soak up some of the new profit by unraveling a huge amount of bureaucratic red tape, rather than instituting a coherent legal framework; as Overholt states, "Americans could not imagine how many laws, regulations and licenses can be created by a bureaucracy thirsty for a stream of capitalist income." Beijing itself recognizes that by relaxing central control in the interest of rapid capitalization, it has encouraged the proliferation of white-collar crime and corrupt legal practices at the regional and local levels.

In contrast, Hong Kong offers access to the Chinese market without the risk inherent in a direct mainland venture. Of the 14 million PRC private enterprises that have sprung up since 1979, many have invested heavily in Hong Kong; there, they can establish "off-shore" operations under Hong Kong laws. The colony's standardized exchange and monetary stability have set an example that the PRC will need to follow if it is to improve its reputation in the international market. Indeed, China has already attempted to address this problem in a sweeping tax and banking reform plan introduced in January 1994. China's ability to regulate its economy by Western standards will be fundamental to gaining admission to the General Agreement on Tariffs and Trade (GATT) talks.

The Patten Factor

In the context of Hong Kong's increasingly important economic relationship with China, Governor Christopher Patten's proposed electoral reform has had quite an impact. Hong Kong's traditionally small and non-interventionist political structure, headed by an elite circle of native Hong Kong business leaders and British officials, has for years served the interests of a handful of well-connected corporations. Patten's planned legislation aims at reforming this corporate-biased system.

At present, even after the considerable reforms of the last decade, only 10 of the 21 "functional constituencies," or electoral districts, vote by an electoral college. The others vote by groups of corporations (three are a mixture of both corporate and electoral constituencies). Under this system, representatives of the business community have direct influence over the political decision-making process. The governor has proposed to eliminate the exclusively corporate voting constituencies, expand the size of the constituencies to extend the vote to all Hong Kong civil servants and ensure the separation of the legislative and executive branches.

Taken at face value, the governor's changes in the direction of democracy for the 1994–95 elections are relatively slight. As Harvard scholar William Kirby has noted, the new reform would only bring Hong Kong to a level of democracy comparable to that of Great Britain after the passage of the 1832 Reform Act, which extended suffrage to small property owners while continuing to exclude the working classes from the vote. Thus, even after the Patten reforms, Hong

Kong would remain far removed from the contemporary Western standard of full-suffrage democracy.

The Sino-British controversy about Patten's proposed reforms has centered not on the issue of democracy itself, but on two important precedents: the 1984 Joint Declaration, and the change in Sino-Hong Kong relations that took place after the 1989 Tiananmen Square uprising. According to the Declaration's "one country/two systems" concept, Hong Kong is to retain its self-governed free-market capitalism for 50 years following the 1997 transition. The accord states that after 1997, "the current social and economic systems in Hong Kong will remain unchanged and so will the lifestyle. Private property, ownership of enterprises, legitimate right of inheritance and foreign investment will be protected by law." Hong Kong's large-scale reaction to the Tiananmen Square crackdown, however, has cast the implementation of "one country/two systems" into doubt.

Patten contests that Beijing's "fundamental review of [its] attitude toward Hong Kong" since the colony's reaction to the 1989 Tiananmen Square crackdown threatens to undermine the Declaration. As he stresses, "one can't underestimate the impact of Tiananmen and the reaction in Hong Kong to the Chinese government." In the politicized atmosphere that has pervaded Hong Kong since the 1989 protests, the PRC may fear that Hong Kong self-rule as mandated in the "one country/ two systems" clause could pose a threat to Beijing's authority which Patten's "eleventh hour" liberalization would exacerbate. The governor, concerned with this possible PRC sentiment, emphasizes the need to safeguard the spirit of the Joint Declaration and Britain's interpretation of self-rule.

The PRC, however, has accused Patten of violating the Joint Declaration. The accord stipulates that any British changes which would affect Hong Kong after 1997 would first require "consultation" with China; the PRC has interpreted consultation to mean *formal authorization*. Furthermore, the 1990 Basic Law, Beijing's official constitution for Hong Kong after 1997 included a "non-subversion clause" designed to prevent the reinterpretation by either of the parties of the 1984 agreement. While Patten claims that several weeks before he officially proposed the legislation on October 7, 1992, he submitted the plans to an upper-level Chinese official who acknowledged them, the PRC counters that the governor never received *authorization* from Beijing to announce the reform. According to China, the governor has not only bypassed the requisite consultation with the PRC, but has unilaterally reinterpreted the Joint Declaration, in breach of the Basic Law.

According to the PRC, Patten's reform not only politicizes the Hong Kong community, but attempts to ensure the success of pro-British politicians in the final colonial elections in 1994 and 1995. Legal issues aside, China has perceived the Hong Kong governor's proposed changes not as the low-key internal political statement the British would have them see, but as a pitched battle between Great Britain's declining commercial interests in the colony and the mainland's budding entrepreneurialism. After many prosperous years of conservative business-oriented rule, Beijing argues, the Hong Kong government's proposed reform would destabilize the colony's economy and remove executive control from the hands of the corporate technocrats-the Hong Kong natives who dominate the colony's business sector.

Hong Kong's low-profile corporate leadership has provided a seemingly ideal model for the PRC's developing one-party capitalism; as Overholt points out, Hong Kong's "consultative colonialism"—the system whereby an appointed head of state is consulted by a range of formal and informal advisors—is structurally similar to China's "democratic centralism." In the economic sector, this parallel has particular relevance; just as Hong Kong's leadership has operated largely in the interest of a big-business economy, China's policy of "corporatizing" larger state enterprises and privatizing smaller ones while keeping power in the hands of the Central Committee will require the state to address the needs of the expanding business community. From China's standpoint, Patten's attempt to reform Hong Kong's corporate oligarchy directly opposes Beijing's interests in Hong Kong.

Who Profits?

After 17 fruitless rounds of Sino-British negotiations, China's portrayal of the governor's reform as a sly attempt to protect British economic interests in the colony and disrupt the Hong Kong business community may prove increasingly effective. A case in point has been the planned US$22 billion airport and container terminal. Of the project's 48 consulting contracts, 35 went to British companies, while joint American and native Hong Kong firms were awarded the remaining 13. While Beijing was infuriated by the apparently biased system used by the Hong Kong government to award contracts, the US Chamber of Commerce accused the Patten government of favoring British companies over superior American engineering firms.

The short-term profits for British companies in the colony derived from government favoritism may be offset by China's political and economic leverage with Britain in the reform negotiations. Indeed, by the end of 1993, China had already begun what some reporters have called "economic punishment" of Britain in financial negotiations on the planned airport, whose development lies in the hands of the near-bankrupt Provisional Airport Authority. While the airport project is unrelated to the Patten legislation, Beijing has effectively conflated the two. As Chinese Prime Minister Li Peng stated last March, "If the current relationship [with Great Britain] should deteriorate . . . it cannot be said that the economic relations will not be affected."

Even after the Patten reforms, Hong Kong would remain far removed from the contemporary Western standard of full-suffrage democracy.

According to a 1991 "memorandum of understanding" between China and Britain, the PRC must approve any Hong Kong project that would reach completion after the transition to Chinese rule in 1997. The new airport, whose original completion date of early 1997 has now been pushed back to spring 1998, conveniently falls under the agreement. China has stalled its approval of the project, forcing the Hong Kong government to seek funds from its own Legislative Council. Not only is the expedient completion of the airport vital to Hong Kong's commercial interests, but the government estimates that every six months of delays in construction will increase costs for the British by US$500 million. Arguing that the ambitious project will leave the PRC mired in debt when Britain bows out in 1997, officials in Beijing are asking Patten's government to post more equity in the project, and delaying approval has proven effective in opening British coffers.

The PRC's recently created 57-member Preliminary Working Committee (PWC) has presented another obstacle to the airport project. The PWC, composed of Beijing officials and Hong Kong businessmen, serves in theory as an instructive body to prepare Beijing for the 1997 transition. The organization's behavior, however, has resonated startlingly with Li Peng's threatened "second stove," or shadow government. According to Li, the second stove will promote China's interests in Hong Kong and begin to make the transition to mainland rule even before the official 1997 deadline, if Patten attempts to go through with his legislation unilaterally.

While China has demonstrated more bark than bite in implementing the second stove, the PWC has become an effective leveraging device: China insists that a senior Hong Kong official must train the PWC in management issues in the colony before it grants approval for the near-bankrupt airport project. For the British, this sort of political blackmail, and any other influence the PWC can garner in the coming months, may become the most damaging part of Li's strategy. If Beijing were to successfully implement the shadow administration, the colonial government's authority on economic issues might diminish *before* the 1997 transition.

Drawing on Li's threats, Great Britain claims that it is China's corrupt management, not Patten's, that may ultimately inflict long-standing damage on the Hong Kong investment community. The Patten reforms arguably have been intended to curb corruption. As the governor emphasizes, even if Beijing does not clamp down on Hong Kong with a "second stove," a laissez-faire system, whether along the lines of Hong Kong's existing system or closer to the PRC's policy of relaxed central economic control, would provide a breeding ground for the corruption that plagues mainland enterprise. As Patten remarks, "Hong Kong is unique because it lives by the rule of law. If Hong Kong rapidly got the reputation that the rule of law was under threat, the international community would move its cash elsewhere, and they would not take very long to do it."

Winning the support of the Hong Kong economic sector against Patten may ultimately prove as difficult for China now as in 1997. Whether or not Patten's warning to the Hong Kong business community holds true, the colony has been reluctant to support any move from either side that could compromise its current prosperity in the international community. In 1993, despite the colony's political rift with the PRC, the Hang Seng stock index climbed nearly 78 percent. Despite the protracted Sino-British discord and Li's bitter denunciations of Patten, a number of prominent Hong Kong businessmen have simply ignored the dispute. Patten has given them little cause to believe that their concerns will be disturbed in the immediate future, and they have weathered China's threats before.

China, indeed, has proven unwilling to mar the Hong Kong economy in its harangue of the colonial government. While the Chinese prime minister's increasingly overt threats may give firms like Jardine Matheson cause for concern, Beijing's real interest seems to be in strengthening Hong Kong's economic sector before the 1997 transition, as it has shown in its under-the-table financial backing for the Western Harbor Tunnel Project.

The tunnel, which will add a third underwater crossing to the mainland, has been financed by a consortium of 22 banks. The Bank of China, by accepting or declining to participate financially in a Hong Kong project, has traditionally served as an indicator of Beijing's attitude toward any proposed development in the colony; its absence from the consortium represents the PRC's official withholding of approval of the project until Britain concedes on the airport negotiations. The combined 35 percent stake of both the Pacific and Hong Kong branches of the influential China International Trade and Investment Corporation, however, proves that in real terms the PRC will fund the tunnel project regardless of the airport situation. More significantly, the PRC has clearly prioritized its policy to its own economic advantage: while the tunnel project directly affects China in that it will greatly facilitate commuter traffic to and from the mainland, the airport will primarily cater to Hong Kong's burgeoning international business traffic.

Perhaps the greatest menace to Hong Kong's economic growth lies neither in the Patten plan nor in any retaliatory PRC measures, but in the source of its prosperity: China's own economic growth. The possibility of the mainland's growth overheating by rampant inflation has begun to raise moderate concern among Western analysts, who envision a possible Hong Kong market crash if inflation becomes explosive; by Western standards, Hong Kong's current inflation rate of eight to nine percent is already steep. China's 1993 inflation rate of 15.9 percent does not reflect the inflationary pressures present in the large commercial cities of southern China, where consumer prices continue to rise more than 20 percent annually.

A New Economic Landscape

While inflation poses an economic threat to the PRC, Beijing has shown little desire to curb the pace of economic change. Behind the dynamic leadership of Vice Premier Zhu Rongji, China has boldly forged ahead with a plan (scheduled to be endorsed in the spring of 1994) for economic reform that will overhaul the cumbersome and loss-incurring state enterprises; dramatically redesign and centralize the banking system according to Western models; and revise the revenue system by implementing such devices as a value-added tax. As a prominent Chinese economist has noted, by forwarding Zhu's plan, the Chinese leadership is acknowledging that "there is no way for it to go back . . . if it does, it collapses."

The same can be said for Hong Kong. China recognizes that the colony has prospered under free-market capitalism too long to be brought under stricter state control. Given its recent economic savvy, China is unlikely to adopt a policy line with Hong Kong that would significantly hurt the port's economic growth. The PRC has become the leading foreign investor in Hong Kong, and the destruction of Hong Kong's self-government and rule of law would be equivalent to economic suicide for the colony.

Even so, Li's threats against the Patten government may carry just enough weight to keep Hong Kong slightly off-balance until the 1997 transition; it will be very much in China's interest in the next three years to learn to manage the port city, whose powerful economy threatens to polarize China's economic transformation on the southern coast. Already, for instance, Beijing has responded coolly to the Hong Kong–Mass Transit Rail Corporation's proposal for a second subway line in the next decade; the PRC has clearly prioritized spending on the mainland, as most Chinese cities do not yet have a subway at all. By keeping Hong Kong economically healthy while restraining the colony's infrastructural spending, China may seek to tailor the port's economy to the interests of the mainland, whose rapidly modernizing economy still remains decades behind that of Hong Kong.

The PRC, in fact, has already begun to imitate Hong Kong's brand of capitalism. In addition to the rise of such economic centers as Shenzen, which has earned the nickname "little Hong Kong," in 1993 Beijing approved a US$1.3 billion port and manufacturing center to be built in Yangpu, on the Chinese island of Hainan, southwest of Hong Kong. A consortium of foreign interests will develop the planned commercial center, which the PRC has designated an unrestricted economic zone modeled after Hong Kong. The Yangpu project not only represents China's willingness to experiment with Western capitalism from the foundations up, but also may demonstrate a Chinese interest in taking some of the economic heat off of Hong Kong.

As China's interest in Hong Kong is primarily economic, the status of the colony vis-à-vis the mainland's economy will likely determine its political future. In a transformation that would parallel that of Imperial China in the 1840s, after the Opium War ended the Canton single-trading-port system and opened China's coastal cities to Western trade, the successful proliferation of economic centers such as Yangpu could gradually end the PRC's "Hong Kong system" of Western investment. If China's economy achieves a measure of stability the availability of other free ports on the mainland may render Hong Kong less important to the West and less crucial to the PRC's economic transformation.

Whether or not Hong Kong remains China's primary international trading port, the fate of the colony's economy will hold little sway over Great Britain's support of the Patten legislation. Britain's economic interests in Hong Kong have already waned, and American and German claims already far outstrip the British stake in the region. Far from protecting British interests, the governor's legislation strives to ensure that "Hong Kong people rule Hong Kong" under the rule of law. The governor recognizes that Hong Kong's economy is more than predominantly controlled by Hong Kong natives; unlike the British and other foreign expatriates who are free to leave in 1997, the local population will suffer the consequences of any changes under the PRC. As Patten said, "if we have put some panes of glass in the window and China decides that she wants to smash them after 1997 . . . I think that will need some explaining both in the community in Hong Kong and more generally internationally."

> *The colony's continued resilience in the face of an unsure political future could prove the decisive separation between politics and economics in international relations.*

The danger of Patten's philosophy lies in its fundamental assumption that the "window" needs a "pane" from a British colonial government in its final years of rule; from the earliest confrontations of Western colonialism with China, the mainland has abhorred taking orders from an outsider. Patten's, and hence Britain's, suggestion that China may not follow through on the Basic Law and Joint Declaration comes as a direct insult to the Chinese.

Given China's interests in preserving Hong Kong's international reputation as well as its own, a subtle PRC policy of economic retaliation against Britain itself may prove the most effective and safe response to any unilateral measures taken by Patten. What will Britain lose? As one senior British official said, given successful relations, "[Britain could have] five percent of an import market worth [US$225 billion], worth to us [US$11.25 billion]." In this respect, the argument of former British Ambassador to China, Sir Percy Craddock, that Britain should "cooperate with China on the best terms [it] can get" has a powerful logic.

For Great Britain, the question remains whether or not an "outsider" like Patten can make a lasting stand on an issue China regards as internal. Without the PRC's authorization, the reform package, which would have to be in place by July 1994, may have little impact on Hong Kong's political system after 1997. However, if Patten has only succeeded in further politicizing Hong Kong the point will have been well made.

For China, the debate is economic, not political. At a time when the PRC hopes to preserve its Most Favored Nation status and gain market credibility in hopes of joining GATT, it must support the continued growth of Hong Kong. China's argument for the separation of politics and trade at the November 1993 economic summit in Seattle will only work to the extent that Beijing's politics do not interfere with Hong Kong's economy. As Patten stated recently, "what's true in Seattle is just as true in [Beijing]"; certainly he hopes that what is true for Hong Kong's economy today remains true after 1997.

The colony's continued resilience in the face of an unsure political future could prove the decisive separation between politics and economics in international relations. Ironically, it is Britain, by pursuing a political agenda in the international economic port of Hong Kong, that may ultimately capitulate this turning point in international diplomacy.

Article 33

The World Today, May 1994

China, Britain and Hong Kong: Policy in a cul-de-sac

Sir Percy Cradock

One of the great practitioners of traditional foreign policy, Sir Eyre Crowe, Permanent Under-Secretary at the Foreign Office until 1925, used to say that he deplored all public speeches on foreign affairs. It is a point of view with which I have some sympathy. But I have a feeling that in our time things have gone well beyond that ideal condition. Foreign policy, which in the public estimation is not a particularly demanding discipline, has become a sort of public park, where anyone is free to kick a ball about. The professionals have to put up with that. All they can ask is that discussion is reasonably informed and reasonably balanced and that the various points of view are fairly represented. The reason why I propose to discuss China and Hong Kong here is the sense that we are not having this balanced public discussion on the subject today; that we in Britain have been hearing only one half of the story; and that as a result we find ourselves now in a serious crisis with China without really knowing how we got there and how we might begin to extricate ourselves.

In what follows I shall try to remedy that defect. I shall try to explain how the current troubles arose, what the consequences are likely to be, what the prospects are for Hong Kong and British relations with China, and what the alternative policy might have been. I do not pretend that it will be a very cheery story. But it may be instructive, and even elevating, in the way that the best tragedies are supposed to be.

To set the scene, I have to go back a little way. The need for cooperation between Britain and China over Hong Kong has been imposed by a number of facts, geographical, historical, and politico-military. First, the fact of Hong Kong as a tiny island on the southern rim of the Chinese landmass. Then the existence of a lease, with only three years to run now, covering 92 per cent of the territory, the remaining 8 per cent being unviable on its own. Hong Kong has to revert to China; the only question concerns the terms of that reversion. Next, the fact that, on this issue at least, there is overwhelming superiority of power in Chinese hands: the lease, military preponderance, the dependence of Hong Kong on the mainland for food and water, and so on. Finally, British responsibility to do everything possible to protect Hong Kong and its people in the unenviable circumstances in which they find themselves.

Cooperation does not mean automatic acquiescence in China's views. Tough negotiation has always been necessary and has always been practised. But it does mean recognising that unilateral action and confrontation with China are more damaging to Hong Kong in its special circumstances than a negotiated settlement and are therefore inconsistent with our responsibility to do our best for the territory. The long-term welfare of Hong Kong must be the sole criterion.

It was in this spirit that we negotiated with the Chinese over Hong Kong from 1979 onwards; and this approach produced a series of important and beneficial agreements, which could not have been secured in any other way. Foremost among them, of course, was the Joint Declaration of 1984, which provided the most complete protection possible for the territory for at least 50 years from 1997. Another very important agreement in the same spirit was that on directly elected seats of February 1990, which greatly increased the number of directly elected seats in the Legislative Council (Legco) and ensured a steadily rising curve of such seats in the future: 18 in 1991; 20 in 1997; 24 in 1999; and 30—that is half the legislature—in 2003. This meant that, though Hong Kong was far from full Westminster democracy, there was an assurance of steady progress, with Chinese agreement, as expressed in the Basic Law, so that the arrangements would stick. This last aspect was crucial: there was little point, and considerable danger, in measures that would only last until 1997 and then be torn down in acrimony, with damage to the whole structure.

These two main agreements, in 1984 and 1990, established a political and constitutional settlement for Hong Kong which should have assured stability and continuity, plus a fair level of democracy, over the watershed of 1997 and into the next century. The arrangements were not all-inclusive: there were some loose ends relating to the 1995 elections and Britain reserved the right to try again for more directly elected seats in 1995. But the Chinese made it very clear that they would make no further concessions on numbers. They also warned that British attempts to go further, without Chinese agreement,

would provoke serious consequences. I was told myself in December 1989 that if we tried unilateral action, they would impose their own conflicting arrangements in 1997, the so-called 'through train' would break down, and there would be, as they put it, 'big trouble'.

That, in summary outline, was the situation between governments in the summer of 1992. But the outline neglects certain more elusive but influential factors, namely the strains the policy of cooperation imposed, the criticism it evoked, particularly in the British press, and the developments inside China which, according to one school of thought, only served to justify that criticism.

The Tiananmen effect

The principal development was, of course, Tiananmen in 1989. The killings there naturally provoked universal condemnation, in which the British government joined. They also created a mood of emotion and outrage on the subject of China which was not at all conducive to sensible policy-making. In that mood the value of any dealings with Peking came under question; and, in Britain at least, the rationale of the Joint Declaration was forgotten. I recall leading articles in *The Times* and *The Spectator* urging a review, or even a denunciation, of the Joint Declaration, though it was never clear what that would achieve, apart from terminal damage to Hong Kong.

The same mood bred impatience with the compromises and accommodations inseparable from a policy of cooperation with China over Hong Kong. Those responsible for that policy were regularly attacked in the press for cringing or 'kowtowing' to China, though, curiously, officials rather than the responsible Ministers were seen as the principal villains. It was alleged that the negotiators in 1982–84 had been too supine, that passes had been sold; and a new conviction developed that there was an alternative policy, which would be tougher with China and would secure greater benefits for Hong Kong. We were told we should stand up to China. We should, inter alia, introduce more democracy in Hong Kong, if need be in disregard of Peking.

In Hong Kong, as in Britain, Tiananmen greatly increased the enthusiasm for democracy and the belief that it would be in some way an infallible bulwark against political pressure from the mainland. In the elections of September 1991 a group of Legislative Councillors was elected who went further and, under Martin Lee, saw special merit in defying the mainland.

In Peking, on the other hand, the effect of Tiananmen was to deepen suspicions of democracy and cause it to be seen as a source of instability and a threat to the regime. Extension of democracy in Hong Kong was readily interpreted as a British plot to give Hong Kong a form of independence, or to use it, with the help of foreign powers, as a base for proselytising or subverting on the mainland. Sino-British relations over Hong Kong came to be seen as a form of struggle rather than cooperation. It became a clearer Chinese aim to extend a dominant influence over the territory as rapidly as possible, regardless of the undertaking in the Joint Declaration that Britain should retain undisturbed rule until 1997.

So the situation in 1992 was volatile and difficult. The two governments remained committed to cooperation, but forces were at work on both sides which threatened that cooperation. On the British side, in particular, there was a popular belief that tougher policies would pay off and that there was a unique virtue in more democracy in Hong Kong, regardless of the Chinese reactions to such a move. Nevertheless, it remained a basically manageable situation.

Enter the new Governor

The element that broke the fragile accord and provoked a crisis was the advent of a new Governor, a politician, with new policies.

The Governor's proposals for more democracy, though stopping short of a direct challenge to the agreement on directly elected seats, sought to circumvent those arrangements by greatly enlarging the popular electorate with the help of new-style functional constituencies. Given the situation I have outlined, it was not surprising that such ideas provoked strong Chinese hostility. The proposals incensed the Chinese both as regards manner (the refusal of prior consultation) and as regards content (the increase in the popular vote). They were seen in Peking as a complete U-turn in British policy and as a breach of the constitutional and political settlement enshrined in the Joint Declaration, the agreement on directly elected seats and the Basic Law. Several months of angry public exchanges followed, then some seven months of confidential negotiations, all without success. Though the British made some significant concessions, the Chinese remained unyielding on all major issues. Eventually, at the end of 1993, the British and Hong Kong governments decided to take unilateral action; and early this year the first package of legislation enacting the Governor's reforms was put before Legco in Hong Kong.

Responsibility for this impasse must be borne by both sides. The Chinese have always been difficult over Hong Kong. Dealing with them has demanded unnatural reserves of ingenuity and patience. This was particularly true after Tiananmen; also during the latest negotiations. it is not in their tradition, or their interests, to seek to humiliate their opponents; but this is what they seem to have tried. The rigidity may well reflect the fact that they had reached what they saw as a settlement on Hong Kong and, as they repeatedly told us, they had nothing more to give. Or it may be that in the atmosphere attending the coming demise of Deng Xiaoping, nobody felt confident enough to be flexible. We can only speculate.

On the British side, a greater responsibility must lie. The Chinese position, however extreme and unreasonable it may have been, was well known: there was plenty of evidence and warning. Given the balance of power between the two sides, it was a factor to be given great weight. This does not seem to have happened: the limits of Chinese tolerance were consistently misread. The public approach made sensitive exploration and dignified retreat equally difficult. The Duke of York had marched his men to the top of the hill with all the regimental bands playing and to the applause of the assembled British press. It was naturally harder to get them down again. British sights were set unreasonably high and, despite concessions, were kept that way. The eventual choice faced in November was in consequence painful: either a drastic lowering of objectives, or a decision in favour of unilateral action and defiance. Faced with that choice, which was partly of their own making, the government opted for unilateral action. That was, I think, a serious mistake, since it will bring greater damage to Hong Kong than the alternative course.

We are now in a state of lasting political confrontation with China. Assurances by the British government that, after the passage of legislation in Hong Kong, they will be ready to pick up the threads again are unreal. Each side is now too involved, their face and credit too far engaged, to allow the sort of manoeuvres that might lead to a compromise. It could be argued that after the famous speech of 7 October 1992, the die was cast: the rest would follow like a Greek tragedy. Whether that is so or not, we are now in an unpleasant stand-off on political issues which could last until the summer of 1997. We had better batten down.

The consequences of confrontation

That brings me to the consequences. The Chinese have said, repeatedly and formally, that, in these circumstances, when they take over in 1997 they will repeal any unilateral legislation and that they will dismantle the legislature itself and replace it with something more to their liking. There is little doubt that they will carry out their threat, though there are apparently still some illusions on that score. The effect will be that, after some two years of improved democracy, from the 1995 elections to 1997, the Legislative Council will come to an end and will be replaced by a more subservient assembly. There will be a permanent setback to democracy, not just for a year or so, but for good. Even on the terms the Governor has set, the policy will be self-defeating.

The Chinese have also declared their intention of replacing the top hamper of the Hong Kong administration when they come in in 1997. They speak of setting up their own political structures. As a result, valuable civil servants, who have served the present Hong Kong administration loyally, know that they are under sentence, to be succeeded by less qualified personnel of the right political colour. Hong Kong is bound to suffer; and that continuity of administration which we struggled for in the negotiations from 1983 onward will be lost.

The Chinese have also spoken of restructuring the judiciary. I do not know how serious that intention is; but nothing could be more damaging to the rule of law, on which all Hong Kong's freedoms depend.

These are all things we must reckon will happen in 1997. But in addition to these slightly more distant dangers, there are serious Chinese reactions occurring now. They are stoking up their 'second kitchen', an alternative centre of government for the territory, which will ensure divided authority for the rest of the transitional period. They are likely to prove recalcitrant over the great backlog of legal and administrative work that has to be cleared if Hong Kong is to have a chance of a smooth transition. Unilateral action by the Governor is unlikely to be recognised, so that, come 1997, there could be a legal vacuum, which the Chinese will feel they have discretion to fill.

Because of the political dispute, the Chinese have been even more obstructive than usual over the great construction projects which are needed if Hong Kong is to retain its commercial leadership. I do not rule out an eventual deal on the airport; but the container terminal looks much more doubtful.

Most serious of all, Chinese commitment to the Joint Declaration, the colony's sheet anchor, is being weakened. By acting unilaterally, the British government gives Peking the perfect pretext for doing the same. I think the bulk of the Joint Declaration will survive; but the Chinese are now tinkering with it, and with some excuse.

This is a rough survey of the damage to Hong Kong likely to flow from the present rupture with China. It naturally raises the question why the government and the Governor are prepared to incur these heavy penalties for the territory for which they remain responsible. There are two categories of official answer: that a number of these things will not, or should not, happen; and that in any case the price is worth paying.

In the first place it is argued that once the new reforms are enacted and in operation, the Chinese will quietly acquiesce in them. This is a dangerous illusion, which disregards the intensity of Chinese feeling on this matter of recovering national territory lost in humiliating circumstances in the nineteenth century and doing so on tolerable terms. It neglects the repeated public and formal statements of Chinese intentions. It neglects the consideration that, from the Chinese point of view, in dismantling the latest legislation they will be doing no more than reverting to the settlement of 1984 and 1990 and simply erasing the unilateral additions by the British. They will undertake the work of demolition with relish. They were never enamoured of the British arrangements, or the increasingly assertive legislature. If we had played our hand right they would reluctantly have acquiesced in them. Now they have a prime excuse for doing what they have always wanted. Finally, this line of argument neglects wiser thinking by Ministers on the same subject in the recent past. In February 1990, when commending the agreement on directly elected seats to the Commons, the Foreign Secretary, Douglas Hurd, said: 'Those who suggest that, whatever we do now, China will be obliged to accept in 1997 are out of touch with reality.' I could not put it better.

Another scenario painted is what might be called 'Rescue by the US Cavalry'. It is contended that China will be deterred from tampering with democracy by the United States. The United States is, of course, sympathetic to the cause of democracy in Hong Kong; it also has some leverage with China. But it also has its own problems, its own agenda. Not surprisingly, it will concentrate on that, as in a similar situation in 1982–84. Even if it were to intervene, the effect would almost certainly be highly counterproductive.

Then there is the argument, or, more precisely, the hope that on the death of Deng Xiaoping a liberal regime will emerge in Peking and all will fall into place in Hong Kong. A less plausible situation is hard to imagine. Deng's death is unlikely to usher in immediate fundamental change: the present regime has great tenacity. Even if it did, any more liberal government in Peking would be intent on showing that, in this highly sensitive matter of the recovery of lost national territory, it was no less nationalist and patriotic than its Communist predecessor. There is, I am afraid, no salvation from that quarter.

On a different tack, namely that we cannot afford to drop these reforms, it is argued that only through them can Hong Kong enjoy open, fair and credible elections. This is a very vague and elastic argument; but, however expressed, it carries the clear implication that the existing electoral system in Hong Kong is in some way corrupt. Yet no one, I think, would venture to argue that the 1991 elections, held under the present system, under which the United Democrats, following Martin Lee, did so well, were in any sense rigged. Besides, if we are talking about securing more fair and open elections, how will the current reforms contribute to that end? They will only provoke a Chinese backlash, resulting in a more subservient legislature and greatly increased political intrusion from the mainland. We are, in fact, ensuring a much less fair and open system in 1997 than would have been the case had we left matters alone.

In the same vein, it is argued that only in this way can the rule of law be preserved in the territory. But the rule of law depends crucially on Annex I of the Joint Declaration, which contains all the vital provisions. And by acting unilaterally we present the Chinese with a perfect excuse for doing likewise and tinkering with the Joint Declaration. As I have indicated, they even talk about restructuring the judiciary. How can that possibly help the rule of law?

We are told that, whatever the objections may be to the new reforms, the Hong Kong legislature has approved them; how can we interfere with this exercise in parliamentary democracy? Of course, the Legco members have not yet approved the substance of the proposed reforms; the package could well be substantially amended before final enactment. But, for the sake of argument, let us overlook that and assume general endorsement by the legislature. The fact remains that final responsibility for Hong Kong rests with the British government until 1997. Only it can settle with China or disagree with China, and China will not deal with any other party. It is not open to Britain to shuffle off responsibility for Hong Kong to a subordinate body in the shape of the colonial legislative assembly and blame the consequences upon them.

This is even more true when that assembly has not been left in a position to reach a considered view on the basis of a fair assessment of the prospective gains and losses flowing from current policy. The consequences of the present course have not been spelt out to them. On the contrary, the Hong Kong public have been assured that the Chinese threats are bluff and that the course of instant improved democracy will not be attended by any of the inevitable penalties. Moreover, instead of a free vote on the solemn subject of Hong Kong's future, they are being pressed to endorse the Governor's plans by all the considerable powers of persuasion at the disposal of Government House. The whips are on with a vengeance; and Hong Kong is being driven forward into a modern version of the Charge of the Light Brigade.

A further line of defence, or plea in mitigation, is that this is an unfortunate but irrelevant dispute: Hong Kong is in effect already part of China, and doing very well out of it. What is all the fuss about? It is, happily, true that the Hong Kong economy, because of close mainland ties, is insulated from the political rift in a way that was not possible in the early 1980s. But that does not mean that human rights and freedoms, the rule of law and democracy, the attributes of a liberal society, have become less valuable or relevant. Much of the British effort has over recent years been directed to this vital area, and rightly so. On this point the Governor and his critics are

at one. In time, no doubt, these trials will all be seen as blips on the great historical screen. But they involve real people here and now, and Britain's responsibilities to them.

The final justification is that all this may be true, but that at least we shall have done our best; we shall have gone down fighting and honour will be preserved. But it will not be the British who go down fighting—they will have left the battlefield. The Hong Kong population, or the less moneyed part of it, who lack the papers and the means to set up abroad, will remain. They will have been led into a confrontation they did not want and left to face the music. There is little honour in that situation.

The outlook for Hong Kong

The political prospects are bleak for Hong Kong. Economically, the territory should continue to flourish; it is now tightly bound to the booming economy of southern China. Obviously every effort must be made in damage limitation; and some cooperation over the airport may be manageable. But in all other respects—in terms of democracy, the rule of law, the attributes of a free and liberal society, not to mention the smooth running of the administration—Hong Kong will find itself worse off after 1997 as a result of the present policy than it was in 1992. Or than it would have been if cooperation with China had been continued. It is here that the full, zany, 'Alice-in-Wonderland' quality of current policy is manifest. Far from helping democracy, it damages it. After the briefest of interludes, Western values in Hong Kong will lose rather than gain. And at one and the same time, current policy has succeeded in deeply antagonising China, a rising superpower and a vast new market. This is a negative achievement of a high order, calling for special talents. I seem to recall the phrase 'a double whammy'. This is a notable example.

We have also to think of the effects on Britain's wider relations with China. So far I have argued the case solely in terms of the impact on Hong Kong. That is right: the welfare of Hong Kong must be the decisive criterion. But other British interests, particularly trade with China, are bound to suffer. The evidence of discrimination will not be easy to collect: the Prime Minister, Li Peng, is not going to announce a formal ban or emulate Malaysia's Prime Minister, Dr Mahathir. He also has to think about China's candidature for the General Agreement on Tariffs and Trade (GATT). But there will undoubtedly be a commercial fall-out; the majority of contracts will go to our competitors. Nor are our European Union partners likely to lose much sleep over our predicament. French behaviour is instructive. After selling arms in quantity to Taiwan—sales from which they continue to receive the revenues—they have executed a U-turn that would do credit to a London taxicab. They have expressed penitence and have been welcomed back into the fold like the prodigal son. On his visit to China, Mr Balladur will, no doubt, enjoy the fatted calf in the shape of a number of lucrative contracts. Whereas Britain, formerly on the inside track as a result of a sensible policy on Hong Kong, is now on the outside track—or perhaps not on the track at all. To exclude ourselves from the world's fastest growing market in this way is no mean feat.

Could it have been different? Or would the Chinese have treated the last British Governor in the same way, whoever he had been? It could have been very different, though it would be wrong to claim that we could have extracted big concessions in terms of more democracy for Hong Kong. If the Governor had quietly approached Peking in the autumn of 1992, explained his difficulties and sought their help, he would have got something. Not much—the Chinese had gone as far as they were prepared to go in previous negotiations. But they would have made some small concessions to give him face and as an earnest of continuing cooperation. We could then have got on with the demanding task of preparing for a smooth transition with full British input, localising the legislation, writing in the fine print. It would not have been easy: in that environment it never is. But the Legislative Council would have been preserved; mainland political intrusion would have been infinitely less; we could have got on with the airport; Britain would have remained on the inside track as regards China trade; we would have retained influence over Hong Kong's future up to the last moment; the Joint Declaration would have remained intact. We could honestly have said that we

had ensured the best possible conditions for the territory's survival in the form in which we had established it. Whereas now we have ensured a rough reversion, an angry landlord, and a series of retaliatory measures, the precise extent of which cannot be predicted with certainty, but which will clearly be injurious. And in addition we have abdicated any influence on the future in the last three years of transition. The future of Hong Kong is being worked out in Peking by the Chinese government with its huddle of Preliminary Working Committee advisers; and there is no Hong Kong or British government voice in that vital process.

This, then, is the story: a crisis of large proportions and lasting consequences, seriously damaging Hong Kong as a liberal society and Britain in its relations with China. An unnecessary crisis. One brought about by a fatal misreading of Chinese attitudes and tolerance, and by the pressures of an uncomprehending press and Parliament.

It is a story that it is necessary to tell, since relatively little of it has appeared in the British media. They have confined themselves to the primitive litany: democracy good, Governor good, China bad. The real and longer-term consequences of official policy for the 6m people in our charge have been prudently veiled. But there is a serious case to answer. Historically, Sino-British relations, both over Hong Kong and on other matters, have been full of blunders: they are a catalogue of misunderstandings and misperceptions. But in the past we were cushioned by superior strength. Not any more. We have waited to make our biggest mistake until the last minute, when there is no time for a second chance and when the balance of power is heavily against us.

Article 34   *Far Eastern Economic Review*, November 24, 1994

Hollow House

Beijing floats idea of a 'provisional' legislature

Louise do Rosario in Hong Kong

Amidst the skyscrapers of central Hong Kong, an impressive Edwardian-style building stands elegantly aloof from the expanses of mirror glass. This is the home of the colony's Legislative Council, or Legco, a body of 60 elected and appointed politicians who debate government policy. Thanks to pro-democracy reforms introduced since the mid-1980s, Legco has become an increasingly independent and assertive institution.

That's how it was meant to remain after Hong Kong's looming reversion to Chinese sovereignty. But there's been a change of plan on Beijing's side, a change not provided for in any blueprint for the colony's future.

On July 1, 1997, Hong Kong's first day under Chinese rule, a very different body is likely to replace the current Legco. The members of this "provisional" legislature will probably be hand-picked by China in early 1997, and at most they will serve a term of one year. Local liberals, however, fear that Beijing will use this period to roll back some of the colony's political freedoms and safeguards against repression.

When London and Beijing agreed to the handover in 1984, it was understood—if not explicitly stated—that all elected institutions, including Legco, would continue operating with little disruption after 1997. Under this "through-train" scenario, the last Legco elected under British rule (in 1995) would serve out its four-year term. That was why the Basic Law, China's mini-constitution for post-handover Hong Kong, provides for elections in 1999 rather than 1997.

Beijing has hinted that the job of choosing the provisional legislature will be given to a 400-member selection committee. How the choosers will themselves be chosen hasn't been decided.

China has promised that the interim legislature would have a limited mandate, tackling only the most important is-

sues relating to the takeover. These include the passage of new electoral laws and the budget, as well as the appointment of judges and key government officials.

The interim legislature would also be expected to deal with emergencies, such as a monetary crisis. But many in Hong Kong worry that Beijing could turn the body into a rubber stamp and use it to tighten its grip on the colony's political life. "It is part and parcel of a Beijing-controlled [Hong Kong] government," columnist Margaret Ng wrote recently in the *South China Morning Post*.

Beijing may get its way after 1997, but political activists in the colony are making desperate attempts to salvage what they can of their fledgling democracy now. "We have to fight. We may not have much political clout in Beijing's eye, but public opinion is on our side," says Lo Chi-kin, a member of the Democratic Party, the colony's largest political group. Lo's party colleague, Cheung Man-kwong, has called for a signature campaign to oppose the Chinese plan.

The idea of a provisional Legco was first raised in early October by the Preliminary Working Committee (PWC), a Beijing-appointed body that advises China on handover matters. Though committee members stress that the plan is only for discussion, many in Hong Kong believe it is a trial balloon for Beijing. Indeed, Lu Ping, one of the most senior Chinese officials dealing with Hong Kong, has pronounced on it. Columnist Ng says the PWC is merely Beijing's "mouthpiece."

The 57-member working committee argues that a provisional body is necessary because there will be no legislature to govern Hong Kong on July 1, 1997. The reason: In its quarrels with the British and Hong Kong governments, a testy China has vowed to scrap all existing elective bodies on Day One; although Beijing says it will organise fresh elections, the through-train has been derailed.

The train began to wobble when the colony's leadership changed hands in 1992 and new Governor Chris Patten introduced electoral reforms designed to extend democracy. The proposals, which angered China, passed in a charged Legco debate in June.

They include enlarging, to 30 from 21, the number of seats assigned to so-called functional constituencies. These divisions have previously been narrowly focused on small professional groups such as lawyers, doctors and accountants; the nine new ones, however, will encompass much of the local workforce. In addition, the Legco seats currently filled by government appointees will be abolished. In their place, 10 seats will be filled by members of the colony's elected district boards.

Thus, when polls are held next year, Legco will be fully elected—one way or another—for the first time in its history. Beijing, accusing Patten of stirring up trouble for the future sovereign power, has refused to accept the reforms. Basically, it seems to think Patten's actions have been premature; the Basic Law envisages a more gradual expansion of the electorate.

Until recently, a few optimists in the colony still dared to hope that Beijing would relent, allowing most of the pre-1997 Legco to stay on except, perhaps, for a few members it regards as hostile to China. Most other observers believed Beijing would hold fresh Legco elections, under a narrower franchise, soon after the handover.

Instead, Beijing appears to be pursuing a plan not provided for in either the Basic Law or the Sino-British Joint Declaration of 1984, which sealed the colony's fate. "There is no legal basis for the new body," says Lo of the Democratic Party.

The fear among local liberals is that with no written rules on how the caretaker legislature should be run, Beijing could at a stroke remove all the mechanisms for fair elections that Hong Kong has established over the years. If that happens, they say, China would clearly be breaking its promise that Hong Kong will retain a high degree of autonomy after 1997.

"It is increasingly clear what China has in mind. It wants to control everything in Hong Kong," says Lo. Another party colleague, legislator Huang Chenya, charges that China wants to "create an institution to enable it to change the rules of the game." Lo and Huang fear Beijing will use the provisional body to pass draconian laws without open debate and set back Hong Kong's political evolution. "With such a legislature, any law can be passed and any can be repealed," adds another Democratic legislator, Szeto Wah.

Some politicians, however, call for pragmatism. "A provisional Legco is the by-product of non-cooperation between Britain and China," says legislator Henry Tang, a member of the moderate Liberal Party. "In the absence of a better alternative, the plan is a practical solution." Adds pro-China legislator Chim Piuchung: "The fact is that there will be no through-train in 1997, and that the new government needs a legislature to function properly. We should not be prejudiced and criticise whatever China proposes."

To reassure a nervous Hong Kong, Lu Ping, director of China's Hong Kong and Macau Affairs Office, has said the caretaker legislature would deal with only the most urgent issues. It would not, he stressed, scrap Hong Kong's Bill of Rights, even though this legislation, passed in 1991, has been another bone of contention between China and local liberals. Prodemocracy activists see the bill as a safeguard against repression; China has vowed to scrap it, saying it could provide a haven for lawbreakers.

Tsang Yok-sing, a member of the Beijing-appointed PWC, says there are four entities that China could pass Hong Kong's law-making powers to: a provisional Legco, the colony's chief executive, the Chinese parliament or the Preparatory Committee, a body that will be set up in 1996 to organise the first post–1997 Hong Kong Government. He says the last three weren't considered acceptable because they would allow these entities to act independently of the authority of the local legislature.

Dorothy Liu, who represents Hong Kong in China's parliament, the National People's Congress, notes that Beijing has softened its tone over the provisional Legco idea in recent weeks, following the outcry against it in Hong Kong. Others see it differently. "Beijing is merely giving us time to digest the bad news," says Lo of the Democratic Party.

Glossary of Terms and Abbreviations

Ancestor Worship Ancient religious practices still followed in Taiwan, Hong Kong, and the People's Republic of China. Ancestor worship is based on the belief that the living can communicate with the dead and that the dead spirits to whom sacrifices are ritually made can bring about a better life for the living.

Brain Drain A migration of professional people (such as scientists, professors, and physicians) from one country to another, usually in search of higher salaries or better living conditions.

Buddhism A religion of East and Central Asia founded on the teachings of Siddhartha Guatama (the Buddha). Its followers believe that suffering is inherent in life and that one can be liberated from it by mental and moral self-purification.

Capitalist A person who has capital invested in business, or someone who favors an economic system characterized by private or corporate ownership of capital goods.

Chinese Communist Party (CCP) Founded in 1921 by a small Marxist study group, its members initially worked with the Kuomintang under Chiang Kai-shek to unify China and, later, to fight off Japanese invaders. Despite Chiang's repeated efforts to destroy the CCP, it eventually ousted the KMT and took control of the Chinese mainland in 1949.

Cold War A conflict carried on without overt military action and without breaking off diplomatic relations.

Communism Theoretically, a system in which most goods are collectively owned and are available to all as needed; in reality, a system of government in which a single authoritarian party controls the political, legal, educational, and economic systems, supposedly in order to establish a more egalitarian society.

Confucianism Often referred to as a religion, actually a system of ethics for governing human relationships and for ruling. It was established during the fifth century B.C. by the Chinese philosopher Confucius.

Contract Responsibility System A system of rural production in which the land is contracted by the village to individual peasant households. These households are then responsible for managing the production on their contracted land and, after fulfilling their production contracts with the state, are free to use what they produce or to sell it and pocket the proceeds. Such a system has been in place in China since the late 1970s and has replaced the communes established during the Maoist era.

Cultural Revolution Formally, the Great Proletarian Cultural Revolution. In an attempt to rid China of its repressive bureaucracy and to restore a revolutionary spirit to the Chinese people, Mao Zedong (Tse-tung) called on the youth of China to "challenge authority" and "make revolution" by rooting out the "reactionary" elements in Chinese society. The Cultural Revolution lasted from 1966 until 1976. It seriously undermined the Chinese people's faith in the Chinese Communist Party's ability to rule and led to major setbacks in the economy.

De-Maoification The rooting-out of the philosophies and programs of Mao Zedong in Chinese society.

Democratic Centralism The participation of the people in discussions of policy at lower levels. Their ideas are to be passed up to the central leadership; but once the central leadership makes a decision, it is to be implemented by the people.

Exco The Executive Council of Hong Kong, consisting of top civil servants and civilian appointees chosen to represent the community. Except in times of emergency, the governor must consult with the Exco before initiating any program.

Feudal In Chinese Communist parlance, a patriarchal bureaucratic system in which bureaucrats administer policy on the basis of personal relationships.

Four Cardinal Principles The Chinese Communists' term for their commitment to socialism; the leadership of the Chinese Communist Party; the dictatorship of the proletariat; and the ideologies of Karl Marx, Vladimir Lenin, and Mao Zedong.

Four Modernizations A program of reforms begun in 1978 in China that seeks to modernize agriculture, industry, science and technology, and defense by the year 2000.

Gang of Four The label applied to the four "radicals" or "leftists" who dominated first the cultural and then the political events during the Cultural Revolution. The four members of the Gang were Jiang Qing, Mao's wife; Zhang Chunqiao, former deputy secretary of the Shanghai municipal committee and head of its propaganda department; Yao Wenyuan, former editor-in-chief of the *Shanghai Liberation Daily*; and Wang Hongwen, a worker in a textile factory in Shanghai.

Great Leap Forward Mao Zedong's alternative to the Soviet model of development, this was a plan calling for the establishment of communes and for an increase in industrial production in both the cities and the communes. The increased production was to come largely from greater human effort rather than from more investment or improved technology. This policy, begun in 1958, was abandoned by 1959.

Great Proletarian Cultural Revolution See *Cultural Revolution*.

Gross Domestic Product (GDP) A measure of the total flow of and services produced by the economy of a country over a certain period of time, normally a year. GDP equals gross national product (GNP) minus the income of the country's residents earned on investments abroad.

Guerrilla A member of a small force of "irregular" soldiers. Generally, guerrilla forces are used against numerically and technologically superior enemies in jungles or mountainous terrain.

Han Of "pure" Chinese extraction. Refers to the dominant ethnic group in the P.R.C.

Ideograph A character of Chinese writing. Originally, each ideograph represented a picture and/or a sound of a word.

Islam The religious faith founded by Muhammad in the sixth and seventh centuries A.D. Its followers believe that Allah is the sole deity and that Muhammad is his prophet.

Kuomintang (KMT) The Chinese Nationalist Party, founded by Sun Yat-sen in 1912. Currently the ruling party on Taiwan. See also *Nationalists*.

Legco Hong Kong's Legislative Council, which reviews policies proposed by the governor and formulates legislation.

Long March The 1934–1935 retreat of the Chinese Communist Party, in which thousands died while journeying to the plains of Yan'an in northern China in order to escape annihilation by the KMT.

Mainlanders Those Chinese in Taiwan who immigrated from the Chinese mainland during the flight of the Nationalist Party in 1949.

Mandarin A northern Chinese dialect chosen by the Chinese Communist Party to be the official language of China. It is also the official language of Taiwan.

Mao Thought In the post-1949 period, originally described as "the thoughts of Mao Zedong." Mao's "thoughts" were considered important because he took the theory of Marxism-Leninism and applied it to the concrete conditions existing in China. But since Mao's death in 1976 and the subsequent reevaluation of his policies, Mao Thought is no longer conceived of as the thoughts of Mao alone but as the "collective wisdom" of the party leadership.

May Fourth Period A period of intellectual ferment in China, which officially began on May 4, 1919, and concerned the Versailles Peace Conference. On that day, the Chinese protested what was considered an unfair secret settlement regarding German-held territory in China. The result was what was termed a "new cultural movement," which lasted into the mid-1920s.

Nationalists The KMT (Kuomintang) Party. The ruling party of the Republic of China, now in "exile" on Taiwan.

Newly Industrialized Country (NIC) A term used to refer to those developing countries of the Third World that have enjoyed rapid economic growth. Most commonly applied to the East Asian economies of South Korea, Taiwan, Hong Kong, and Singapore.

Offshore Islands The small islands in the Formosa Strait that are just a few miles off the Chinese mainland but are controlled by Taiwan, nearly 90 miles away.

Opium A bitter, addictive drug made from the dried juice of the opium poppy.

Opium War The 1839–1842 conflict between Britain and China, sparked by the British import of opium into China. After the British victory, Europeans were allowed into China and trading posts were established on the mainland. The Treaty of Nanking, which ended the Opium War, also gave Britain its first control over part of Hong Kong.

People's Procuracy The investigative branch of China's legal system. It determines whether an accused person is guilty and should be brought to trial.

People's Republic of China (P.R.C.) Established in 1949 by the Chinese Communists under the leadership of Mao Zedong after defeating Chiang Kai-shek and his Nationalist supporters.

Pinyin A new system of spelling Chinese words and names, using a Latin alphabet of 26 letters, created by the Chinese Communist leadership.

Proletariat The industrial working class, which for Marx was the political force that would overthrow capitalism and lead the way in the building of socialism.

Republic of China (R.O.C.) The government established as a result of the 1911 Revolution. It was ousted by the Chinese Communist Party in 1949, when its leaders fled to Taiwan.

Second Convention of Peking The 1898 agreement leasing the New Territories of Hong Kong to the British until 1997.

Shanghai Communique A joint statement of the Chinese and American viewpoints on a range of issues in which each has an interest. It was signed during U.S. President Richard Nixon's historic visit to China in 1971.

Socialism A transitional period between the fall of capitalism and the establishment of "true" communism. Socialism is characterized by the public ownership of the major means of production. Some private economic activity and private property are still allowed, but increased attention is given to a more equal distribution of wealth and income.

Special Administrative Region (SAR) A political subdivision of the People's Republic of China that will be used to describe Hong Kong's status after it comes under Chinese sovereignty in 1997. The SAR will have much greater political, economic, and cultural autonomy from the central government in Beijing than do the provinces of the P.R.C.

Special Economic Zone (SEZ) An area within China that has been allowed a great deal of freedom to experiment with different economic policies, especially efforts to attract foreign investment. Shenzhen, near Hong Kong, is the largest of China's Special Economic Zones.

Taiwanese Independence Movement An organization of native Taiwanese who want to overthrow the Mainlander KMT government and establish an independent state of Taiwan.

Taoism A Chinese mystical philosophy founded in the sixth century B.C. Its followers renounce the secular world and lead lives characterized by unassertiveness and simplicity.

United Nations (UN) An international organization established on June 26, 1945, through official approval of the charter by delegates of 50 nations at a conference in San Francisco. The charter went into effect on October 24, 1945.

Yuan Literally, "branch"; the different departments of the government of Taiwan, including the Executive, Legislative, Judicial, Control, and Examination Yuans.

Bibliography

CHINA

Periodicals and Newspapers

The following periodicals and newspapers are excellent sources for coverage of Chinese affairs:

Asian Survey
Australian Journal of Chinese Affairs
Beijing Review
China Business Review
China Daily
China Quarterly
Far Eastern Economic Review
Foreign Broadcasts Information Service (FBIS)
The Free China Journal
Free China Review
Joint Publications Research Service (JPRS)
Journal of Asian Studies
Modern China
Pacific Affairs

General

Kwang-chih Chang, *The Archaeology of China,* 4th ed. (New Haven: Yale University Press, 1986).
____, *Shang Civilization* (New Haven: Yale University Press, 1980).
Two works by an eminent archaeologist on the origins of Chinese civilization.

Brian Hook, ed., *The Cambridge Encyclopedia of China* (New York: Cambridge University Press, 1982).
An excellent encyclopedia of Chinese history, geography, and culture from the earliest times up to the 1980s. Nicely illustrated.

Nicholas D. Kristof and Sherly WuDunn, *China Wakes* (New York: Times Books, 1994).
The authors are *New York Times* reporters who won the Pulitzer Prize in journalism for their reporting on the Tiananmen crisis of 1989. This insightful book is a highly readable composite of their memories and perspectives on China since the late 1980s.

Mark Salzman, *Iron and Silk* (New York: Random House, 1987).
An insightful and delightfully written account of the experiences of a young American teacher in China in the early 1980s. Provides a sense of life (for both foreigners and Chinese) in post-Mao China.

Christopher J. Smith, *China: People and Places in the Land of One Billion* (Boulder: Westview Press, 1991).
An introductory text with the purpose of offering a "regional geography" that introduces students to geography and China at the same time. A commentary on society and the impact of reforms in China since 1979.

History

Lucien Bianco, *Origins of the Chinese Revolution, 1915–1949* (Stanford: Stanford University Press, 1967).
The best short account of the collapse of the empire, the foundations of the republic, the civil war, and the victory of the CCP.

Jung Chang, *Wild Swans: Three Daughters of China* (New York: Simon and Shuster, 1992).
A superb biographical account that illuminates what China was like for one family over three generations. Insightful and well-written.

John King Fairbank, *China: A New History* (Cambridge: Harvard University Press, 1992).
Examines essential motivating forces in China's history that define it as a coherent culture from its earliest recorded history to 1991. Looks at the multifaceted, often contradictory aspects of Chinese civilization that have been the source of both its unity and its internal conflicts. Superbly written and often humorous.

William Hinton, *Fanshen: A Documentary of Revolution in a Chinese Village* (New York: Random House, 1968).
Based on the author's witness to the process of land reform carried out by the CCP in the north China village of Long Bow, 1947–1949. The story is exciting and gripping. Hinton updated Long Bow's story in a sequel, *Shenfan: The Continuing Revolution in a Chinese Village* (New York: Random House, 1983); and his daughter, Carma, made several superb films about life in Long Bow in the 1980s (available from Long Bow Film Group, 617 West End Ave., New York, NY).

Makers of the 20th Century: Deng Xiaoping (London: Sphere Books, 1990).
Covers the life of one of China's leading political figures in the twentieth century, from his birth in 1904 through his many victories, defeats, and "mistakes," to his role as China's "paramount leader" in the 1980s, and, finally, to his image as "the butcher of Beijing." Does not cover the post-Tiananmen Square period, in which Deng has been restored to a leader of nearly heroic proportions in the minds of the people.

Tony Saich and Hans Van de Ven, eds., *New Perspectives on the Chinese Communist Revolution* (Armonk: M. E. Sharpe, Inc., 1995).
Articles provide new perspectives on the CCP's rise to power. Looks at how the CCP operated, the role of intellectuals and women in the Communist movement, the peasants' responses to the CCP's efforts at mobilization, and other topics related to the ultimate success of the CCP.

Edgar Snow, *Red Star Over China* (New York: Grove Press, 1973).

This book, which first appeared in 1938, is the author's account of the months he spent with the CCP Red Army in Yanan in 1936, in the midst of the Chinese civil war. It is a thrilling account of the revolution in action, and includes Mao's own story (as told to Snow) of his early life and his decision to become a Communist.

Jonathan D. Spence, *The Search for Modern China* (New York: W. W. Norton & Co., 1990).

A lively, fascinating, and comprehensive history of China from the seventeenth century to 1989. Looks at the cyclical patterns of collapse and regeneration, revolution and consolidation, growth and decay. Examines how forces in Chinese history—intellectual, political, cultural, economic, emotional—have shaped the China of today.

Politics, Economics, Society, and Culture

Julia F. Andrews, *Painters and Politics in the People's Republic of China, 1949–1979* (Berkeley: University of California Press, 1994).

A fascinating presentation of the relationship between politics and art from the beginning of the Communist period until the eve of major liberalization in 1979. Examines how vacillating political requirements for art, political repression of artists, the influence of the Soviet Union, and the shift from a traditional Chinese style (landscape) to socialist realism and traditional medium (ink on silk) to oil on canvas affected the art world. Looks at China's art education, careers of artists, and values, fears, and ideals that motivated China's painters. Includes 150 reproductions of paintings, drawings, and block prints.

Ma Bo, *Bloodred Sunset* (New York: Viking, 1995).

Perhaps the most compelling autobiographical account by a Red Guard during the Cultural Revolution. Responding to Mao Zedong's call to youth to "make revolution," the author captures the intense emotions of exhilaration, fear, despair, and loneliness. Takes place in the wilds of Inner Mongolia.

Nien Cheng, *Life and Death in Shanghai* (New York: Grove Press, 1987).

A gripping autobiographical account of a woman persecuted during the Cultural Revolution because of her earlier connections with a Western company, her elitist attitudes, and her luxurious lifestyle.

Qing Dai, *Yangtze! Yangtze!* (Toronto: Probe International, 1994).

A collection of documents concerning the debate over building the Three Gorges Dam on the upper Yangtze River in order to harness energy for China. Among opponents are many scientists, committed Communists who argue the dam will lead to environmental disaster. The book was banned in China in 1989.

William Theodore De Bary, ed., *Sources of Chinese Tradition,* Vols. I and II (Columbia: Columbia University Press, 1960).

A compilation of the major writings (translated) of key Chinese figures, from Confucius through Mao Zedong. Gives readers an excellent understanding of intellectual roots of development of Chinese history.

Michael S. Duke, ed., *World of Modern Chinese Fiction: Short Stories & Novellas from the People's Republic, Taiwan & Hong Kong* (Armonk: M. E. Sharpe, Inc., 1991).

A collection of short stories written by Chinese authors from China, Taiwan, and Hong Kong during the 1980s. The 25 stories are grouped by subject matter and narrative style. One group uses modernist narrative techniques to question the meaning of recent Chinese history as defined by the Communist Party. A second group examines personal issues of romance, the struggles of ordinary people, and family relationships.

B. Michael Frolic, *Mao's People: Sixteen Portraits of Life in Revolutionary China* (Cambridge: Harvard University Press, 1980).

A must-read. Through composite biographies of 16 different types of people China, the author offers a humorous but penetrating view of "unofficial" Chinese society and politics. Biographical sketches reflect political life during the Maoist era, but the book has enduring value for understanding China.

David S. G. Goodman, *Beijing Street Voices: The Poetry and Politics of China's Democracy Movement* (London: Marion Boyars, 1981).

An analysis of the 1978–1979 "democracy movement" and its participants. Includes translations from wall posters posted on "democracy wall" in Beijing, the first prodemocracy movement to occur in the P.R.C.

David S. G. Goodman and Beverly Hooper, eds., *China's Quiet Revolution: New Interactions Between State and Society* (New York: St. Martin's Press, 1994).

Articles examine the impact of economic reforms since the early 1980s on the social structure and society generally, with focus on changes in wealth, status, power, and newly emerging social forces.

Ruth Hayhoe, *Education and Modernization: The Chinese Experience* (New York: Pergamon Press, 1992).

Examines the role that education has played in China's modernization, from Confucian education in imperial China to Marxist education in the Communist period. Looks at pedagogical issues and how women and minority groups are treated in the educational system.

Liang Heng and Judith Shapiro, *Son of the Revolution* (New York: Vintage, 1984).

A gripping account of the Cultural Revolution by a Red Guard. Offers insights into the madness that gripped China during the period from 1966–1976 and how the politics of the Maoist era affected individuals and families.

Alan Hunter and Kim-kwong Chan, *Protestantism in Contemporary China* (New York: Cambridge University Press, 1993).

Examines historical and political conditions that have affected the development of Protestantism in China. Chinese cultural beliefs and religious practices have shaped Protestantism, as have the government's policies toward religion. Includes a comparative chapter on Buddhism and Catholicism.

William R. Jankowiak, *Sex, Death, and Hierarchy in a Chinese City* (New York: Columbia University Press, 1993).

Written by an anthropologist with a discerning eye, this is one of the most fascinating accounts of daily life in China. Particularly strong on rituals of death, romantic life, and the on-site mediation of disputes by strangers (e.g., with bicycle accidents). Although the book is based on fieldwork done in the capital of Inner Mongolia, the majority of the population there is now Chinese, as is the people's approach to most issues.

Maria Jaschok and Suzanne Miers, eds., *Chinese Patriarchy: Women's Submission, Servitude and Escape* (Atlantic Highlands: Humanities Press International, Inc., 1993).

Examines Chinese women's roles, the sale of children, prostitution, Chinese patriarchy, Christianity, and feminism, as well as social remedies and avenues of escape for women.

James T. Myers, *Enemies Without Guns: The Catholic Church in China* (New York: Paragon House, 1991).

Interrelates history of the Chinese Catholic Church with the course of Chinese domestic politics, with an emphasis on the persecution and oppression of Chinese Catholics. Commentary and documents of communications between Rome and Beijing reveal the clash between two regimes, each claiming "infallibility"—the pope and the Chinese Communist Party.

Suzanne Ogden, *China's Unresolved Issues: Politics, Development, and Culture,* 3rd ed. (Englewood Cliffs: Prentice-Hall, 1995).

A thematic and issue-oriented approach to Chinese politics. Presents the ongoing issues in Chinese politics in terms of the interaction between Chinese culture, politics/ideology, and development. Includes a chapter on pre-1949 Chinese history and one on the meaning of socialism in China in the 1990s.

Suzanne Ogden, Kathleen Hartford, Lawrence Sullivan, and David Zweig, eds., *China's Search for Democracy: The Student and Mass Movement of 1989* (Armonk: M. E. Sharpe, 1992).

An excellent collection of wall posters, handbills, and speeches of the prodemocracy movement of 1989. These documents capture the passionate feelings of the student, intellectual, and worker participants. Covers the period from Hu Yaobang's death in April 1989 through the crackdown on June 4, 1989, and is arranged chronologically. Each of the six sections is introduced by an editor's analysis of the documents.

Michel Oksenberg, Lawrence R. Sullivan, and Marc Lambert, eds., *Beijing Spring, 1989: Confrontation and Conflict: The Basic Documents* (Armonk: M. E. Sharpe, 1990).

A collection of the major official documents of the Chinese government and Communist Party in the period immediately preceding and during the prodemocracy movement in the spring of 1989. An excellent research tool.

Tony Saich, ed., *The Chinese People's Movement: Perspectives on Spring 1989* (Armonk: M. E. Sharpe, 1990).

A collection of essays on the prodemocracy movement of 1989. Topics include the Chinese tradition of student protests, the political economy, the lack of organization in the student leadership of the movement, the emergence of civil society, and the changing role of the Chinese media. A chronology of the student demonstrations is appended.

Martin Schoenhals, *The Paradox of Power in a People's Republic of China Middle School* (Armonk: M. E. Sharpe, 1993).

An in-depth study of aspects of Chinese culture as revealed in the educational system. Themes include the persistent evaluation of superiors by their subordinates on the basis of their morality and competence; the Chinese obsession with ranking; the competitiveness that ranking engenders; and the resulting tension that this constant evaluation, criticism, and ranking generates not only between subordinates and superiors but also among "equals" and friends.

Ezra F. Vogel, *One Step Ahead in China: Guangdong Under Reform* (Cambridge: Harvard University Press, 1989).

A case study of Guangdong Province, which abuts "Special Economic Zones" and Hong Kong. Demonstrates how Guangdong has raced ahead of the rest of China through economic liberalization and the problems and opportunities created by a mixed economy. Focuses on the importance of Hong Kong to Guangdong's development.

Robert P. Weller, *Resistance, Chaos, and Control in China: Taiping Rebels, Taiwanese Ghosts, and Tiananmen* (Seattle: University of Washington Press, 1994).
Addresses issues of tacit cultural resistance, which may or may not become a political movement or armed rebellion. It uses three cases to illustrate forms cultural resistance may take: the Taiping Rebels in the nineteenth century, ghost worship in Taiwan, and efforts of the Chinese people to resist cultural control after the Tiananmen crisis of 1989 led to cultural repression.

Chihua Wen, *The Red Mirror: Children of China's Cultural Revolution* (Boulder: Westview Press, 1995).
A former editor and reporter for New China News Agency in Beijing presents the heart-rending stories of a dozen individuals who were children at the time the Cultural Revolution started. It shows how rapidly changing policies of the period shattered lives of its participants and left them cynical adults 20 years later.

Foreign Policy

Harry Harding, *A Fragile Relationship: The United States and China Since 1972* (Washington, D.C.: The Brookings Institution, 1992).
Traces U.S.–China relations from President Richard M. Nixon's visit to China in 1972 to the 1990s. Takes a U.S. perspective to interweave commentary on issues of U.S.–China relations with the corollary issue of U.S.–Taiwan relations. Examines how Washington has dealt with issues concerning China's human rights, strategic concerns, economic relations, exchanges, and how the United States might redesign its China policy.

Thomas Robinson and David Shambaugh, eds., *Chinese Foreign Policy: Theory and Practice* (New York: Oxford University Press, 1994).
Provides the most comprehensive study to date of China's foreign policy since 1949. Carefully documents the historical, cultural, domestic, perceptual, economic, ideological, geopolitical, and strategic issues influencing China's formulation of foreign policy. Also applies international relations theories to China's foreign policy.

TAIWAN

Politics, Economics, Society, and Culture

Joel Aberbach et al., eds., *The Role of the State in Taiwan's Development* (Armonk: M. E. Sharpe, 1994).
Articles address technology, international trade, state policy toward the development of local industries, and the effect of economic development on society, including on women and farmers.

Hsiao-shih Cheng, *Party-Military Relations in the PRC and Taiwan* (Boulder: Westview Special Studies on China and East Asia, 1990).
Argues that military participation in government, not the control of the military through the political commissar system, is the key stabilizing factor in both the P.R.C. and Taiwan.

Bih-er Chou, Clark Cal, and Janet Clark, *Women in Taiwan Politics: Overcoming Barriers to Women's Participation in a Modernizing Society* (Boulder: Lynne Rienner Publishers, 1990).
Examines the political underrepresentation of women in Taiwan and how Chinese culture on the one hand and modernization and development on the other are affecting women's status.

Hill Gates, *Chinese Working Class Lives: Getting By in Taiwan* (Ithaca: Cornell University Press, 1987).
An in-depth, well-written account of the culture of Taiwan's working people. Includes nine individual histories. Particularly strong on Taiwan's culture, religious traditions, family relations, status of women, and the political economy of working-class people.

Stevan Harrell and Chun-chieh Huang, eds., *Cultural Change in Postwar Taiwan* (Boulder: Westview Press, 1994).
A collection of essays that analyzes the tensions in Taiwan's society as modernization erodes many of its old values and traditions. Includes such topics as the government's cultural policy; Taiwan's quest for a cultural identity today; trends in religion, recreation, and ethnic relations; and how cultural change is expressed in literature and the arts.

David K. Jordan, *Gods, Ghosts, and Ancestors: The Folk Religion of a Taiwanese Village* (Berkeley: University of California Press, 1972).
A fascinating analysis by an anthropologist of folk religion in Taiwan, based on field study. An essential work for understanding how folk religion affects the everyday life of people in Taiwan.

Murray Rubinstein, ed., *The Other Taiwan: 1945 to the Present* (Armonk: M. E. Sharpe, 1994).
Articles focus on those groups within Taiwan whose views of Taiwan differ from those of the establishment. Critical perspectives on the "Taiwan miracle." Contributors suggest that policies of Taiwan's elites led to the disaffection that has resulted in greater political awareness, gender consciousness, environmental protests, spiritual rebirth, and ethnic identification.

N. T. Wang, ed., *Taiwan's Enterprises in Global Perspective* (Armonk: M. E. Sharpe, Inc., 1992).
A series of articles on Taiwan's economy, including such topics as Taiwan's personal-computer industry, the inter-

nationalization of Taiwan's toy industry, liberalization and globalization of the financial market, and Taiwan's economic relationship with mainland China.

Foreign Policy

Dennis Hickey, *United States–Taiwan Security Ties: From Cold War to Beyond Containment* (Westport: Praeger, 1994).
Examines U.S.–Taiwan security ties from the cold war to the present and what Taiwan is doing to ensure its own military preparedness. Also assesses the P.R.C.'s security threat to Taiwan.

Robert G. Sutter and William R. Johnson, *Taiwan in World Affairs* (Boulder: Westview Press, 1994).
Articles give comprehensive coverage of Taiwan's involvement in foreign affairs. Topics include Taiwan's role in the economic development of East Asia; Taiwan in the international arms market, Taiwan's efforts to gain legitimacy as an international actor, Taiwan's relations with the P.R.C., and the implications of Taiwan's international role for U.S. foreign policy.

Nancy Bernkopf Tucker, *Patterns in the Dust: Chinese–American Relations and the Recognition Controversy, 1949–1950* (New York: Columbia University Press, 1983).
An excellent account of the Truman government's efforts to make the right decision about how to treat both the Chinese Communists when they gained control of China's government and the Chinese Nationalists who had fled to Taiwan.

HONG KONG

Politics, Economics, Society, and Culture

"Basic Law of Hong Kong Special Administrative Region of the People's Republic of China," *Beijing Review,* Vol. 33, No. 18 (April 30–May 6, 1990), supplement.

John Gordon Davis, *Hong Kong Through the Looking Glass* (Hong Kong: Kelly & Walsh Ltd., 1977).
A humorous, informed, and insightful presentation of life in Hong Kong, through narrative and photographs. Gives readers a feel for life in Hong Kong.

Berry Hsu, ed., *The Common Law in Chinese Context,* in a series entitled *Hong Kong Becoming China: The Transition to 1997* (Armonk: M. E. Sharpe, Inc., 1992).
Examines common-law aspects of the "Basic Law," the mini-constitution that will govern Hong Kong after 1997.

Looks at such common-law concerns as presumption of innocence, the right to remain silent, judicial independence, and the jury system, and how these assumptions of British law do and do not fit into the Chinese cultural context of Hong Kong (or of China).

Benjamin K. P. Leung, ed., *Social Issues in Hong Kong* (New York: Oxford University Press, 1990).
A collection of essays on select issues in Hong Kong such as aging, poverty, women, pornography, and mental illness.

William McGurn, *Perfidious Albion: The Abandonment of Hong Kong 1997* (Washington, D.C.: Ethics and Public Policy Center, 1992).
A condemnation of the British selling out of the interests of the people of Hong Kong beginning in 1984 in the interests of strengthening Sino–British ties. Discusses Hong Kong people's emigrating and the refusal of Britain to issue them British passports.

Foreign Policy

Ming K. Chan, ed., *Precarious Balance: Hong Kong between China and Britain, 1842–1942* (Armonk: M. E. Sharpe, 1994).
A collection of essays concerning Hong Kong's efforts to balance its relations with China and Great Britain from the time it became a British colony in 1842 to 1992. Includes topics such as Chinese nationalism in Hong Kong, Hong Kong as a point of contention between China and Britain, and race-based discriminatory legislation in Hong Kong.

Robert Cottrell, *The End of Hong Kong: The Secret Diplomacy of Imperial Retreat* (London: John Murray, 1993).
Exposes the secret diplomacy that led to signing of the "Joint Declaration on Question of Hong Kong" in 1984, the agreement to end 150 years of British colonial rule over Hong Kong and return it to Chinese rule. Puts forth the thesis that Britain was reluctant to introduce democracy into Hong Kong before this point because it thought it would ruin Hong Kong's economy and lead to social and political instability; notes support of this position by many members of Hong Kong political elite.

Mark Roberti, *The Fall of Hong Kong: China's Triumph and Britain's Betrayal* (New York: John Wiley & Sons, Inc., 1994).
A fast-paced, drama-filled account of the decisions Britain and China have made about Hong Kong's fate since the early 1980s. Based on interviews with 150 key players in the secret negotiations between China and Great Britain.

Credits

PEOPLE'S REPUBLIC OF CHINA

Page 88 Article 1. © 1994 by The Royal Institute of International Affairs. Reprinted by permission.

Page 91 Article 2. Reprinted from *Commentary,* April 1994, by permission of *Commentary* and the author. All rights reserved.

Page 95 Article 3. ©1992 by Ross Terrill and "Mr. X." Reprinted by permission.

Page 98 Article 4. © 1994 by *U.S. News & World Report.*

Page 102 Article 5. Reprinted by permission of *Foreign Affairs,* May/June 1994. © 1994 by the Council on Foreign Relations, Inc.

Page 108 Article 6. © 1992 by Harvard International Review.

Page 111 Article 7. © 1994 by The Economist, Ltd. Distributed by The New York Times Special Features.

Page 114 Article 8. Reprinted with permission from *Current History* magazine, September 1992. © 1992 by Current History, Inc.

Page 119 Article 9. Reprinted by permission from *Asiaweek,* April 6, 1994.

Page 120 Article 10. This article originally appeared in *World Policy Journal,* Vol. X, No. 3, Fall 1994.

Page 124 Article 11. © 1994 by Xia-huang Yin. Reprinted by permission.

Page 128 Article 12. © 1994 by Review Publishing Company, Ltd. Reprinted by permission from *Far Eastern Economic Review,* Hong Kong.

Page 130 Article 13. © 1993 by The New York Times Company. Reprinted by permission.

Page 133 Article 14. © 1993 by The New York Times Company. Reprinted by permission.

Page 136 Article 15. © 1994 by The Christian Science Publishing Society. All rights reserved.

Page 138 Article 16. © 1994 by The Christian Science Publishing Society. All rights reserved.

Page 141 Article 17. © 1994 by The New York Times Company. Reprinted by permission.

Page 146 Article 18. © 1994 by Dow Jones & Company, Inc. All rights reserved worldwide.

Page 148 Article 19. © 1994 by Time Inc. Reprinted with permission.

Page 150 Article 20. This article appeared in *The World & I,* December 1994. Reprinted with permission from *The World & I,* a publication of The Washington Times Corporation. © 1994.

Page 155 Article 21. © 1993 by *U.S. News & World Report.*

Page 157 Article 22. This article appeared in *The World & I,* October 1989. Reprinted with permission from *The World & I,* a publication of The Washington Times Corporation. © 1989.

Page 161 Article 23. © 1994 by The Nation Company, Inc.

Page 165 Article 24. Reprinted by permission of *Sinorama Magazine.*

TAIWAN

Page 167 Article 25. Reprinted by permission of *Foreign Affairs,* November/December 1994. © 1994 by the Council on Foreign Relations, Inc.

Page 173 Article 26. © 1994 by Dow Jones & Company, Inc. All rights reserved worldwide.

Page 175 Article 27. Reprinted from *Free China Review,* March 1994.

Page 176 Article 28. © 1994 by Review Publishing Company, Ltd. Reprinted by permission from *Far Eastern Economic Review,* Hong Kong.

Page 177 Article 29. Reprinted from *Free China Review,* January 1988.

Page 180 Article 30. Reprinted from *Free China Review,* January 1988.

Page 184 Article 31. Reprinted by permission of *Sinorama Magazine.*

HONG KONG

Page 188 Article 32. Reprinted with permission of the *Harvard International Review.*

Page 192 Article 33. © 1994 by The Royal Institute of International Affairs. Reprinted by permission.

Page 198 Article 34. © 1994 by Review Publishing Company, Ltd. Reprinted by permission from *Far Eastern Economic Review,* Hong Kong.

Sources for Statistical Reports

U.S. State Department, *Background Notes* (1993).

C.I.A. *World Fact Book* (1994).

World Bank, *World Development Report* (1994).

UN *Population and Vital Statistics Report* (January 1994).

World Statistics in Brief (1994).

Statistical Yearbook (1994).

The Statesman's Yearbook (1994–1995).

World Almanac (1995).

Demographic Yearbook (1995).

Index